How to
Grill
Everything

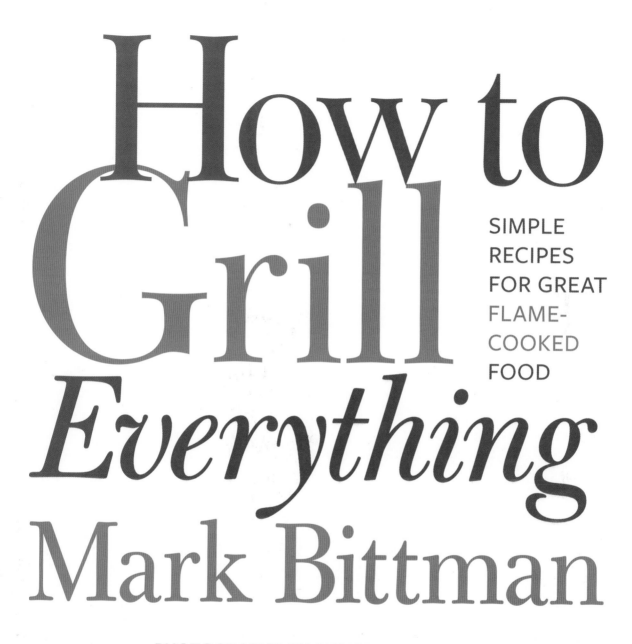

How to Grill Everything

SIMPLE RECIPES FOR GREAT FLAME-COOKED FOOD

Everything

Mark Bittman

PHOTOGRAPHY BY CHRISTINA HOLMES

HOUGHTON MIFFLIN HARCOURT

Boston | New York | 2018

For information about permission to reproduce selections from this
book, write to trade.permissions@hmhco.com or to Permissions,
Houghton Mifflin Harcourt Publishing Company, 3 Park Avenue,
19th Floor, New York, New York 10016.

hmhco.com

Library of Congress Cataloging-in-Publication Data is available.
ISBN 978-0-544-79030-8 (hardcover)
ISBN 978-0-544-79082-7 (ebook)

Book design by Toni Tajima

Printed in China

SCP 10 9 8 7 6 5 4 3 2 1

Contents

Acknowledgments

Everyone knows grilling is fun, but codifying the world's most primitive cooking method, especially one that's grown to cult status, was not easy. Pam Hoenig, with whom I've been working since the original edition of *How to Cook Everything* was conceived (1994!), did the brunt of the work on this tome. Kerri Conan, as usual, contributed mightily, and nothing in the world of me and books happens without Angela Miller.

Others on the team included recipe testers Karin Huggens and Cara Wood-Ginder, who got their grilling groove on. The spectacular photography is down to Christina Holmes, who did the shooting with assistants Spencer Wells and True O'Neill, and food stylist Chris Lanier—who, with Dana McClure, hosted at Ravenwood, their beautiful Catskills barn—plus assistants Frída Kristinsdóttir and Erika Joyce. The prop styling was done by Kaitlyn DuRoss. Netherton Foundry and Hawkins New York supplied some of the cast-ironware for the shoot.

You can't write a grilling book without meat, and a few Putnam County people really helped us get our hands on not only the best meat, but some of the hardest-to-come-by cuts. Chris Pascarella of Marbled Meat Shop in Cold Spring always did us right, and the meat team of Donald Arrant and Stephanie Pittman at Glynwood (an awesome institution led by my awesome partner, Kathleen Frith) kept me well-supplied with perfectly raised meat for my testing chores.

A shout-out, too, to Erin Harrison of Broil King, who supplied us with what are really the best gas grills I have ever used (and I was an early adopter of gas). I wouldn't say it if it weren't true.

I have editors, publishers, marketers, publicists, and so on, and they've all been great: My esteemed higher-ups Bruce Nichols, Deb Brody, and Ellen Archer; editor Stephanie Fletcher, copy editor Suzanne Fass, and managing editor Marina Padakis Lowry. Plus art director Melissa Lotfy, designer Toni Tajima, and production coordinator Kevin Watt, and the marketing and publicity team of Lori Glazer and Adriana Rizzo.

To my friends and family, thank you, as always. To Kate and Emma, you're more impressive and faboo than ever. To my mom: Keep it UP! And to Kathleen, and a future of grilling and eating together.

Mark Bittman
Cold Spring, New York, 2017

Why Grill?

Cooking is the same whether you do it on a range or a grill. That is, the same skills apply: You control heat, tune into your senses, and learn to recognize doneness. Only with grilling the flame is always visible. And often neither pot nor pan comes between the food and the fire.

That directness makes grilling outdoors exhilarating, intimate, elemental, fun. The lure of food sizzling on a grate over burning embers is powerful. And with the wide selection of modern equipment and fuels now available, it's no more difficult than turning on the stove.

Anything you can do in an oven or on a stove you can do on the grill. As with all the How to Cook Everything books, here you'll find variations for changing components, techniques, and flavors, and inspiration for trying your own ideas. But while these recipes open the door to many new possibilities—especially with vegetables and desserts—they also show you when and how not to fuss. There are lots of options for hot and fast cooking that will have dinner on the table on harried weeknights, as well as slow-and-low "project" recipes like pulled pork and brisket, perfect for leisurely weekend cooking for friends and family.

Then there's the whole being outdoors with friends and family thing. Standing at the grill you've usually got some help or at least a friend to keep you company. And a cool drink is probably in arm's reach. Cooking doesn't get any better.

Grilling Basics

Grilling gurus searching mainly for new recipes might want to skim this chapter. Everyone else—especially if you don't already have a grill or are in the market for a new one—listen up. This is the part where I tell you that what you cook on (or over) hardly matters. With a little technique and honest ingredients, you can enjoy excellent grilled meals with virtually any rig.

Gas Versus Charcoal

In the great debate played out in backyards across America, I'm either preaching to or insulting the choir, since I believe both types of grills have value. The decision is deeply personal and depends on everything from your climate and how often you entertain to how committed you are to learning new skills. My job is to provide successful recipes for both types of grills, covering several different variables. Maybe after reading this section you'll want to own gas *and* charcoal grills. (They're affordable enough that might be a real possibility.)

Gas makes grilling convenient. You open a propane tank or natural gas line, press an ignition button, and in 15 minutes—less time than it takes to prep most dinners—you've got adjustable flames and a blazing hot cooking surface. Now you can decide to cook something lean and mean (and fast) over direct heat or move it to the cool side of the grill for a slow roast. And the precision and predictability of gas are appealing, especially if you regularly cook for a crowd.

Getting a charcoal grill ready doesn't take a whole lot longer, but it sure can seem like it when you're messing with lighting, spreading, and building the coals.

When cooking direct (meaning the food is positioned over the flames), I've gotten awesome results with both gas and charcoal grills, including absolutely delicious char-broiled steaks and burgers, boneless chicken, shrimp, vegetables, you name it. Hardcore charcoal grillers argue that the gas grill can't get hot enough (read 800° to 900°F) for the perfect sear, but I have been plenty happy with the outcomes I have gotten with my gas grill.

About heat: Many new gas grills push their thermometers all the way into the red, achieving temperatures above 700°F. That's plenty hot—hotter than you usually want. Getting and maintaining a charcoal fire at this sort of hard-core searing heat is tough without special equipment or the inclination to cook food directly on the coals (fun and totally doable; see page 226). Everyday grilling doesn't require you go to such extremes.

Gas is also criticized for its performance with slow-and-low cooking (where the food is positioned away from the flames and cooked at a relatively low temperature, between 225° and 275°F) and with smoking. On both points, I disagree. While it's true that some gas grills have difficulty maintaining super-low temperatures like, say, 225°F, many can and do meet the challenge. So if slow grill-roasting is important to you and you still think you'll use gas more frequently than charcoal, look for a gas grill with burners that work well at low heat, and that maintains heat well.

Trying to generate smoke when cooking at a low temperature is even more specialized barbecue cooking that I encourage you to try at least once. (See the "Smoking" section on pages 10–12.) It's not impossible on gas—but it can be more difficult to get smoke going and collected, since gas grills are purposely built *not* to have a good seal, for safety reasons (see "Lid Up or Down?" on page 10). On the other hand, you can smoke quite effectively in an inexpensive kettle or drum charcoal grill.

Bottom line: Buy the grill or grills you'll use the most. Otherwise, what's the point?

Buying a Grill

A lot of these considerations are universal for charcoal and gas, although some won't apply to the most bare-bones grills.

Price

First, establish the intersection between how much you want to spend and which features you think are mandatory. A higher price doesn't always mean a better grill. Some of the best—and cheapest—grills are simple kettles or drums. Decide on a maximum and then compare apples to apples across different brands. Take advantage of the internet—especially legit sources for reviews and questions—to do your initial research; company websites are helpful to access detailed specifications on most every feature. Then go shopping in person, even if you plan to buy online, and take a look at the grills you're considering up close.

Overall Size and Cooking Surface Area

Both gas and charcoal grills vary greatly in size and shape, from tabletop hibachis to mega platforms with grates on pulleys. Ask yourself some questions: How much room do you have to safely operate a grill away from the house and low-hanging tree branches, for example? What do you like to cook, and how much of it will you be cooking at a time? If it's you and one other person, plus occasionally having folks over, then perhaps go smaller. Frequent entertainers or big families obviously require larger equipment. Ditto for accommodating multiple or big cuts (racks of ribs, a whole turkey or brisket, a bone-in pork shoulder, and so on) that you will likely cook using both direct and indirect heat.

In fact, if you plan to do a lot of slow, indirect cooking, you'll want a grill with enough surface area to move food to different zones. This is particularly an issue for gas grills, where you need at least two burners under the lid—and preferably three or four—situated in such a way that you have plenty of room to set food over unlit burners. Burners that run from front to back are better for this kind of cooking, though side-to-side orientation can work if the grilling surface is deep enough.

Finally, the lid: For grilling those large cuts, make sure there's enough headroom in the grill when you shut the lid so that the air can circulate well. If the grill includes a warming rack, make sure it is removable, for the same reason.

Heat Output

Regardless of the number and placement of burners on gas grills, most specs reference Btus. ("British thermal unit," a universal way of measuring the heat, is the amount of heat needed to heat a pound of water 1°F.) The range of available Btus is shocking; the higher the number, the hotter the grill can go. A high number also usually means that the grill will maintain heat better at lower temperatures.

For charcoal grills, the capacity to build and maintain a hot fire depends on how big it is; remember big can mean vertical space, not just horizontal. And it's important to have a way to add coals during cooking. Sometimes there's a hinged grate; in other styles, a trap door on the side. Beware of any grill that makes stoking the fire at all dangerous or difficult while there's food on the grate.

Construction

You want to buy a grill with solid construction, whether it is manufactured from steel (stainless, or powder- or enamel-coated), cast aluminum, or ceramics. Check out all its moving parts and look at how the pieces and seams are put together. Are the materials strong or flimsy? Is the workmanship solid? Does the lid close tightly? How well are the accessories attached? If it has wheels, how easy is it to roll? Do the wheels feel like they're coming off?

Grates

For the main cooking surface, cast iron or stainless steel are the best choices. In terms of maintenance and performance, the difference is the same as between iron and stainless pans: Cast iron conducts and retains heat better, but requires oiling to prevent rusting; stainless steel is reliable for even cooking and easy cleaning. Stainless steel rails are also usually narrower, so you get more but less-thick grill marks. Some manufacturers offer multiple features and styles of grate, so it's important to research the options as part of your decision.

Thermometer

Even though the thermometer (temperature gauge) set into the lids of grills can be inaccurate (see "Taking Your Grill's Temperature," page 9), it's better to have one than not. It gives you a general base-point temperature to work from in terms of knowing how hot a fire you have.

Warming Rack

This is a shallow grate at the back, running the length of the grill's interior above the cooking grate. I've got one in both my charcoal and gas rigs and I love it. But be careful when using it to keep cooked food warm or you risk overcooking. Instead, try it as another cooking option. A wide one is especially great for spatchcocked chicken (see page 195). With the rack high enough above the fire, flare-ups can't get to it, so you can cook the chicken more quickly over direct heat and develop a crisper skin. Just make sure the rack is removable, otherwise it will limit the height of what you can put on the grill. For more on using your warming rack to cook, see "Top-Shelf Grilling," page 194.

Fat Trap

Gas grills are almost always constructed so any fat that drips off the food and isn't incinerated is collected in a trap you can remove and empty. If you grill regularly and you like to cook things that are fatty, like pork and poultry (particularly duck and goose, which can shed a pint or more), you want a sizeable fat trap or the ability to put a heatproof bowl or pan under it to catch the overflow. Another option during indirect cooking is to put a pan on the unlit burners of the grill, under the food. But you're still going to need some way to capture fat during direct cooking, so the fat trap is worth checking out. (For charcoal grilling, simply put a disposable foil pan under the food).

Smoker Box

If you've decided on buying a gas grill and have intentions of smoking, I highly recommend you buy a grill equipped with a smoker box. This is an inset metal box with a perforated lid that sits over its own dedicated burner. Fill the box with chips, turn the burner on, and, after a few minutes, you'll have smoke; you can control how much by turning the burner up or down and it's easy to replenish the chips when they burn down. (See "Smoking in a Gas Grill," page 11.)

Side Burner

More and more gas grills offer an additional burner that is not under the lid of the grill. It's handy for preparing a sauce for your grilled food, boiling corn or pasta outside, and cooking sides and/or keeping them warm.

Rotisserie

A luxury, to be sure, but if you're into the idea of roasting more than just chickens this way you might consider it. Pork or lamb roasts, ducks or turkeys, dramatic presentations of slowly grill-roasted whole vegetables like eggplants, potatoes, and winter squashes are an unexpected benefit. Just make sure the rotisserie spins close enough to the heat to brown and cook the food, but with enough room to put a drip pan under it. You'll need access to an outdoor socket for the electric rotor mechanism.

Propane Tank Connection

Depending on configuration, connecting the fuel line to the propane tank can be awkward. Check to make sure the setup makes the process as easy as possible.

Vents

When buying a charcoal grill, be sure it has a bottom vent as well as one in the lid to allow for heat regulation and flow. The top vent also helps to draw smoke up and over the food when cooking.

Ash Removal and Disposal

Convenience is king here. Different brands and models have their own methods to get cooled ashes out of the bottom of the grill. In some, you've got to remove the charcoal grate to dump or shovel them out; others have catchers underneath that are easily removed for emptying.

Shelving

Having a landing spot right next to the grill is a real plus. You need someplace from which to load stuff onto the grill, to hold it when you take it off, to brush it with a glaze, and to hold utensils and accessories. You choose: Have a table or small cabinet nearby, or buy a grill with a built-on shelf or two. Otherwise you'll go nuts.

Wheels

Invaluable for moving the grill. All the better if they lock.

Getting Started

After the equipment, but before there can be cooking, there must be fire. Here's what you need to know for both gas and charcoal grills.

Grill Placement

Take commonsense precautions when finding a spot for your grill: Don't put it against an exterior wall of your house or garage. Avoid covered porches or balconies. Don't grill in the garage, regardless of

USING A CHIMNEY STARTER

STEP 1 Stuff the bottom of the chimney with newspaper and then fill the top with lump charcoal or briquettes. Light the newspaper in several places.

STEP 2 Let the coals heat for about 15 minutes, until flaming hot and white.

STEP 3 Once the coals are hot, pour them onto the grill.

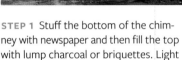

how tempting that might be. Cement patios provide a safer spot than a wood or composite deck; check the manufacturer's instructions for recommended surfaces and other safety guidelines. With charcoal grills, you do sometimes get sparks blown around when it's windy, so don't put it in a place where there is the possibility that dry leaves or grass could catch fire.

Firing Up a Charcoal Grill

The only method I recommend for starting a fire with briquettes or lump charcoal is a chimney starter (see above). It's easy: Tightly crumple a few sheets of newspaper or a brown paper bag and stuff them in the bottom of the chimney from underneath, then fill the chimney with your fuel of choice.

Find a safe surface to set the chimney. For the first batch, that will be in the bottom of the grill, probably on the charcoal grate above or near the vent. Later, to replenish the fire with properly ashed coals, you can start it in a metal tub or on your driveway or another concrete surface; be sure it's not in a place where kids or pets might knock it over.

Light the paper in several places and wait to see smoke to make sure it's caught. In about 15 minutes, you should have flaming hot, white-crusted coals ready to pour out the top into the grill. If the coals on top are still more black than white, give the chimney a gentle shake and check back in 5 minutes. Be careful about grabbing the handle: Depending on the construction of the chimney, it can get superheated, so it is best to wear a barbecue mitt or use a heavy-duty pot holder or dry, doubled-up kitchen towel. (Never grab anything hot with a damp towel, even if it is doubled up; within seconds, the towel in your hand will be screaming hot with steam.)

Once the coals are dumped into the bottom of the grill (which usually means on the charcoal grate), you can spread or move them with tools as you like. For an even hotter fire, top them off with a handful or two of unlit coals.

Firing Up a Gas Grill

Assuming your grill isn't fueled by a natural gas hookup, you'll have to buy liquid propane, which is sold in standard 20-pound refillable tanks. Exchanging stations are usually cages set up outside house-and-garden and hardware stores and even some supermarkets. You usually shell out fifty bucks or so for the first full tank, and then much less when you bring the empties to be refilled or swapped for full tanks. You can also just buy an empty tank and find a place to fill it; but then you have the responsibility of maintaining the connection hardware.

The problem with propane tanks is that they don't have gauges. So I strongly recommend that you invest in two tanks. There is nothing more aggravating than running out of propane when you are in middle of cooking and having to run to the store for a refill.

Follow the manufacturer's directions for connecting the tank. Here's the usual drill: First, make sure the knob at the top is closed and turned all the way clockwise. (Remember: "right tight, left loose.") Remove any plastic cap from the valve on the tank or where the grill's regulator attaches to the tank. Insert the nipple of the grill regulator into the valve, making sure the threads match, and turn it all the way clockwise, until it won't go any further. Getting the threads right can be a pain the first time and you may have to redo it until you have a snug fit, but you'll get the hang of it. Do all tightening and untightening by hand; never use a tool.

DEALING WITH FAT AND FLAMES

Regardless of how you capture the fat during cooking, a lot sticks to the grate. Many gas grill manufacturers tell you to burn the fat off the grate—and remember, fat accumulates underneath, too—before cooking. I like to do it afterwards, and then sometimes again before. Unless you scrupulously keep the grate and interior clean, residual fat will drip down into the fire and ignite, sometimes spectacularly so. When that happens, your grill can become a fireball, even with the lid down.

If this happens, don't panic and dump water on the flames; water and fat don't mix, and flaming droplets of fat can splatter, resulting in a much bigger fire. If you have a charcoal grill, put the lid down and wait it out. Once the fat's all burnt up, the fire will settle down. If you have a gas grill, turn all the burners off, turn off the propane tank, put the lid down, and wait until the flames die down. Usually that first big flameout has taken care of the vast majority of the leftover fat; if it flares up again, it will be at a much more manageable level that will settle down quickly.

When grilling fatty items with indirect heat, gas grillers also need to know where the pilot lights are on their burners and position food away from them. After heating the grill, when the indirect burners are turned off, the pilot lights sometimes stay on and if rendering fat hits that flame, you'll have flare-ups.

For the same reason you don't throw water on a grease fire, don't spray down flare-ups caused by dripping fat with a water bottle when cooking. Do this with a duck or goose breast and you'll light the inside of your grill on fire. To minimize flare-ups on cuts like steaks and chops, trim as much exterior fat off as you can; this is largely the culprit. If you're still getting too much flare-up, move the food to the edges of the fire or next to but not directly over the fire.

When you're ready to light the fire—and only then—open the knob at the top of the propane tank all the way. (Again: "left loose.")

Different gas grills can have different methods of ignition, so follow the instructions in the owner's manual. As you turn on the flow of propane to each burner, immediately ignite it. If you are having trouble getting a burner to ignite, turn the dial off while you try to figure out what the problem is. It's important to remember that once you turn the knob to an "ignite" position, propane is being fed into the burner. And if it's not ignited, it doesn't just dissipate into the air; since propane is heavier than air, it will pool in the bottom of your grill. If enough of it accumulates, when you finally get the burner to ignite, you can have an explosion. So when you are igniting your gas grill, pay attention and take precautions.

To heat any gas grill, fire up all the burners to high, close the lid, and let it heat for 15 minutes before adjusting the heat levels as indicated in the particular recipe.

Direct Versus Indirect Heat

Direct cooking on a grill means that the food is put on the grate directly above the heat source—directly over the coals, or for a gas grill, directly over a turned-on burner or burners. Indirect cooking involves positioning the food away from the heat. You may see this described as a two-zone or three-zone fire, referring to the fact that there is a hotter area and one or two cooler areas in the

SETTING UP DIRECT AND INDIRECT HEAT FIRES

FOR A TWO-ZONE FIRE on a charcoal grill, push all the coals to one side, creating a direct heat zone on one side and indirect heat on the other.

FOR A THREE-ZONE FIRE on a charcoal grill, divide the coals so that they flank a cooler zone in the middle.

grill. With indirect cooking you will almost always be taking advantage of hot and cool parts of the grill. In fact, even for direct cooking, it's handy to create some cool spots, in case you need a place to move something that's starting to scorch.

For an indirect charcoal fire, once your coals are ready, pour them into the grill and push them all to one side, creating a cooler space large enough to accommodate whatever you're cooking that has no coals underneath it; that is a two-zone fire. For a three-zone fire, divide up the coals, arranging them so they flank the cool zone on either side. This is my preferred way to cook whole poultry

(see page 155 for more). Either way, be sure to place a disposable foil pan underneath the grate and the food (unless it's vegetables or fish) to catch any rendering fat.

For an indirect fire on the gas grill, if there are three or more burners, I much prefer to go with a three-zone setup, the outer burners turned on, the inner burner(s) turned off to create the cool indirect zone. No need for a drip pan, as the fat trap will capture it.

Some recipes call for both indirect and direct heat, with direct heat applied either at the very beginning of cooking or at the end to sear or brown the food. In those cases, you build an indirect fire and simply put the food right over the flames for the amount of time directed.

Taking Your Grill's Temperature

Having an accurate read on the interior temperature of your grill—especially when beginning—makes for more successful outcomes. If your grill has a temperature gauge set in the lid, it may not be accurate, and could be off by a lot; the thermometer in the lid measures the air temperature at the top of the grill. If you use a surface thermometer, you can accurately measure the temperature exactly where the food is being cooked, which is particularly important when you are going slow-and-low. I highly recommend you purchase a grill thermometer you can hang from the warming rack inside the grill or a surface thermometer that can sit right on the grate. See page 3 for more about thermometers and their use.

Take the temperature as guidance, not dogma. So many variables are at play. For example, if I'm looking to cook a large piece of meat at 325° or 300°F, I have no worries about putting it on when the grill

temperature is at a max of 400°F, since I know the temperature will start to fall within 30 minutes and soon be in the range I want it.

Regulating Temperature and Replenishing Charcoal

For gas grills, use the burners' control knobs to fine-tune your temperature. The high, medium, and low positions on your control knobs do not necessarily line up with the heat ranges indicated in "How Hot a Fire?" at left. In fact, I can almost guarantee they don't. If you have all your burners on with the knobs in what you would consider the medium position, you very likely are at around 500°F. If you have a thermometer in the lid, use that as a guide; if your gas grill doesn't have a lid thermometer, you absolutely need to buy one for the inside of the grill.

Hitting particular temperatures on a charcoal grill is a little trickier. If the temperature is too high, you can bring it down by closing the bottom vent or opening the grill to release stored heat. If you're losing temperature, light a chimney-full of charcoal or briquettes and pour it into the grill when the coals are flaming hot.

If what you are cooking is going to take several or many hours, you need to get into a groove for replenishing the coals. My method is to wait until the grill temperature drops down to my preferred temperature, at which point I light a chimney of coals. By the time they are ready, the temperature usually has dropped down below my optimum, and the added coals will bring the grill back up to heat. I continue to add more fuel in this way.

To keep a charcoal fire going for long cooking, you need to be able to easily access the coals (see the "Heat Output" discussion on page 3). Adding a few unlit briquettes or charcoal lumps to the burning fire isn't as ideal as adding prepared coals, but it works just fine. The fire will spike a bit is

The lid must always be down on a gas grill for safety reasons, with the obvious exception of opening it to maneuver or check on the food. Open, you run the risk of a pilot light blowing out, and if you don't immediately notice, propane will continue to flow into the grill, pooling in the bottom (propane is heavier than air), until it is ignited by one of the lit burners and explodes.

When grilling on a windy day, be super careful opening and closing the lid, keeping an eye on all your burners to make sure they're still flaming. If any of them gets blown out and you're not certain when it happened, turn all the burners off and open the lid for 10 to 15 minutes before reigniting them.

Even when cooking on a charcoal grill, I often cook with the lid down—an unpopular position among grillers striving to get a perfect sear on a steak before moving it off to the cool side of the grill to finish, but it works for me, especially if the meat is thick and the fire is hot.

Also, always close the lid when you are done grilling. For a charcoal grill, this will keep any embers contained. For both types of grills, it will protect the inside of the grill from the elements, helping to ward off rust.

---

all, and have a bit of extra smokiness. Just don't do too many at a time. If you don't want to bother with the fuss of repeatedly lighting chimneys of charcoal, try this easier method and see what you think.

If what I am cooking is going to be done in an hour or a little over an hour, I rarely replenish the fire, unless for some reason the temperature drops rapidly early on. Just put a chicken or a pork roast on indirect when the temperature is 400° to 450°F, and then keep the lid down and let it cook as the grill temp gradually drops. So long as you start with a big enough fire, equivalent to around 80 briquettes, the fire will hold its heat for quite a while.

Smoking

Smoke is created as a byproduct of burning wood—chunks, chips, pellets, or branches. The smoke surrounds and flavors the food on the grill. When grillers talk about smoking, they're usually talking about true barbecue: food cooked indirect (away from the fire) at a relatively low temperature, usually 225° to 275°F, surrounded by wood smoke for part of the cooking time. You can also smoke at higher temperatures.

Smoke contains lots of different compounds, and two in particular are responsible for the smoke flavor we love so much in food: guaiacol and syringol. To release these specific compounds, you want a well-oxygenated fire—one with good airflow—that yields white smoke; if your fire is producing black or otherwise dark smoke, it's not getting enough air and the results are not going to be particularly tasty. Prepare the fire and position the food on the grate so the smoke will be drawn up and over it as it exits the top vent. Basically, build the fire as far away from the top vent as possible and position the food directly under the vent.

In terms of fuel, when smoking on a charcoal grill, I prefer to burn chunks of wood, even thicker branches or small pieces of firewood. They burn slower, longer, and more evenly than chips, which disappear almost immediately and have to be replenished constantly. Just add one or two fist-sized pieces of wood or branches to the fire, close the lid, and wait for smoke to come out the top vent. After the food is on, monitor the smoke through the vents on the lid; when it starts to peter out, add more wood. If you only have access to chips or are doing a quick smoke, add about 1 cup of chips at a time to the fire.

Woods for Smoking

During grilling season, you'll find bags of different kinds of wood chips and chunks at home-and-garden and hardware stores. Go online and the choice widens even further—hickory, oak, ash, apple, cherry, pecan, mesquite, even chips from retired bourbon and wine barrels. Serious grillers will tell you they can distinguish the smoke flavors generated by these different woods. I'm happy just to have wood to burn (and frequently pick up dried sticks from the yard or during a hike), but I'll tell you in the recipe what smoking woods are traditionally used. Experiment and see if you can tell the difference, and keep track of the woods you like best with specific foods. One wood—

mesquite—definitely generates a distinctive smoke, so much so that you need to be judicious with your use of it, which leads to the question of timing.

How Long to Smoke?

In recipes that suggest smoking, I'll tell you how much smoking time I think is enough. The sweet spot in smoking is just enough time to infuse the food without the smoke overpowering the natural flavor of what's cooking. When I bite into something, I don't want it to taste overpoweringly like smoke. Start with less smoke rather than more, then tweak the timing to suit your palate as you gain experience. I max out at about two hours for pulled pork and brisket. For poultry, an hour is enough. For fish, vegetables, and cheese, 20 to 30 minutes is plenty.

Smoking in a Gas Grill

If you have a built-in smoker box in your gas grill, follow the instructions in the owner's manual for using it. If not, there's a work-around. The challenge with smoking in a gas grill is that the lid and body are purposely constructed to *not* fully seal. So smoke tends to dissipate rather than accumulate and circulate around the food. Here are two methods to try, both using chips (in the case of the gas grill, faster ignition is a good thing) and a disposable foil pan.

METHOD 1

Before turning the grill on, remove the grate over the burner(s) you intend to use for smoking, then remove the heat diffuser(s) over the burner(s). The heat diffuser (also referred to as a "flavor bar" or "flavorizer") is a V-shaped length of metal that sits directly under the grate and is positioned over the port holes of each burner. It's easy to pop it off. The reason to remove it is to expose the bottom of a foil pan directly to the flames.

Put the grate back on.

Put about a cup of chips in the foil pan, set it on the grate positioned directly over the burner, ignite the burner(s), set the burner(s) to high, and close the lid.

METHOD 2

This method works best for a gas grill with four burners. Remove the grate over the two burners you will leave on. Leave the heat diffusers in.

You'll need a long, narrow foil pan for the chips, just the right size to place between the burners. The lip of the pan, on either long side, will sit on top of the two diffusers, allowing the bottom of the pan to hang down, close to the flames (for my grill, a 6½- × 13-inch pan is the perfect size).

Add the chips, turn on the burners, and close the lid. Leave the grate off while you cook so that you can replenish the chips as they burn down.

I have also tried putting wood chunks next to the flames—don't ever put anything directly on the port holes; you don't ever want to interfere with the flow of propane. They catch fire nicely; the problem is the smoke can dissipate as it floats up.

If you are able to get smoke going, it might require a higher temperature in the grill than you are aiming for. To that I say fine. To get smoke, I have had my grill at 350°F for two hours when smoking a brisket and still ended up with a tasty, tender result. If you are intent on smoking in a gas grill, you've got to do what you've got to do to make it happen.

Grill Cleanup

For the best cooking results and to maximize the lifespan of your grill and avoid mishaps, take care of your grill.

Ash Removal

For a charcoal grill, remove the ashes before preparing a new fire. Frequent grillers should buy a covered galvanized steel or aluminum trash can to hold spent ashes. Even though you might not see any live embers, ashes from grilling the night before very likely still contain them and can start a fire in your household trash bin. After three or more days, dispose of the ashes.

Fat Trap

For a gas grill, check on the fat trap before every session; if it's full, or close to full, empty it. After grilling, if you keep a can for fat, empty the fat into that, otherwise, put some paper towels in a plastic bag and pour it into that, then wash the trap well with soap and water before returning it to the grill.

Grates

It's easiest to clean grates when they are hot, as the high heat will incinerate and/or loosen any food particles left behind. You can do this before you shut the grill down, or while you are readying the grill to cook. (Or both, if the job was messy.) For a gas grill, when you are done preheating, run a grill brush vigorously over the grates to clean them, working between the rows.

For a charcoal grill, once you've got the coals flaming in the bottom, put the grates back on and close the lid for 5 minutes; then take a brush to them. Check the grates for stray bits of wire, plastic, or metal. (Hey, it happens.) Remember that residue also builds up underneath the grates, so periodically turn them over and clean the bottom as well.

Grill Accessories

You can go totally crazy when it comes to grill accessories, but they are largely unnecessary. The ones listed here are tools, utensils, and pieces of equipment I use over and over again. They make my grilling experience easier and contribute greatly to getting good results.

Grill Cover

They rarely come with the grill, but most manufacturers offer them specifically fitted for their models. Consider getting one to protect your grill from the elements. Only put it on after the grill is fully cooled.

Chimney Starter

This is a metal (most commonly steel or aluminum) cylinder open on top, with an inset perforated grate at the bottom; it allows you to light lump charcoal or briquettes without using lighter fluid or some other accelerant. To use a chimney starter, see "Firing Up a Charcoal Grill," page 5. They are generally about 12 inches high and 6½ to 8 inches across, holding 4 to 6 pounds of charcoal; there are also compact versions available that hold considerably less fuel.

Hinged Grate

If you want to cook indirect or slow-and-low, or smoke on a kettle or other similar grill, this is a necessity. The hinge allows you to pull up the grates on both sides (or the center, depending) to feed the fire.

Grill Thermometer

Absolutely necessary to have if your grill doesn't have a thermometer inset in its lid, and highly recommended even if you do have one, to confirm its accuracy. These operate like an oven thermometer and can be set on the grill or hung from a warming rack, if you have one. Other options are the more high-tech remote thermometers and probes, which allow you to place a sensor inside the grill to track the temperature and display the temperature outside. Be sure to buy thermometers meant for the grill, that max out at 800°F.

Grill Surface Thermometer

To measure the temperature exactly where the food is sitting. I find this valuable when I am cooking indirect, particularly when cooking slow-and-low. The grill thermometer might be clocking in at 350°F, but the temperature on the indirect side registers 250°F, just where I want it.

Digital Instant-Read Thermometer

This is the easiest, quickest way to check the interior doneness of all foods. Yes, you can use a small sharp knife to nick and peek—I often do, and you will, too—but it can be awkward over a searing hot fire.

Be sure to check doneness in a few places on larger cuts. Then you can reposition the meat for more even cooking. Do not leave your instant-read thermometer in whatever you are cooking. Leave it in long enough and the plastic bit will melt, but even before that happens, subjecting the electronics to high heat for even 5 to 10 minutes fries them—and yes, I've learned this from experience.

Perforated Grill Pan

Also called a "grill topper," this is a rimmed metal pan with holes cut into the bottom—and sometimes the sides—so whatever goes inside it makes contact with the fire. I use it often for small pieces of food; it can replace the use of skewers. Cherry tomatoes, broccoli and cauliflower florets, Brussels sprouts, green beans, and shrimp get tossed into the pan and arranged in a single layer and then the pan is set on the grill. Give the pan a couple of shakes a few times to turn things while grilling. Super easy.

Cast-Iron Skillet

If you want to try your hand at paella (page 149) or grill-baking (see page 482), an absolute must.

Skewers

Even though I often use a perforated grill pan for small items, I still like skewers for kebabs and many appetizers. Both metal and bamboo or other wooden skewers are available in a wide range of sizes. Avoid anything longer than 12 inches; they get too heavy and are unwieldy on the grill. Flat-bladed metal skewers will keep your food from spinning around when you try to turn them. And when using wooden skewers, soak them for at least 30 minutes before using to keep them from scorching on the grill.

Metal Spatula

At least one is necessary for turning burgers and fish; wielding two can help keep even the most delicate foods intact. Make sure they have long handles.

Tongs

I prefer spring-loaded tongs. For the same reason you need to buy a long-handled spatula, buy tongs that are at least 12 inches long.

Basting Brush

It's good to have several of these on hand to apply sauces or glazes to your grilled items. Silicone brushes are heat resistant. I also like spray bottles for oiling the food.

Barbecue Mitt

Depending on the material used, a heat-resistant barbecue mitt or glove can offer you protection from temperatures up to 500°F, which is plenty when you're moving food on and off the grill. Make sure it's comfortable and secure in your hand.

Disposable Foil Pans

I always have these on hand in a range of sizes. Use them for drip pans, for smoking chips on the gas grill, and as baking and serving pans.

Grill Brush

An absolute must. (Even though you're not supposed to use them on cast-iron grates, I do.) Most have stainless-steel bristles, some have brass. After you brush the grates, check them for stray bits of wire or metal. You can also purchase grate cleaners fitted with scrub pads, or made from plastic and wood (these are designed to be used when the grates are cool). See what works best for your equipment.

Headlamp

Don't laugh. Even if you think you have good outdoor lighting, inside the grill can be pretty dark sometimes.

The Grilling Pantry

Keep these select ingredients in your pantry or fridge and you'll have the makings for most of the sauces, glazes, and rubs in the book. Supplement these staples with fresh herbs and you can pivot in a multitude of directions, depending on what you have a taste for.

1. **SALT AND PEPPER.** You often need nothing more. Coarse noniodized salt is best—I use kosher for the recipes in this book. You can always use sea salt if you prefer. Freshly ground pepper is more intense than preground, but both are fine.

2. **OIL.** I predominantly use good-quality olive oil but also use a good-quality vegetable oil when a less-pronounced flavor is required. By "good-quality" I mean a minimally processed and refined, often unfiltered oil that actually has some flavor and never tastes rancid, chemical, or metallic.

3. **MUSTARD.** Dijon is nice but in a pinch any kind will work.

4. **MAYONNAISE.** To make your own, see page 460.

5. **VINEGAR.** Keep a collection on hand: red wine, rice, sherry, distilled white, balsamic.

6. **KETCHUP.** To make your own, see page 462; to see options for flavoring store-bought ketchup, see page 256.

7. **SOY SAUCE**

8. **SRIRACHA AND/OR OTHER HOT SAUCES**

9. **WHITE AND/OR BROWN SUGAR.** In the recipes, if just "brown sugar" is called for, either light or dark is fine; also, always measure brown sugar packed down into the measuring cup.

10. **HONEY**

11. **HOISIN SAUCE**

12. **FISH SAUCE**

13. **PAPRIKA, REGULAR AND SMOKED (PIMENTÓN)**

14. **DRIED AND GROUND HERBS AND SPICES,** like thyme, red pepper flakes, cumin, cayenne, and five-spice powder.

15. **LEMONS AND LIMES.** Citrus is a great flavor brightener. For even more pop, use the grated zest.

16. **GARLIC.** Mostly fresh; very rarely garlic powder (exclusively for use in rubs)—be sure it is 100 percent dehydrated garlic.

17. **FRESH GINGER**

How to Use This Book

Every recipe in the book is really four recipes in one—the main ingredients and directions, followed by three flavor variations.

The time shown under each recipe title includes 15 minutes for the grill to come to temperature (except for the handful that don't get grilled). For charcoal grilling, that includes getting the fire started; for gas grilling, that means heating the grill with all burners on high and the lid down.

All of the recipes include icons:

Ⓓ means direct fire

Ⓘ means an indirect fire

Ⓜ means some portion of the recipe can be made ahead

Ⓥ means the recipe includes a vegetarian option (it could be the entire recipe and its variations or just one)

The directions are written to help you coordinate ingredient prep with grill prep. If anything can be accomplished while the grill is coming up to temperature, you're instructed to get the fire going first. When the components can be done hours or even a day ahead, then you'll wait to get the fire going when you are ready to cook. In these cases, the make-ahead aspect will be clearly stated.

Timing and Temperature

If I've learned anything over years of grilling, it's that cooking with fire outdoors is imprecise. No matter how good your skills or equipment, you can't always control all the variables that might affect the outcome. So you need to observe and rely on your senses.

The chart "How Hot a Fire?" on page 9 defines the levels referenced throughout the book in temperature ranges, often with the caveat, "depending on how hot the fire is." And I know there will also be times when I'm calling for a hot fire (over 550°F) but when you check on the coals you'll realize your fire is at 350°F. You can start another chimney of charcoal, or you can go ahead and get your food on the grill, accepting that it might take a bit longer. And it's better to pull something from the grill early than too late. Just leave the fire going until you're sure the food is cooked to the desired doneness; you can always pop it back on to finish.

Grilling is imprecise, yes, and that's going to teach you to be an even better, more observant cook. To be a good griller, you need to pay attention. You need to judge the heat of the fire, then track the progress of your food by poking, smelling, and tasting so you can make adjustments on the fly. These recipes are loaded with all sorts of visual cues and tips to put you on the road to success.

Appetizers
and Snacks

Once you've fired up the grill, it only makes sense to stoke appetites with a savory bite before the main event—even on a weeknight. From garlicky toast to restaurant-style marrow bones, there's something here for every occasion. And many of these recipes are on and off in the grill in a matter of minutes.

Some specific serving suggestions are scattered throughout, but I usually offer appetizers as a free-for-all on big plates with dipping sauces and condiments within easy reach. For less casual occasions, it's fun to plate them individually and sometimes even nibble away with a knife and fork.

A word about setup: You can get the grill going for the main course—for direct or indirect cooking—and choose an appetizer that requires the same configuration. Or prepare the grill specifically for the first course and then adjust the heat before proceeding. In those cases, changing the settings on gas grills involves nothing more than turning the knobs and waiting. With charcoal, you'll almost certainly have to replenish the fire even if the type of fire and heat remain the same. Add more coals when you take the appetizers off the grill, and the fire will probably be ready again by the time you are.

Best-case scenario: You're cooking the appetizer over direct heat while dinner is working over the indirect side of the grill. Fortunately, the bulk of these appetizers allow you to do just that.

10 APPETIZERS TO MAKE FOR A LIGHT LUNCH OR DINNER

Almost anything in this chapter qualifies as a meal if you eat enough of it. Here are some serving ideas to get you thinking in that direction:

1. **Portobello Mushroom Wedges with Smoked Swiss and Soppressata** (page 43): One portobello cap (sliced or left whole) served on top of a simply dressed green salad is all you'll need

2. **Provoleta** (page 47): A panful spread on baguette slices is perfect for two, especially with some pickles on the side. It's like eating smoky free-form grilled cheese sandwiches

3. **Cheesy Jalapeño Quesadillas** (page 51) and its variations: One whole quesadilla per person sounds about right to me any time of day

4. **Pizza Bianca** (page 52) and its variations: Add Fennel with Olive Oil and Lemon (page 414) and any of these will serve two to four for lunch or dinner

5. **Spicy Squid with Lemon** (page 72) makes an exceptional pasta dinner for four when simply tossed with a pound of linguine, some of the pasta water, and a little more olive oil. Ditto the Korean- and Thai-Style variations, only use softened rice noodles

6. **Hot-Smoked Fish** (page 61): 1 cup flaked fish over lemony dressed arugula or spinach makes a satisfying salad, especially with croutons

7. **Chicken Negimaki Bites** (page 79) and its variations: Cut the grilled rolls as described—or not—and serve with soba noodles, in hot broth or tossed with sesame oil

8. **Chipotle Chicken Wings with Lime Crema Dipping Sauce** (page 82) and its variations: No one will complain about having wings for dinner! Will serve three to four

9. **Rosemary-Garlic Chicken Liver and Onion Skewers** (page 85): Divide the skewers over four servings of buttered kasha or other cooked whole grain, add steamed broccoli or cauliflower, and call that dinner for four

10. **Cajun-Style Grilled Shrimp** (page 63): Make a double batch, add corn on the cob (page 404), and gather eight people around the table. No one gets up until the last bite is gone

D direct fire   I indirect fire   M make ahead   V vegetarian option

Bruschetta

Makes: 4 servings	Time: 20 to 25 minutes	Ⓓ Ⓜ Ⓥ

You'll learn a lot about observing and controlling heat on your grill from making toast. I like to cut the bread thickly so the outside gets crunchy and the inside stays tender; you may prefer the bruschetta thinner and crisp all the way through. Pull any extra toppings together while the grill heats.

8 1-inch slices baguette or Italian bread

¼ cup good-quality olive oil

1 or 2 cloves garlic, peeled

1 Start the coals or heat a gas grill for medium-high direct cooking. Make sure the grates are clean.

2 Lightly brush both sides of the bread slices with the oil. Put them on the grill directly over the fire. Close the lid and toast, turning once, until the bread develops grill marks, 1 to 3 minutes per side. Transfer the slices to a platter. When the bread has cooled just enough that you can handle it, rub one or both sides of the bread with the garlic, and serve.

---

11 SIMPLE WAYS TO TOP BRUSCHETTA

1. Chopped fresh tomatoes (about 1 cup)
2. Chopped fresh basil (1 cup packed)
3. Shaved or grated Parmesan cheese (about ½ cup)
4. Sliced fresh mozzarella (8 ounces)
5. Ricotta cheese (about ½ cup); jazz it up by stirring in grated citrus zest or chopped fresh herbs
6. Chopped pitted olives (½ cup) or capers (¼ cup)
7. Grated lemon or orange zest (2 tablespoons)
8. Sliced apples, pears, or plums (1 or 2 should do it, depending on their size)
9. Anchovy fillets or smoked sardines (1 or 2 per slice)
10. Thinly sliced salami, prosciutto, or other smoked or cured meat (about 4 ounces, number of slices per bruschetta will depend on the size of the slice; for prosciutto, you might want to use half a slice)
11. Crumbled cooked sausage or bacon (about 4 ounces when raw)

• recipe continues →

Bruschetta with Tomatoes, Red Onion, and Mint	Best during peak tomato season: Chop 2 large fresh tomatoes and combine with 1 cup chopped fresh mint and ¼ cup chopped red onion. (For a mellower onion flavor, soak the chopped onion in cold water for a few minutes, drain, and pat dry with paper towels first.) Sprinkle with salt and pepper and toss a few times to release the juices.
Bruschetta with Lemon and Dill White Bean Spread	You can make the spread up to a day ahead, cover, and refrigerate: Rinse and drain one 15-ounce can cannellini beans. Put them in a blender or food processor with the grated zest of 1 lemon, 2 tablespoons each fresh lemon juice and good-quality olive oil, a few sprigs fresh dill, and some salt and pepper; pulse to a rough purée. After rubbing the bruschetta with garlic in Step 2, spread on the bean mixture and garnish each with a small sprig dill.
Bruschetta with Shrimp, Feta, and Capers	More substantial: Mash 4 ounces feta cheese with 2 tablespoons drained capers and 1 tablespoon fresh lemon juice. Thread 8 peeled medium shrimp onto skewers and brush with 1 tablespoon good-quality olive oil. Put the shrimp directly over the fire as you grill the bread and cook, turning once, until they're opaque, about 5 minutes total (see "Grilling Shrimp," page 125). Spread the feta mixture over the bruschetta, top each with a shrimp, and squeeze the juice of half a lemon over all.

---

10 MORE TOPPERS AND DIPS FOR BRUSCHETTA

As is, roughly mashed, or fully puréed, these recipes all work perfectly with grilled bread.

1. Hot-Smoked Fish (page 61)
2. Smoky Guacamole (page 26)
3. Roasted Peppers (page 34)
4. Baba Ghanoush (opposite)
5. Rosemary-Garlic Chicken Liver and Onion Skewers (page 85)
6. Creamy Chicken Liver Spread (page 86)
7. Queso Frito with Salami (page 48)
8. Sliced Beef or Lamb Heart (page 86)
8. Any of the cheeses in "7 Other Cheeses on the Grill" (page 47)
10. Provoleta (page 47)

Ⓓ direct fire   Ⓘ indirect fire   Ⓜ make ahead   Ⓥ vegetarian option

Baba Ghanoush

Makes: 6 to 8 servings | Time: About 1 hour, largely unattended   Ⓓ Ⓜ Ⓥ

Fire transforms a whole eggplant. The flesh goes from firm to silk inside its skin and is infused with smokiness.

2 medium-large eggplants (about 2 pounds total), with stems on

⅓ cup tahini

¼ cup fresh lemon juice

2 large cloves garlic, or to taste, minced

Salt and pepper

4 pita breads (to make your own, see page 492) for serving

Good-quality olive oil for drizzling

¼ cup chopped fresh parsley for garnish

1 Start the coals or heat a gas grill for hot direct cooking. Make sure the grates are clean.

2 Pierce the eggplants in several places with a thin knife or skewer. Put them on the grill directly over the fire and close the lid. Cook, turning every 10 minutes or so, until the eggplants are blackened on all sides and collapsed, 25 to 30 minutes. Transfer to a bowl.

3 Whisk the tahini and lemon juice in a small bowl until smooth. Stir in the garlic and sprinkle with salt and pepper.

4 When the eggplants are cool enough to handle, peel off and discard the burnt skin. Mash the flesh with a fork. Beat in the tahini mixture until the dip is smooth. Taste and adjust the seasoning. (You can make the dip up to 3 days in advance; cover and refrigerate.)

5 Toast the pita directly over the fire, turning once, until they're warm and have grill marks, 1 to 2 minutes per side. Cut into wedges. Transfer the baba ghanoush to a shallow serving bowl, drizzle the top with olive oil, sprinkle with the parsley, and serve with the warm pita wedges.

• recipe continues →

Fire-Smoked Eggplant, Garlic, and Lemon Dip	My favorite way to cook eggplant, if you're game (for a charcoal grill only): Omit the tahini, lemon juice, and minced garlic. Put the eggplants directly on the coals along with an unpeeled head of garlic and a whole lemon (first puncture it in several places with a knife or skewer). Leave the eggplants, garlic, and lemon on the coals, turning them occasionally, until their skins blister and blacken and the flesh softens; this will take 15 to 20 minutes for the eggplants and garlic and 5 to 10 minutes for the lemon. When the eggplants are cool enough to handle, peel and mash them as described in Step 4. Halve the lemon and squeeze in the juice (be careful, it's hot), and press as many of the garlic cloves as you like out of their skins into the bowl. Stir with a fork, mashing the mixture until smooth. Sprinkle with salt and pepper, taste and adjust the seasoning, and serve.
Baingan Bharta	My spin on the Punjabi dish to serve as a dip or side: Omit the tahini, lemon juice, and parsley. Cook and mash the eggplants as described in Steps 2 and 4. Warm 2 tablespoons good-quality vegetable oil in a skillet over medium-high heat; add 1 teaspoon cumin seeds and shake the pan until they pop, about a minute. Stir in 1½ cups chopped onion, the garlic, and 1 or 2 chopped seeded jalapeños; cook, stirring, until soft and fragrant, about 5 minutes. Add 1½ cups chopped fresh tomatoes and sprinkle with salt and pepper. Cook until they're soft and the pan is mostly dry, about 5 minutes. Add 1 teaspoon each ground coriander and garam masala and ½ teaspoon ground turmeric and stir for 1 minute. Add the eggplant and let the mixture bubble until thick, 5 to 10 minutes. Add ½ cup chopped fresh cilantro. Taste and adjust the seasoning. Serve hot, cold, or at room temperature with grilled chapati (page 487).
Creamy Eggplant Dip with Pomegranate and Mint	Omit the tahini, lemon juice, and parsley. Cook and mash the eggplants as described in Steps 2 and 4. Add ½ cup yogurt and 1 tablespoon pomegranate molasses to the eggplant along with the garlic and ¼ cup chopped fresh mint; stir to combine. Drizzle with the olive oil, garnish with pomegranate seeds, and serve.

Smoky Guacamole

Makes: 6 to 8 servings	Time: 30 to 35 minutes	Ⓓ Ⓜ Ⓥ

Throwing peeled avocado halves on the grill for a few minutes adds just the right amount of charred flavor to guacamole. Be sure to use avocados that give only a bit to pressure. Serve with tortilla chips and salsa or as part of a taco table.

3 medium or 2 large ripe Hass avocados

Good-quality olive oil for brushing

1 lemon, halved

¼ cup minced onion

½ teaspoon minced garlic, or to taste

1 serrano or jalapeño chile, seeded and minced, or cayenne to taste (optional)

1 teaspoon chili powder or any mild pure chile powder like ancho, or to taste

Salt and pepper

¼ cup chopped fresh cilantro for garnish

1 Start the coals or heat a gas grill for medium direct cooking. Make sure the grates are clean.

2 Cut the avocados in half. Carefully strike a chef's knife into the avocado pit, then wiggle it a bit to lift and remove it. Repeat with the other avocado(s).

Insert a spoon underneath the flesh against the skin and run it all the way around to separate the entire half of the avocado. Repeat with the remaining halves, brush them with oil, and squeeze one of the lemon halves over all so they don't discolor.

3 Put the avocados on the grill directly over the fire. Close the lid and cook, turning once, until grill marks develop, 2 to 3 minutes per side. Transfer to a bowl and mash with a fork or potato masher. Add the onion, garlic, chile if you're using it, chili powder, salt, pepper, and the juice from the remaining lemon half. Taste and adjust the flavors as necessary.

4 Garnish with the cilantro and serve right away. Or cover with plastic wrap, pressing it down on the surface to minimize discoloration, and refrigerate for up to 4 hours before garnishing.

Smoky Guacamole with Tomatoes	Increase the cilantro to ½ cup. Halve 1 large fresh tomato, squeeze to remove most of the seeds, and chop. Add it and the cilantro after mashing the avocado in Step 3.
Minted Avocado-Tomato Raita	Try serving with grilled naan or as a sauce for fish: Halve 1 large fresh tomato, squeeze to remove most of the seeds, and chop. Peel, seed, and chop 1 small cucumber. Grill the avocados as directed; when done, cut them into cubes instead of mashing. Toss with 1 cup yogurt, the cucumber and tomato, ¼ cup chopped fresh mint, 1 teaspoon ground cumin, and juice of 1 lime.
Avocado, Mango, and Basil Salsa	Grill the avocados as directed; cut into cubes instead of mashing. Toss with 1 ripe mango, peeled, pitted, and cubed; the onion; ¼ cup chopped fresh basil; and the juice of 1 lime.

Ⓓ direct fire Ⓘ indirect fire Ⓜ make ahead Ⓥ vegetarian option

Fire-Roasted Tomatillo Salsa with Grilled Tortilla Wedges

Makes: About 2 cups (6 to 8 servings)	Time: 25 to 30 minutes	Ⓓ Ⓜ Ⓥ

Fresh tomatillos are available most of the year now. Look for firm, unshriveled fruit still covered with tight husks. You can refrigerate the salsa for up to several hours in advance.

1 pound tomatillos

3 scallions, trimmed

1 jalapeño chile, seeded and minced (leave the seeds in if you want more heat)

2 cloves garlic, minced, or to taste

¼ cup chopped fresh cilantro

3 tablespoons fresh lime juice, or to taste

Salt and pepper

8 small corn or flour tortillas

Good-quality olive oil for brushing

1 Start the coals or heat a gas grill for medium-high direct cooking. Make sure the grates are clean.

2 Remove the husks from the tomatillos, then rinse off the tacky residue and pat dry.

3 Put the tomatillos and scallions on the grill directly over the fire. Close the lid and cook until they soften and blacken in spots, turning them to cook evenly, 5 to 10 minutes total. Transfer to a food processor or blender and add the jalapeño, garlic, cilantro, lime juice, and some salt and pepper; pulse a few times until the mixture comes together but isn't completely smooth. Taste and adjust the seasoning, adding more garlic or lime if you like.

4 Brush the tortillas on both sides with oil. Put them on the grill directly over the fire, close the lid, and toast, turning once, until they are warm and grill marks develop, 1 to 2 minutes per side. Cut into wedges and serve with the salsa.

Fire-Roasted Green Tomato Salsa	Substitute green tomatoes for the tomatillos. Cut them in half and grill on both sides.
Fire-Roasted Pico de Gallo	Grill fresh red tomatoes as for Fire-Roasted Green Tomato Salsa. After grilling, chop the tomatoes and scallions, then combine in a serving bowl with the remaining ingredients.
Fire-Roasted Jícama-Ginger Salsa	Refreshing and crunchy: Substitute 1 peeled jícama for the tomatillos and 1 tablespoon minced fresh ginger for the garlic. Cut the jícama into ¼-inch-thick slices and lightly brush with good-quality olive oil. Cook, turning once or twice to develop grill marks, 4 to 5 minutes per side; chop, then combine with the remaining ingredients.

TOP TO BOTTOM: Ancho-Dusted Jícama Sticks with Lime, Radishes with Butter and Sea Salt (page 30), and Rosemary and Garlic Olives (page 31)

Ancho-Dusted Jícama Sticks with Lime

Makes: 6 to 8 servings	Time: 35 to 45 minutes	Ⓓ Ⓥ

A popular Mexican street food delivers a winning combination of crunch, smoke, heat, and fruit, especially when you start it on a grill. Enjoy these on their own as "fries," with chips and salsa, or as part of a crudité spread. Select a jícama that feels heavy for its size, with smooth skin.

1 2-pound jícama, trimmed and peeled

2 tablespoons good-quality olive oil

2 teaspoons ancho chile powder

Salt

1 lime, cut into wedges

> **9 DIPS FOR GRILLED CRUDITÉS**
>
> 1. Lemon Aïoli (page 38)
> 2. Za'atar Yogurt Sauce (page 38)
> 3. Tofu Herb Sauce (page 123)
> 4. Lime Crema Dipping Sauce (page 82)
> 5. Tzatziki (page 322)
> 6. Minted Yogurt (page 323)
> 7. Green Goddess Dressing (page 334)
> 8. Pepper Jelly Mayo (page 271)
> 9. Blue Cheese Dressing (page 436)

1 Start the coals or heat the gas grill for medium-high direct cooking. Make sure the grates are clean.

2 Cut the jícama into ½-inch slices. Brush the slices on both sides with the olive oil. Put the slices on the grill directly over the fire. Close the lid and cook, turning once, until they develop grill marks, 7 to 10 minutes per side.

3 Transfer the jícama to a cutting board and cut the slices into ½-inch-wide sticks. Put on a serving platter and sprinkle with the ancho powder and salt to taste, turning them to coat evenly. Squeeze the lime wedges over them, again turning to coat evenly, and serve.

Chipotle-Dusted Jícama Sticks with Lime and Cilantro	Amp up the heat: Substitute 1 teaspoon chipotle powder for the ancho powder. (You can always add more.) In Step 3, sprinkle with 3 tablespoons minced fresh cilantro after adding the lime juice.
Cumin- and Pimentón–Dusted Jícama Sticks with Orange	Substitute 1 teaspoon smoked paprika (pimentón) and ½ teaspoon ground cumin for the ancho powder and ½ orange for the lime.
Sesame and Five-Spice Jícama Sticks with Lime and Soy Sauce	Replace the olive oil with sesame oil and the ancho powder with 1 teaspoon five-spice powder. Omit the salt. Toss the sticks with a mixture of the juice of 1 lime and 1 teaspoon soy sauce.

Radishes with Butter and Sea Salt

Makes: 6 to 8 servings	Time: 20 to 25 minutes	Ⓓ Ⓥ

Grilling the radishes for this classic French combination accomplishes three things: It tames their pepperiness, warms them gently, and leaves you with the tangy greens as a bonus. I recommend using radishes no more than an inch and a half around so they cook quickly and evenly. (See the photo on page 28.)

1 pound whole radishes, with greens attached

2 tablespoons good-quality olive oil

8 tablespoons (1 stick) butter, softened

1 to 2 tablespoons sea salt

1 Start the coals or heat the gas grill for hot direct cooking. Make sure the grates are clean.

2 Trim the root ends and remove any discolored leaves from the radishes. Rinse, pat them dry with paper towels, and toss with the oil until completely coated, including the greens.

3 Put the radishes on the grill directly over the fire. Close the lid and cook, turning once, until they warm through and char in places, 2 to 3 minutes per side. Transfer to a platter and serve with the butter and salt in small bowls for dipping.

Sliced Radish and Tomato Salad	Reduce the radishes to 8 ounces and omit the butter. After grilling the radishes, cut the greens off and reserve. Slice 1 pound fresh tomatoes thickly and put them on a platter. Thinly slice the radishes and scatter them on top. Sprinkle with salt. Top with the radish greens, a little more salt, drizzle with a good-quality olive oil, and serve as a side.
Radish Salsa	Works equally well as a spicy foil for chicken or fish or with a bowl of tortilla chips: Omit the butter. After grilling, chop the radishes and their greens and combine in a bowl with 1 diced peeled Kirby cucumber, ¼ cup chopped red onion, 1 thinly sliced scallion, 1 tablespoon minced fresh hot chile, 2 tablespoons fresh lemon juice, ¼ cup chopped fresh cilantro, and a sprinkle of salt and pepper.
Radish and Cotija Quesadilla	Crunchy and cheesy: Omit the butter. Reduce the radishes to 8 ounces. After grilling them, chop the greens and thinly slice the roots. Brush one side of four 8-inch flour tortillas with good-quality olive oil. With the oiled side down, sprinkle 1 cup shredded Cotija cheese over two of the tortillas, dividing it evenly. Scatter the radishes over the cheese, then the top with the remaining tortillas, oiled side up. Grill over medium-high direct heat, turning once, until the tortillas have grill marks and the cheese is melted, 2 to 3 minutes per side. Transfer to a platter, let sit for a minute to let the cheese set, then cut each into 8 wedges and serve.

Ⓓ direct fire   Ⓘ indirect fire   Ⓜ make ahead   Ⓥ vegetarian option

Rosemary and Garlic Olives

| Makes: 6 to 8 servings | Time: 30 to 45 minutes, plus marinating time | Ⓓ Ⓜ Ⓥ |

These beat marinated olives from a jar—or bar. The trip to the grill evaporates some of their moisture, which concentrates the olive flavor. (See the photo on page 28.)

2 cups olives (12 to 16 ounces; green, black, or a mixture; pitted or unpitted)

About ¼ cup good-quality olive oil

8 cloves garlic, lightly crushed with the side of a knife

4 4-inch sprigs fresh rosemary, cut into pieces

4 long strips lemon zest, removed using a vegetable peeler

1 Drain the olives well and put them in an airtight container with the oil, garlic, rosemary, and lemon zest. Cover and shake until the olives are coated with the oil. Refrigerate for at least 4 hours and as long as 2 days, shaking them every so often to make sure they're evenly coated.

2 Start the coals or heat a gas grill for hot direct cooking.

3 Put a perforated grill pan over a baking sheet to catch the oil and pour in the olives. (Or punch a lot of holes in a disposable foil pan with a skewer.) Pick out the garlic and rosemary and put them in a serving bowl. Discard the lemon zest.

4 Put the pan on the grill directly over the fire. Close the lid and let the olives sizzle, shaking the pan several times to keep them from scorching, until they have the degree of char and smokiness you like, 10 to 20 minutes total. Transfer the olives to the serving bowl and toss with the garlic and rosemary. Serve warm or at room temperature. Or cover and refrigerate for up to several weeks; bring to room temperature before serving.

Spicy Olives with Orange Zest and Aleppo Pepper	An Eastern Mediterranean spin: In Step 1, substitute one 3-inch cinnamon stick for the rosemary and orange zest for the lemon zest, and add 1 teaspoon Aleppo pepper or red chile flakes.
Boozy Martini Olives	For those who like their martinis dirty. It's best to make these with unpitted olives; otherwise, the juniper berries can get lodged inside—not the tastiest of things to bite down on. Omit the garlic and rosemary and use the zest of the entire lemon. Add ¼ cup gin and 1 tablespoon juniper berries in Step 1.
Olives and Bacon	If you like, use a flavored bacon that works with the olive seasonings: Cut 4 ounces slab bacon into ½-inch chunks. In Step 3, add them to the grill pan. Grill, stirring to cook the cubes evenly, until the bacon has browned. (These don't keep more than a day or 2.)

Quick-Pickled Charred Vegetables

| Makes: 8 or more servings | Time: 45 to 50 minutes, plus several hours pickling time | D M V |

I'm finicky about my pickles, and declare this technique nothing short of amazing. The only trick is to avoid vegetables that soften quickly, like summer squash, because they need to char but retain some crunch for the brining step. Some specifics: Cut broccoli and cauliflower into florets. Firm vegetables—like fennel, kohlrabi, daikon, onion, and jícama—should be grilled in ½-inch-thick slices, then cut into sticks. Cook whole green beans and okra (a real treat), but grill radishes whole or cut in half, depending on their size. Cucumbers hold up remarkably well on the grill; cut them into spears. And don't forget their cousins, melons. Carrots should be left whole, halved, or quartered so the pieces are no thicker than your pinky.

1½ cups distilled white vinegar or cider vinegar

½ cup sugar

1 teaspoon salt

1 teaspoon mustard seeds

1 teaspoon coriander seeds

1 teaspoon black peppercorns

2 bay leaves

2 cloves garlic, sliced

2 pounds vegetables of your choice

1 Make the brine: Put the vinegar, sugar, salt, mustard seeds, coriander seeds, peppercorns, and bay leaves in a small saucepan over medium heat. Stir until the sugar dissolves. Remove from the heat and add the garlic. When it cools, pour it into a large, nonreactive metal or glass bowl.

2 Start the coals or heat a gas grill for medium-high direct cooking. Make sure the grates are clean.

3 Prep the vegetables as described above. Put the vegetables on the grill directly over the fire. (For smaller pieces, use a perforated grill pan, or skewer them to make them easier to handle.) Close the lid and cook the vegetables, turning them as necessary, until they brown deeply on all sides without softening; how long this takes will depend on the vegetable and how hot the fire is, but figure between 5 and 15 minutes total for most vegetables. Stay close to the grill, check them early and often, and move them to cooler parts of the grill to control the coloring.

4 As they finish, transfer them to the bowl with the brine. When all are done, toss the vegetables with the brine to coat. Cover the bowl and refrigerate, tossing the vegetables every 30 minutes so, until the flavor and texture fully develop, at least 3 hours. Serve right away, or keep in an airtight container in the refrigerator for up to a week.

Quick-Pickled Charred Vegetables with Chile, Lime, and Star Anise	Perfect with Vietnamese noodles, soups, and salads: For the brine, use 1½ cups rice vinegar, ½ cup sugar, 1 teaspoon salt, and 5 pods star anise. After the liquid simmers, add the grated zest of 1 lime and 1 sliced jalapeño or Thai bird chile (remove the seeds for less heat).
Sweeter Quick-Pickled Charred Vegetables with Ginger	Akin to sweet-and-sour Chinese and Korean pickles: For the brine, use 1 cup each rice vinegar and sugar, ½ cup water, 1 teaspoon salt, and ⅓ cup thinly sliced or julienne fresh ginger. After the sugar dissolves in Step 1, let the brine bubble gently for another 15 minutes to develop the ginger flavor.
Spicy Dilly Pickled Vegetables	Terrific made with green beans or okra: In Step 1, substitute 1 tablespoon dill seeds and 2 teaspoons red chile flakes for the mustard and coriander seeds. After adding the vegetables, toss in several fresh dill sprigs if you like.

Roasted Peppers

Makes: 4 to 8 servings	Time: 45 to 50 minutes	Ⓓ Ⓜ Ⓥ

Cooked on a gas or charcoal grill, these peppers are just about perfect. The technique here works with all colors, shapes, and sizes of sweet and hot peppers, though those with thin flesh can be more challenging to peel.

8 bell peppers (about 2 pounds)

Good-quality olive oil for drizzling

Salt (optional)

Lemon wedges for serving (optional)

1 Start the coals or heat a gas grill for hot direct cooking. Make sure the grates are clean.

2 If you are using a charcoal grill, start the peppers just as the flames begin to die down. Put the peppers on the grill directly over the fire, without crowding them. (You may have to grill them in batches.) Close the lid and check on them every few minutes. As they blacken, turn them so they char on all sides, 15 to 25 minutes total. Transfer them to a bowl. Repeat with the remaining peppers, if necessary; pile them on top of the peppers already in the bowl. (Bundling peppers and chiles with thin flesh or thick skin in a foil package can help make them easier to peel.)

3 When the peppers are cool enough to handle, you should be able to easily peel off the skins with your fingers or a small knife. Cut the peppers open and remove the seeds and stems. Using as little water as possible, you can rinse any remaining seeds and skin from the peppers if you like, but a few seeds and bits of skin are fine.

4 Put the peppers on the serving plate and drizzle with lots of olive oil. Sprinkle with salt and squeeze over some lemon juice if desired. (These will keep in an airtight container in the refrigerator for at least a week.)

---

7 IDEAS FOR A GRILLED ANTIPASTO PLATTER

Here are some possibilities in addition to roasted peppers and their variations.

1. Mushrooms with Fresh Mozzarella and Prosciutto (page 43)
2. Crisp Baby Artichokes with Lemon Aïoli (page 38)
3. Rosemary and Garlic Olives (page 31)
4. Pizza Bianca (page 52) or New Haven–Style Fresh Clam Pizza (page 54), cut into 2-inch squares
5. Prosciutto-Wrapped Melon (page 44), each slice cut into 2 or 3 pieces, or Prosciutto-Wrapped Asparagus (page 44)
6. Rosemary Polenta Squares with Orange Crème Fraîche and Olives (page 60)
7. Bruschetta with Lemon and Dill White Bean Spread (page 22)

Ⓓ direct fire   Ⓘ indirect fire   Ⓜ make ahead   Ⓥ vegetarian option

ROASTING PEPPERS

STEP 1 Grill the peppers until charred on all sides, then transfer to a bowl to cool.

STEP 2 Peel off the skin with your fingers.

STEP 3 Remove the stems and seeds and cut the peppers into strips if you like.

Roasted Peppers and Anchovies	Cut the roasted, peeled peppers into 1-inch-wide strips and set a drained oil-packed or pickled white anchovy fillet on each one.
Roasted Red Pepper–Basil-Mozzarella Bites	Use all red bell peppers. After peeling, cut them into 1-inch-wide strips. Wrap a fresh basil leaf around a small fresh mozzarella ball (bocconcino), then wrap a pepper strip around and secure with a toothpick. You can also serve the components on a platter, drizzled with olive oil, and offer toothpicks on the side for guests to spear their own.
Ajvar	This purée is traditional with the Balkan-style beef kebabs known as *ćevapi* (see page 265). It also makes a rich vegetable dip for crudités or a spread for crackers or Bruschetta (page 21): Roast and peel 3 red bell peppers as directed. Grill 1 pound eggplant until collapsed, 20 to 30 minutes; when cool enough to handle, peel. Purée the vegetables in a blender or food processor with ¼ cup good-quality olive oil, 2 tablespoons chopped garlic, 1 tablespoon red wine vinegar, and a sprinkle of salt and pepper. Taste and adjust the seasoning. Store in an airtight container in the refrigerator for up to a week. Makes 2½ to 3 cups.

Appetizers and Snacks

Jalapeño Poppers with Smoked Gouda

Makes: 4 to 6 servings	Time: 25 to 30 minutes	Ⓓ Ⓜ Ⓥ

The moderate heat of jalapeños is a perfect counterbalance to this rich filling, a combination of cream cheese and smoked Gouda. The results are nothing like the breaded, deep-fried apps you get in sports bars.

12 large jalapeño chiles

4 ounces cream cheese

1 cup finely shredded smoked Gouda (to smoke your own, see page 45)

Salt

Chopped fresh cilantro for serving

1 Start the coals or heat a gas grill for medium direct cooking. Make sure the grates are clean.

2 Cut the jalapeños in half lengthwise but leave the halves connected at the stem. With your finger or a pointed spoon (like a grapefruit spoon), remove the seeds and white ribs from the halves. (Wear rubber gloves, or be careful not to touch your skin after handling the chiles.)

3 Put the cream cheese and Gouda in a medium bowl with a little salt; mash until combined. Fill the jalapeño halves evenly with a small spoon and press the halves back together to close. (You can fill and refrigerate the jalapeños up to a day ahead.)

4 Put the jalapeños on the grill directly over the fire. Close the lid and cook, carefully turning once, until the peppers have softened and browned (it's okay if they char in spots) and the cheese has melted, 5 to 10 minutes. Transfer to a platter, sprinkle with cilantro, and serve.

Honey-Orange Jalapeño Poppers	Tangy with a hint of sweet: In Step 3, fill the jalapeños with a mixture of 1½ cups crumbled fresh goat cheese (6 ounces), 2 tablespoons honey, 1 tablespoon grated orange zest, and salt to taste.
Jalapeño Poppers with Pimento Cheese and Pepper Jelly	South by Southwest: In Step 3, fill the jalapeños with with a mixture of 1 cup grated extra-sharp cheddar cheese (4 ounces), ¼ cup each chopped drained pimentos and mayonnaise, and a dash of Worcestershire sauce. Serve topped with a dab of pepper jelly.
Pesto Jalapeño Poppers with Mozzarella	In Step 3, fill the jalapeños with a mixture of 1½ cups shredded mozzarella (6 ounces) and ¼ cup Basil Pesto (page 475). Serve the poppers topped with fresh basil leaves if you like.

Crisp Baby Artichokes with Lemon Aïoli

Makes: **2 to 4 servings**	Time: **40 to 45 minutes**	Ⓓ Ⓜ Ⓥ

Baby artichokes are much easier to prepare than the mature globes, with the added benefit that every bite is edible. I clean them in advance earlier in the day, so they are ready to go on the grill when guests arrive. And if they discolor despite coating them with lemon juice, don't worry—after grilling you won't notice that at all.

2 tablespoons good-quality olive oil

Grated zest and juice of 1 lemon

8 baby artichokes

½ cup mayonnaise (to make your own, see page 460)

1 teaspoon minced garlic, or more to taste

Salt and pepper

1 Whisk the oil and lemon juice in a large bowl. Peel away and discard the outer layers of each artichoke until the leaves are half yellow and half green. With a sharp knife, cut across the top of the artichoke to remove the green tops. Leave 1 inch of stem and use a paring knife or vegetable peeler to trim the bottom so no green remains. Cut the artichoke in half lengthwise from top to bottom. As each artichoke is trimmed, add it to the olive oil mixture and toss to coat evenly; this helps delay discoloring. (You can cover the bowl and refrigerate for up to several hours.)

2 Start the coals or heat a gas grill for medium-high direct cooking. Make sure the grates are clean.

3 Make the aïoli: Put the mayonnaise, garlic, and lemon zest in a small bowl, sprinkle with salt and pepper, and whisk to combine. Taste and adjust the seasoning.

4 Put the artichokes cut side down on the grill directly over the fire. Close the lid and cook, turning once, until tender and charred, 4 to 5 minutes per side. Transfer to a plate and serve with the aïoli for dipping.

Crisp Baby Artichokes with Za'atar Yogurt Sauce	Another creamy citrus combo: For the dipping sauce, combine ½ cup yogurt, 2 teaspoons za'atar (page 456), and ½ teaspoon red chile flakes.
Crisp Baby Artichokes with Lime-Basil Vinaigrette	Use this vinaigrette as a dunk or drizzle it over the grilled artichokes before serving: Omit the lemon zest, mayonnaise, and garlic. In Step 3, whisk together ½ cup good-quality olive oil and ¼ cup fresh lime juice until it thickens. Season with salt and pepper and stir in ¼ cup thinly sliced fresh basil leaves.
Crisp Baby Artichokes with Grilled Lemon	The easiest of all: Omit the lemon zest, mayonnaise, and garlic and skip Step 3. While grilling the artichokes, also grill 1 lemon, halved, with the cut sides down. When the artichokes are done, squeeze the juice over them and serve.

Ⓓ direct fire　Ⓘ indirect fire　Ⓜ make ahead　Ⓥ vegetarian option

Brussels Sprout Skewers with Green Olive Dipping Sauce

Makes: 4 to 6 servings	Time: 20 to 25 minutes	Ⓓ Ⓜ Ⓥ

A recipe that preaches to the choir *and* makes converts: The fire crisps the outer layers of the sprouts, creating a delicious foil for the nutty, creamy insides. Try to grab small Brussels sprouts all of a similar size so they cook evenly and can be devoured in one bite. Blanching makes the sprouts easier to pierce and lets you crank up the fire to put on the perfect char. You can prepare the skewers and sauce up to several hours in advance and refrigerate; bring both to room temperature while the grill heats.

Salt

16–36 small Brussels sprouts

3 tablespoons good-quality olive oil

1 cup lightly packed fresh parsley leaves

2 tablespoons fresh lime juice

1 small clove garlic, peeled

½ cup pitted green olives

1 If you're using bamboo or wooden skewers, soak them in water for 30 minutes. Meanwhile, start the coals or heat a gas grill for hot direct cooking. Make sure the grates are clean.

2 Bring a large pot of salted water to a boil. Trim the Brussels sprouts and remove any discolored outer leaves. Add the sprouts and blanch until just soft enough to pierce with a skewer, 8 to 12 minutes. Drain, then pat dry with paper towels. Toss with 1 tablespoon of the oil in a bowl. When cool enough to handle, thread 4 to 6 sprouts on each skewer.

3 Make the dipping sauce: Put the parsley, lime juice, garlic, and remaining 2 tablespoons oil in a blender or food processor and process until chopped, stopping to scrape down the side of the container if necessary. Add the olives and pulse until the mixture is a rough purée. Taste and add a little salt if you'd like. Transfer to a small serving bowl.

4 Put the skewers on the grill directly over the fire. Close the lid and cook, turning once or more, until the Brussels sprouts are tender all the way through and browned, 3 to 5 minutes per side. Transfer to a serving plate and serve with the dipping sauce on the side.

• recipe continues →

Brussels Sprout and Soppressata Skewers	This Italian salami—or any good salami for that matter—is a nice switch from the usual bacon: You'll need 1 thin slice soppressata for every sprout. Reduce the oil to 1 tablespoon and use it only to coat the sprouts. Omit the parsley, lime juice, garlic, and olives and skip Step 3. Skewer a sprout, then fold a slice of soppressata into quarters, and push it up against the sprout on the skewer so it fans a little. Repeat with the remaining sprouts and salami. Grill until the soppressata is crisp, even charred in spots.
Brussels Sprout Skewers with Parsley-Cilantro Pesto	A bright, herbal alternative: Omit the olives, and in Step 3, add 1 cup lightly packed fresh cilantro leaves and some salt; process until smooth.
Okra Skewers with Green Olive Dipping Sauce	In Step 1, build a medium direct fire. Substitute small okra pods for the Brussels sprouts. Trim their stems; there is no need to blanch them. Okra is easier to handle if you skewer several crosswise using two skewers, threading the tops with one and the tips with another. Or skip the skewers and put the okra right on the grill if they're large enough. Cook, turning once or more, until they're bright green and you can insert a knife through the center of one without resistance, 3 to 4 minutes per side. Serve with the sauce.

D direct fire   **I** indirect fire   **M** make ahead   **V** vegetarian option

Mushrooms with Smoked Swiss and Soppressata

Makes: 4 servings	Time: 20 to 25 minutes	D M V

Stuffed mushrooms are a breeze on the grill. Instead of the usual bread crumbs or sausage, I often fill them with a rich combination of cheese and very thinly sliced salami or ham for an unbeatable combination of crisp, creamy, and earthy. You choose how decadent to go; the quantities listed are for single and double layers. And if you can't find smoked cheese, plain Swiss is still really good.

12 small to medium button or cremini mushrooms, brushed clean, stems discarded

2 tablespoons good-quality olive oil

3 or 6 thin slices soppressata, quartered

12 or 24 thin 1-inch squares smoked Swiss cheese

1 Start the coals or heat a gas grill for medium-high direct cooking. Make sure the grates are clean.

2 Brush the bottoms of the mushrooms with the oil. Put a piece of soppressata on the stem end of each mushroom. Top with a square of cheese. If you like, repeat the layering. (You can assemble the mushrooms up to several hours in advance and refrigerate until ready to grill.)

3 Put the mushrooms on the grill directly over the fire. Close the lid and cook until the mushrooms have visibly softened and the soppressata crisps, even chars in places, 4 to 5 minutes. (The cheese will retain its shape even when melted.) Transfer to a platter and serve hot.

Mushrooms with Fresh Mozzarella and Prosciutto	Prosciutto has a lot less fat than soppressata but also gets crunchy when hit with fire: Substitute prosciutto for the soppressata and fresh mozzarella for the Swiss. Low-moisture mozzarella will work fine.
Mushrooms with Herbed Goat Cheese and Toasted Walnuts	A meatless alternative: Omit the soppressata and replace the Swiss with a 4-ounce log herbed goat cheese, cut into 12 slices. Toast 12 walnut halves on a baking sheet in a 350°F oven until lightly browned and fragrant, 8 to 10 minutes. Top each mushroom with a slice of cheese, then a walnut half, pushing it in just a bit to secure. Grill until the cheese and mushrooms heat through and soften.
Portobello Mushroom Wedges with Smoked Swiss and Soppressata	Replace the mushrooms with 3 medium portobello mushrooms. Use 3 (or 6) full slices each cheese and soppressata. After brushing the cap with oil, top each mushroom with a full slice of soppressata, then a slice of Swiss; repeat if you like. Grill as directed; portobellos will take 10 to 20 minutes to soften. Transfer to a platter, slice each portobello into 4 or more wedges, and serve.

Prosciutto-Wrapped Melon

Makes: 8 servings	Time: 20 to 25 minutes	(D) (M)

Frizzled ham and juicy, warm melon—you may never eat this classic cold again. Serve each wedge as a plated first course with a knife and fork—and a salad even—or cut them across into bite-sized pieces to pass on toothpicks. You can wrap the melon slices several hours ahead of time, cover with plastic wrap, and refrigerate until you're ready to grill.

1 ripe cantaloupe

Salt and pepper

16 thin slices prosciutto

1 Start the coals or heat a gas grill for medium direct cooking. Make sure the grates are clean.

2 Cut the cantaloupe in half lengthwise and scoop out all the seeds. Cut each half into 8 wedges, then cut away the rind from each wedge. Sprinkle with salt and pepper and wrap each wedge with a slice of prosciutto, covering as much of the cantaloupe as possible.

3 Put the wedges on the grill directly over the fire. Close the lid and cook, turning once, until the prosciutto shrivels, browns, and crisps in places, 2 to 3 minutes per side. Serve hot or at room temperature.

Prosciutto-Wrapped Asparagus	Substitute 16 medium-thick asparagus spears for the melon wedges. You'll only need 8 prosciutto slices; cut each in half lengthwise before wrapping. Grill until the asparagus is crisp-tender, turning a few times, 1 to 2 minutes per side.
Virginia Ham–Wrapped Peach Slices with Five-Spice Powder	A bold and juicy spin: Substitute 4 large ripe peaches for the melon. Pit and cut each into 6 wedges. Sprinkle the wedges very lightly with five-spice powder. You'll only need 12 thin slices deli Virginia ham. Cut each in half across and wrap one piece around each peach wedge. Grill as directed. For each serving, set 3 peach wedges on a leaf of Bibb lettuce.
Pancetta-Wrapped Watermelon Skewers	Crunchy and refreshing: Cut seeded or seedless watermelon into sixteen 1- × 2-inch sticks and wrap each with a thin slice of pancetta just big enough to wrap around it. Grill until the pancetta is crisp, turning as needed, about 2 minutes per side.

(D) direct fire   (I) indirect fire   (M) make ahead   (V) vegetarian option

Smoked Cheese

Makes: as much as you'd like	Time: 30 to 45 minutes	Ⓘ Ⓜ Ⓥ

It turns out that cheese—soft and hard—takes very well to smoke. And it's easy. No cheese takes longer than 30 minutes, and some are ready in as little as 15, depending on the cheese and how much smoke you're producing. I prefer a light touch: A short hop on the grill lightly infuses them with flavor—you want it to be about the cheese, not the smoke.

A few technical tips: Any cheese that holds its shape on a board will work, even the softer types like fresh goat cheese, feta, and paneer. Don't pat the cheese dry before putting it on the grill; the moisture helps capture the smoke. Keep the temperature in the grill at 275°F or below and position the cheese as far away from the fire as you can; at most, you want the cheese to gently warm through. No need to turn the cheese; the smoke surrounds and colors it pretty evenly.

It's your choice of cheese and quantity. Look for cheese with a higher melting point; it also helps if it is soft and/or somewhat moist/wet, as long as it will hold its shape.

1 Start the coals or heat a gas grill for medium-low indirect cooking. (Position the coals so that the smoke will be pulled over the food and out the top vent.) Make sure the grates are clean. When the grill is ready, put 1 cup wood chips in the grill (see "Smoking," pages 10–12) and close the lid.

2 If you have a large piece of cheese, cut it in half or several pieces to increase the surface area.

3 As soon as the grill fills with smoke, put the cheese on the indirect side as far away from the fire as you can. Close the lid and cook until the cheese has lightly colored, 15 to 30 minutes; you may need to add more wood to keep the smoke going. Taste occasionally; when it's as smoky as you like, transfer the cheese to a platter or board and serve right away. Or wrap tightly and refrigerate until you're ready to serve; let come back to room temperature for serving.

• recipe continues →

Smoked Ricotta	Now you can add a touch of smoke flavor to baked pasta dishes or Calzones (page 371): To help keep the ricotta from drying out, spread it in a shallow heatproof baking dish so that the layer is 1 to 1½ inches deep. Smoke as directed for 15 to 20 minutes; you may see it start to color at that point. Stir the ricotta and taste. If it doesn't quite have the degree of smokiness you want, smooth it out again and let it go another 5 to 10 minutes. Remove from the grill, let cool, then refrigerate in an airtight container until you are ready to use it.
Smoked Yogurt	For an elusive flavor that's wonderful in dips and sauces both savory and sweet: Put the yogurt in a shallow heatproof bowl. Smoke as directed for 20 minutes; it probably won't have colored at all by then; stir and taste. You're not looking for overt smokiness, but the yogurt will start to sweeten and caramelize a bit when it's ready. It might take another 5 minutes.
Smoked Goat Cheese Spread with Fruit and Nuts	Delicious and pretty: Smoke two 4-ounce logs fresh goat cheese as directed. Put in a medium bowl and mash together with 2 tablespoons sour cream or yogurt. Add ½ cup each minced dried fruit and chopped nuts, and cream together. (I like cranberries, figs, apricots, cherries, or a mix.)

D direct fire   I indirect fire   M make ahead   V vegetarian option

Provoleta

Makes: 4 to 6 servings	Time: 30 to 35 minutes, largely unattended	Ⓓ Ⓥ

I love everything about this dish, starting with the name: Provoleta. Crusty bread spread with seared, melted provolone cheese is a traditional part of the Argentinian *asado* or grill meal. A cast-iron pan is a must for this, preferably small. (A 5-inch square pan is the perfect size for a ¾-inch-thick slice of cheese; a 6-inch round pan is runner-up.)

Good-quality vegetable oil for the pan

1¾- to 1-inch-thick slice provolone cheese (about 8 ounces)

1 tablespoon chopped fresh oregano (optional)

1 teaspoon red chile flakes (optional)

1 baguette, sliced, for serving

1 Start the coals or heat a gas grill for hot direct cooking. Pour a little bit of oil on a paper towel and lightly grease a small cast-iron pan. Put the pan on the grill directly over the fire, close the lid, and let it heat for 10 minutes.

2 Put the cheese in the hot pan and sprinkle with the oregano and red pepper, if you're using them. Close the lid and cook until the cheese melts to fill the pan and gets bubbly and crusty at the edges, 4 to 5 minutes. Carefully transfer the extremely hot skillet to a trivet and serve with the baguette slices.

---

7 OTHER CHEESES ON THE GRILL

All of these cheeses can go right on the grate, directly over the fire.

1. **Kasseri:** A pungent and salty semihard cheese made in Greece and Turkey from unpasteurized sheep's milk
2. **Kefalotyri:** A salty hard cheese made from sheep's or goat's milk, traditional to Greece and Cyprus
3. **Manouri:** A semisoft goat and sheep's milk cheese from Greece made from the whey left over from making feta cheese.
4. **Paneer:** A fresh cheese popular throughout India, Pakistan, and other South Asian countries made by curdling water buffalo's milk or buffalo's and cow's milk
5. **Feta:** A brined white cheese made from sheep's milk or sheep's and goat's milk
6. **Queso fresco:** A mild Mexican fresh cheese usually made from cow's milk
7. **Bread cheese:** "Bread cheese" is the translation of this cheese's original name, *juustoleipa*; it has been made in Finland and Sweden for several hundred years, from reindeer milk. It came to this country with Scandinavian immigrants; here it is made from cow's milk and part of the cheesemaking process is baking it.

recipe continues →

Appetizers and Snacks

Raclette	Once hard to find but now increasingly available: Substitute raclette cheese for the provolone and omit the oregano and red chile flakes. Serve with cornichons, pickled onions, and boiled fingerling or other small potatoes.
Halloumi Cheese with Balsamic Glaze and Pomegranate Seeds	A semihard brined cheese from Cyprus, halloumi is a sheep's and goat's milk blend with a very high melting point. Grilling it is kind of amazing; you can brown it, even char it, and it won't change its shape: Substitute 8 ounces halloumi for the provolone; omit the oregano and red chile flakes. Put the cheese on the grill directly over the fire. Close the lid and cook, turning once, until heated through and deeply browned, 10 to 12 minutes per side. Transfer to a serving plate and make several cuts in the top to facilitate breaking it apart. Drizzle the top with 1 to 2 tablespoons Balsamic Syrup (page 467) and sprinkle with ¼ cup pomegranate seeds. Serve with crackers.
Queso Frito with Salami	Made from cow's milk, *queso frito* (also sold as *queso de freir* or *queso para freir*) is a staple of Central American and Caribbean cooking, most often served fried (as the name implies). Look for it in the refrigerator section of the supermarket where corn tortillas are sold: Grill one 10-ounce package queso frito as directed for the halloumi variation above. Serve with slices of salami. If you want even more smoke flavor, you can grill the unsliced salami before slicing it, turning to let it brown on all sides, 5 to 8 minutes total.

Real Grilled Cheese Bites

Makes: 2 to 4 appetizer servings or 1 lunch serving	Time: 25 to 30 minutes	Ⓓ Ⓜ Ⓥ

When something is *really* good, all you need is a bite. So like pizza or quesadillas, a well-made sandwich easily doubles as an appetizer. The most important thing is to avoid the sin of overstuffing. How much you use depends on the cheese.

1–2 ounces cheese, sliced

2 slices country-style bread

1 tablespoon good-quality olive oil or softened butter

1 Start the coals or heat a gas grill for medium direct cooking. Make sure the grates are clean.

2 Put the cheese between the pieces of bread. Brush or spread the oil or butter over both sides of the sandwich.

3 Put the sandwich on the grill directly over the fire. (If you like, you can set a pan on top of the sandwich, to press the sandwich into the grate.) Close the lid and cook, turning once, until the bread turns golden brown and the cheese has melted, 3 to 5 minutes per side. Transfer to a plate and let sit for 1 or 2 minutes for the cheese to set. Cut into quarters or eighths and serve right away.

---

9 CHEESES TO TRY IN REAL GRILLED CHEESE BITES

1. Mozzarella
2. Fontina
3. Monterey Jack
4. Havarti
5. Muenster
6. Asiago
7. Gouda
8. Provolone
9. Taleggio

Cubano Bites	Use a Swiss cheese like Gruyère, Jarlsberg, or Emmental. First layer in 1 or 2 thin slices roast pork, then the cheese, then 1 or 2 slices boiled ham, then a layer of dill pickle chips. Spread yellow mustard on the inside of the top piece of bread. Grill as directed. Try to cut the pieces so that each bite contains a full pickle chip.
Cheddar-Apple Bites	Use cheddar cheese and add thin slices of red or green apple.
Brie and Fig Bites	Brie softens on the grill rather than melts, and it's delicious this way: Use thinly sliced Brie cheese (slice it along one of the cut edges if you have a wedge) and top with thinly sliced ripe figs. Or spread the inside of one slice of bread with store-bought fig jam. Leave the sandwich on the grill for a good 5 minutes before turning it.

Cheesy Jalapeño Quesadillas

| Makes: 4 appetizer servings or 2 light lunch servings | Time: 20 to 25 minutes | Ⓓ Ⓥ |

You have unlimited options for varying these: Try a grated Mexican-style melting cheese like Chihuahua or Oaxaca, which are now easy to find in supermarkets. Serrano or Anaheim chiles will punch up the heat, and pickled peppers are a fun twist. Once off the grill, an easy way to cut quesadillas quickly and neatly into wedges is to use a pizza cutter.

Good-quality vegetable oil for brushing

4 8-inch flour tortillas

1 cup grated Monterey Jack cheese

1 large jalapeño chile, or to taste, seeded if you like, chopped

1 Start the coals or heat a gas grill for medium-high direct cooking. Make sure the grates are clean.

2 Lightly brush one side of 2 of the tortillas with oil. With the dry sides facing up, scatter half the cheese over each; top with the jalapeño. Cover with the remaining tortillas and brush the tops with oil.

3 Put the quesadillas on the grill directly over the fire. Close the lid and cook, turning once, until the tortillas turn golden brown and the cheese has melted, 2 to 3 minutes per side. Transfer to a cutting board and let sit for 1 or 2 minutes to let the cheese set. Slice each quesadilla into 8 wedges and serve hot.

Quesadillas with Black Beans and Fresh Tomato	Omit the jalapeño. Chop 1 medium fresh tomato. Rinse, drain, and mash one 15-ounce can black beans; season with salt and pepper and 1 teaspoon ground cumin. In Step 2, spread the dry side of the tortillas with a thin layer of the black bean mixture; refrigerate the rest for another use. Top with the cheese, then the tomato. Finish and grill the quesadillas as directed.
Quesadillas with Cheddar, Avocado, and Cilantro	Omit the jalapeño; substitute cheddar for the Monterey Jack. Pit, peel, and thinly slice 1 ripe avocado. In Step 2, divide the avocado between the quesadillas, layering it over the cheese; sprinkle each with 1 to 2 tablespoons roughly chopped fresh cilantro, and finish and grill as directed.
Hoisin Quesadillas with Scallions and Basil	Use Thai basil here if you can find it: Omit the jalapeño; substitute mozzarella or Oaxaca cheese for the Monterey Jack. For each quesadilla, brush one side of 2 of the tortillas with 1 tablespoon hoisin sauce, top with the cheese, and sprinkle with 1 thinly sliced scallion and 2 large fresh basil leaves, thinly sliced. Finish and grill the quesadillas as directed.

Pizza Bianca

Makes: 2 or more small pizzas	Time: 2 to 3 hours, largely unattended, if making own dough	D M V

White pizza has no sauce or cheese, just a sprinkle of coarse salt and rosemary and a drizzle of good-quality olive oil. It's essentially bread—only way better. Serve this as is with dinner, as a vehicle for a spread or dip, or to make sandwiches.

3 cups all-purpose or bread flour, plus more as needed

2 teaspoons instant yeast

2 teaspoons kosher or coarse sea salt, plus more for sprinkling

2 tablespoons good-quality olive oil, plus more for drizzling

1 tablespoon or more chopped fresh rosemary

1 Whisk the flour, yeast, and salt together in a large bowl. Add the oil and 1 cup water and mix with a heavy spoon. Continue to add water, 1 tablespoon at a time, until the dough forms a ball and is slightly sticky to the touch. In the unlikely event that the mixture gets too sticky, add flour 1 tablespoon at a time until you have the right consistency.

2 Lightly flour a work surface and turn out the dough onto it. Knead by hand for a minute until smooth, then form into a round ball. Put the dough in a bowl and cover with plastic wrap; let rise in a warm spot until it doubles in size, 1 to 2 hours. You can cut this rising time short if you're in a hurry, or you can let the dough rise more slowly, in the refrigerator, for up to 8 hours. You can freeze the dough at this point for up to a month: Wrap it tightly in plastic wrap or put in a zipper bag. Thaw in the refrigerator; bring to room temperature before shaping.

3 To shape, divide the dough into 2 or more pieces; roll each piece into a round ball. Put each ball on a lightly floured work surface, sprinkle lightly with flour, and cover with plastic wrap or a towel. Let rest until slightly puffed, 25 to 30 minutes.

4 Start the coals or heat a gas grill for medium direct cooking. Make sure the grates are clean.

5 Roll or lightly press each ball into a flat, round disk, lightly flouring the work surface and the dough as necessary to keep it from sticking (use only as much flour as you need). To stretch the dough, push down at the center and outward to the edge, turning the round as you do. Continue pushing down and out and turning the dough until the round is the size you want; if you're making 2 pizzas, aim for rounds 10 to 12 inches in diameter. Sprinkle the tops evenly with the rosemary and a pinch or so coarse salt, then drizzle lightly with olive oil.

6 Put the crusts on the grill directly over the fire. Close the lid and cook until the bottoms firm up and brown and the tops are cooked through, 5 to 10 minutes, depending on how hot the fire is; the top side of the dough will bubble up from the heat underneath but likely won't take on much color. Transfer to a cutting board and use a pizza cutter to slice into wedges or small pieces and serve.

● recipe continues →

D direct fire   I indirect fire   M make ahead   V vegetarian option

Margherita Pizza (page 54)

Margherita Pizza	So insanely good during peak tomato season; in the heat of the grill, the slices concentrate to a sauce-like consistency: Omit the rosemary, salt, and olive oil. For the two pizzas, you'll need about 8 ounces thinly sliced mozzarella cheese and 2 medium tomatoes, sliced ¼ inch thick. Top each crust with mozzarella, then tomato. After the crust has cooked and the cheese melted, transfer to a cutting board and let cool a couple minutes. Scatter with fresh basil leaves, slice, and serve.
Pizza with Mozzarella and Prosciutto	Salty, crisp, and creamy all at the same time: Omit the rosemary, salt, and olive oil. You'll need about 8 ounces each of thinly sliced mozzarella cheese and prosciutto for 2 pizzas. Top the crusts with mozzarella, then fully cover all the way to the edge of the pie with thinly sliced prosciutto. Grill and serve as directed.
New Haven–Style Fresh Clam Pizza	Based on Frank Pepe's famous clam pizza: Omit the rosemary and salt. Shuck 32 littleneck clams, removing them from their shells (see page 76, or have your fishmonger do this). In a small bowl, mix together ¾ cup freshly grated pecorino Romano cheese, 4 cloves garlic, minced, and 1 tablespoon minced fresh oregano; use this mixture to top the pizzas. Put the clams on top, then drizzle very lightly with olive oil. Grill as directed until the crusts brown and the clams are hot.

---

7 WAYS TO FLAVOR PIZZA DOUGH

Knead any of these ingredients into the dough in Step 2:

1. 2 tablespoons chopped or mashed Grill-Roasted Garlic (page 464)
2. ¼ cup freshly grated Parmesan, pecorino Romano, or other hard cheese
3. 2 slices bacon, fried until crisp then chopped, or 2 ounces diced pancetta, fried until crisp
4. 1 ounce thinly sliced salami (hard, Genoa, soppressata, capicola, pepperoni), chopped
5. 2 tablespoons pesto of your choice (to make your own, see page 475) or chopped oil-packed dried tomatoes
6. 1 tablespoon chopped fresh rosemary or basil
7. 2 tablespoons chopped black olives

D direct fire   I indirect fire   M make ahead   V vegetarian option

PIZZA ON THE GRILL

Cooking pizza this way is nothing short of a miracle. (Like: why doesn't the dough slip through the grate?) The only challenge is transferring the topped dough to the grill. If you're going to be grilling pizza frequently, think about investing in a peel. This tool makes getting the dough onto and off the grill a lot easier, especially if you get one of those stainless-steel paddles that look like a giant spatula. You can use an inverted baking sheet, or just wait to add the toppings until after the dough is on the grill and work quickly. Don't be tempted to make one large pie—it'll be too unwieldy and you'll end up with disappointing results—and go easy on the toppings. This should be about the crust.

Smoked Nuts

Makes: 2 cups	Time: 45 minutes, or longer to taste	Ⓘ Ⓜ Ⓥ

No one can eat just one . . . handful. Raw nuts can go south fast, so be sure to taste them before starting. My favorite nuts for smoking are walnuts, almonds, and pecans, but pine nuts, peanuts, macadamias, and cashews are all fine. Blanched hazelnuts also work. For me, 30 minutes of smoke time is ideal for most nuts, but start tasting before that to pinpoint what you like.

2 cups shelled unsalted raw nuts

2 tablespoons good-quality vegetable oil

2 teaspoons salt

1 Start the coals or heat a gas grill for medium indirect cooking. Position the coals so that the smoke will be pulled over the food and out the top vent.

2 Put the nuts, oil, and salt in a disposable foil pan large enough to hold the nuts in a single layer. Toss to coat.

3 When the grill is ready, put a generous handful of wood chips in the grill (see "Smoking," pages 10–12) and close the lid. As soon as the grill fills with smoke, put the pan of nuts on the indirect side of the grill and close the lid again.

4 Smoke the nuts, shaking the pan every 10 minutes or so, until they're as smoky and crisp as you like, at least 20 minutes. Replenish the wood as needed to keep the grill filled with smoke. Remove the nuts from the grill and serve when they're cool enough to handle. Or cool completely, transfer to an airtight container, and refrigerate for up to a few weeks or freeze for several months; bring to room temperature before serving.

Sweet and Salty Smoked Nuts	In Step 2, add 2 tablespoons sugar to the pan along with the nuts, oil, and salt.
Hot and Sweet Nuts	Reduce the salt to 1 teaspoon. In Step 2, add 2 tablespoons sugar and 2 teaspoons chili powder, 1 teaspoon chipotle chile powder, or ½ teaspoon cayenne.
Umami Nuts	Omit the salt and replace the oil with ¼ cup tamari.

MORE SPICE MIXTURES YOU CAN USE WITH SMOKED NUTS

After tossing the nuts with the oil, toss them with 2 to 3 tablespoons of any of the spice mixes until evenly coated, then grill as directed. Or, you can toss them with ¼ cup Balsamic Syrup (page 467) or Ponzu Sauce (page 468), or any of their variations, before smoking.

- The seasoning mix from Cajun-Style Grilled Shrimp (page 63) and its variation
- Star Anise Grill Salt (page 222)
- Baharat Rub (page 254)
- Smoky Cumin Grill Salt (page 204) and its variations
- Chris's Best Ever Rub and its variations (page 455)
- Lime-Ancho Grill Salt (page 279)
- Jerk Seasoning (page 456)
- Garam masala (mix it with 2 teaspoons salt before adding)
- Curry powder (mix it with 2 teaspoons salt before adding)
- Spiced Brown Sugar Rub (page 112)
- Chipotle-Cumin Grill Salt (page 209)

Polenta Squares with Chive Sour Cream and Salmon Roe

| Makes: **48 squares** | Time: **60 to 70 minutes, plus cooling time** | Ⓓ Ⓜ |

Elegant and unexpected, these luxe little morsels will have guests singing your praises. And you'll have time to bask in the spotlight since you made most of it before they arrived. Be sure to cook the polenta to the thickness described in the recipe; otherwise it will never firm up enough for you to slice and grill it.

1 tablespoon butter, plus more for the pan

1 cup medium or coarse polenta

½ cup milk (preferably whole)

Salt and pepper

1 cup sour cream

¼ cup minced chives

Grated zest and juice of 1 lemon

Good-quality olive oil for brushing the polenta

2–3 ounces salmon roe

1 Butter a 9- × 13-inch baking pan. Put the polenta in a medium saucepan with 1 cup water and whisk to form a smooth slurry. Whisk in the milk and a large pinch salt and set the pan over medium-high heat. Heat until the mixture boils, then lower the heat to medium and cook, whisking frequently and adding more water a little at a time to prevent lumps and keep the mixture somewhat soupy. Expect to add another 2½ to 3½ cups water before the polenta is ready. It will be thick and creamy, with just a little grittiness, and the mixture will pull away from the side of the pan when you stir, 15 to 30 minutes, depending on the grind. Stir in the butter until incorporated and taste for salt and pepper. Pour the polenta into the prepared pan and spread into an even layer; it should be about ½ inch thick. Let stand at room temperature until fully cooled (or cover and refrigerate overnight).

2 Start the coals or heat a gas grill for medium-high direct cooking. Make sure the grates are clean.

3 Whisk the sour cream, chives, and lemon zest in a small bowl. Add lemon juice to taste.

4 With a serrated knife, cut the polenta in half across the short side so that you have two pieces, each 6½ × 9 inches. Lift them out of the pan with a spatula, being careful not to break them apart. Lightly brush them with oil on both sides. Put them on the grill directly over the fire. Close the lid and cook, turning once, until they are brown and heated through, 3 to 5 minutes per side.

5 Carefully transfer the grilled polenta to a cutting board. With the serrated knife, cut each half into 4 strips along the short side, then cut each strip into 6 equal pieces. Transfer the squares to a platter. Dollop 1 teaspoon of the sour cream mixture on each square, top with a few salmon eggs, and serve.

● recipe continues →

Polenta Squares with Dilled Sour Cream and Smoked Salmon	Substitute chopped fresh dill for the chives and smoked salmon (lox) for the salmon roe; one 4-ounce package should be enough. Top the sour cream with a small piece of salmon. If your store carries smoked salmon trimmings, this is the perfect use for it.
Rosemary Polenta Squares with Orange Crème Fraîche and Olives	Replace the sour cream with crème fraîche, and the lemon with orange zest and juice. In Step 1, add 1 tablespoon chopped fresh rosemary. In Step 5, top the crème fraîche mixture with chopped pitted kalamata olives.
Polenta Squares with Dried Tomato–Basil Goat Cheese and Chorizo	Omit the sour cream, chives, and lemon. Mash 8 ounces fresh goat cheese with ¼ cup each chopped oil-packed dried tomatoes and chopped fresh basil. In Step 5, spread the mixture on each polenta square and top with a very thin slice of Spanish chorizo (alternatively, chop about 4 ounces chorizo and sprinkle it over the top).

D direct fire I indirect fire M make ahead V vegetarian option

Hot-Smoked Fish

Makes: **8 servings**	Time: About 1 hour, plus marinating/ brining time largely unattended	Ⓘ Ⓜ

Once you try this easy technique, you'll never buy expensive smoked fish again. Infusing the fish with smoke using indirect heat dries and firms the flesh. The results beg to be flaked and served on a cracker. The wet marinade adds another layer of flavor but is totally optional.

1 cup bourbon (optional)

Leaves from 5 sprigs fresh rosemary (optional)

2 pounds fish fillets (ideally no more than 1 inch thick each)

¾ cup brown sugar

½ cup salt

1 tablespoon crushed black peppercorns

1 If you are using the wet marinade, pour the bourbon in a baking dish that will fit the fillets in a single layer. If the fillets are skinless, coat them on both sides with the bourbon and sprinkle both sides with the rosemary leaves. If the fillets are skin-on, sprinkle the rosemary over the bourbon and put the fillets in the dish skinless side down. Cover and refrigerate for 2 hours, turning them once if they are skinless. Remove the fish from the bourbon, rinse, and pat dry with paper towels. Discard any remaining marinade. Wash and dry the baking dish.

2 Stir the sugar, salt, and peppercorns together in a small bowl to make a dry brine. Work the mixture into the fillets, skinless side(s) only and put back into the baking dish. Refrigerate, uncovered, for 2 hours.

3 Start the coals or heat a gas grill for medium indirect cooking. Position the coals so that the smoke will be pulled over the food and out the top vent. Make sure the grates are clean. When the grill is ready, add wood to the grill (see "Smoking," pages 10–12) and close the lid.

4 When the grill fills with smoke, put the fish on the indirect side of the grill. Close the lid and cook until the fillets break into flakes when you press down on them, 25 to 45 minutes, depending on the thickness of the fish and how hot the fire is. Transfer to a platter and serve warm, at room temperature, or chilled. (To store, let the fish cool completely, then wrap tightly and refrigerate for up to 1 week or freeze up to 1 year; thaw in the refrigerator before serving.)

• recipe continues →

Hot-Smoked Fish with Gravlax Flavors	Substitute gin for the bourbon and dill for the rosemary.
Sriracha and Five-Spice Hot-Smoked Fish	Omit the bourbon and rosemary. For the wet marinade, whisk together ¼ cup sriracha and the juice of 2 limes. Brush this over the skinless side(s) of the fish. Add 1 tablespoon five-spice powder to the dry brine. Proceed as directed.
Hot-Smoked Fish Spread	Here is a basic recipe you can tweak as you like, depending on the type of fish and its seasonings: Put one 8-ounce package cream cheese, 1 cup flaked smoked fish, ½ cup crème fraîche or sour cream, the juice of ½ lemon, 1 tablespoon each grated lemon zest and minced chives, and 1 teaspoon Worcestershire sauce in a medium bowl and mash together with a fork or the back of a spoon until thoroughly combined. Serve with crackers or small toasts. Makes 10 or more servings.

---

11 FISH FOR HOT-SMOKING

Buy fillets that are about the same thickness for even cooking, no more than 1 inch thick so the smoke time doesn't end up being too long. And make sure the fish is super fresh; if you're in doubt, choose something else.

1. Black cod
2. Bluefish
3. Catfish
4. Eel
5. Mackerel

6. Mahi-mahi
7. Salmon
8. Tilapia (not my favorite, but it's popular)

9. Trout (I like to use butterflied trout; if you prefer, you can cut the heads off before starting)

10. Tuna
11. Whitefish

D direct fire   I indirect fire   M make ahead   V vegetarian option

Cajun-Style Grilled Shrimp

Makes: 6 to 8 appetizer servings or 4 main-course servings	Time: 25 to 30 minutes	D M

When it comes to seafood, shell-on versus shell-off can open a heated discussion. I find cooking in the shell almost always enhances the natural flavor of the sea. (And you don't have to do all the peeling!) It's your choice. Just be sure to serve these with plenty of napkins on hand. If you go with small shrimp, skewer them or use a perforated grill pan. You can also make this with crawfish, though most folks will have to buy frozen crawfish tails. Because of their smaller size, you'll have to cook them in a grill pan so they don't fall through the grate.

1 teaspoon salt

1 teaspoon paprika

1 teaspoon garlic powder

1 teaspoon cayenne

½ teaspoon dried oregano

½ teaspoon black pepper

2 pounds extra-large or jumbo shrimp, peeled and deveined if you like

2 tablespoons good-quality olive oil

1 Start the coals or heat a gas grill for medium-high direct cooking. Make sure the grates are clean.

2 Put the salt, paprika, garlic, cayenne, oregano, and pepper in a small bowl; whisk to combine. Put the shrimp in a large bowl and toss with the oil. Sprinkle the spice mix over the shrimp and toss until evenly coated with the spices. (You can prepare the shrimp up to several hours ahead, cover, and refrigerate until you're ready to grill.)

3 Put the shrimp on the grill directly over the fire (see "Grilling Shrimp," page 125). Close the lid and cook, turning once, until the shrimp are opaque all the way through and the spice mix looks crusty, 3 to 5 minutes per side depending on their size and how hot the fire is. Transfer the shrimp to a serving platter, let cool for a few minutes, then have at it.

• recipe continues →

Rosemary and Red Pepper Grilled Shrimp	So incredibly aromatic: Substitute red chile flakes for the paprika and omit the cayenne, oregano, and black pepper. In Step 3, toss the shrimp with 2 tablespoons chopped fresh rosemary and the grated zest of 1 lemon when they come off the grill (adding these seasonings at the last minute will keep their flavors vibrant).
Smoked Paprika and Orange Grilled Shrimp	Pimentón intensifies and sweetens the smokiness: Substitute smoked paprika (pimentón) for the regular paprika and ground cumin for the cayenne; omit the oregano and black pepper. In Step 3, toss the shrimp with the grated zest of 1 orange when they come off the grill.
Chipotle and Oregano Grilled Shrimp	Even hotter: Substitute chipotle chile powder for the paprika, ground cumin for the cayenne, and 2 tablespoons chopped fresh oregano for the dried oregano. Squeeze the juice of 1 lime over the grilled shrimp before serving.

D direct fire   I indirect fire   M make ahead   V vegetarian option

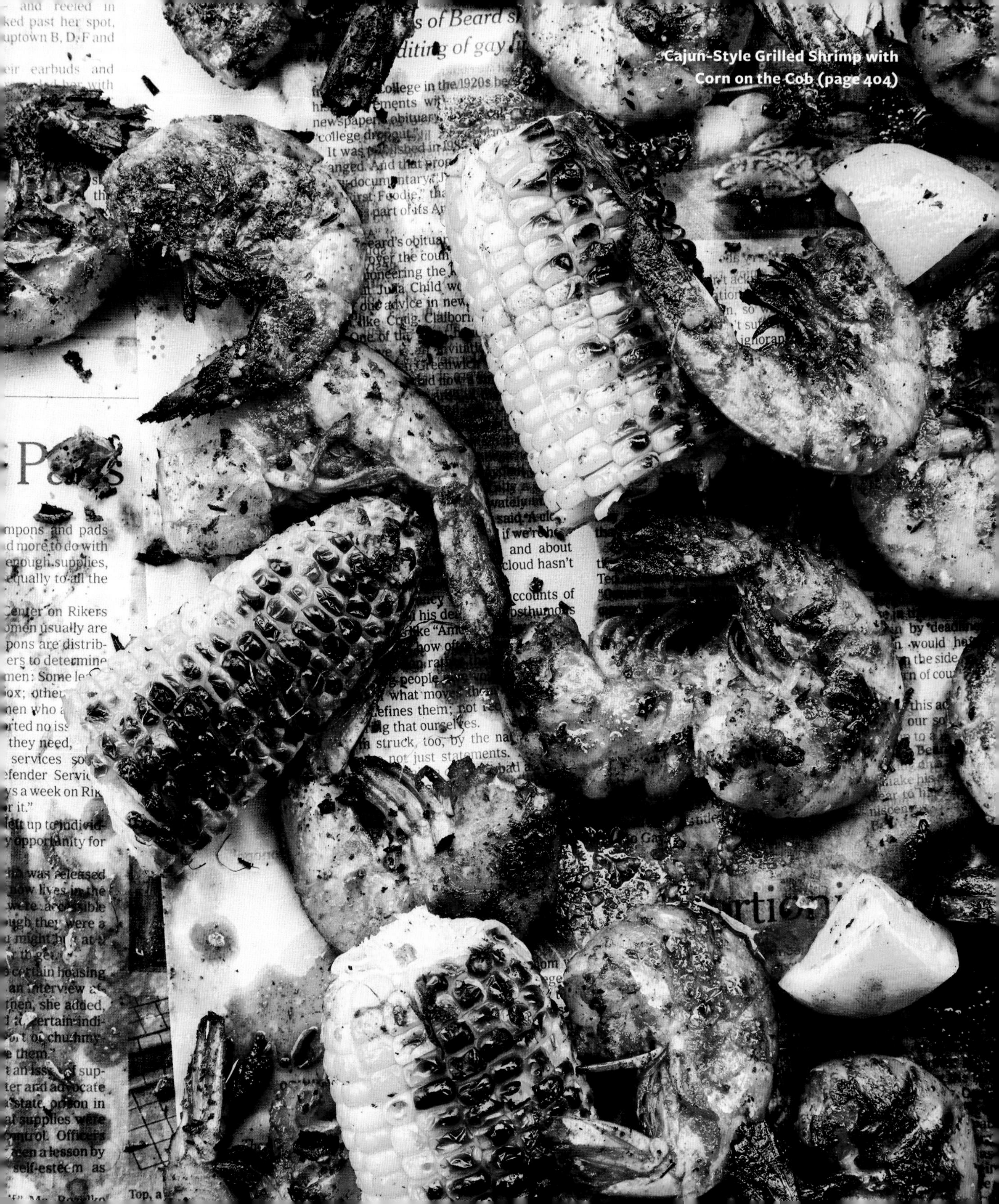

Cajun-Style Grilled Shrimp with Corn on the Cob (page 404)

Capicola-Wrapped Scallops

Makes: 6 servings	Time: 20 to 25 minutes	Ⓓ Ⓜ

I've grilled enough bacon-wrapped scallops to know they're a pain. I take the easy way out here, using very thinly sliced capicola, which doesn't require precooking. (You can also use soppressata or any other deli salami of your preference.) By the time the scallop is done, the capicola will be charry, a delicious counterpoint to the sweet creaminess of the scallop. Don't forget to clean the grill grates well, otherwise the scallops will stick.

1 pound sea scallops (16–20), trimmed of any tough connective tissue

Good-quality olive oil for brushing the scallops

16–20 thin slices capicola

1 Start the coals or heat a gas grill for medium-high direct cooking. Make sure the grates are clean.

2 Pat the scallops dry with paper towels, then brush lightly with oil. For each scallop, roll up a slice of capicola, push down to flatten it, then wind it around the side of a scallop. Secure both ends with a toothpick. (You can do this up to several hours ahead. Cover and refrigerate until ready to grill.)

3 Put the scallops on the grill directly over the fire. Close the lid and cook, turning once, until they're golden brown in spots, 3 to 5 minutes per side. You want a good sear on the outside of the scallop, with the center still ever so slightly translucent. The capicola should be crisp. Transfer to a platter and serve.

Salami and Scallops	Another way to enjoy this combo: Omit the capicola. Buy a stick of your favorite dry salami and cut it into ¼-inch-thick slices. Set a scallop on each slice and run a toothpick through the center to secure them. Put them salami side on the grill and cook until the salami gets really crisp, 3 to 4 minutes, then turn over and cook just until the scallops are done, 1 to 2 minutes.
Bacon-Wrapped Water Chestnuts	Rumaki without the chicken liver; spectacular with fresh water chestnuts: Substitute 18 whole peeled water chestnuts for the scallops and 6 slices bacon for the capicola. Combine ¼ cup soy sauce and 1 tablespoon each brown sugar and minced fresh ginger in a large bowl, add the water chestnuts, and toss to coat well. Cut the bacon across into thirds. Wrap each water chestnut in a piece of bacon and secure with a toothpick. Grill over medium direct heat until the bacon gets crisp on all sides, 4 to 8 minutes total. If the bacon looks like it's burning instead of browning, move the chestnuts to the outer edges of the fire.
Bacon-Wrapped Dates	Simple and richly delicious: Substitute 18 pitted dates for the scallops and 6 slices bacon for the capicola. Cut the bacon across into thirds. Wrap each date in a piece of bacon and secure with a toothpick. Grill over medium direct heat until the bacon gets crisp on all sides, 4 to 8 minutes total. If the bacon looks like it's burning instead of browning, move the dates to the outer edges of the fire.

Scallop and Mango Salad

Makes: 6 to 8 servings	Time: 25 to 30 minutes	Ⓓ

Properly cooked scallops are as creamy and sweet as fruit, only they taste more like the sea. To turn this plated salad into finger food, chop everything into pea-sized pieces and serve with chips.

2 tablespoons fresh lime juice

1 tablespoon fish sauce

1 tablespoon rice vinegar

1 tablespoon warm water

1 tablespoon sugar

2 ripe mangoes, peeled and flesh cut off the pit into 1-inch pieces

Grated zest of 1 lime

½ cup packed fresh mint leaves

½ cup packed fresh cilantro leaves

1½ pounds sea scallops, trimmed of any tough connective tissue

Good-quality olive oil for brushing the scallops

Salt and pepper

Lime wedges for serving

1 If you're using bamboo or wooden skewers, soak them in water for 30 minutes. Start the coals or heat a gas grill for hot direct cooking. Make sure the grates are clean.

2 Make the dressing: Whisk the lime juice, fish sauce, vinegar, water, and sugar together in a small bowl until the sugar dissolves.

3 Put the mango and lime zest in a medium bowl; toss with 1 tablespoon of the dressing. Put the mint and cilantro leaves in another bowl; toss with 2 tablespoons of the dressing.

4 Pat the scallops dry with paper towels. Lightly brush them on both sides with oil and sprinkle with salt and pepper. Thread them onto skewers.

5 Put the skewers on the grill directly over the fire. Close the lid and cook, turning once, until the scallops are golden brown in spots, 3 to 5 minutes per side. You want a good sear on the outside of the scallops, with the centers still ever so slightly translucent. Transfer the scallops to individual plates or a platter.

6 Add the mango and herbs to the scallops, drizzle with the remainder of the dressing, and serve with lime wedges.

Ⓓ direct fire   Ⓘ indirect fire   Ⓜ make ahead   Ⓥ vegetarian option

Scallop Salad with Kiwi and Star Fruit	For the dressing, substitute 3 tablespoons good-quality olive oil and 1 tablespoon each cider vinegar, fresh orange juice, and honey for the lime juice, fish sauce, vinegar, water, and sugar. Replace the mangoes with 1 or 2 star fruit, cut across into ¼-inch slices, and omit the lime zest and wedges. Peel and chop 2 kiwis. For each salad, include 2 star fruit slices and sprinkle the scallops with the kiwi.
Scallop Salad with Oranges and Pine Nuts	For the dressing, substitute 3 tablespoons good-quality olive oil and 1 tablespoon each pomegranate molasses and red wine vinegar for the lime juice, fish sauce, vinegar, water, and sugar. Instead of the mangoes, peel and section 3 medium or 4 small oranges. Omit the lime zest and wedges. In Step 6, sprinkle the salad with ¼ cup toasted pine nuts before serving.
Scallop Salad with Papaya and Basil	Substitute two 12- to 16-ounce ripe papayas for the mangoes; peel, cut in half, scoop out the seeds, and cube. Substitute basil sprigs for the mint.

Chesapeake-Style Crab Sliders with Classic Tartar Sauce

Makes: **8 sliders**	Time: **40 to 50 minutes, plus chilling time**	Ⓓ Ⓜ

Turning a crab cake into a grillable burger is a balancing act: It's got to be full of big, sweet flakes of crab without falling to pieces. I count on softened cracker crumbs and time to chill. For the best flavor, use fresh, unpasteurized picked crab if you can find it, or if you have the energy, boil and shell your own. Otherwise, choose refrigerated canned or jarred crab, not the shelf-stable stuff sold next to the canned tuna. I prefer claw meat; it's far cheaper than lump and backfin and tastes great. Don't be afraid of setting the patties over high heat; that will create a good sear that allows you to turn them over without sticking.

4 tablespoons (½ stick) butter, melted and cooled slightly

1 egg

2 tablespoons fresh lemon juice

1 teaspoon Worcestershire sauce

¼ cup saltine cracker crumbs

1 pound crabmeat (see headnote), picked over for shells and cartilage

½ cup mayonnaise (to make your own, see page 460)

1 tablespoon chopped bread-and-butter pickles or cornichons

½ teaspoon pickle juice, or more to taste

½ teaspoon spicy brown mustard

Salt and pepper

8 slider buns (like potato or dinner rolls)

Lemon wedges

1 Put the butter, egg, 1 tablespoon of the lemon juice, and the Worcestershire in a medium bowl; whisk until smooth. Fold in the cracker crumbs with a rubber spatula until fully incorporated. Add the crabmeat and gently fold until fully incorporated.

2 With your hands, form the mixture into 8 equal-sized sliders. Without handling them too much, press each just enough so it stays together without gaps and cracks. Put the patties on a plate, cover, and refrigerate for at least 3 hours for the butter in the mixture to completely harden.

3 To make the tartar sauce, put the mayonnaise, pickles and pickle juice, mustard, and the remaining 1 tablespoon lemon juice in a small bowl; whisk to combine. Sprinkle with salt and pepper; taste and adjust the seasoning. Refrigerate until you're ready to serve.

4 Start the coals or heat a gas grill for hot direct cooking. Make sure the grates are clean.

5 Put the crab patties on the grill directly over the fire. Close the lid and cook, turning once, until they brown and heat through, 4 to 5 minutes per side. While the second side is browning, toast the buns on the grill if you like. Squeeze some lemon juice over the sliders and serve on the buns, topped with a dollop of tartar sauce.

Ⓓ direct fire　Ⓘ indirect fire　Ⓜ make ahead　Ⓥ vegetarian option

Creole Crab Sliders with Rémoulade	Add heat to both the crab and sauce: Substitute 2 teaspoons Louisiana-style hot sauce for the Worcestershire. In Step 3, omit the pickles and juice, substitute 1 tablespoon Creole or other stone-ground mustard for the spicy brown mustard, and add 1 tablespoon each ketchup, chopped celery, and chopped scallion, and 1 teaspoon each hot sauce and paprika.
Capered Crab Sliders with Tarragon Mayo	A natural and underused herb with crab: Add 2 tablespoons chopped drained capers to the crab along with the cracker mixture. Substitute chopped fresh tarragon for the pickles and juice in the sauce.
Lobster Roll Sliders with Lemon Mayo	For a flavor reminiscent of a Maine lobster roll: Substitute lobster meat for the crab, cutting any large pieces so they're in ½- to ¾-inch chunks. Omit the Worcestershire and add ¼ cup chopped celery to the lobster along with the cracker mixture. Substitute the grated zest of 1 lemon for the pickles and juice. In Step 4, before toasting the buns, spread the cut sides lightly with about 2 tablespoons softened butter.

---

11 BURGERS YOU CAN TURN INTO SLIDERS

Any of these burgers and their variations can be turned into sliders:

1. The Real Deal Burger with Fiery Ketchup (page 255)
2. Green Chile Cheeseburgers (page 257)
3. Garlicky Pork Burgers (page 304)
4. Tzatziki Lamb Burgers (page 322)
5. Caesar Salad Poultry Burgers (page 168)
6. Basil-Ginger Shrimp Burgers (page 130)
7. Salmon Burgers (page 115)
8. Chana Chaat Burgers (page 338)
9. Beet Burgers with Dates and Ginger (page 340)
10. Scallion-Sesame Tofu Sliders (page 336)
11. Design-Your-Own Nut Burgers (page 341)

Spicy Squid with Lemon

Makes: 6 to 8 servings	Time: 20 to 25 minutes	Ⓓ

You'll never go back to fried calamari after trying squid on the grill—smoke and fire add so much to its texture and flavor. It's a practical appetizer choice, too, since you can grill the squid while the fire is still too hot to start the main course.

2 pounds cleaned squid, bodies and tentacles

1 tablespoon good-quality olive, plus more for drizzling

2 lemons, 1 halved, 1 cut into wedges

1 teaspoon red chile flakes, or more to taste

Salt

1 Start the coals or heat a gas grill for hot direct cooking. Make sure the grates are clean.

2 Pat the squid dry with paper towels. Toss with the oil in a medium bowl until evenly coated.

3 Put the lemon halves on the grill directly over the fire, then the squid, arranging the bodies perpendicular to the grate. (Let the tentacles straddle a grate and hang down toward the fire if you like the tips really crisp.) Turn the squid after 1 minute, and cook until opaque on both sides and charred in spots, 1 to 2 minutes more.

4 Transfer the tentacles to a serving bowl and the bodies to a cutting board. Cut the bodies across into 1-inch-wide rings with scissors or a sharp knife. Add the rings to the tentacles. Drizzle with more oil and sprinkle with the red pepper and salt to taste. Remove the lemon halves from the grill. Holding them with a kitchen towel, carefully squeeze each one over the squid. Toss to coat evenly and serve with the lemon wedges.

DRY EQUALS CRISP

For calamari with a crunch, *do not* skip drying the squid before grilling it. Squid has a ton of moisture and because it cooks so fast, if you haven't dried it, it will essentially steam in its own juice when it hits the hot grill. Not that there's anything wrong with that—it will still be tender inside; you just won't get any browning.

Squid with Spicy Tomato Sauce	A play on the traditional marinara dipping sauce for fried calamari: Grill the squid as directed above, omitting the lemon and sprinkling of red pepper flakes. Instead, before you grill the squid, toss 8 ounces cherry tomatoes with 1 tablespoon good-quality olive oil and pour them onto a perforated grill pan in a single layer or skewer them. Put on the grill directly over the fire. Close the lid and cook, turning several times, until they start to look wrinkled, 5 to 8 minutes total. Transfer the tomatoes to a bowl, add ½ teaspoon red chile flakes or to taste, and salt to taste, purée with an immersion blender, and serve with the grilled squid.
Korean-Style Spicy Squid	In Step 2, toss the squid with sesame oil instead of olive oil. Instead of the olive oil and red pepper in Step 4, toss the grilled squid with a mixture of 2 tablespoons each gochujang and mirin (or 1 tablespoon each honey and water mixed together instead of the mirin), 2 teaspoons soy sauce, 1 teaspoon minced fresh ginger, and 1 teaspoon minced garlic. Omit the grilled lemon. Substitute lime wedges for the lemon and serve sprinkled with 1 tablespoon sesame seeds and 2 chopped scallions.
Thai-Style Spicy Squid	In Step 2, substitute peanut oil for the olive oil. In Step 4, toss the grilled squid with a mixture of 2 tablespoons each coconut milk and fresh lime juice, 1 tablespoon fish sauce, 2 cloves garlic, minced, and 1 green chile, minced. Omit the grilled lemon. Substitute lime wedges for the lemon and serve sprinkled with ¼ cup chopped fresh cilantro.

Clams Casino

Makes: 4 to 6 servings	Time: 25 to 30 minutes	D M

For classic clams casino, clams are steamed until they open, the meat removed, chopped, mixed with a bread-crumb filling, then loaded back in the shells for a quick trip under the broiler. In this version, the clams are opened, leaving them on the half shell, and the filling piled on top of the whole clams before putting them on the grill. It's faster and it yields fantastic clam flavor. Buy only littlenecks—preferably the day you plan to prepare them. Refrigerate the clams in the bag they come in; just be sure it's ventilated, and set the bag in a bowl to catch any drips. One last tip: This stuffing is insanely good. Make a double batch and use the extra to sprinkle over asparagus and any other kind of vegetable you can imagine before roasting it.

1 slice bacon

1 tablespoon good-quality olive oil

1 tablespoon minced shallot

2 teaspoons minced garlic

¼ cup dry bread crumbs

2 tablespoons chopped fresh parsley

2 tablespoons freshly grated Parmesan cheese

24 littleneck clams, rinsed

Lemon wedges for serving (optional)

1 Start the coals or heat a gas grill for medium-high direct cooking.

2 In a medium skillet over medium heat, cook the bacon, turning several times, until crisp. Transfer to a paper towel to drain. Add the oil, shallot, and garlic to the fat in the pan; cook, stirring a few times, until the shallot and garlic are soft, 2 to 3 minutes. Add the bread crumbs and cook, stirring, until golden, 2 to 4 minutes. Add the parsley and stir for 1 minute. Remove from the heat and let cool for a few minutes. Finely chop the bacon and stir it into the crumbs along with the Parmesan. (You can prepare the stuffing earlier in the day or even the day before, cover, and refrigerate it.)

3 Open the clams (see "Opening Clams," page 76), leaving the meat on the bottom shells. Discard the top shells. Divide the stuffing between the clams, about 1 teaspoon or a little less per clam, depending on their size.

4 Put the clams on the grill directly over the fire. Close the lid and cook until the clams are hot and the crumbs brown a bit, 3 to 5 minutes. Transfer to a platter and serve with lemon wedges if you like.

● recipe continues →

D direct fire   I indirect fire   M make ahead   V vegetarian option

Portuguese-Style Stuffed Clams	A play on the flavors in the Rhode Island stuffie: Substitute 2 tablespoons chopped Spanish chorizo or Portuguese linguiça for the bacon; sauté it with the shallot and garlic in 2 tablespoons good-quality olive oil in a medium skillet until a little crisp, 2 to 3 minutes, then add the bread crumbs and parsley. Use grated Manchego cheese instead of Parmesan.
North African–Style Stuffed Clams	Substitute 4 ounces merguez (lamb) sausage, removed from its casing, for the bacon. Cook it with the olive oil in a medium skillet over medium-high heat, breaking it up with a wooden spoon, until no longer pink, then add the shallot and garlic. Omit the Parmesan. When adding the bread crumbs and parsley, stir in 1 teaspoon ground cumin and 2 teaspoons minced preserved lemon or 1 teaspoon finely grated lemon zest. If the mixture is too dry, add another tablespoon olive oil.
Ginger and Wasabi Stuffed Clams	Substitute 2 teaspoons minced fresh ginger for the shallot and good-quality vegetable oil for the olive oil. Use panko instead of bread crumbs and cilantro instead of parsley. Omit the Parmesan; stir 1 teaspoon each wasabi powder, soy sauce, and sesame oil into the stuffing. Serve with lime wedges instead of lemon, if you like.

OPENING CLAMS

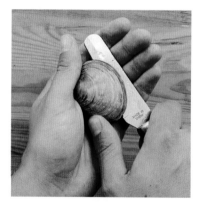

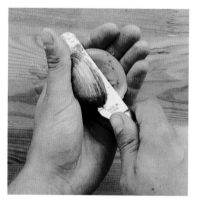

STEP 1 Use a blunt knife—preferably a clam knife, which is made for this purpose. Hold the clam in your cupped hand and wedge the edge of the knife into the shell opposite the hinge.

Once you get it there, twist the knife to pry open the clam.

STEP 2 Run the knife along the shell and open up the clam.

STEP 3 Run the knife under the clam to detach it, leaving it on the bottom half of the shell. Try to keep as much of the juice (clam liquor) inside the shell as you can. Discard the top shell.

ⅅ direct fire   ⅼ indirect fire   Ⓜ make ahead   Ⓥ vegetarian option

BBQ Oysters à la Tomales Bay

Makes: 4 servings	Time: 40 to 45 minutes, plus chilling time	Ⓓ Ⓜ

Located just north of San Francisco Bay, Tomales Bay is known for its oysters. A popular way of serving them there is to grill the oysters on the half-shell, topping them first with a garlicky, chipotle-fired compound butter.

8 tablespoons (1 stick) butter, softened

3 cloves garlic, minced

1 tablespoon minced canned chipotle chile in adobo sauce, or to taste

16 oysters, scrubbed

1 Put the butter, garlic, and chipotle in a small bowl; mash together until thoroughly mixed. Shape the compound butter into a log, wrap it in plastic, and refrigerate for at least an hour or up to 1 week.

2 Start the coals or heat a gas grill for medium direct cooking.

3 If you're handy with an oyster knife, carefully open the oysters, preserving as much of the liquor in the bottom shell as possible; discard the top shell.

OPENING OYSTERS

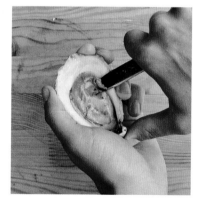

STEP 1 Use an oyster knife, which comes to a point. For safety's sake, put the oyster on a cutting board and hold it steady with a folded clean dish towel. Hold the knife with your dominant hand. Work the point of the knife into the hinge, but don't force it or the knife might slip.

STEP 2 When you gain purchase, twist the knife, which will pop the top shell off.

STEP 3 Run the knife under the oyster to detach it, leaving it on the bottom half of the shell. Try to keep as much of the juice (oyster liquor) inside the shell as you can. Discard the top shell.

● recipe continues →

If you're not comfortable opening oysters, skip to Step 4.

4 Cut the butter into 16 equal-sized pats. Put the oysters on the grill directly over the fire. If you've opened them, set a piece of compound butter on top of each. If you haven't, as soon as their shells pop open, slip a pat of butter inside. Close the lid. Check on the oysters every 2 minutes or so. When the butter melts and starts bubbling, remove the oysters from the grill, being careful not to spill their juices, and serve right away.

BBQ Clams, Tomales Bay Style	Because of the clams' smaller size, the technique needs a little tweak: Substitute 24 littleneck clams for the oysters. Don't open them. To make the compound butter, melt the butter in a small saucepan over low heat, then add the garlic and let it simmer for 3 to 5 minutes to soften; don't let it brown. Stir in the chipotle; remove from the heat. Grill the clams with the lid down, transferring them to a bowl as their shells open; start checking after 2 minutes. When they've all opened, pour the chipotle butter over the clams and serve.
BBQ Oysters or Clams with Andouille-Garlic Butter	Substitute ¼ cup minced andouille sausage for the chipotle. Put the andouille and 1 tablespoon good-quality olive oil in a small skillet over medium-high heat and cook, stirring occasionally, until the sausage crisps up, 3 to 4 minutes. Add to the butter (let it cool first if preparing this for oysters) along with the garlic and 2 tablespoons fresh lime juice.
BBQ Oysters with Sherry Vinegar–Pimentón Mignonette	A twist on the classic raw oyster accompaniment: Omit the butter, garlic, and chipotle. In a small bowl, stir together ¼ cup sherry vinegar, 1 tablespoon minced shallot, and ½ teaspoon smoked paprika (pimentón). Don't open the oysters; grill them until the shells open, then serve topped with some of the mignonette.

D direct fire   **I** indirect fire   **M** make ahead   **V** vegetarian option

Chicken Negimaki Bites

Makes: 8 to 10 appetizer servings or 4 main-course servings	Time: 45 to 50 minutes	D M

These bite-sized scallion-stuffed rolls make a truly impressive appetizer. And since you can serve them at any temperature—hot off the grill, warm, room temperature, even straight out the refrigerator—they're perfect to make ahead.

It will cost you a bit extra at the supermarket, but buying thinly sliced chicken breast makes this even quicker; the chicken should be no more than ¼ inch thick. You can also leave the rolls whole and enjoy them as a main course.

½ cup soy sauce

½ cup mirin (or ¼ cup honey mixed with ¼ cup water)

1 tablespoon minced garlic

1 bunch scallions, trimmed

1½ pounds thinly sliced chicken breast

Salt and pepper

Sesame oil, as needed

Lime wedges for serving

1 Put the soy sauce, mirin, garlic, and scallions in a medium skillet over medium-low heat. Cook until the liquid comes to a gentle boil, 3 to 4 minutes, turning the scallions several times. Turn off the heat.

2 Sprinkle the chicken with salt and pepper on both sides and pound gently to flatten to about ¼ inch thick. Divide the scallions evenly among the slices, putting them along one long edge, with some scallion sticking out on either end; aim for 2 or 3 scallions per slice. Roll each slice around the scallions from the long edge and secure the roll in two or three places with toothpicks or butcher's twine. Lightly brush the rolls with sesame oil. (You can transfer the rolls to a platter at this point, cover, and refrigerate for several hours.) Transfer the soy sauce mixture to a small bowl.

3 Start the coals or heat a gas grill for medium-high direct cooking. Make sure the grates are clean.

4 Put the rolls on the grill directly over the fire. Close the lid and cook, brushing several times with the reserved soy mixture and turning each piece once or twice, until cooked through, 10 to 15 minutes total. Transfer the rolls to a cutting board and cut across into 1-inch pieces; remove any toothpicks or twine. Put the pieces on a platter, cut side up, and serve with lime wedges.

● recipe continues →

Chicken Bites with Asparagus	Substitute 1 bunch thin asparagus for the scallions, and snap off the tough bottoms. When the soy sauce mixture comes to a boil, let it simmer until the asparagus are tender but still put up just a tiny bit of resistance when pierced with a knife, 3 to 5 minutes. Use 1 asparagus spear per roll.
Chicken Bites with Baby Bok Choy	Substitute 2 or 3 heads baby bok choy for the scallions. Trim the bottoms and quarter them lengthwise. Simmer as directed for the asparagus variation. Use 1 piece bok choy for each roll.
Steak Negimaki Bites	Try this with any of the suggested fillings: Replace the chicken with 1½ pounds skirt steak, sliced and pounded thin. After grilling, cut each roll in two or three pieces.

D direct fire   I indirect fire   M make ahead   V vegetarian option

Chicken Skewers with Peanut Sauce

Makes: 6 to 8 servings	Time: 30 to 35 minutes	D M V

Because the chicken is so thin, it's important to start with a clean grill. (Ditto the pork and tofu variations.) Otherwise, the chicken will form a crust on the grill, and when you try to pick it up it will stick or just shred away. Use 6-inch skewers.

1 pound boneless, skinless chicken thighs

½ cup creamy peanut butter

¼ cup coconut milk

2 tablespoons fresh lime juice

2 tablespoons soy sauce

2 tablespoons minced garlic

2 tablespoons minced fresh ginger

Chopped fresh cilantro for garnish

1 Slice the chicken about ⅛ inch thick (it's easier if you freeze it for 15 to 30 minutes first). Whisk the peanut butter, coconut milk, lime juice, soy sauce, garlic, and ginger together in a large bowl until smooth and fully combined. Transfer half the sauce to a small bowl. Put the chicken in the large bowl and stir to coat evenly with the sauce. Let sit at room temperature, tossing occasionally, as the grill heats up. Or cover and refrigerate for up to 24 hours.

2 If you're using bamboo or wooden skewers, soak them in water for 30 minutes. Start the coals or heat a gas grill for hot direct cooking. Make sure the grates are clean.

3 Thread 1 or 2 slices of chicken lengthwise onto each skewer, stretching out the slices. Put the skewers on the grill directly over the fire. Close the lid and cook, turning once, until the chicken cooks all the way through, 2 to 3 minutes per side. Transfer the skewers to a platter, sprinkle with cilantro, and serve with the reserved peanut sauce for dipping.

Pork Skewers with Peanut Sauce	Substitute thinly sliced boneless pork shoulder, loin, or pounded sirloin cutlets for the chicken. Grill for 3 to 4 minutes per side.
Shrimp Skewers with Peanut Sauce	Substitute 1 pound peeled shrimp for the chicken. If you use large shrimp (31/35 count), use 3 shrimp per skewer for 10 to 11 skewers. With jumbo (21/25 count), use 2 per skewer, for 10 to 12 skewers. Grill, turning once, until the shrimp are fully opaque, 2 to 4 minutes per side.
Tofu Skewers with Peanut Sauce	Heat the grill for medium direct cooking. Substitute one 14- to 16-ounce package extra-firm tofu, cut into 12 long sticks, for the chicken. In Step 3, thread 1 stick onto each skewer. Grill, turning once, until the tofu develops a crust and releases easily from the grate, 5 to 10 minutes per side.

Chipotle Chicken Wings with Lime Crema Dipping Sauce

Makes: 6 to 8 servings	Time: 45 to 55 minutes	Ⓘ Ⓓ

The secret to grilling saucy bone-in chicken without burning it is to keep it over the cooler part of an indirect fire until it's cooked through. Then toss the pieces with sauce and put directly over the heat for a final crisping. Some of the sauces in the variations contain more sugar than others, so be vigilant to avoid scorching; you may have to move the wings to the edges of the fire. Look for *crema* in the refrigerated section with other Hispanic dairy products. And if you want to save some time, buy "party wings"—already separated into drumettes and wingettes—instead of whole chicken wings.

3 pounds chicken wings

¾ cup Mexican *crema*, yogurt, or sour cream

¼ cup fresh lime juice

¼ cup chopped fresh cilantro

Salt and pepper

⅓ cup chipotle hot sauce

4 tablespoons (½ stick) butter, melted

1 tablespoon distilled white vinegar

1 Start the coals or heat a gas grill for hot indirect cooking (see "Grilling Bone-in Poultry Parts," page 155). Make sure the grates are clean. If using charcoal, put a drip pan under the indirect side of the grill; for gas, empty and clean the fat trap.

2 With a chef's knife, cut the wings at each joint into 3 sections; save the wing tips for stock if you like.

3 Whisk the *crema*, lime juice, and cilantro together in a small serving bowl with some salt; taste and adjust the seasoning. (You can make the sauce ahead, cover it, and refrigerate for up to a day.)

4 Put the wings on the indirect side of the grill as close to the fire as possible without any danger of fat dripping onto the flames, or the pilot lights of the unlit burners on a gas grill. Close the lid and cook until most of the fat has been rendered from the skin and the wings are cooked through, 25 to 35 minutes. After 10 to 15 minutes, turn the pieces over and rotate 180 degrees for even browning.

5 While the wings cook, whisk the chipotle sauce, butter, vinegar, and salt and pepper to taste in a large bowl. When the wings are cooked, add them to the sauce and toss to coat evenly. Put the wings on the grill directly over the fire and cook, turning once, until they're browned and the sauce caramelizes, 2 to 5 minutes per side, depending on how hot the fire is. If you are cooking with a gas grill, turn the heat down to medium or low as needed to keep the sauce from burning. Transfer to a platter and serve with the *crema* dipping sauce.

• recipe continues →

Ⓓ direct fire   Ⓘ indirect fire   Ⓜ make ahead   Ⓥ vegetarian option

Pomegranate-Ginger Chicken Wings with Lime Crema Dipping Sauce	Tart, sweet, and spicy: Replace the chipotle sauce, butter, and vinegar with ¼ cup pomegranate molasses, 3 tablespoons honey, 1 tablespoon each fresh lime juice, soy sauce, and minced fresh ginger, and a generous amount of black pepper.
Buffalo Chicken Wings with Blue Cheese Dressing	The classic: Substitute sour cream for the *crema*, ½ cup crumbled blue cheese for the cilantro, and 2 tablespoons lemon juice for the lime juice. Substitute ⅓ cup hot sauce for the chipotle sauce (if you want to be true to the original recipe, use Frank's RedHot) and add 1 tablespoon minced garlic.
Honey Mustard Chicken Wings	Omit the dipping sauce. Replace the hot sauce, butter, vinegar, and salt and pepper with ¼ cup each honey and Dijon mustard, 2 tablespoons good-quality olive oil, and 1 tablespoon balsamic vinegar.

---

5 OTHER GLAZES TO USE WITH CHICKEN WINGS

1. Maple-Orange Glaze (page 128)
2. Sherry-Honey Glaze (page 215)
3. Hoisin-Ginger Glaze (page 300)
4. Spicy Miso Glaze (page 126)
5. Balsamic-Honey Glaze (page 279)

D direct fire I indirect fire M make ahead V vegetarian option

Rosemary-Garlic Chicken Liver and Onion Skewers

Makes: 6 to 8 servings	Time: 30 to 35 minutes	Ⓓ

As delicate as they are, chicken livers are delicious grilled. There are several secrets for success. First, make sure the grill grates are super clean; otherwise the livers will stick. Next, skewer them using thin skewers; you don't want the livers to tear as you skewer them or transfer them to the grill. Last, cook them hot and fast. Keep a close eye out, since they'll go from perfect to shoe leather in a matter of minutes. Onions are a classic accompaniment to chicken livers but because the cook time on the livers is so fast, make sure you cut the onions into very small wedges, or just thread one or two layers of onion on the skewer at a time. Use 4- or 6-inch skewers for this.

½ cup good-quality olive oil

8 cloves garlic, smashed

6 sprigs fresh rosemary

1 pound chicken livers

Salt and pepper

1 medium onion, cut into thin wedges and each wedge halved across

1 If you're using bamboo or wooden skewers, soak them in water for 30 minutes.

2 Meanwhile, put the oil, garlic, and rosemary in a small saucepan over the lowest heat possible; warm the mixture, stirring occasionally, until the garlic turns golden, 8 to 10 minutes. Turn the heat off and let the oil cool.

3 Start the coals or heat a gas grill for hot direct cooking. Make sure the grates are clean.

4 Trim the chicken livers of any fat or membranes; pat dry with paper towels.

5 Transfer half the oil to a medium bowl; sprinkle generously with salt and pepper. Add the livers and turn them gently to coat. Double-skewer the livers, alternating 2 or 3 livers with 2 or 3 onion wedges on each.

6 Put the skewers on the grill directly over the fire. Close the lid and cook, turning once, until the livers are well browned but still a bit pink in the center, 2 to 3 minutes per side. Transfer to a platter, drizzle with the remaining oil, and serve.

• recipe continues →

Lamb or Veal Kidney Skewers with Sherry Vinegar	Kidney is a popular part of the South American *asado* grill tradition; it browns quickly and has a deep liver-like taste: Substitute lamb or veal kidneys for the chicken livers, and omit the oil, garlic, rosemary, and onions. Skip Step 2. When cleaning the kidneys, remove all the fat, including the hard plug of fat that protrudes from the center of the kidney. The best way to remove it is to run your knife down the side of it all around, then cut under it. Cut the kidneys into ½-inch pieces and toss with ¼ cup sherry vinegar; marinate for 10 to 15 minutes. Skewer the kidney pieces and grill as directed.
Sliced Beef or Lamb Heart	Another traditional *asado* appetizer: You can sometimes find already cleaned heart sold in slices, which is a great shortcut. Otherwise, cut away all the fat and connective tissue, then cut into 1-inch slices and season with salt and pepper. Omit the oil, garlic, rosemary, and onions. You can skewer the slices if you like or not, your choice. Heart cooks up like steak, with a steak-like flavor that has undertones of liver. Don't cook it beyond medium-rare, which will take 1 to 2 minutes per side. Let them rest a minute or 2, then cut into ½- to ¾-inch slices.
Creamy Chicken Liver Spread	You can also make this using Smoked Chicken Livers (page 177): Omit the oil, garlic, rosemary, and onions and skip Step 2. Instead, melt 2 tablespoons butter; remove from the heat. In Step 5, toss the cleaned livers with the butter and grill as directed. Transfer to a blender or food processor. Add 6 tablespoons (¾ stick) butter, ⅓ cup cream, 1 tablespoon brandy (or more to taste), 1 teaspoon black pepper, ¼ teaspoon each ground allspice and coriander, and a pinch ground cloves. Process until smooth, taste, add salt as needed, and correct the spices. Transfer to a small bowl and refrigerate until set, 2 to 3 hours. Serve with crackers or thin small toasts.

Ⓓ direct fire Ⓘ indirect fire Ⓜ make ahead Ⓥ vegetarian option

Sweetbread Skewers with Lemon

Makes: **8 or more servings**	Time: **1¼ to 1½ hours, plus soaking time**	Ⓓ Ⓜ

Sweetbreads are the thymus gland of a calf or lamb. It's an odd-looking organ, kind of a cauliflower from space. To me, sweetbreads have the same rich flavor as the delicious fat along the edge of a good steak. In restaurants, they are often presented fried as an appetizer, but grilling produces the same contrast in texture—a creamy interior with a crunchy crust. The technique is easy, even though there are several steps. Make sure the sweetbreads you buy are absolutely fresh, and prepare them the day you buy them.

1½ pounds veal or lamb sweetbreads

1 tablespoon salt

1 tablespoon black peppercorns

2 lemons, 1 halved and 1 cut into small wedges

2 tablespoons good-quality olive oil

1 Put the sweetbreads in a large bowl and cover with cold water. Soak in the refrigerator for at least 2 hours or overnight, changing the water several times to remove any blood. Drain and rinse.

2 Prepare an ice bath in a large bowl. In a large pot, combine 8 cups water, the salt, and the peppercorns. Squeeze the juice from the lemon halves into the water and add the reamed-out shells as well. Bring to a boil, reduce the heat to a very gentle simmer (bubbles just barely breaking the surface), and add the sweetbreads. Poach just until firm, 6 to 10 minutes. Drain and transfer to the ice water to stop the cooking.

3 When the sweetbreads have cooled, using your fingers, pull away as much of the membrane as you can, along with any fat, gristle, and hard bits. Break the sweetbreads into 1- to 2-inch pieces. (They will largely come apart on their own.) Toss with the oil. (You can prepare them to this point up to a day before cooking; cover and refrigerate.)

4 If you're using bamboo or wooden skewers, soak them in water for 30 minutes. Meanwhile, start the coals or heat a gas grill for medium direct cooking. Make sure the grates are clean.

5 Alternate 2 or 3 pieces of sweetbreads per skewer, depending on their size, with a wedge of lemon. Put the skewers on the grill directly over the fire. Close the lid and cook, turning several times, until the sweetbreads are crisp on the outside and heated through, 8 to 15 minutes total, depending on the size of the pieces. Serve hot or warm for the best flavor.

Sweetbread Skewers with Roasted Red Peppers	Instead of a lemon wedge, thread a strip of grill-roasted red pepper (page 34) between the sweetbread pieces.
Pancetta-Wrapped Sweetbread Skewers	Omit the lemon wedges. Before skewering the sweetbreads, wrap each in a thin slice of pancetta. Grill until the pancetta crisps up.
Sweetbread Skewers with Green Chimichurri	Omit the lemon wedges. Serve the skewers with Green Chimichurri (page 229) on the side.

Appetizers and Snacks

Marrow with Garlic Crostini

Makes: 4 servings	Time: 35 to 40 minutes	Ⓓ

Nature's savory pudding. It's so easy to make this fabulously rich restaurant-style indulgence. Grill the bones just until the marrow inside melts enough so you can spoon it out, then eat as is or spread on crostini. The only trick is timing: heating them to the point that the marrow is the right consistency but not so long that it drains from the bones into the fire. If your meat store sells long lengths of bones (4 to 8 inches), have the butcher cut them in half lengthwise. Then you can fearlessly give the marrow side a good sear and turn them to finish, with the bone cradling the softening marrow. If all you can find are shorter lengths (2 to 3 inches), where the marrow is exposed on both sides, just keep a close eye on their progress and have a platter at hand to get them off the grill as soon as they are ready.

1 baguette, cut into ½-inch slices

¼ cup good-quality olive oil

1 clove garlic, peeled

4 4- to 6-inch-long beef marrow bones, halved lengthwise, or eight 2- to 3-inch lengths

Salt and pepper

1 Start the coals or heat a gas grill for medium-high direct cooking. Make sure the grates are clean.

2 Brush the baguette slices with the oil on both sides, then toast directly over the fire until they have good color, 1 to 2 minutes per side. Transfer to a platter and rub one side with the garlic clove.

3 Sprinkle the bones with salt and pepper. Put them on the grill directly over the fire and close the lid. For long and short bones, put them cut side down; for long bones, let them sear for 4 to 5 minutes, then turn marrow side up and cook until the marrow is hot and jelly-like in consistency. For short lengths, turn them every 2 to 3 minutes, from cut side to cut side, checking on the marrow's progress by inserting a skewer all the way into the center. As soon as there is no resistance in the marrow, transfer the bones to a platter and serve with the crostini, small knives for spreading the marrow, and salt and pepper for sprinkling.

Marrow with Watercress and Lemon	Don't rub the crostini with garlic. Spread the marrow on the crostini, top with sprigs of watercress, and serve with lemon wedges.
Marrow with Mint and Lime	The crostini are optional. Sprinkle the grilled marrow while still in the bones with chopped fresh mint and serve with lime wedges.
Marrow Butter Toasts	When the marrow is ready, transfer it from the bones to a bowl and let cool. Add 2 tablespoons softened butter and a squeeze of lemon; sprinkle with salt and pepper. Whisk until fluffy. Spread on toast points to serve.

Fish and Shellfish

Seafood and fire have a natural affinity. From clambakes and oyster roasts to fresh catch cooked over a campfire, the briny, sweet taste of fish and shellfish are perfect for the smoke and char of the grill. And almost everything is ready in minutes. If you've tried grilled shrimp, salmon, or tuna and enjoyed it, then dive deep into this chapter and explore.

Let's start by debunking two myths: First, seafood can be affordable if you shop well and are willing to make substitutions for freshness, sustainability, and value. This chapter helps you with that part. And second, fish behaves better on the grill when you cook it fast and don't fuss over it. The next section provides more detail to ensure you have the tools to buy and prepare all kinds of fish and shellfish with consistent success.

The Basics of Grilling Seafood

With the exception of Hot-Smoked Fish (page 61), I grill all seafood directly over the fire, and it's usually a hot one. Sometimes, as with medium-to-large whole fish, it's a good idea to tone down the heat to medium-high so the skin doesn't burn before the inside cooks. But almost everything else benefits from assertive cooking.

As long as you stay close to the grill and pay attention to the cues, you'll do fine. Since there's not much margin between just-right and overcooked, have everything you need for the fish assembled and handy, and the sides ready to eat. Then you can hang out by the grill and focus on getting the food off the moment it's done.

Buying Seafood

Fish in all its forms is highly perishable, so it's important to find a reliable source—a fish market, supermarket, or specialty food store. Let your nose be your guide. Quality fish should have a clean or saltwater smell. Anything stronger is a warning sign.

The flesh should always look firm and solid, never "gaping." When buying fillets or steaks, their surface should be bright and reflective, with no dullness or discoloration. This is the case whether the fish is labeled as fresh or previously frozen. When buying whole fish, look for fish with red gills (located right behind the head); bright, reflective skin; firm flesh; undamaged scales; and no browning. It should look alive, as if it just came out of the water.

Mussels and clams should be tightly shut or should close when gently tapped; live crustaceans like lobsters should be moving. If buying frozen seafood, look for packages with little or no ice crystal buildup inside. And nothing should look slimy, discolored, or dry.

Making Sustainable Seafood Choices

Fish now comes from all over the globe, but some of it is in short supply; dozens of kinds have been overfished nearly to the point of extinction. In some countries, in an attempt to allow these species to reach commercial quantities again—or, in some cases, just to survive—their fishing is forbidden or restricted by government mandate. Other fish are raised in farms—a type of production known as aquaculture—as an alternative to wild fishing, but often in ways that pollute the environment without regulation.

Not all countries are responsible fishery stewards, so there are watch groups that track fish populations and make recommendations about environmentally responsible choices, including alternatives to threatened species. Be an informed consumer and check with these groups regularly, as the health of the world's fisheries is in constant flux, with some populations recovering while others go into decline. My go-to references for seafood sustainability are:

- safinacenter.org/seafoods (The Safina Center Seafood Ratings)

- seafood.edf.org (Environmental Defense Fund Seafood Selector)

- seafoodwatch.org (Monterey Bay Aquarium Seafood Watch)

Storing Seafood

Get in the habit of cooking seafood the day you buy it, unless you buy it frozen. Head home as soon as possible—especially in warm weather—and refrigerate your purchase immediately in the coldest section of your refrigerator. If you have bought live seafood—like crabs, lobsters, mussels, clams, or oysters—make sure the bag or container is not sealed; if it is, they'll die. For the same reason, don't put mussels, clams, or oysters in water.

Thaw frozen seafood in the refrigerator over-night. You can also thaw shrimp by putting them in a large bowl filled with cold water and changing the water a few times until they are no longer frozen. Smaller shrimp will thaw in a minute or so under cold running water.

Avoiding Stuck-On Fish

Next to overcooking, the biggest challenge when grilling fish and scallops is to avoid sticking and tearing. The two are actually related. By the time the fish releases easily, it can be dry inside. I can't promise that nothing will ever stick, but I've got some suggestions to hedge your bets: First, start with scrupulously clean grates. Get the grill screaming hot—the hotter, the better to incinerate any stuck-on grime—then scour any bits and ash away with a stiff brush.

Next, just before grilling, pat the fish dry with paper towels and brush with oil. This way, when you cook over direct heat, you'll get an immediate sear—assuming the fire is still hot enough that the food sizzles when it hits the grates. Once the piece has browned, it will release; without the barrier of that crust, it will stick. Also, it helps to put the fish on perpendicular to the grate, or at least at an angle. To test whether it's ready, insert a large serving fork under the fish between two rails, and gently try to pull up. If the fish releases, switch to a metal spatula, lift the fish up and, using another spatula or your hand (carefully, to prevent burning yourself) turn it over to the uncooked side and lower it back down onto the grill intact. If it doesn't release, keep cooking another minute or so and try again.

Choose thick fillets and steaks over thin ones. Cut cubes for kebabs on the big side. And finally, focus on species that hold up best on the grill. (The list on page 94 offers some ideas.)

Anticipating Doneness

It's better to pull fish and shellfish off the grill under-done than overdone; you can always put it back on. After turning the fish, start checking the interior soon and often. Poking, pressing, and peeking are the only ways to know for sure. In most cases, the fish should be just opaque at the center, and will flake with some pressure. It shouldn't look dry at all. A few fish (like tuna) are best still rare inside. Some, like salmon, dry out quickly; try to catch them right before the center turns fully opaque.

Lobster, crab, and shrimp will change color on the outside and the interiors will lose their translucence, as will squid. Creatures enclosed between two shells will open. In all cases, remove from the heat one stage of doneness shy of where you ultimately want it to be.

9 FISH THAT HOLD UP WELL ON THE GRILL

Fish steaks, which are slices cut crosswise from thick fillets or whole fish—think tuna, swordfish, halibut, and salmon—are perfect for the grill. Fillets can be trickier, particularly when thin and from white-fleshed fish, not only because of their thinness but also because of their flakiness. Even with well-oiled, super-clean grates, some fish (sole and cod, for instance) can start to come apart on the grill as they cook through. Cooking them with the skin still on, if that is an option, can help.

Here are the fish fillets that grill best:

1. Salmon
2. Halibut (usually sold with inedible skin; leave it on during cooking and it will shrivel and peel off easily after)
3. Catfish
4. Tilapia (I'm not a fan, but many people are)
5. Trout
6. Bluefish
7. Mahi-mahi
8. Red snapper
9. Mackerel

D direct fire　I indirect fire　M make ahead　V vegetarian option

Salt-and-Pepper Fish Fillets or Steaks

Makes: **4 servings**	Time: **20 to 25 minutes**	Ⓓ

Adjust for different types of fish and this becomes a master recipe. Fillets and steaks can vary greatly in thickness and in the density of their flesh; both will affect cooking time. For white-fleshed fish, to check for doneness insert a skewer or sharp, thin knife at the thickest point; as soon as it goes in without resistance, the fish is done. For darker, dense fish, nick with the knife and peek inside. Before cooking fish, read "Avoiding Stuck-On Fish" and "Anticipating Doneness" on page 93.

1½ pounds fish fillets or steaks

Good-quality olive oil for brushing the fish

Salt and pepper

Lemon wedges for serving

1 Start the coals or heat a gas grill for hot direct cooking. Make sure the grates are clean.

2 Pat the fillets or steaks dry with paper towels, then brush them with oil and season with salt and pepper on both sides.

3 Put the fish skin side down (if it has skin) on the grill directly over the fire, perpendicular to the grate. Close the lid and cook until the bottoms brown and release easily, 3 to 7 minutes. Carefully turn the fillets or steaks over, using a second spatula to keep them from breaking apart. Close the lid and cook until a skewer or thin knife inserted at the thickest point of the fish easily pierces it all the way through, 2 to 4 minutes, depending on the fish and the thickness. Transfer to a platter and serve with lemon wedges.

Orange-Cumin Fish Fillets or Steaks	Whisk 1 teaspoon ground cumin and the grated zest of 1 orange into the oil before brushing. Substitute orange wedges for the lemon wedges.
Sesame-Sriracha Fish Fillets or Steaks	Sesame oil has a strong flavor that has no problem standing up to heat of sriracha. A dynamite and simple combination: Substitute 1½ tablespoons sesame oil for the olive oil and whisk it with 2 teaspoons sriracha. Substitute lime wedges for the lemon wedges.
Dijonnaise Fish Fillets or Steaks	Instead of brushing the fish with oil, use a mustard-flavored mayonnaise: Replace the oil with a mixture of 2 tablespoons mayonnaise, 2 teaspoons (or more) Dijon mustard, 1 teaspoon fresh lemon juice, and salt and pepper.

Fish Fillets with Avocado-Cilantro Salsa

Makes: 4 servings	Time: 20 to 25 minutes	Ⓓ

Grilled fish and fresh salsa is one of my favorite combinations. The salsas here and in the variations are slightly offbeat, with vibrant flavors and textures that perfectly complement the mild sweetness of the fish. When fillets still have their skin on—the thin kind that's edible—all the better. The fire will crunch it up for even more contrast. Bass and salmon are both great choices to try. These salsas also pair great with seared sea scallops.

2 ripe avocados, pitted, peeled, and diced

½ cup chopped fresh cilantro

¼ cup chopped red onion

Juice of 1 lime, or more to taste

Salt and pepper

1½ pounds fish fillets (preferably skin-on)

Good-quality olive oil for brushing the fish

1 Start the coals or heat a gas grill for hot direct cooking. Make sure the grates are clean.

2 Put the avocados, cilantro, onion, and lime juice in a small bowl, sprinkle with salt and pepper, and gently toss to combine (take care not to mash the avocado). Taste and adjust the seasoning.

3 Pat the fillets dry with paper towels, then brush them with oil and season with salt and pepper on both sides.

4 Put the fish on the grill (skin side down, if it has skin), perpendicular to the grate. Close the lid and cook until the bottoms brown and release easily, 3 to 7 minutes. Carefully turn the fillets over, using a second spatula to keep them from breaking apart. Close the lid and cook until a skewer or thin knife inserted at the thickest point of a fillet easily pierces it all the way through, 2 to 4 minutes, depending on the fish and the thickness. Transfer the fish to a platter, top with the salsa, and serve.

Fish Fillets with Mango-Mint Salsa	So incredibly refreshing and still rich: Substitute mint for the cilantro and 1 large or 2 medium-sized ripe mangoes for the avocados. Peel, cut the flesh off the pit, and dice.
Fish Fillets with Papaya-Cilantro Salsa	Substitute 1 firm but ripe 12- to 16-ounce papaya for the avocados. Peel and seed before dicing.
Fish Fillets with Avocado-Tomato Salsa	Substitute basil for the cilantro and 1 fresh medium tomato for one of the avocados. Seed the tomato if you like; chop.

Ⓓ direct fire   Ⓘ indirect fire   Ⓜ make ahead   Ⓥ vegetarian option

Baja-Style Fish Tacos with Grilled Slaw and Chipotle Mayo

Makes: 4 servings	Time: 40 to 45 minutes	Ⓓ Ⓜ

Traditionally the fish for Baja-style tacos is batter-fried, but cooking the fillets on the grill makes more sense. It's much quicker and a lot less messy. And grilling the cabbage before turning it into slaw adds another layer of smokiness. To retain heat for cooking the fish, keep the lid of the grill down while you put together the slaw and chipotle mayonnaise.

1 quarter-wedge of 1 medium head green cabbage, cored

Good-quality olive oil for brushing

Salt and pepper

½ cup chopped fresh cilantro

Juice of 2 limes

½ cup mayonnaise (to make your own, see page 460)

1 tablespoon canned chipotle chile mashed with some of its adobo, or to taste

1½ pounds skinless white fish fillets

8 6-inch corn tortillas (or 16 if you like to double 'em up)

Lime wedges for serving

1 Start the coals or heat a gas grill for hot direct cooking. Make sure the grates are clean.

2 Brush the wedge of cabbage on all sides with 1 tablespoon oil and sprinkle with salt. Put on the grill directly over the fire. Close the lid and cook, turning once or twice, until grill marks develop, 4 to 5 minutes per side. Transfer to a cutting board until cool enough to handle, then cut across into thin ribbons. Put in a serving bowl along with the cilantro and lime juice and sprinkle with pepper. Toss to combine; taste and adjust the seasoning.

3 Put the mayonnaise and chipotle in a small serving bowl and whisk until combined; add a little salt if you like. (You can make the slaw and sauce up to a day before. Cover and refrigerate them until you're ready to serve.)

4 Pat the fish dry with paper towels. Brush with oil and sprinkle with salt and pepper on both sides.

5 Put the fillets on the grill directly over the fire, at an angle or perpendicular to the grate. Close the lid and cook until the bottoms brown and release easily, 3 to 7 minutes. Carefully turn the fillets, using a second spatula to keep them from breaking apart. Close the lid and cook until a skewer or thin knife inserted at the thickest point of a fillet easily pierces it all the way through, 2 to 4 minutes, depending on the fish and the thickness. Transfer the fillets to a platter.

6 Heat the tortillas on the grill (see page 100) and wrap in foil or a clean kitchen towel to keep warm. Break the fish into large pieces and serve, passing the tortillas, slaw, mayo, and lime wedges at the table for building the tacos.

• recipe continues →

Baja-Style Shrimp Tacos with Grilled Slaw	Substitute 2 pounds peeled large shrimp (deveining is optional) for the fish fillets. For easier handling, skewer the shrimp or put them in a perforated grill pan; cook, turning once, until they're opaque all the way through, 2 to 3 minutes per side.
Fish Tacos with Minted Grilled Slaw	Switching the herb in the slaw changes everything: Substitute mint for the cilantro.
Fish Tacos with Grilled Slaw and Sweet Chili Mayo	With just a bit of heat: Substitute 2 tablespoons Thai sweet chili sauce for the chipotle chile and adobo. (It's available in supermarkets as *nam chim kai*, translated as sweet chili sauce, sweet red chili sauce, or sweet chili dipping sauce.)

HEATING TORTILLAS

The best way to heat corn or flour tortillas is directly on the grill. Over a hot fire with the lid closed, it takes less than a minute and you can do several at a time—just don't stack them. They often puff up like the Indian bread poori, but deflate off-grill. Then you can distribute them among waiting plates or wrap loosely in foil or a clean kitchen towel to pass warm at the table. It's definitely worth the short wait, but if you can't—or prefer a softer texture—wrap the tortillas in one or more foil packages and put them on the grill during the last few minutes of cooking (the warming rack is an ideal place).

D direct fire   I indirect fire   M make ahead   V vegetarian option

Whole Fish with Basil-Orange Oil

| Makes: **4 servings** | Time: **35 to 40 minutes** | Ⓓ |

Whenever possible, I grill fish whole. Whole fish are easy to handle, and the skin crisps and protects the delicate flesh so it stays moist. Start larger fish first over direct heat, then move to indirect after the skin releases. Smaller fish require more attention but less time: Fish less than 1½ pounds before cleaning can be cooked over direct heat the entire time so the skin chars without burning and the inside is cooked through. If the fish isn't already cleaned (scaled and gutted) and you don't want to do it, they'll do that where you buy it. Just be sure to leave the head and tail on.

¼ cup good-quality olive oil, plus more for brushing the fish

2 cloves garlic, thinly sliced

1 orange

2 1½-pound or 4 12- to 16-ounce whole fish, scaled and gutted

Salt and pepper

8–12 large sprigs fresh basil

2 tablespoons chopped fresh basil

1 Start the coals or heat a gas grill for medium direct cooking. Make sure the grates are clean.

2 Put the oil and garlic in a small saucepan or skillet over the lowest heat possible. When the garlic begins to sizzle, swirl the oil a bit, then turn the heat off; don't allow the garlic to brown.

3 Grate 2 teaspoons zest from the rind of the orange, then slice the orange thinly, removing any seeds.

4 Pat the fish dry with paper towels. Brush them on both sides with olive oil and sprinkle with salt and pepper on both sides and in the cavity. Divide the orange slices between the fish, overlapping them in the cavities. Put the basil sprigs on top of the orange slices and close the fish.

5 Put the fish on the grill directly over the fire, at an angle or perpendicular to the grate. Close the lid and cook until the skin browns and the fish release easily, 10 to 12 minutes. Carefully turn the fish, using a second spatula to lower them back down to the grate. Close the lid and cook until a skewer or thin knife inserted at the thickest point easily pierces it all the way through, 4 to 6 minutes. Transfer the fish to a platter.

6 Heat the oil and garlic again over low heat (or set the pan on the grill over indirect heat to warm). When the garlic begins to sizzle, stir in the orange zest and chopped basil and remove from the heat.

LEAVE THE HEAD (AND TAIL) ON!

I like to serve whole fish with the fillets cut free from the bones—it's still dramatic, but less messy at the table. I also serve the tail, which crisps up beautifully and makes for great eating. The head is lagniappe for those enthusiasts happy to root around for the cheeks or the tasty morsels that can be found around the "collar" just above the fillets.

• recipe continues →

Fish and Shellfish

7 Remove the fillets from both sides of the fish by cutting horizontally between the flesh and the bones with a sharp knife and a spatula. Try to keep them intact, and remove as many bones as possible. Drizzle the warm orange-basil oil over the fillets and serve the carcass alongside if you like.

WHOLE FISH, THE EASIEST WAY

One of my favorite ways to cook whole fish is to sprinkle them with salt and pepper inside and out, rub them with good-quality olive or vegetable oil, and stuff the cavity with some chopped garlic and a few fresh herb sprigs like rosemary, thyme, or parsley. You can add lemon slices inside if you like or just serve the fish with wedges of citrus.

Whole Fish with Lemon-Parsley Oil	Substitute 2 lemons for the orange and the grated zest of 1 of the lemons for the orange zest, and substitute parsley sprigs and chopped parsley for the basil.
Whole Fish with Lemon-Dill Oil	Substitute 2 lemons for the orange and the grated zest of 1 of the lemons for the orange zest, and substitute dill sprigs and chopped dill for the basil.
Whole Fish with Lime-Cilantro Oil	Substitute 1 tablespoon chopped fresh ginger for the garlic, 2 limes for the orange and the grated zest of 1 of the limes for the orange zest, and cilantro sprigs and chopped cilantro for the basil.

Sardines with Lemon and Thyme

Makes: 2 servings	Time: 25 to 30 minutes	Ⓓ

Grilled sardines are the bomb. These rich, firm little fish are easy to work with, and they cook in minutes—so fast that you shouldn't stray from the grill. They're best when the skin takes on some char and gets quite crisp. Hit them with lemon juice and a final pinch salt and you'll understand why fresh sardines are popular throughout the Mediterranean.

The only challenge is finding them. Specialty seafood markets or the best supermarket counters have them, or can order them. Anytime you see them looking shiny and brightly colored, grab some. You can have your fishmonger clean the sardines, but it's really not hard: First, rake a small, sharp knife along both sides of the fish from the tail to the head to remove the scales. Then insert the knife in the belly at the tail and slit up the middle to the head. Pull out the innards with your finger, running it from one end of the fish to the other. Then rinse and pat the sardines dry with paper towels. After cooking, the head and inedible bones are easily removed. You can use this recipe to prepare other small fish, like whiting, and it's easily multiplied to cook in batches for a crowd.

1 pound fresh sardines, cleaned (see the headnote)

Good-quality olive oil for brushing the fish

Salt and pepper

1 small bunch fresh thyme

Lemon wedges for serving

1 Start the coals or heat a gas grill for medium-high direct cooking. Make sure the grates are clean.

2 Pat the fish dry with paper towels. Brush them with oil and season with salt and pepper on both sides and in the cavity. Tuck in the thyme sprigs—or wait and scatter them over the fish after turning.

3 Put the fish on the grill directly over the fire, at an angle or perpendicular to the grate. Cook, turning once, until the skin is charred in places and the fish release easily, 2 to 4 minutes per side, depending on their size and how hot the fire is. The easiest way to test for doneness is to insert a skewer or thin knife through the thickest point. If it goes in without resistance, the fish is done. Transfer the fish to a platter and serve with lemon wedges and a final sprinkle of salt.

Ⓓ direct fire   Ⓘ indirect fire   Ⓜ make ahead   Ⓥ vegetarian option

Sardines with Red Onion and Olive Oil	Omit the thyme and lemon. Halve a red onion, slice thinly into half moons, and separate the layers. After grilling the sardines, put them on a platter, scatter with the onion, sprinkle with ½ cup chopped fresh parsley, and drizzle generously with more good-quality olive oil.
Sardines with Garlic, Lemon, and Oregano	Omit the lemon wedges. In a small bowl, stir together 6 tablespoons good-quality olive oil, 2 tablespoons chopped fresh oregano, 3 cloves garlic, chopped, and the juice of 1 lemon. In Step 3, pour the dressing over the grilled sardines and serve.
Sardines with Tomatoes, Olives, and Vinegar	Omit the lemon wedges. In a small bowl, stir together 1 cup chopped fresh tomato, ¼ cup chopped pitted black olives, 2 tablespoons chopped fresh parsley, and 1 tablespoon red wine vinegar. Top the grilled sardines with the tomato mixture.

11 FISH TO GRILL WHOLE

To use different fish in the recipes that call for grilling them whole, all you need is to add up the total pounds and substitute the same weight of another species; the number of fish doesn't matter. The same visual cues apply and will help you adjust the cooking time accordingly. Here's a list of some good ones to try. It's always best to buy whatever is sustainable in your area (see page 92 for some websites to check).

1. Porgy
2. Seabass
3. Perch
4. Trout
5. Sardines
6. Mackerel
7. Rockfish
8. Branzino
9. Grouper
10. Small salmon
11. Red snapper

Bacon-Wrapped Butterflied Trout with Lemon-Scallion Relish

Makes: 4 servings	Time: 35 to 45 minutes	D M

This is a real indulgence: One, bacon; and two, a serving is an entire fish. You can do it. Or just hack the trout crosswise into manageable pieces. The preserved lemon for the relish can be tricky. You can buy good ones from a Mediterranean market (or make your own), but if you can't find them you can make a quick ersatz version: Up to a day before serving, chop one whole lemon. Remove any seeds, toss the lemon with ½ teaspoon salt, and mash and stir with a fork. Then finish the relish as described in Step 3. Feel free to substitute fresh sardines or other small whole fish here.

4 8- to 12-ounce trout, cleaned and butterflied

1 tablespoon good-quality olive oil, plus more for brushing

Salt and pepper

8 slices bacon

1 good-quality preserved lemon (or see the headnote to use fresh lemons)

2 scallions, trimmed and chopped

2 tablespoons chopped fresh mint

1 Start the coals or heat a gas grill for medium direct cooking. Make sure the grates are clean.

2 Pat the fish dry with paper towels. Brush them with oil and sprinkle with salt and pepper on both sides. Wrap each fish with 2 slices bacon, covering as much of the body as possible (don't worry about the head).

3 Cut the rind off the lemon and chop it (discard the rest of the lemon). Put the lemon rind in a small bowl along with the scallions, mint, and 1 tablespoon oil; stir to combine. (You can wrap the trout and prepare the relish several hours ahead; cover both and refrigerate until you're ready to grill.)

4 Put the fish on the grill directly over the fire, at an angle or perpendicular to the grate. Close the lid and cook until the bacon browns on the bottom, 4 to 6 minutes, moving it or adjusting the heat as necessary to brown without burning. Carefully turn the fish, using a second spatula to lower them back down to the grate. Close the lid and cook until the bacon browns on the other side and a skewer or thin knife inserted at the thickest point easily pierces it all the way through, 4 to 6 minutes. Serve the trout sprinkled with the relish.

• recipe continues →

Bacon-Wrapped Salmon Fillet with Lemon-Scallion Relish	These two should get together more often: Substitute four 4- to 6-ounce skin-on salmon fillets for the trout. Depending on the size and shape of the fillets, you may only need 1 slice bacon to wrap each fillet; you want some of the skin showing. Start the fillets skin side down.
Bacon-Wrapped Trout with Scallions	Instead of serving with the relish, grill scallions right along with the fish: Increase the scallions to 8 and trim but do not chop them. In Step 2, put 2 scallions on top of each trout before wrapping it with the bacon. Start the fish scallion side down on the grill.
Prosciutto-Wrapped Trout with Basil-Citrus Gremolata	Prosciutto is absolutely delicious after it's hit with fire: Substitute 8 thin slices prosciutto (¼ to ⅓ pound total) for the bacon. In Step 4, instead of the relish, combine ¼ cup chopped fresh basil, 2 teaspoons grated lemon zest, and 1 teaspoon grated orange zest in a small bowl to serve with the trout.

---

13 SEAFOOD RECIPES FOR THE GRILL ELSEWHERE IN THIS BOOK

1. Clams Casino (page 74) and its variation
2. New Haven–Style Fresh Clam Pizza (page 54)
3. BBQ Oysters à la Tomales Bay (page 77) and its variations
4. Bruschetta with Shrimp, Feta, and Capers (page 22)
5. Shrimp Skewers with Peanut Sauce (page 81)
6. Piri-Piri Shrimp (page 182)
7. Capicola-Wrapped Scallops (page 66) and its variations
8. Spicy Squid with Lemon (page 72) and its variations
9. Squid Adobo (page 186)
10. Hot-Smoked Fish (page 61) and its variations
11. Whole Fish en Escabeche (page 162)
12. Jerk Whole Fish (page 184)
13. Polenta Squares with Chive Sour Cream and Salmon Roe (page 59) and its variations

D direct fire I indirect fire M make ahead V vegetarian option

Crab-Stuffed Trout

Makes: 4 to 8 servings	Time: 30 to 35 minutes	Ⓓ Ⓜ

Butterflied whole trout are such a pleasure to eat, no matter how they're cooked. Stuffed, they're out of this world. The skin holds the fine-flaked fillets together, and with no bones to worry about, you can cut into the fish like a steak. This is a good place to use less expensive crab claw meat since it's not the star. One of these makes for a very hearty dinner. For smaller portions serve them on a platter, cut in half.

12 ounces crabmeat, picked over for shells and cartilage

1 cup chopped seeded fresh tomato, drained if necessary

Grated zest of 1 lemon

1 tablespoon good-quality olive oil, plus more for brushing the fish

2 scallions, trimmed and chopped

Salt and pepper

4 8- to 10-ounce rainbow trout, cleaned and butterflied

Lemon wedges for serving

1 Start the coals or heat a gas grill for medium direct cooking. Make sure the grates are clean.

2 Put the crab, tomato, and lemon zest in a medium bowl. Put the oil and scallions in a small skillet over medium heat; cook, stirring occasionally, until softened, 2 to 3 minutes. Add to the crab, sprinkle with salt and pepper, toss gently, and taste and adjust the seasoning.

3 Pat the trout dry with paper towels. Brush them with oil and sprinkle with salt and pepper on both sides. Divide the crab mixture between the trout, filling their cavities. Pull the two sides closed, pushing the filling in, if needed, to keep it from spilling out. (You can prepare the fish earlier in the day, cover, and refrigerate until you're ready to grill.)

4 Put the trout on the grill directly over the fire, at an angle or perpendicular to the grate, with the open side of the fish facing you. Close the lid and cook until the skin browns and the fish release easily, 8 to 10 minutes. Carefully turn the fish, using a second spatula to lower them back down to the grates. Close the lid and cook until the stuffing is heated through and a skewer or thin knife inserted at the thickest point of a fish easily pierces it all the way through, 4 to 5 minutes. Transfer the trout to a platter and serve with lemon wedges.

● recipe continues →

Crab-Stuffed Trout with Ginger and Cilantro	Substitute ½ cup chopped fresh cilantro for the tomato, lime zest for the lemon zest, and lime wedges for the lemon. Add 1 tablespoon chopped fresh ginger to the scallions, and whisk 1 tablespoon soy sauce with the olive oil before brushing the fish.
Crab-Stuffed Trout with Lemon, Olives, and Basil	Substitute ¼ cup chopped fresh basil for the tomato and 2 cloves garlic, chopped, for the scallions. Add ¼ cup chopped pitted black olives to the stuffing.
Spinach-Stuffed Trout with Bacon and Pine Nuts	A totally different take: Chop 2 slices bacon and cook in a large skillet over medium-high heat, stirring occasionally, until the fat has rendered and the bacon is crisp, about 5 minutes; drain on a paper towel. Add 2 cloves garlic, chopped, to the bacon fat and stir for 1 minute. Add 1 pound baby spinach and stir until completely soft, 2 to 3 minutes; pour out any liquid from the pan. Stir in the bacon along with 2 tablespoons toasted pine nuts and salt and pepper to taste; use this mixture to stuff the trout as directed in Step 3.

D direct fire　　I indirect fire　　M make ahead　　V vegetarian option

Crisp-Skin Salmon with Maple-Ginger Glaze

Makes: 4 to 6 servings	Time: 25 to 30 minutes	Ⓓ

Lots of contrasts and a gorgeous presentation make this one of my favorite ways to grill salmon. I like mine on the rare side; take it further if you prefer but be careful not to overdo it to dryness. Since you cook the fillet skin down, the glaze caramelizes without burning.

1 2-pound skin-on salmon fillet

1 tablespoon good-quality vegetable oil

Salt and pepper

¼ cup maple syrup

1 tablespoon Dijon mustard

1 tablespoon minced fresh ginger

1 Start the coals or heat a gas grill for medium-high direct heat cooking. Make sure the grates are clean.

2 Pull any remaining pin bones from the salmon. With a sharp knife, score the skin in a crosshatch pattern.

3 Pat the fish dry with paper towels and put it on a large baking sheet. Brush the skin side with the oil, sprinkle with salt and pepper on both sides, and turn it skin side down. Put the maple syrup, mustard, and ginger in a small bowl and stir to combine. Brush the glaze over the top.

4 Put the salmon skin side down on the grill directly over the fire, at an angle or perpendicular to the grate. Close the lid and cook, without turning, until the thickest part is as opaque as you like, 5 to 10 minutes; nick with a sharp knife and peek inside to check a couple of times. Transfer the salmon to a cutting board, cut into 4 or 6 pieces, and serve.

Crisp-Skin Honey-Chipotle-Garlic Salmon	Up the heat factor: Substitute honey for the maple syrup, mashed canned chipotle chiles with some of their adobo for the mustard, and garlic for the ginger.
Crisp-Skin Sweet Soy-Lime Salmon	The soy adds a bit of umami and the lime zest a citrus pop: Replace the maple syrup, mustard, and ginger with 2 tablespoons each soy sauce and honey and the grated zest of 1 lime. If you like, garnish the salmon with chopped fresh Thai basil.
Crisp-Skin Lemon-Dijon Salmon with Dill	Instead of glazing the salmon, drizzle it with a vinaigrette when it comes off the grill: Omit the maple syrup, mustard, and ginger and use good-quality olive oil instead of vegetable oil. Whisk together ¼ cup olive oil, 2 tablespoons fresh lemon juice, 1 tablespoon minced fresh dill, and 1 teaspoon each grated lemon zest and Dijon mustard (use more mustard if you like). Drizzle the grilled salmon with the vinaigrette before serving.

Cedar-Planked Salmon

| Makes: 4 to 6 servings | Time: 25 to 30 minutes, plus soaking time | D |

The brown sugar in the rub forms a spicy-sweet crust that's like savory candy. Remember to plan ahead; the planks need to soak for a while. See "Plank-Grilling" on page 114 for more about this technique.

2 tablespoons brown sugar

1 tablespoon salt

1 teaspoon black pepper

1 2-pound skin-on salmon fillet, any remaining pin bones removed

1 At least 3 hours before you plan to grill, soak a plank big enough to hold the fish in water to cover; you'll need to weight the wood with something to keep it from floating.

2 Put the brown sugar, salt, and pepper in a small bowl and use your fingers to thoroughly combine the seasoning rub. Pat the fillet dry with paper towels, then work the rub into it on both sides. Let sit at room temperature while the grill heats up.

3 Start the coals or heat a gas grill for medium-high direct cooking. Have a spray bottle of water handy in case the plank catches fire in a big way.

4 Remove the wood from the water and put it on the grill directly over the fire. Close the lid. When you smell cedar and hear crackling, quickly open the grill and put the fillet, skin side down, on the plank. Close the lid and cook, without turning, until the thickest part is as opaque as you like, 5 to 10 minutes; nick with a sharp knife and peek inside to check a couple of times. Transfer the salmon to a cutting board. Completely spray down the plank once you remove the fillet. (Otherwise, even if you move the plank away from the fire or turn the burners off, it will continue to burn.) Cut the salmon into pieces and serve.

Cedar-Planked Salmon with Five-Spice–Brown Sugar Rub	Five-spice powder adds fragrance and flavor and works really well with salmon: Substitute five-spice powder for the black pepper.
Cedar-Planked Salmon with Smoked Paprika–Brown Sugar Rub	Another layer of smokiness: Add 1 tablespoon smoked paprika (pimentón) to the rub.
Cedar-Planked Salmon with Spiced Brown Sugar Rub	This rub includes many of the spices found in the Middle Eastern mixture known as baharat: Decrease the brown sugar to 1 tablespoon. Add 1 teaspoon each ground coriander, cumin, and paprika, ½ teaspoon ground allspice, ¼ teaspoon ground cinnamon, and a pinch each ground cardamom, cloves, and nutmeg.

• recipe continues →

D direct fire   **I** indirect fire   **M** make ahead   **V** vegetarian option

PLANK-GRILLING

Using planks to cook fish has been traced back to the indigenous people of the Pacific Northwest, who would attach salmon fillets to cedar planks and set them in front of a fire to smoke. The technique has changed and now the planks are first soaked in water, so they don't immediately combust, and put directly over the fire in a grill and close the lid. When you smell the cedar smoke and hear the boards starting to crackle, then set the salmon on top of the plank and cook with the lid down. The smoke will infuse the salmon with cedar flavor, as will the steam rising off the plank as it heats.

Plan ahead. The shorter the soak, the quicker the plank catches fire. So figure 3 hours or more before grilling. Keep water in a spray bottle handy to control the flaming; you need some fire to build flavor, but you want to avoid a conflagration.

You can find cedar planks (as well as other woods like pecan, alder, maple, and hickory) in some supermarkets and specialty food shops, and at grilling, home-and-garden, and hardware stores. They come in a range of sizes (13×5½ inches, 8×6 inches, 6×3 inches, and others) and thicknesses (up to ½ inch). Pick the size that best works for you. I prefer thicker planks because they give you a little leeway should they catch fire; some planks are a bit too thin for my comfort. Make sure the wood hasn't been treated with any chemicals, especially if you're shopping at a nonfood store.

Although salmon is traditional for plank-grilling, it's fine to expand your horizons. Any kind of fish fillet or steak will work; you can also plank whole fish or any of the seafood burgers in this chapter.

D direct fire   I indirect fire   M make ahead   V vegetarian option

Salmon Burgers

Makes: 4 burgers or 8 to 10 sliders	Time: 35 to 45 minutes, plus chilling time	Ⓓ Ⓜ

The secret to getting these burgers to hold together is to process some of the salmon into a paste; then add the rest and pulse just until chopped. And the trick to keeping the burgers from sticking on the grill is to clean the grates well.

1½ pounds salmon fillet, skin and any remaining pin bones removed, cut into chunks

2 teaspoons Dijon mustard

3 scallions, trimmed and chopped

¼ cup bread crumbs (preferably fresh)

Salt and pepper

Good-quality olive oil for brushing

4 sesame hamburger buns or 8–10 slider buns (like potato or dinner rolls)

1 large tomato, cut into 4 thick slices (omit for sliders)

1 Put about one quarter of the salmon and the mustard in a food processor and purée into a paste. Add the rest of the salmon and pulse until chopped. Transfer to a bowl, add the scallions, bread crumbs, and a sprinkle of salt and pepper. Mix gently just enough to combine. Form into 4 burgers ¾ to 1 inch thick (or 8 to 10 sliders). Transfer to a plate, cover with plastic wrap, and chill until firm, at least 2 or up to 8 hours.

2 Start the coals or heat a gas grill for medium-high direct cooking. Make sure the grates are clean.

3 Brush the burgers with oil on both sides, then put them on the grill directly over the fire. Close the lid and cook until the bottoms are browned and the burgers release easily, 4 to 5 minutes. Carefully turn them with a spatula and cook another 4 to 5 minutes, until firm and cooked through but not dry. Cooking time for sliders will be a minute or two less per side. Remove the burgers from the grill.

4 Put the buns on the grill, cut side down, close the lid, and toast for 1 to 2 minutes. Serve the burgers on the buns, topped with the tomato if using.

Lox Burgers	Use 1¼ pounds salmon fillet and 4 ounces cold-smoked salmon (belly lox or nova). Add the smoked salmon to the food processor with the second addition of salmon fillet in Step 1. Serve the burgers, on toasted bialys if you like, with a schmear of cream cheese, a slice of red onion, and a sprinkle of capers.
Lemon-Dill Fish Burgers	Substitute catfish, cod, or haddock fillets for the salmon and ¼ cup chopped dill for the scallions. Add 3 tablespoons mayonnaise and the grated zest of 1 lemon along with the bread crumbs. Cut the zested lemon into wedges to serve alongside.
Ginger-Hoisin Tuna Burgers	Substitute tuna steaks for the salmon and 1 tablespoon hoisin sauce for the mustard. Add 1 tablespoon minced fresh ginger with the crumbs.

Sesame-Crusted Tuna Steaks with Lime Dipping Sauce

Makes: 4 servings	Time: 20 to 25 minutes	Ⓓ Ⓜ

You know this tuna—seared on the outside in a screaming hot skillet. So why not take it outdoors? Cook the steaks to the doneness you like: After 1 minute on each side, the outside will be seared, the inside raw. Four to five minutes on each side should yield tuna cooked all the way through. The sesame seeds can be all black, all white, or a mixture, known as a tuxedo blend.

1½ pounds 1-inch-thick tuna steaks

1 tablespoon sesame oil

½ cup sesame seeds

¼ cup fresh lime juice

2 tablespoons soy sauce

1 tablespoon rice vinegar

1 tablespoon sugar

1 tablespoon minced fresh ginger

1 tablespoon minced garlic

Chopped scallion for garnish (optional)

1 Start the coals or heat a gas grill for hot direct cooking. Make sure the grates are clean.

2 Pat the tuna steaks dry with paper towels. Brush with the oil on both sides. Put the sesame seeds on a small plate and dredge the steaks in them, coating the tuna completely, even the sides.

3 Whisk the lime juice, soy sauce, vinegar, sugar, ginger, and garlic together in a small bowl until the sugar dissolves. (You can dredge the tuna and make the dipping sauce several hours in advance, cover, and refrigerate until ready to grill.)

4 Put the steaks on the grill directly over the fire. Close the lid and cook 1 to 5 minutes per side, depending on the desired doneness (see the headnote); nick with a small knife to peek inside as necessary. Transfer the tuna to individual serving plates, garnish with scallion if you like, and serve with small bowls of dipping sauce. Or slice the tuna and serve family style, passing the sauce at the table.

• recipe continues →

Fish and Shellfish

Sesame-Crusted Wasabi Tuna Steaks with Lime Dipping Sauce	For that sushi bar nose-burning heat: Omit the sesame oil. In a small bowl, whisk together 2 tablespoons each warm water and wasabi powder. Before dredging them in the sesame seeds, brush the steaks with as little or as much of the mixture as you like.
Sesame-Crusted Salmon Fillets with Lime Dipping Sauce	Salmon is delicious this way, but keep the skin on for extra crunch: Substitute skin-on salmon fillet for the tuna steaks but dredge only the skinless side in the sesame seeds. Put the dredged salmon skin side down on the grill, close the lid, and cook until the bottom has browned and easily releases from the grill, 4 to 5 minutes. Turn, close the lid, and cook to your desired degree of doneness, 1 to 5 minutes more.
Tuna au Poivre	Tuna gets the classic French treatment: Coarsely crack ¼ cup black peppercorns by putting them in a zipper bag and running a rolling pin back and forth over them, or use a mortar and pestle; these replace the sesame seeds. Substitute Dijon mustard for the sesame oil. Omit the dipping sauce.

D direct fire **I** indirect fire **M** make ahead **V** vegetarian option

Swordfish in Salmoriglio

Makes: **4 servings**	Time: **23 to 25 minutes**	**D**

Though the word comes from the Sicilian word for "brine," salmoriglio is an olive oil and citrus sauce traditionally paired with grilled fish. It's a great choice for dark-fleshed species like mackerel and bluefish, the citrus balancing their richness. It also works well drizzled over grilled whole fish (see pages 101–103). For a bigger kick of citrus, add up to 1 tablespoon grated zest to the sauce.

Swordfish holds together wonderfully on the grill and turns a lovely ivory-white. Often it comes with the tough inedible skin still attached to one side of the steak, which will flake away once it's done. You'll want to put the sauce on everything, so serve the steaks with a baked potato or plain rice on the side—or break up the fish and toss the whole thing with pasta.

½ cup good-quality olive oil

¼ cup fresh lemon juice

2 tablespoons chopped fresh oregano

2 tablespoons chopped fresh parsley

¼ teaspoon red chile flakes, or more to taste

2 cloves garlic, minced

Salt

1½ pounds 1-inch-thick swordfish steaks

1 Start the coals or heat a gas grill for hot direct cooking. Make sure the grates are clean.

2 Whisk the oil and lemon juice in a small bowl until it thickens. Stir in the oregano, parsley, red pepper, garlic, and salt to taste. Transfer 2 tablespoons of the sauce to a small bowl and brush the steaks with it on both sides.

3 Put the steaks on the grill directly over the fire. Close the lid and cook until the bottoms develop grill marks and the fish releases easily from the grates, 4 to 5 minutes. Turn the steaks, close the lid, and cook until they lose their translucence in the center, 4 to 5 minutes; at that point, you should be able to insert a skewer or thin knife through the center with no resistance. Transfer the steaks to a platter, pour over the remaining salmoriglio, and serve.

Swordfish in Red Salmoriglio	After removing the 2 tablespoons sauce for brushing the fish, stir 1 fresh tomato, chopped, into the remaining sauce.
Swordfish with Orange-Herb Sauce	Orange pairs beautifully with the oregano: Substitute fresh orange juice for the lemon juice.
Swordfish with Lime-Basil Sauce	Substitute lime juice for the lemon juice and ¼ cup chopped fresh basil for the oregano and parsley.

Seafood Skewers with Croutons and Orange

Makes: **4 servings**	Time: **25 to 30 minutes**	Ⓓ

You can take these skewers in many directions. Use all fish, alternate fish with sea scallops or shrimp, or mix them all up; the flavors play well together and the cook times are pretty much the same. Oranges bring freshness, especially if you're grilling in winter. To include onions in the mix, either put wedges on a separate skewer and start them at least 5 minutes before the seafood, or thread single layers of onion between the cubes of fish. This is one time you can't assemble the skewers too long before grilling or the bread will get soggy.

1½ pounds 1-inch-thick skinless fish fillets or steaks

1 loaf crusty Italian bread

6 tablespoons good-quality olive oil

Salt and pepper

3 oranges

1 If you're using bamboo or wooden skewers, soak them in water for 30 minutes. Meanwhile, start the coals or heat a gas grill for medium-high cooking. Make sure the grates are clean.

2 Cut the fish and the bread into 1- to 1½-inch cubes. Toss the fish with 2 tablespoons of the oil in one bowl and the bread with the remaining 4 tablespoons oil in another. Season with salt and pepper.

3 Slice off the peel at the top and bottom of an orange and set it, flat side down, on a cutting board. Cut downward to remove the peel, pith, and membrane to reveal the fruit. Then cut each orange section on both sides to remove it from the membrane. As you work, put the sections in a bowl. Repeat with the remaining oranges. Thread the fish, bread, and orange sections onto skewers, alternating them; save any juice that has accumulated in the bowl.

4 Put the skewers on the grill directly over the fire. Close the lid and cook until the croutons are golden and the fish is just cooked through (peek inside in a few places to check), 4 to 5 minutes per side. Transfer to a platter, pour over any reserved orange juice, and serve.

---

5 FISH TO USE FOR KEBABS

These fish offer good flavor and will keep together on the skewer.

1. Tuna
2. Swordfish
3. Salmon
4. Mahi-mahi
5. Bluefish

• recipe continues →

Ⓓ direct fire   Ⓘ indirect fire   Ⓜ make ahead   Ⓥ vegetarian option

Seafood Skewers with Croutons and Apricots	A surprising combination that works particularly well with tuna, salmon, and swordfish: Substitute ¾ pound fresh apricots for the oranges; halve them to remove the pits, then quarter them if they're big. Serve with lime wedges.
Balsamic-Glazed Seafood Skewers with Croutons and Figs	Substitute 1 pound ripe figs for the oranges. Depending on their size, you can leave them whole, halve, or quarter them. Drizzle Balsamic Syrup (page 467) over the skewers before serving.
Seafood Skewers with Croutons and Mango	Substitute 1 large ripe mango for the oranges. Peel, slice the flesh off the seed, and cut into 1- to 1½-inch pieces. Serve with lime wedges.

D direct fire **I** indirect fire **M** make ahead **V** vegetarian option

Shrimp with Yogurt-Herb Sauce

Makes: 4 servings	Time: 25 to 30 minutes	⒟ Ⓜ

Yogurt makes a great base for a quick grill marinade. It clings well to deliver a tangy backdrop for all sorts of herbs, spices, and seasonings. And the browned crust that forms when yogurt hits the fire is sublime. This marinade and its variations also work well with chicken and pork.

4 scallions, trimmed and cut into pieces

2 cloves garlic, peeled

1 small bunch fresh parsley, thick stems removed (thin stems are fine)

1 cup yogurt

Salt and pepper

2 pounds large or jumbo shrimp, peeled (and deveined if you like)

Lemon wedges for serving

1 Put the scallions, garlic, parsley, and yogurt in a blender or food processor, sprinkle with salt and pepper, and purée until smooth. Transfer to a large bowl, add the shrimp, and toss to coat fully with the marinade. Marinate at room temperature while the grill heats up, or cover and refrigerate for up to several hours.

2 Start the coals or heat a gas grill for hot direct cooking. Make sure the grates are clean.

3 Put the shrimp on the grill directly over the fire. (See "Grilling Shrimp," page 125.) Close the lid and cook, turning once, until the shrimp are opaque all the way through, 3 to 5 minutes per side, depending on their size and how hot the fire is. Discard any remaining marinade. Transfer to a platter and serve with lemon wedges.

Tandoori-Style Shrimp	Omit the parsley; add a ½-inch piece peeled fresh ginger, cut into slices, 1 tablespoon ground cumin, 1 teaspoon ground coriander, and ¼ teaspoon cayenne to the yogurt before puréeing.
Shrimp with Yogurt-Pomegranate Sauce	If you can't find the molasses, reduce ½ cup pomegranate juice to a syrup in a small saucepan and use that: Substitute cilantro for the parsley and add 2 tablespoons pomegranate molasses before puréeing. Garnish the shrimp with pomegranate seeds and serve with lime wedges.
Shrimp with Tofu-Herb Sauce	A dairy-free option for the main recipe or any of the variations: Substitute 1 cup silken tofu for the yogurt.

Garlic Shrimp

| Makes: 4 to 6 servings | Time: 25 to 30 minutes | Ⓓ Ⓜ |

The traditional version of this iconic Spanish dish—*gambas al ajillo*—is done on the stovetop in a skillet. It doesn't make sense to take simple dishes out to the grill without a compelling reason, but in this case there is one. Tossing char-grilled shrimp in warm garlic-and-chile-infused olive oil is even better than cooking them together. Let the two get acquainted in the pan; the flavors will mingle while you grill the bread. Then use the toast to mop up all the oil. I like to use huge shrimp so they can develop a brown crust without overcooking.

¾ cup good-quality olive oil, plus more for brushing the bread

8 cloves garlic, thinly sliced

½ teaspoon red chile flakes

2 pounds large or jumbo shrimp, peeled (and deveined if you like)

Salt and pepper

¼ cup chopped fresh parsley

4 to 8 thick slices crusty bread

1 Start the coals or heat a gas grill for hot direct cooking. Make sure the grates are clean.

2 Put the oil, garlic, and red pepper in a medium skillet over low heat or a cool part of the grill. Let the garlic simmer in the oil, stirring occasionally, just until it starts to color, 6 to 10 minutes, then immediately take the pan off the heat. Keep a close eye on it; the garlic can quickly go from golden to burnt. (You can make the sauce up to several hours ahead; gently rewarm it before grilling the shrimp.)

3 Pat the shrimp dry with paper towels. Put them in a large bowl and toss with 2 tablespoons of the infused oil and sprinkle with salt and pepper.

4 Put the shrimp on the grill directly over the fire. (See "Grilling Shrimp," opposite.) Close the lid and cook, turning once, until they are opaque all the way through, 3 to 5 minutes per side, depending on their size and how hot the fire is. Transfer the shrimp to the pan of sauce, add the parsley, and stir to coat evenly with sauce.

5 Brush the bread with oil on both sides. Toast until it develops grill marks, 1 to 2 minutes per side. Taste the sauce and adjust the seasoning if necessary. Serve the shrimp drizzled with the oil, over—or alongside—the bread.

Ⓓ direct fire   Ⓘ indirect fire   Ⓜ make ahead   Ⓥ vegetarian option

Shrimp Scampi on the Grill	An Italian American favorite: Substitute 12 tablespoons (1½ sticks) butter for the olive oil and omit the red chile flakes. Substitute basil for the parsley. Melt the butter over low heat with the garlic. When you take the pan off the heat, stir in 2 tablespoons fresh lemon juice. Proceed with Step 2. Serve with lemon wedges.
Garlic Shrimp with Cilantro and Lime	Omit the red chile flakes. Substitute ½ cup chopped fresh cilantro for the parsley. Serve with lime wedges.
Garlic-Ginger Shrimp with Sherry	The sherry adds a note of nuttiness: Omit the red chile flakes. Decrease the oil to 6 tablespoons and add 6 tablespoons (¾ stick) butter. When the butter has melted, add the garlic and 2 tablespoons minced fresh ginger. When the garlic starts to color, stir in 2 tablespoons dry sherry; let the mixture come to a simmer and bubble for another minute before removing from the heat. Serve with lime wedges.

GRILLING SHRIMP

The recipes in this section will work for any size shrimp, though I make some specific suggestions. I generally prefer shell-on American varieties, most of which have been previously frozen—so buying them that way is fine, too, as long as they don't look too frosted. I don't bother to devein them, though you can remove any dark lines with a sharp knife. Starting with shelled shrimp is also okay; figure somewhere between 1½ and 2 pounds for the following recipes.

You've got lots of ways to cook shrimp over fire. I usually just tumble large or jumbo shrimp onto the grill, spreading them in a single layer with tongs. Or you can put them on one by one for more strategic placement. Another alternative—especially with smaller sizes—is to use a perforated grill pan. Set the pan over a rimmed baking sheet to catch any drippings and get the shrimp in a single layer before bringing them out to the grill. When using the pan, you can use spatula to turn the shrimp simply like a stir-fry. The last option is to thread them on skewers. This might seem like more work if you're cooking a lot of shrimp, but you can do it ahead, and the skewers keep medium-size shrimp from falling between the grate, so it's often worth it. Larger shrimp work great threaded between two skewers so they lie flat and can be easily maneuvered.

Butterflied Shrimp with Spicy Miso Glaze

Makes: 4 servings	Time: 20 to 25 minutes	Ⓓ Ⓜ

Why bother to butterfly when shrimp already cook so fast? More surface area. And that means more of what you love about grilled shrimp. The quick searing time gives you an opportunity to use more sugar-heavy glazes which might otherwise risk burning over high heat. Don't bother fussing with anything smaller than jumbo shrimp or you'll go nuts. If you're not a big fan of hot sauce, leave out the sriracha or go with something milder.

½ cup any miso

¼ cup mirin (or 2 tablespoons each honey and water mixed together)

1 tablespoon sriracha or other garlicky hot sauce

Salt and pepper (optional)

2 pounds jumbo or colossal shrimp (21/25 or under 15 count), peeled

2 tablespoons chopped scallion greens

1 Start the coals or heat a gas grill for hot direct cooking. Make sure the grates are clean.

2 Whisk the miso, mirin, and sriracha together in a small bowl until smooth. Taste and add a little salt and pepper if you like.

3 Butterfly the shrimp (see "Butterflying Shrimp," page 128). Spread the butterflied shrimp out in a single layer on a rimmed baking sheet. (You can butterfly the shrimp and make the glaze up to several hours ahead and refrigerate until ready to grill.) Brush the shrimp with the glaze, then turn them all over and brush the other side.

4 Put the shrimp on the grill directly over the fire one at a time, flattening them quickly by hand or with tongs as you work. Close the lid and cook, turning once, until the shrimp are opaque all the way through and the glaze is browned, 2 to 4 minutes per side, depending on their size and how hot the fire is. Garnish with the scallion greens and serve.

---

5 OTHER GLAZES AND SAUCES FOR BUTTERFLIED SHRIMP

1. Sweet Rosemary-Orange Glaze (page 179)
2. Lime-Cilantro Oil (page 103)
3. Lemon Finadene Dipping Sauce (page 215)
4. Pomegranate BBQ Sauce (page 199)
5. Mustard-Garlic Vinaigrette (page 432)

• recipe continues →

Ⓓ direct fire   Ⓘ indirect fire   Ⓜ make ahead   Ⓥ vegetarian option

Butterflied Shrimp with Spicy Miso Glaze and Thai-Style Coleslaw (page 398)

Butterflied Shrimp with Ginger-Honey Glaze	Replace the miso, mirin, sriracha, and salt and pepper with ½ cup honey, 2 tablespoons fresh lime juice, 1 tablespoon soy sauce, and 1 inch peeled fresh ginger, cut into slices. Put in a blender and purée until smooth.
Butterflied Shrimp with Maple-Orange Glaze	Maple syrup and shrimp? Trust me, it works: Replace the miso, mirin, sriracha, and salt and pepper with ½ cup maple syrup, 3 tablespoons soy sauce, and 1 tablespoon each orange juice and grated orange zest.
Sesame Shrimp	A take on Chinese sesame chicken: Replace the miso, mirin, sriracha, and salt and pepper with ¼ cup sugar, and 2 tablespoons each sesame oil, soy sauce, and dry sherry. Add 1 tablespoon sesame seeds, 2 teaspoons minced fresh ginger, and 1 clove garlic, minced. Omit the scallions— or not.

BUTTERFLYING SHRIMP

STEP 1 Cut through the back of the shrimp with a small knife until you almost cut all the way through—to the tail, if there is one.

STEP 2 If you'd like, remove the vein.

STEP 3 Holding the shrimp on either side, open it until it lies flat.

D direct fire   **I** indirect fire   **M** make ahead   **V** vegetarian option

Coconut-Rum Shrimp and Pineapple Skewers

Makes: 4 to 6 servings	Time: 35 to 40 minutes	Ⓓ Ⓜ

The version in restaurants is usually too sweet for me, but the components—when left alone—are naturally balanced. And the tropical flavors get even better over a hot fire. If you can't find or don't want to make your own ras el hanout, for a different but equally nice flavor, substitute five-spice powder (to make your own, see page 456). Serve the skewers on a bed of fragrant jasmine rice, on either individual plates or a platter.

½ cup coconut milk

¼ cup dark or spiced rum

¼ cup fresh lime juice

1 teaspoon ras el hanout (to make your own, see page 456)

Salt and pepper

2 cloves garlic, chopped

2 pounds large or jumbo shrimp, peeled (and deveined if you like)

1 ripe pineapple, peeled, cored, and cut into 1½-inch cubes

Lime wedges for serving

1 Stir the coconut milk, rum, lime juice, ras el hanout, and garlic together in a large bowl. Add the shrimp and toss to coat completely. Marinate at room temperature while you prepare the grill, or cover and refrigerate for up to 1 hour.

2 If you're using bamboo or wooden skewers, soak them in water for 30 minutes. Meanwhile, start the coals or heat a gas grill for medium-high direct cooking. Make sure the grates are clean.

3 Alternate the shrimp and pineapple cubes on skewers. Discard any remaining marinade. Put the skewers on the grill directly over the fire. (See "Grilling Shrimp," page 125.) Close the lid and cook, turning once, until the shrimp are opaque all the way through and the pineapple browns in spots, 4 to 8 minutes per side, depending on their size and how hot the fire is. Transfer the skewers to a platter and serve with lime wedges.

Coconut-Chile Shrimp and Tomato Skewers	Now with Southeast Asian flavors: Substitute 3 tablespoons fish sauce for the rum and add minced fresh red hot chile to taste; omit the ras el hanout. Substitute 2 cups cherry or grape tomatoes for the pineapple.
Curried Coconut Shrimp and Pineapple Skewers	Omit the rum and substitute 1 tablespoon curry powder for the ras el hanout.
Coconut Shrimp and Orange (or Tomato) Skewers with Smoked Paprika	For winter, or summer: Omit the rum and substitute 1 tablespoon smoked paprika (pimentón) for the ras el hanout. Substitute 2 or 3 oranges for the pineapple, peeling and sectioning them before threading on the skewers (see page 534). Or cut wedges from 2 or 3 fresh tomatoes.

Basil-Ginger Shrimp Burgers

Makes: 4 burgers or 8 to 10 sliders	Time: 25 to 30 minutes, plus chilling time	Ⓓ Ⓜ

Like the Salmon Burgers on page 115, puréeing some of the shrimp here helps hold the remaining ingredients together in a burger that can stand up to the grill. To prevent sticking, make sure to clean the grates well and oil them generously.

1 large clove garlic, peeled

1 1-inch piece fresh ginger, peeled and sliced

1½ pounds shrimp, peeled (and deveined if you like)

½ cup lightly packed fresh basil leaves

¼ cup roughly chopped shallots, scallions, or red onion

Salt and pepper

Sesame oil for brushing the burgers

4 sesame hamburger buns or 8–10 slider buns (like potato or dinner rolls)

Lime wedges for serving

Lettuce, sliced tomato, and other condiments for serving (optional)

1 Put the garlic, ginger, and one-third of the shrimp in a food processor; purée until smooth, stopping the machine to scrape down the sides as necessary. Add the remaining shrimp, the basil, and shallots, season with salt and pepper, and pulse to chop. Form into 4 burgers about ¾ inch thick (or 8 to 10 sliders). Transfer to a plate, cover with plastic wrap, and chill until firm, at least 1 or up to 8 hours.

2 Start the coals or heat a gas grill for medium-high direct cooking. Make sure the grates are clean.

3 Brush the burgers on both sides with oil, then put them on the grill directly over the fire. Close the lid and cook until the bottoms brown and they release easily, 5 to 7 minutes. Carefully turn and cook until opaque all the way through, 3 to 5 minutes.

4 Put the buns, cut side down, on the grill to toast. Serve the burgers on the toasted buns with lime wedges, as is or dressed however you like.

Ⓓ direct fire   Ⓘ indirect fire   Ⓜ make ahead   Ⓥ vegetarian option

Ginger Scallop Burgers with Orange Zest	Omit the garlic and basil. Substitute 1½ pounds sea scallops for the shrimp; trim any tough connective tissue if necessary. Double the ginger if you like, use red onion, and add the grated zest of 2 oranges.
Shu Mai Burgers	Decrease the amount of shrimp to 8 ounces and add 1 pound coarsely ground pork (preferably from the shoulder; see page 260 for information on grinding your own). Substitute cilantro for the basil. Pulse the garlic, ginger, cilantro, scallions, and all the shrimp in the food processor until chopped. Transfer to a bowl and fold in the pork along with 1 teaspoon soy sauce. Season with salt and pepper and mix well. Shape and grill as directed; cook time may be a few minutes longer.
Chorizo-Shrimp Burgers	Double the garlic and omit the ginger. Decrease the shrimp to 1¼ pounds. Substitute parsley for the basil and use red onion. After processing, transfer the shrimp mixture to a bowl, work in about 5 ounces fresh Mexican chorizo squeezed from its casing, 1 teaspoon smoked paprika (pimentón), and the grated zest of a lime. Stir gently to combine. Shape and grill as directed; cook time may be a few minutes longer.

Seared Scallops with Beurre Blanc

Makes: 4 servings	Time: 30 to 35 minutes	Ⓓ

Beurre blanc, or "white butter," is an easy-to-make classic French butter sauce that pairs beautifully with grilled scallops as well as simply grilled fish fillets, lobster, mussels, clams, and much more. Where you take it is up to your imagination. Once you get the hang of making it, you can whip up a batch in the time it takes the grill to heat.

Two secrets for success: First, the butter should be firm and ice cold to achieve a good emulsion. It's best to cube the butter, then return it to the fridge or freezer until you need it. Second, watch the heat; if it's too high when you're adding the butter, the sauce will separate or "break." It may not be pretty but it will still taste good; toss the sauce with the scallops before serving and no one will be the wiser.

2 tablespoons minced shallot

⅓ cup white wine vinegar or rice vinegar

⅓ cup dry white wine

Salt and pepper

2 pounds sea scallops, trimmed of any tough connective tissue

Good-quality olive oil for brushing the scallops

8 tablespoons (1 stick) cold butter, cut into ½-inch cubes

1 Start the coals or heat a gas grill for hot direct cooking. Make sure the grates are clean.

2 Put the shallot, vinegar, and wine in a small saucepan over medium heat. Sprinkle with salt and pepper and simmer, stirring a few times, until the liquid reduces to 2 to 3 tablespoons, 8 to 10 minutes. Remove from the heat and let cool for 2 minutes.

3 Pat the scallops dry with paper towels. Brush them with oil and season with salt and pepper on both sides.

4 Finish the sauce. Put the pan over a burner with the heat as low as possible and whisk in the cold butter 4 or 5 cubes at a time until fully incorporated before adding the next batch. When all the butter is added and the sauce is smooth and creamy, you're done. Immediately remove the pan from the heat; taste and adjust the seasoning. (If the sauce needs to wait, pour it into a thermos or set the saucepan in a pan of warm water or in the oven at its lowest setting.)

5 Put the scallops on the grill directly over the fire. Close the lid and cook, turning once, until they are seared and golden brown in spots, with the centers still ever so slightly translucent, 3 to 5 minutes per side. Transfer the scallops to a platter, drizzle with the beurre blanc, and pass the remaining sauce at the table.

Ⓓ direct fire   Ⓘ indirect fire   Ⓜ make ahead   Ⓥ vegetarian option

Seared Scallops with Tarragon Beurre Blanc	Tarragon is a classic pairing with fish: In Step 4, stir 1 tablespoon minced fresh tarragon into the beurre blanc after adding all the butter.
Seared Scallops with Soy-Chive Beurre Blanc	Just a little soy sauce goes a long way in adding a welcome savoriness: In Step 4, stir 1 tablespoon minced fresh chives and 1 teaspoon soy sauce into the beurre blanc after adding the butter.
Seared Scallops with Grapefruit Beurre Blanc	The addition of grapefruit produces a lovely rose-colored sauce and tastes terrific with scallops: Substitute ½ cup red grapefruit juice for the wine (you might need 2 large grapefruits) and grate the zest. The added volume will increase the time the sauce takes to reduce in Step 2 by a couple minutes. In Step 4, stir 1 teaspoon grated grapefruit zest (or more to taste) into the beurre blanc after adding the butter.

BUYING SCALLOPS

When you buy scallops, make sure to buy "dry" or "dry-pack." "Wet," "soaked," or "treated" scallops have been soaked in a phosphate solution to whiten and plump them, which can increase their weight by up to 30 percent. And the extra water makes treated scallops tough to sear, since they will ooze water when they hit the grill or pan.

In their natural dry state, scallops are more ivory (or even beige or pinkish) than white. If the scallops being sold at your fish counter are not marked, ask. And if you have no choice, soak them in a couple of changes of fresh water, gently squeeze them dry in your hands between paper towels, and refrigerate them on a wire rack over a pan or plate, loosely covered with parchment or wax paper, for up to several hours before grilling. This will help improve their flavor and dry them out for searing.

Seared Scallops with Parsley-Lemon Stuffing

Makes: 4 servings	Time: 25 to 30 minutes	Ⓓ Ⓜ

One of my all-time favorites, I've made this recipe many ways over the years. Each bite combines just the right amount of crust with a taste from the little flavor pocket inside. Try brushing the scallops with oil before stuffing them; they're easier to handle at that stage. And be sure to clean your grates extra well, otherwise the scallops will stick and tear.

½ cup minced fresh parsley

2 teaspoons grated lemon zest

1 clove garlic, minced

Salt and pepper

1½ pounds sea scallops, trimmed of any tough connective tissue

Good-quality olive oil for brushing the scallops

Lemon wedges for serving

1 Start the coals or heat a gas grill for hot direct cooking. Make sure the grates are clean.

2 Stir the parsley, lemon zest, and garlic together in a small bowl and sprinkle with a little salt and pepper if you like.

3 Pat the scallops dry with paper towels. Brush them with oil and season with salt and pepper on both sides. With a small thin knife, make a 1- to 1½-inch-long horizontal slit in the side, going almost all the way through. Jiggle the knife from side to side to enlarge the pocket without cutting through the side. Using a small spoon with a pointed tip, like a grapefruit spoon, fill each scallop with the stuffing. (You can prepare and refrigerate the scallops up to several hours in advance.)

4 Put the scallops on the grill directly over the fire. Close the lid and cook, turning once, until they're seared and golden brown in spots, with the centers still ever so slightly translucent, 3 to 5 minutes per side. Transfer the scallops to a platter and serve with lemon wedges.

Seared Scallops with Mint-Lime Stuffing	Substitute mint for the parsley, lime zest for the lemon zest, and lime wedges for the lemon for serving.
Miso-Glazed Scallops with Cilantro-Chile Stuffing	Substitute cilantro for the parsley and lime zest for the lemon zest; add 2 teaspoons (more or less to taste) minced seeded hot green chile (like jalapeño or Thai) to the stuffing. Instead of olive oil, brush the scallops with a mixture of 1½ tablespoons each fish sauce, mirin or honey, and any kind of miso. Serve with lime wedges.
Honey-Tangerine-Glazed Scallops with Chive-Ginger Stuffing	Substitute chives for the parsley, tangerine zest for the lemon zest, and 1 teaspoon minced fresh ginger for the garlic. Instead of olive oil, brush the scallops with a mixture of 1 tablespoon each fresh tangerine juice and honey and 2 teaspoons Vietnamese chili-garlic sauce. Omit the lemon wedges.

Ⓓ direct fire   Ⓘ indirect fire   Ⓜ make ahead   Ⓥ vegetarian option

Stuffed Squid with Tomatoes, Ginger, and Basil

Makes: **4 servings**	Time: **30 to 35 minutes**	Ⓓ Ⓜ

This presentation is memorable. And the assembly is as easy as it is dramatic. The advice to cook squid super-quick holds here so don't stray far from the grill while they cook. A Filipino recipe inspired this version; the original calls for calamondin juice (also called calamansi); it has kind of a sour tangerine flavor.

¼ cup fresh lime juice

¼ cup soy sauce

1 tablespoon crushed black peppercorns, plus more to taste

1 tablespoon sugar

1½ pounds cleaned squid (you need an equal number of bodies and tentacles)

1 cup seeded and chopped fresh tomatoes

½ cup chopped red onion

¼ cup chopped fresh basil

1 tablespoon chopped fresh ginger

Salt

Lime wedges for serving

1 Stir the lime juice, soy sauce, peppercorns, and sugar together in a medium bowl until the sugar dissolves. Add the squid and toss to coat with the marinade, opening up the bodies so that the marinade coats the insides. Let sit at room temperature while you make the filling.

2 Drain the tomatoes of any excess juice and put them in a small bowl with the onion, basil, and ginger; taste and add a little salt if you like, remembering the marinade has soy sauce in it.

3 Remove the squid from the marinade; discard any remaining marinade. Working with a teaspoon, fill the bodies with the tomato mixture; don't pack it in and leave a little space at the opening. Take a set of tentacles and insert into the opening. Run a toothpick straight across the opening, catching the body on both sides and running it through the center of the base of the tentacles. (You can cover and refrigerate the stuffed squid up to several hours in advance.)

4 Start the coals or heat a gas grill for hot direct cooking. Make sure the grates are clean.

5 Put the squid on the grill directly over the fire, at an angle or perpendicular to the grate. Close the lid. Turn the squid after 2 to 3 minutes and again close the lid. The squid are ready when they're just opaque all the way through and the filling is hot, 2 to 3 minutes per side. Serve hot or at room temperature with lime wedges.

• recipe continues →

Fish and Shellfish

Stuffed Squid with Tomatoes, Garlic, and Mint	Substitute mint for the basil and garlic for the ginger.
Sicilian-Style Stuffed Squid	Omit the lime juice, soy sauce, peppercorn, and sugar marinade and the tomato, onion, basil, and ginger stuffing. In a small skillet over medium heat, sauté ½ cup bread crumbs (preferably fresh) and 1 tablespoon chopped garlic in 2 tablespoons good-quality olive oil until golden, 3 to 4 minutes. Remove from the heat and add ½ cup chopped fresh parsley and ¼ cup grated Parmesan cheese; taste and add salt and pepper if you like. Use this mixture to stuff the squid, then brush them with olive oil and sprinkle with salt and pepper before grilling. Serve with lemon wedges.
Pork-Stuffed Squid with Cilantro and Garlic	Pork and squid pair deliciously in this play on a Thai dish: Omit the tomato, onion, basil, and ginger stuffing. Instead, stuff the squid with a mixture of 8 ounces ground pork, ¼ cup chopped fresh cilantro, 1 tablespoon each fish sauce and dark soy sauce, and 4 cloves garlic, chopped. They are done when there is no pinkness left in the filling; depending on the size of the squid, that can take 5 to 7 minutes per side. Serve with lime wedges.

CLEANING SQUID

Already cleaned squid is widely available. But in case your find yourself with the whole, somewhat messy shebang, here's how to do it yourself.

1. Pull apart the tentacles and head. Discard the head.
2. Reach inside the body to pull out and discard the hard, plastic-like quill and the ink sac.
3. Peel off the skin, using a knife if necessary, and rinse all the pieces in a colander.

Octopus with Lemon and Oregano

| Makes: 4 servings | Time: 1½ hours, largely unattended | Ⓓ Ⓜ |

Char-grilled octopus is near perfect—ethereal on the inside, with crunchy blackened bits on the outside. On restaurant menus, it's usually offered as an appetizer but with some fingerling potatoes and an arugula salad, I make a meal of it.

Now that cleaned octopus is more available at the fish counter or in the frozen section, grilling it well is a snap. All you have to do is set aside some time to simmer and tenderize the octopus before last-minute finishing on the grill. This extra step provides make-ahead flexibility and gives you two opportunities to vary the flavors, via either the simmer liquid or the ingredients in the dressing.

3 lemons

3 pounds cleaned octopus, thawed if frozen

6 cloves garlic, peeled

4 sprigs fresh oregano

2 bay leaves

Salt and pepper

3 tablespoons good-quality olive oil

Minced fresh oregano for garnish

1 Halve one of the lemons. Put the octopus, garlic, oregano sprigs, bay leaves, a large pinch of salt, and lemon halves in a large pot with enough water to cover by a couple of inches. Bring to a boil, adjust the heat so the liquid bubbles gently but steadily, and cook, turning occasionally with tongs, until the octopus is tender, 30 to 90 minutes. (Check with the tip of a sharp knife; it should go in easily.) Drain; discard the seasonings. (You can cover and refrigerate the octopus for up to 24 hours.)

2 Start the coals or heat a gas grill for hot direct cooking. Make sure the grates are clean.

3 Squeeze the juice 1 of the remaining lemons and whisk it with the oil and salt and pepper to taste. Cut the octopus into large serving pieces and toss with the oil mixture.

4 Put the octopus on the grill directly over the fire. Cover the grill and cook until heated through and charred, 4 to 5 minutes per side. Cut the remaining lemon in wedges. Transfer the octopus to a platter, sprinkle with minced oregano, and serve with the lemon wedges.

Red Wine–Braised Octopus with Lemon and Rosemary	Using wine for the simmer liquid completely changes everything, including the color: Replace the water to cover the octopus with one 750-ml bottle red wine. Substitute rosemary for the oregano sprigs and omit the minced oregano.
Octopus with Paprika and Sherry Vinegar	A Portuguese-style twist: Omit the lemons and all the oregano. Add 1 halved orange to the simmer water. In Step 3, whisk the oil with 1 tablespoon each sherry vinegar and paprika.
Octopus and Shrimp Salad with Chickpeas	Use a slightly smaller octopus if you like or plan on more servings: Cook and grill the octopus as directed and cut into bite-size pieces. Toss 1 pound peeled shrimp with 1 tablespoon good-quality olive oil; grill, turning once, as you grill the octopus, until browned, 3 to 5 minutes per side. Put the octopus and shrimp in a bowl with 2 cups drained cooked chickpeas. In a small bowl, whisk together ½ cup good-quality olive oil, ¼ cup each chopped fresh parsley and red onion, 3 tablespoons fresh lemon juice, and 2 tablespoons red wine vinegar; sprinkle with salt and pepper. Add the vinaigrette to the salad and toss until everything is coated and combined; taste and adjust the seasoning. Serve over baby spinach or other tender greens.

Mussels with Pancetta Aïoli

Makes: **4 servings**	Time: **35 to 40 minutes**	Ⓓ Ⓜ

Seafood and pork are cooked together worldwide, and here's another spin. The mussels are steam-grilled in their own juices and then tossed with a garlicky pancetta-spiked mayonnaise. Don't skip toasting the bread; the crispiness offsets the richness of the juices.

This scatter-and-grill technique also works with hard-shell clams, like littleneck, cherrystone, and mahogany (the precious small ocean quahogs harvested off the coast of Maine).

¾ cup mayonnaise (to make your own, see page 460)

1 tablespoon minced garlic, or more to taste

1 4-ounce slice pancetta, chopped

Salt and pepper

4 pounds mussels

8 thick slices Italian bread

¼ cup good-quality olive oil

1 Whisk the mayonnaise and garlic together in a small bowl. Put the pancetta in a cold small skillet and turn the heat to low; cook, stirring occasionally, until most of the fat is rendered and the meat turns golden and crisp, about 5 minutes. Drain on a paper towel, then stir into the mayonnaise along with 1 teaspoon of the rendered fat from the pan. Taste and add more garlic and some salt if you like. Cover and refrigerate until you're ready to serve. (You can make the aïoli up to several days ahead; refrigerate in an airtight container.)

2 Start the coals or heat a gas grill for hot direct cooking. Make sure the grates are clean.

3 Rinse the mussels and pull off any beards. Discard any that are broken or don't close when tapped.

4 Brush both sides of the bread slices with the oil. Put the bread on the grill directly over the fire. Close the lid and toast, turning once, until it develops grill marks with some charring, 1 to 2 minutes per side. Remove from the grill and keep warm.

5 Scatter the mussels onto the grill directly over the fire, spreading them out so they are in a single layer. Immediately close the lid and cook for 3 minutes. Transfer the open mussels to a large bowl with tongs. If any have not opened, leave them on the grill, close the lid, and cook for another minute or 2, checking frequently and removing open mussels until they are all off the grill.

6 Dollop the aïoli over the tops of the mussels and use a large spoon to turn the mussels over to coat them. Serve the mussels drizzled with their juices, either over (or alongside) the bread.

Ⓓ direct fire   Ⓘ indirect fire   Ⓜ make ahead   Ⓥ vegetarian option

Mussels or Clams with Aïoli and Smoked Sausage	And another twist on the pork-seafood theme: Omit the pancetta. Before the mussels or clams go on the grill, grill your choice of cured sausage until hot all the way through and crisp in spots. (Figure about a pound; Spanish-style chorizo, linguiça, andouille, and kielbasa are all good.) Remove from the grill; chop or slice while you cook the mussels or clams, and add it to the shellfish when you add the aïoli.
Mussels or Clams with Citrus Butter	An assertive citrus punch balances the richness: Omit the mayonnaise, garlic, and pancetta. Melt 12 tablespoons (1½ sticks) butter in a small skillet over medium heat, then add 1 chopped small shallot and cook, stirring occasionally, until softened, 2 to 3 minutes. Remove the pan from the heat, stir in the grated zest of 1 lemon and 1 orange and ¼ cup chopped fresh parsley, and keep warm. Proceed with Steps 2 through 5. Pour the citrus butter over the grilled mussels or clams.
Mussels or Clams with Green Curry Sauce	Make the same dish Thai style with a few substitutions. The directions are long but not difficult: Omit the mayonnaise, garlic, and pancetta. Trim the thick stems from 1 bunch fresh cilantro, and put it in a blender or food processor with a 1-inch piece fresh ginger, peeled and sliced, 2 cloves garlic, 1 small shallot, and ½ jalapeño or other green chile (more or less depending on the heat level you want). Pulse until the mixture forms a rough paste. Put 1 cup coconut milk and 2 tablespoons each sugar and fish sauce in a small saucepan over medium heat and bring to a simmer, stirring until the sugar dissolves. Remove from the heat and stir in the cilantro paste and the juice and grated zest of 1 lime. Proceed with Steps 2 through 5. Pour the sauce over the mussels or clams and serve with lime wedges, over plain white rice if you like.

---

6 TOPPINGS FOR GRILLED MUSSELS OR CLAMS

You can dollop mayonnaises on top as described in the recipe. Cut compound butters into pieces; tossing with the hot shellfish will melt it. For all others, pour or spoon over and toss gently to coat and get it down into the shells.

1. Andouille-Garlic Butter (page 78)
2. Ginger-Scallion Compound Butter (page 466)
3. Basil Mayonnaise (page 461)
4. Tarragon Mayo (page 71)
5. Red Salmoriglio (page 119)
6. Lemon-Parsley Oil (page 103; double the ingredients)

Soft-Shell Crabs

Makes: 4 servings	Time: 35 to 40 minutes	Ⓓ

Soft-shell crabs are blue crabs that are in the middle of shedding their shells, leaving behind a sort of thick edible skin that makes a delicious, crunchy container for the sweet, succulent meat inside. If you've never tried them, run don't walk, starting with this recipe. (The variations are on the long side but relatively simple, to show off how far you can take both soft- and hard-shelled crabs on the grill.)

During the short and regional season—usually early summer—you can buy the crabs live. They need to be cleaned and cooked within a day or two. You can use thawed frozen soft-shell crabs, though they won't be quite the same.

4–8 soft-shell crabs (depending on your appetite and their size)

Salt and pepper

Good-quality olive oil for brushing

Lemon wedges for serving

1 Use a sharp knife or kitchen scissors to cut off the eyes and mouth, then the gills found under both sides of the shell. I usually also remove the apron, (the shell covering the crab's abdomen), as it can be a bit chewy. (On the male, the apron is a flap that looks like a T; on the female it looks like a bell.) Sprinkle the crabs all over with salt and pepper. Refrigerate if not grilling immediately.

2 Start the coals or heat a gas grill for medium direct cooking. Make sure the grates are clean.

3 Brush the crabs with oil and put them on the grill directly over the fire. Close the lid and cook, turning once, until the crabs plump up and are firm to the touch, 3 to 4 minutes per side. Transfer to a platter and serve with lemon wedges.

King or Snow Crab with Lemon and Butter	Too good to be this easy and works with any part of cleaned, cooked king or snow crabs. For an entrée, count on at least 1½ pounds legs or claws per person. King and snow crab legs are always sold frozen; it's best to thaw them so they cook evenly: Slowly melt 2 to 3 tablespoons butter for every serving; don't let it brown, but keep warm. Cut plenty of lemons into wedges. Put the legs on the grill directly over the fire, close the lid, and cook, turning once, until heated through, 3 to 5 minutes per side. (Break one open to make sure.) Transfer to a platter and serve with lemon wedges and the warm butter for dipping. Offer scissors, a mallet, or a nutcracker to liberate the crab from the legs.

Ⓓ direct fire   Ⓘ indirect fire   Ⓜ make ahead   Ⓥ vegetarian option

Barbecued Blue Crabs	The taste of summer: Substitute 12 live blue crabs for the soft-shells. The preparation is different than with soft-shells: Put the crabs in a sink filled with ice-cold water for 5 to 10 minutes; if you pull one out and it's still moving, stick it back, add more ice, and wait another few minutes. Working with one a time, pry off the apron to kill the crab, then pull off the top shell. Repeat with the remaining crabs. To clean them, run each under cold running water to rinse away the spongy feather gills and the greenish brown guts. Put the cleaned crabs in a large bowl with 1½ cups barbecue sauce (see page 457 for a list of those in the book). Toss to coat. Put the crabs on the grill, top side up, and grill as directed until the exposed crabmeat is opaque, 8 to 10 minutes. Do not turn them over. Serve when cool enough to handle, with lots of napkins.
Seafood "Boil"	Single servings steam on the grill in foil packets. Boiled potatoes or grilled bread rounds out the meal: Heat the grill for medium-hot direct cooking. For each serving, tear a 24-inch-long piece of 18-inch-wide heavy-duty aluminum foil. In the center of the sheet, put 1 cleaned blue crab, 2 cooked crab claws, or 1 or 2 cut-up king crab legs; 6 unpeeled large shrimp; 1 shucked ear corn, broken in half; and 8 to 10 steamer clams. Pour over 1 tablespoon white wine, sprinkle with 1 teaspoon Old Bay seasoning, dot with 1 tablespoon butter, cut into bits, and top with 2 lemon slices. Allowing headspace over the seafood for steam to accumulate, bring the short ends together and fold and roll them down; fold up the open sides of the foil and crimp to seal completely. Put the packets on the grill directly over the fire, along with enough chorizo, linguiça, or andouille sausage so that everyone gets a 3-inch piece. Close the lid, and cook until everything is steaming, 10 to 20 minutes, depending on how hot the fire is. Turn the sausage so it browns on all sides. Be careful opening the packets; the steam is super-hot. Serve with the sausage.

Lobster with Drawn Butter

| Makes: 4 servings | Time: 40 to 45 minutes | Ⓓ Ⓜ |

Drawn butter is another name for clarified butter, which is butter that has been melted until the milk solids separate so the fat can be "drawn" off and the milk solids discarded. You can skip this step and just use the straight melted stuff for dipping.

This method dispatches the lobsters relatively easily and is more foolproof than grilling without parboiling. The most important thing is that your lobsters are fresh and lively, not at all sluggish in the tank. If you're at all squeamish, see the second variation.

½ pound (2 sticks) butter

4 live lobsters (1¼ to 1½ pounds each)

Salt and pepper

2 lemons, halved

1 Melt the butter in a small saucepan over low heat until it foams. Remove the pan from the heat and skim away the foam. Let the pan sit for several minutes for the milk solids to settle to the bottom. Ladle the clear yellow butterfat into a microwave-safe bowl. (You can clarify the butter up to a day ahead, cover, and refrigerate it.)

2 Start the coals or heat a gas grill for medium-high direct cooking. Make sure the grates are clean. Bring a large pot of water to a boil and salt it. Fill the sink or a very large bowl with an ice bath.

3 Working in batches if your pot isn't large enough, put the lobsters in the boiling water with tongs. Cover the pot and cook until they turn bright red, about 2 minutes depending on their size. (The water may not return to a boil.) Transfer the lobsters to the ice bath to stop the cooking, then drain; add more ice and repeat the process with the remaining lobsters if necessary.

4 Split the lobsters in half along the back with a sharp knife, in one fell swoop if you can. If you like, use a spoon to clean out the gills and anything that doesn't look like meat from the torso.

5 Put the lobsters shell side down on the grill directly over the fire. Close the lid and cook, checking every couple of minutes and turning once, until they're firm and just opaque at the center, 3 to 5 minutes a side. (If you like, sprinkle the flesh with salt and pepper and brush the cut side with some of the drawn butter before turning it.) When you turn the lobsters, put the lemon halves on the grate, cut side down.

6 Heap the lobsters onto a serving platter. Reheat the butter in the microwave, and serve each lobster with a lemon half and a small bowl of drawn butter for dipping.

---

5 OTHER DIPPING SAUCES FOR LOBSTER

1. Tarragon Beurre Blanc (page 133)
2. Lime Crema Dipping Sauce (page 82)
3. Lemon-Caper Vinaigrette (page 436)
4. Finadene Dipping Sauce (page 213)
5. Citrus Butter (page 141)

Ⓓ direct fire　Ⓘ indirect fire　Ⓜ make ahead　Ⓥ vegetarian option

Lobster with Chive Drawn Butter	After clarifying the butter, stir in 2 tablespoons chopped fresh chives.
Lobster Tails with Drawn Butter	Quicker and easier: Substitute four 6- to 8-ounce tails for the lobsters. If necessary, thaw the tails fully in the refrigerator. Skip Step 3. Prior to grilling, cut each tail in half lengthwise through the top shell without cutting through the bottom shell. Hold the tail on either side of the cut and crack it open like a book. Grill as directed for lobster halves, brushing the cut side with the drawn butter before turning.
Stuffed Lobster with Garlic-Parsley Bread Crumbs	Omit the butter and skip Step 1. Prior to heating the grill, put 4 peeled cloves garlic, 1 cup lightly packed fresh parsley leaves, ¾ cup good-quality olive oil, 2 tablespoons fresh lemon juice, and salt and pepper to taste in a food processor and pulse into a paste. Add 2 cups bread crumbs (preferably fresh) and pulse until just incorporated; add more oil or lemon juice as needed if the mixture seems dry. Proceed with Steps 2 through 4. In Step 5, cook the lobsters cut side down for 3 minutes, then turn, top with the bread crumb mixture, and cook with the lid down until the lobster is just cooked through, 3 to 5 minutes more. Serve with the grilled lemon.

Seafood Salad with Caper-Shallot Vinaigrette

Makes: 4 to 5 servings	Time: 35 to 40 minutes	Ⓓ Ⓜ

Cold seafood salad should be a summertime staple. Especially when you take the cooking outside and pull a glorious meal together in no time flat. Choose a sturdy fish that can be cut into big pieces (see "9 Fish That Hold Up Well on the Grill" on page 94). And don't try to cook all of the seafood at once; the timing is too much to manage without something ending up overcooked.

Serve the salad cold if you have time to chill it, or room temperature if not. I like mine many ways: over a bed of spinach or arugula; tossed with warm rice (Arborio or other short-grain rice is amazing this way), or spooned over grilled bread.

1 pound firm white fish fillets

8 ounces sea scallops, trimmed of any tough connective tissue

8 ounces large shrimp, peeled (and deveined if you like)

½ cup good-quality olive oil

Salt and pepper

1 tablespoon white wine vinegar

1 tablespoon capers, drained and chopped

1 small shallot, minced

1 cup packed fresh parsley leaves, chopped

Lemon wedges for serving

1 Start the coals or heat a gas grill for hot direct cooking. Make sure the grates are clean.

2 Pat the fish, scallops, and shrimp dry with paper towels, then coat with ¼ cup of the olive oil and sprinkle with salt and pepper.

3 Put the remaining ¼ cup oil, the vinegar, capers, and shallot in a small bowl; whisk to combine. Taste and add salt and pepper if you like.

4 Put the scallops on the grill directly over the fire. Close the lid and cook, turning once, until they're golden brown in spots, 3 to 5 minutes per side. You want a good sear on the outside, with the center of the scallop still ever so slightly translucent. Transfer to a large serving bowl.

5 Put the shrimp on the grill, close the lid, and cook, turning once, until opaque all the way through, 3 to 5 minutes per side. Transfer to the bowl.

---

5 OTHER DRESSINGS FOR SEAFOOD SALAD

1. Lime-Basil Vinaigrette (page 38)
2. Sesame-Miso Vinaigrette (page 392)
3. Sherry Vinegar–Pimentón Mignonette (page 78)
4. Ponzu Sauce (page 468)
5. Green Goddess Dressing (page 334)

Ⓓ direct fire   Ⓘ indirect fire   Ⓜ make ahead   Ⓥ vegetarian option

6 Put the fish on the grill (skin side down, if it has skin), perpendicular to the grate. Close the lid and cook until the bottoms brown and release easily, 3 to 7 minutes. Carefully turn the fillets, using a second spatula to keep them from breaking apart. Close the lid and cook until a skewer or sharp knife inserted at the thickest point of a fillet easily pierces it all the way through, 2 to 4 minutes, depending on the thickness. Transfer to the bowl.

7 Add the parsley to the seafood and drizzle the vinaigrette over the top. Very gently toss the salad together, breaking the fish into bite-sized pieces as you do. Serve with the lemon wedges.

Seafood Salad with Calamari and Caper-Shallot Vinaigrette	Substitute squid for the fish fillets, in any combination of bodies and tentacles you like best; if using rings, you'll need a perforated grill pan. Be sure to dry the squid well before tossing with the oil. Grill the squid after the shrimp, laying the bodies perpendicular to the grate and arranging the tentacles so they straddle the grate and hang down toward the fire; you'll get great charring that way. No need to close the lid; by the time you get all the squid on the grill, it will be time to turn the first ones over. Cook until they turn white, 1 to 2 minutes per side. If grilling whole bodies, transfer to a cutting board, cut into rings, then add to the other seafood.
Seafood Salad with Clams and Mussels	Substitute 1 pound each mussels and littleneck, cherrystone, or mahogany clams for the fish fillets. Rinse them all and remove any beards from the mussels. After the shrimp are done, scatter the clams and mussels onto the grill, spreading them into a single layer. Close the lid and cook until the shells open; check on them every 2 minutes, transferring the open ones to the bowl. Leave the shells on or remove them when cool enough to handle.
Seafood Salad with Tomato-Basil Vinaigrette	Substitute ¼ cup chopped fresh tomato and 1 clove garlic, chopped, for the capers and shallot, and use red wine vinegar. Substitute basil for the parsley.

Paella

Makes: 8 to 10 servings	Time: 80 to 90 minutes	Ⓓ Ⓜ

Paella is party food at its finest, served as a communal dish in the center of the table for friends and family to help themselves. And it's so good that no one will want to call it quits until every bit of it is gone. Use this recipe as a template. A short-grain Valencia rice like Bomba or Calasparra is traditional, though I've found that long-grain rice, while completely different, is also quite good. In Spain, paella will often include cut-up Romano beans or cooked lima beans and roasted red pepper or diced carrots and peas. Go ahead and doll it up with pieces of lobster tail or crab. Saffron is the dominant seasoning but so precious I consider it optional. Instead of hacking up bone-in chicken, I call for chicken wings. And the last word: Do not under any circumstances skip the *alioli*, the garlicky mayonnaise that brings the whole thing together. They're minor shortcuts, but you can make the *alioli* and the sofrito several hours ahead and refrigerate them.

7 tablespoons good-quality olive oil

1 large onion, chopped (2–2½ cups)

Salt and pepper

1 teaspoon smoked paprika (pimentón)

6 tablespoons minced garlic (9–10 cloves)

2 fresh medium tomatoes, grated (1½–2 cups)

2 tablespoons fresh lemon juice

6 baby artichokes

2 pounds large or jumbo shrimp, peeled (and deveined if you like)

2 pounds chicken wingettes and drumettes (they're also sold as "party wings") or 2½ pounds chicken wings, cut at the joints, tips discarded

1 pound Spanish or Portuguese smoked sausage (chorizo or linguiça), cut into chunks

2 cups short-grain rice (see headnote)

4 cups chicken broth, or more as needed

2 bay leaves

Generous pinch saffron threads, crushed between your fingers (optional)

1 cup mayonnaise (to make your own, see page 460)

1 Put 4 tablespoons of the oil in a skillet or paella pan at least 12 inches wide on the stovetop over medium heat. When it's hot, add the onion, sprinkle with salt and pepper, and cook, stirring occasionally, until soft, 3 to 5 minutes. Add the paprika and stir until fragrant, just a minute or 2. Add 4 tablespoons of the garlic and stir until you can smell that, 2 to 3 minutes. Add the tomatoes and cook, still stirring occasionally, until most of their liquid evaporates, 15 to 20 minutes; lower the heat so the sofrito bubbles gently. Remove the pan from the heat if it's done before you complete the next step.

2 Meanwhile, whisk 2 tablespoons of the oil and the lemon juice in a medium bowl. Peel away and discard the outer leaves of each artichoke until the leaves are half yellow and half green. With a sharp knife, cut across the top of the artichoke to remove the green tops. Leave 1 inch of stem and use a paring knife or vegetable peeler to trim the bottom so no green remains. Cut the artichoke in half lengthwise from top to bottom. As each artichoke is trimmed, add it to the olive oil mixture, season

● recipe continues →

with salt and pepper, and toss to coat evenly; this helps delay discoloring.

3 Toss the shrimp in a medium bowl with the remaining 1 tablespoon oil. Season with salt and pepper.

4 Start the coals (make a fire with 2 chimney starters full of briquettes, about 80) or heat a gas grill for hot direct cooking. Make sure the grates are clean.

5 Sprinkle the chicken with salt and pepper and put it on the grill directly over the fire. Close the lid and cook, turning once or twice and checking often, until they brown on both sides, 8 to 10 minutes total. Transfer to a platter.

6 Put the shrimp on the grill and cook just until they develop grill marks on the bottom, 2 to 3 minutes. Transfer to the platter.

7 Put the sausage chunks on the grill and cook until they develop grill marks, 2 to 3 minutes per side. Transfer to the platter.

8 Put the artichokes on the grill and cook until they get crisp on one side, 5 to 6 minutes. Transfer to the platter.

9 Once the artichokes are done, close the lid of the grill; if you are cooking on a gas grill, turn the burners down to medium.

10 Cut the sausage chunks into ½-inch slices, then cut the slices in half. Cut the artichoke pieces in half.

11 Return the sofrito to medium heat. When it's hot, add the rice and stir until coated. Add the broth, bay leaves, and saffron if you're using it; stir to combine. Bring to a boil, stirring occasionally to keep the rice from sticking to the bottom. Turn off the heat. Put the chicken on top of the rice in a single layer.

12 Carefully move the pan to the grill, centering it over the coals. Close the lid.

13 Make the *alioli:* Put the mayonnaise and remaining 2 tablespoons garlic in a small bowl; stir to combine. Cover and refrigerate until you're ready to serve.

14 After the rice and chicken have cooked for 20 minutes, check the progress: The broth should have been mostly absorbed by the rice to the point that the top of the paella is dry; stick a fork down into the rice by the edge of the pan and you still should see bubbles. Add the sausage, artichokes, and shrimp, pushing them into the rice as much as you can; it's also okay to have them sit on top of the rice if the pan is overly full. Close the lid.

15 Check again in another 10 minutes: Taste a forkful of rice. If it's tender but the broth isn't fully absorbed, give it a little more time. It shouldn't be soupy at all; in a perfect paella, a tasty crust will develop at the bottom without the rice sticking to the pan. (If the rice is dry and burning, drizzle with a little more stock.) Remove and discard bay leaves.

16 Bring the pan to the table and let sit for 5 to minutes. Then let everyone serve themselves; pass the *alioli* on the side for spooning over the paella.

Seafood-Only Paella	Substitute 2 pounds swordfish steaks for the chicken and 12 to 16 cherrystone or littleneck clams for the sausage. In Step 5, brush one side of the fish with olive oil, then put on the grill, oiled side down, and cook until it develops grill marks, 2 to 3 minutes. Cut it into 1- to 1½-inch chunks and add to the rice in Step 11. The clams do not need grilling; add them to the paella with the artichokes and shrimp in Step 14.
Biryani-Style Rice with Merguez and Chickpeas	Omit the artichokes, lemon juice, shrimp, chicken, bay leaves, and *alioli*. Substitute vegetable oil for the olive oil, 1 tablespoon garam masala for the paprika, and basmati rice for the short-grain; decrease the oil to 4 tablespoons. Add 1 teaspoon cumin seeds with the garam masala and 2 tablespoons minced fresh ginger with the garlic. Use merguez for the sausage and increase it to 2 pounds. Add 2 cups cooked chickpeas along with the rice.
Jambalaya with Chicken, Shrimp, and Sausage	Jambalaya and paella are close cousins, both built on a sautéed flavor base, sofrito for paella and for the jambalaya, the "holy trinity" of onion, bell pepper, and celery: Omit the artichokes, lemon juice, and saffron; substitute ½ teaspoon cayenne for the paprika, long-grain rice for the short-grain, and use andouille for the sausage. Decrease the garlic to 4 tablespoons and the olive oil to 5 tablespoons. In Step 1, add ½ cup each chopped green bell pepper and celery along with the onions. Omit the *alioli* and serve with one of the many Louisiana hot sauces.

THE PACE OF PAELLA

The traditional Spanish way to prepare paella is over an open wood fire. For American gas and charcoal grills, it's important to capture that smokiness. Otherwise, why go to the trouble of dragging everything outside? Pre-grilling some of the components before adding them to the paella is a good solution. This has another benefit over an open fire: By the time you're done with the components, the fire has calmed a bit. Since the rice needs to cook in gently bubbling broth, the temperature should be ideal.

The sofrito provides the foundation of a paella's flavor and can't be rushed. That's where the stovetop comes in, giving you complete control of the heat and the option to make it hours in advance.

A paella pan is nice but not necessary. A 12-inch or larger skillet with high walls will work fine; I prefer to use a cast-iron pan. A deep, heavy-bottomed metal roasting pan is another option.

Poultry

Americans now eat about as much chicken and turkey as pork and beef. Whether you consider this good news or not, the increasing popularity of poultry presents a challenge for grillers, since it's not as forgiving as other meats. The window from done to dry is smaller; you must compensate for the lack of internal fat combined with the presence of a fair amount of surface fat; and the taste can be downright bland— especially with boneless chicken breasts, the most popular cut.

You'll learn how to compensate, with a handful of simple techniques and guidance. Being mindful at the grill will guarantee you cook tender, flavorful cuts of chicken, turkey, duck, so-called game birds—and even rabbit, which, yes, tastes like chicken.

The Basics of Grilling Poultry

Choose a cut; know the fire. Cooking chicken and other fowl over direct versus indirect heat is determined by the bird, the type of meat (white or dark), if it's in pieces or whole, and whether it's still on the bone or not.

Chicken and Turkey Cuts for Grilling

Gone is the day when you had to buy whole birds and cut them up yourself. Both chicken and turkey are commonly sold all sorts of ways.

Boneless, skinless breasts. By far the most popular cut; often called "cutlets." This lean white-meat cut is almost always sold split into halves; if what you bought isn't, cut it down the middle to separate the two halves for grilling. Since breasts come in different sizes and are uneven in thickness, you might choose to pound the thickest part to help them cook evenly. (See the headnote on page 157.) You can also buy just the small muscles on the underside of the breasts as "tenders."

Boneless, skinless thighs. All dark meat and fattier than breasts, and not as uniform in size or shape. These take a little longer to cook but don't dry out as fast as breasts. (They may be called "thigh cutlets" at the supermarket.)

Bone-in parts. The skin will be on, too. You can get entire birds cut up, or you can buy just a single part (like all legs or a whole or split breast), or you can get portions, often sold as quarters, that include the leg and thigh. The bone and skin protect the meat during grilling and add flavor and texture; these take longer to cook than boneless cuts.

Wings. Whole, they consist of three parts connected with joints—the inedible tip (good for making stock), the wingette (the flat part), and the drumette (the drumstick-looking part). Wings are

REVERSE-SEARING POULTRY

It's counterintuitive: Instead of starting bone-in chicken directly over the fire to sear the skin before moving it to the indirect portion of the grill, I get much better results and can control the coloring by reversing the sequence—I cook it over the cooler side until just done, then work it over the fire for a few minutes, mostly skin side down. Since the skin has already crisped and the pieces have rendered most of the fat at that point, there's no chance of it sticking to the grate and less chance that there will be flare-ups.

easier to handle on the grill if they're separated; they're sold that way—usually at a higher price—as "party wings."

Whole birds. Less convenient to cook on the grill than cut-up pieces but always worth the extra effort. And if you split and flatten it—a technique known as spatchcocking—the bird is easy to handle and cooks more evenly while every bit of the skin browns and crisps. See page 155 for more details.

Poultry over Direct Heat

Timing is key to successful direct-heat cooking in all circumstances, but especially with chicken and other birds. Stay close to the grill and don't let yourself get distracted. You need to stay tuned into what's happening so you pull everything off as soon as it's done.

Most boneless poultry should be cooked over direct heat. The exceptions are large pieces like a split turkey breast, which can weigh in anywhere from 2 to 4 pounds, or stuffed or rolled roasts.

For pieces you pound thin—paillards (see page 163) or thin turkey cutlets, for example—hot or medium-high direct heat is ideal, since they only need a quick turn on the grill. High heat will brown the outside and brand the broad surface with grill marks in the time it takes for the inside to cook perfectly.

Even though they're relatively thin, boneless chicken breasts or thighs need more time to cook through, so heat the grill to medium. The moderate heat will slow down the exterior browning and drying, yet give the center time to fully cook and become tender all the way through.

Bone-in chicken breasts also do well over medium direct heat. Let them cook mostly with the bone side down on the grate; the ribcage will protect the tender white meat from the heat somewhat and the relatively high temperature in the closed grill will roast the skin crisp and dark.

Other candidates for direct heat are the smaller dark-meated birds (quails and squabs) as well as white-meated Cornish hens, rabbits, and pheasants. Birds with dark meat have more fat and a different kind of muscle, so they can handle a hotter fire, while Cornish hens, rabbits, and pheasants benefit from somewhat slower cooking over a medium-hot or medium fire. Finally, there are the special cases of boneless duck or goose breasts, which need to be rendered of most their fat (see page 209) before hitting a medium-hot grill for finishing.

Poultry over Indirect Heat

Easy to remember: Bone-in thighs, drumsticks, and wings, as well as whole chickens, turkeys, ducks, and geese, should all be cooked over in-direct heat. Using indirect heat, bone-in poultry will cook evenly all the way through and develop crisp and golden skin on the outside, even on a gas grill. You can always get even more browning by moving whole birds and parts over the hotter part of the grill for short periods at the end of cooking.

COOKING BONE-IN POULTRY PARTS

When I have a lot of chicken parts to cook, I often use three-zone indirect heat to apply the heat equally from both sides of the grill at the same time. For gas, heat the grill with all the burners set on high for 15 minutes, then turn off the inner burner (or burners), leaving the ones on the outside on high or medium-high, depending on how fast you want to cook. For a charcoal grill, after you dump in the lit coals and the flames die down, push them into two roughly equal piles flanking the sides of the drip pan.

If your gas or charcoal grill doesn't have enough room for three-zone cooking without flare-ups, or you have a ton of chicken to cook, set up as usual for two-zone indirect cooking. (Page 8 has more details.)

With gas or charcoal—in either a two- or three-zone configuration—start the poultry pieces skin side up on the indirect zone, as close to the fire as possible. Make sure any dripping fat is away from the flames, including any pilot lights—otherwise you'll have flare-ups and burn the meat. If you're cooking an entire cut-up chicken, position the dark meat pieces closest to the fire and the breast pieces further away. About halfway through cooking, turn them over and rotate the pieces 180 degrees for even cooking and move them as necessary so they're done at approximately the same time.

COOKING WHOLE BIRDS

The challenge of roasting a whole chicken or tur-key in the oven is fully cooking the thighs and legs before the breast becomes dry. This also holds true with birds that have been split and flattened—known as butterflied or spatchcocked (see page 196). In pursuit of perfection throughout, folks employ all kinds of techniques, including complicated brining, cramming butter under the skin, and endless basting and turning. On the grill, what's elusive in the oven is at last attainable: You can subject the bird to uneven heat. Again, the solution can be a three-zone fire.

Whole Birds on a Gas Grill. Heat the grill and turn off the inner burners as described for cooking bone-in parts on page 155. Only this time, leave the ignition burner on high or medium-high and the other outside burner one or two notches lower. Put the bird on the grill breast up, as close to the hottest burner as possible with the legs facing that burner.

Grilling chickens and turkeys this way, after 45 to 60 minutes of cooking the internal temperature of the breast can be as much as 20°F lower than the thighs. So after you check the progress at that point, adjust the heat level on the burner closest to the breast, reverse the position of the bird, or even move the breast directly over the fire, so that breast and dark meat are ready at the same time.

Whole Birds on a Charcoal Grill. You have some options: You can push two-thirds of the charcoal to one side of the drip pan, the remainder to the other side. Or if you have a big enough grill, go with half and half but position the bird so the breast will be farther from the coals than the thighs. You will have to do the same fine-tuning to finish

the breast once the dark meat is done or nearly done, as described for the gas grill above.

WHEN THERE IS NO ROOM FOR A THREE-ZONE FIRE

If your gas grill only has two burners (or three close together) or if a three-zone fire and a drip pan are too tight a squeeze in your charcoal grill, go with a typical two-zone indirect fire (see page 8). If you're grilling bone-in pieces, position them as described on page 155 and then about halfway through the cooking, turn them over, rotate them 180 degrees and swap the position of the pieces closest to the fire with those farther away for even browning. If you're cooking bone-in breasts along with dark meat pieces, put the breasts farthest from the fire.

To grill a whole or spatchcocked bird, position it so the legs are closest to the fire. Cooked this way, depending on the heat retention of your grill, the breast can lag even further behind the thighs and legs. Once the dark meat is done, turn the bird around or even move the breast directly over the fire to finish it. (If you're cooking on a gas grill, make sure the heat is at medium or lower.) Cook times using a two-zone fire will probably be a little longer than for a three-zone fire.

TAKING THE TEMPERATURE OF POULTRY

When grilling whole poultry, owning and using a reliable instant-read thermometer is key to an evenly cooked bird. I recommend that you start checking the temperature in the meatiest portion of the thigh, away from the bone, and in the center of the breast after 30 to 45 minutes, depending on the bird's size, and then every 10 minutes or so in order to track progress and adjust the grill temperature or the bird's position as needed.

I usually take chicken and turkey off when the breast is at 155°F and the thigh is 165° to 170°F.

After resting for a few minutes, the temperature usually rises 5°F; you can always return the bird to the grill if it's still underdone. The same thigh temperature works for the legs of duck and other birds. But if you want medium-rare duck breasts (when you're grilling them on their own), you need to disregard the USDA's recommendation of a 160°F final temperature and pull them off at about 135°F, then give them some time to rest and come up a bit in temperature.

Ⓓ direct fire   Ⓘ indirect fire   Ⓜ make ahead   Ⓥ vegetarian option

Salt-and-Pepper Boneless Chicken

Makes: **4 servings**	Time: **30 to 40 minutes**	Ⓓ

Modern boneless breasts are small roasts, with an uneven thickness that's more pronounced the bigger the breast is. Pounding the thickest part with a meat mallet or rolling pin—or a heavy skillet (see "Paillards," page 163)—will help them spread to the same thickness. It's easiest to put the breasts on a sturdy flat surface, cover them with plastic wrap or parchment paper, and whack them all at once or a couple at a time.

1½ pounds boneless, skinless, chicken breasts

2 tablespoons good-quality olive oil

Salt and pepper

1 Start the coals or heat a gas grill for medium direct cooking. Make sure the grates are clean.

2 Pat the chicken dry with paper towels, then pound to an even thickness if necessary. Brush with the oil and sprinkle with salt and pepper on both sides.

3 Put the chicken on the grill directly over the fire. Close the lid and cook, turning once, until the breasts are no longer pink in the center, 3 to 8 minutes per side depending on their size. (Nick with a small knife and peek inside.) Transfer the chicken to a platter, let rest for 5 minutes, slice across the grain if you like, and serve.

Salt-and-Pepper Bone-In Chicken Breasts	Substitute 2 pounds bone-in, skin-on chicken breasts for the boneless breasts. Start these bone side down for 15 to 20 minutes, then turn and cook 5 minutes; if they are still pink at the bone at the thickest point, turn them skin side up again to finish cooking.
Salt-and-Pepper Boneless Chicken Thighs	Give me thighs over chicken breast any day: Everything is the same but the cook time; thighs will take 7 to 10 minutes per side, depending on their thickness.
Salt-and-Pepper Turkey Cutlets	A nice change from chicken, these are usually cut about ½ inch thick from whole breasts: Cook time will be a bit faster, 2 to 3 minutes per side.

● recipe continues →

9 WAYS TO FLAVOR BONELESS CHICKEN OR TURKEY

It's so easy to change up the flavors of boneless chicken breasts and thighs and turkey cutlets. Follow the directions for Salt-and-Pepper Boneless Chicken (page 157), swapping the fat and seasonings.

FLAVOR PROFILE	FAT (2 tablespoons)	SEASONING
MEDITERRANEAN	Good-quality olive oil	1 tablespoon each minced fresh rosemary, lemon zest, and garlic. Whisk with the oil before brushing.
SPICED	Good-quality olive oil	1 teaspoon each ground cumin, allspice, and ginger, ½ teaspoon ground cinnamon, ¼ teaspoon cayenne, and a pinch freshly grated nutmeg. Mix, then sprinkle over poultry after brushing with oil.
NORTH AFRICAN	Good-quality olive oil	1 tablespoon each honey, orange juice, and minced garlic, and 1 teaspoon ground cumin. Whisk with the oil before brushing.
CITRUSY	Good-quality olive oil	Grated zest and juice of 1 lemon or 2 limes. Whisk with the oil before brushing.
CURRIED	Yogurt	2 teaspoons curry powder. Whisk with the yogurt before brushing.
MIDDLE EASTERN	Yogurt	1 tablespoon each chopped fresh mint and ground sumac, and the juice and grated zest of 1 lime. Whisk with the yogurt before brushing.
THAI	Coconut milk	1 tablespoon each fish sauce, sugar, and chopped cilantro, and the juice of 1 lime. Whisk with the coconut milk before brushing.
PARMESAN	Mayonnaise	2 tablespoons each lemon juice and freshly grated Parmesan cheese, and the grated zest of 1 lemon. Whisk with the mayonnaise before brushing.
CHILE-FIRED	Mayonnaise, good-quality vegetable oil, or coconut milk	1 tablespoon or so Vietnamese chili garlic sauce, sambal oelek, or sriracha (use more or less to taste). Whisk with the fat before brushing.

D direct fire **I** indirect fire **M** make ahead **V** vegetarian option

Crunchy Breaded Chicken Cutlets

Makes: **4 servings**	Time: **30 to 40 minutes**	Ⓓ

You'll never fry a breaded chicken cutlet again. And changing up the dipping liquid and the seasoning for the bread crumbs is a lot of fun. To make this with turkey cutlets or chicken paillards, decrease the cooking time to 2 to 5 minutes per side. To help the crumbs form a crust, be sure to oil the grates well and avoid handling the chicken too much.

Good-quality vegetable oil for the grates

1½ pounds boneless, skinless chicken breasts

Salt and pepper

1 cup dry bread crumbs or panko

¼ cup minced fresh parsley

2 egg whites

Lemon wedges for serving

1 Start the coals or heat a gas grill for medium direct cooking. Make sure the grates are clean, then rub them with vegetable oil–soaked paper towels held with long tongs.

2 Pound the chicken breasts to an even thickness if necessary and sprinkle lightly on both sides with salt and pepper. Combine the bread crumbs and parsley in a large shallow bowl, and season with salt and pepper. Put the egg whites in another large shallow bowl; whisk briefly just to combine. Dip each breast in the egg whites, letting the excess drip off, then dredge in the bread crumb mixture until completely covered. Transfer to a rimmed baking sheet; don't let the coated breasts touch one another or the coating may come off.

3 Put the chicken on the grill directly over the fire. Close the lid and cook, carefully turning once, until the breasts are no longer pink in the center, 3 to 8 minutes per side depending on their size. (Nick with a small knife and peek inside.) If the coating seems to be browning too quickly, turn the heat down to medium-low or move the cutlets to a cooler part of the grill. Transfer to a platter, let rest 5 minutes, slice if you like, and serve with lemon wedges.

Crunchy Chicken Cutlets with Pesto	Omit the parsley and substitute 6 tablespoons Basil Pesto (page 475) for the egg whites. Brush the cutlets with the pesto, then dredge in the crumbs.
Crunchy Coconut Chicken Cutlets	Add more crunch with a bit of sweetness: Substitute unsweetened shredded coconut for ½ cup of the bread crumbs, fresh mint for the parsley, and ½ cup coconut milk for the egg whites. Dip the cutlets in the coconut milk, then dredge in the coconut crumbs. Serve with lime wedges.
Crunchy Soy-Mirin Chicken Cutlets	Use panko; substitute cilantro for the parsley and 3 tablespoons each mirin or honey and soy sauce for the egg whites. Brush the cutlets with the mirin mixture, then dredge in the panko. Serve with lime wedges.

Boneless Chicken Breasts and Red Onion en Escabeche

Makes: **4 servings**	Time: **35 to 40 minutes**	Ⓓ Ⓜ

A dish served *en escabeche* is usually poached or fried fish or chicken that cools in a spiced—sometimes chile-fueled—vinegar-based marinade. In this interpretation, the chicken is grilled with red onion before being topped with a Mexican-style vinaigrette. You can also try it with thick or thin turkey cutlets, salmon, tuna, or swordfish. Turn it into a main-course salad by serving it over baby spinach and adding sliced peaches, mango, or grapes.

½ cup good-quality olive oil, plus more for brushing

3 tablespoons cider vinegar

2 tablespoons fresh orange juice

2 tablespoons fresh lime juice

1 tablespoon minced garlic

½ teaspoon dried oregano (preferably Mexican)

¼ teaspoon ground cloves

¼ teaspoon ground cinnamon

1 tablespoon minced seeded jalapeño chile, or more to taste (optional)

Salt and pepper

1½ pounds boneless, skinless chicken breasts

1 red onion, cut into small wedges

1 If you're using bamboo or wooden skewers, soak them in water for 30 minutes. Meanwhile, start the coals or heat a gas grill for medium direct cooking. Make sure the grates are clean.

2 Make the vinaigrette: Whisk the ½ cup oil, vinegar, and the orange and lime juices together in a small bowl until thickened. Whisk in the garlic, oregano, cloves, cinnamon, and jalapeño if you're using it. Sprinkle with salt and pepper, taste, and adjust the seasoning.

3 Pat the chicken dry with paper towels, then pound the breasts to an even thickness if necessary. Brush with oil and sprinkle with salt and pepper on both sides. Skewer the onion wedges and brush with the vinaigrette.

4 Put the chicken and skewers on the grill directly over the fire. Close the lid and cook the chicken, turning once, until the breasts are no longer pink in the center, 3 to 8 minutes per side depending on their size. (Nick with a small knife and peek inside.) Cook the onions, turning the skewers several times, until they have softened and taken on some color, even some char, 8 to 10 minutes per side. As they finish, transfer the chicken and onions to a deep platter or shallow bowl. Let them rest for 5 minutes.

5 Slice the chicken ½ to ¾ inch thick and return it to the platter. Slide the onions from the skewers and scatter them over the chicken. Pour the vinaigrette over all and serve. Or cover and refrigerate for up to 12 hours and serve cold or at room temperature.

• recipe continues →

Ⓓ direct fire   Ⓘ indirect fire   Ⓜ make ahead   Ⓥ vegetarian option

Jamaican-Style Chicken Escovitch	A spin on a traditional dish prepared with fried fish: For the vinaigrette, substitute dried thyme for the oregano, ½ teaspoon ground allspice for the cloves and cinnamon, and a Scotch bonnet or habanero chile for the jalapeño, and add 1 tablespoon minced fresh ginger. Use a yellow onion. Also grill a red or yellow bell pepper, turning until blackened on all sides; remove the skin, stems, and seeds and cut into thin strips. In Step 5, top the chicken with the pepper and onion, then pour the vinaigrette over everything. Serve with lime wedges.
Whole Fish en Escabeche	In South America and the Caribbean, escabeche is commonly made with fried whole fish: Replace the chicken with two 1½- to 2-pound cleaned and scaled whole fish like red snapper, bass, or mackerel (or more than two if they're smaller). Put the fish on the grill directly over the fire at an angle or perpendicular to the grate. Close the lid and cook until the skin is charred and the fish easily releases, 10 to 12 minutes. Carefully turn the fish using a second spatula. Close the lid and cook until a skewer or thin knife easily pierces the flesh all the way through, 4 to 5 minutes. In Step 5, you can marinate the whole fish topped with the onions or use only the fillets; serve within an hour.
Sweet-and-Sour Boneless Chicken Breasts	Instead of making the escabeche vinaigrette, in Step 3 combine ¼ cup each pineapple juice and rice vinegar, 2 tablespoons honey, and 1 tablespoon soy sauce. Put them in a small saucepan over medium-low heat and let bubble for 2 to 3 minutes. For a shot of heat, add sriracha or other hot sauce to taste before pouring over the grilled chicken and onion. Before grilling the onion, brush it with oil, not the sauce; the sugar in it will burn.

Lemony Chicken Paillards with Asparagus and Feta

Makes: **4 servings**	Time: **20 to 25 minutes**	Ⓓ

The best paillards (see below) are pounded thin enough to at least double the surface area for maximum browning without jeopardizing the juicy and tender center. Chicken paillards are a wonderful vehicle for toppings like asparagus or a simple salad, or they can be sliced after grilling and tossed with dressed greens for a fast main-dish salad.

1 pound thin asparagus

1 tablespoon good-quality olive oil, plus more for brushing

Salt and pepper

1½ pounds boneless, skinless chicken breasts, cut and pounded into paillards (see below)

½ cup crumbled feta cheese

Lemon wedges for serving

1 Start the coals or heat a gas grill for hot direct cooking. Make sure the grates are clean.

2 Cut off the bottoms of the asparagus, then toss the spears with 1 tablespoon oil and sprinkle with salt. Put them on the grill directly over the fire, perpendicular to the grate, close the lid, and cook, turning once, until browned and crisp-tender, 3 to 5 minutes. Transfer to a plate.

3 Brush the paillards with oil and sprinkle with salt and pepper on both sides. Put them on the grill directly over the fire. Close the lid and cook, turning once, until the chicken is no longer pink in the center, 1 to 2 minutes per side. (Nick with a small knife and peek inside.) Transfer to individual plates, top with the asparagus, sprinkle with feta, and serve with the lemon wedges.

PAILLARDS

Lots of different cuts of poultry or meat can become the super-thin, broad cutlets known as paillards. However, pounding alone usually won't get you there. Chicken breasts, for example, must be butterflied—cut almost all the way through horizontally so they can be opened like a book—so the pounding will get the meat flat and even.

This technique also works for pork (fatty boneless pork sirloin steaks especially, or split pork tenderloins), turkey breast (start by thinly slicing across a whole boneless breast, or use turkey cutlets), and veal cutlets. A heavy, round, flat pounder is my favorite tool for the job but you can also use a meat mallet, rolling pin, the bottom of a cast-iron skillet, or a sturdy potato masher. To avoid tearing up the meat, put a piece of plastic wrap or parchment paper on top before pounding.

The shortcut to paillards is to buy thinly sliced chicken breast or whole tenders and then, with less fuss, pound them until thin and even. They might not have the same surface area (and you probably will pay a little more) but you hardly need to do much.

Poultry

• recipe continues →

Chicken Paillards with Mesclun and Tomatoes	Omit the asparagus, feta, and lemon wedges. Whisk 3 tablespoons olive oil and 1 tablespoon red wine vinegar together in a large bowl with some salt and pepper. Add 5 ounces mesclun salad greens (6 cups) and toss to coat; taste and adjust the seasoning. Top the grilled paillards with the salad and serve with tomato wedges.
Dijon Chicken Paillards with Mozzarella	Omit the asparagus, oil, feta, and lemon wedges. Combine 2 tablespoons each mayonnaise and Dijon mustard and use this to brush the paillards. Grill the first side of the paillards. When you turn them, top each with a thin slice of fresh mozzarella, close the lid, and grill until they are cooked through and the cheese has melted, 1 to 2 minutes.
Balsamic Chicken Paillards with Arugula, Prosciutto, and Parmesan	Omit the asparagus, feta, and lemon wedges, and increase the oil to ½ cup. Have about 4 ounces thinly sliced prosciutto handy. Grate 2 tablespoons Parmesan cheese and shave some curls with a vegetable peeler. Whisk the oil and 3 tablespoons balsamic vinegar together in a medium bowl, then stir in the grated Parmesan and salt and pepper to taste. Reserve ¼ cup of the dressing; toss the rest with 5 ounces baby arugula (6 cups). Use the reserved dressing to brush the paillards before grilling (discard any extra dressing). Grill the first side of the paillards. After turning, top each with prosciutto, close the lid, and grill until the chicken is cooked through and the prosciutto is crisp in places. Serve topped with the dressed arugula and garnished with shaved Parmesan.

MAKING PAILLARDS

STEP 1 Slice the meat horizontally almost, but not all the way, through.

STEP 2 Open the piece like a book.

STEP 3 Cover with plastic wrap and pound.

Poultry

Chicken Salad with Mango and Fresh Herbs

Makes: 4 servings	Time: 40 to 50 minutes	Ⓓ Ⓜ

Since chicken breasts have such a mild taste, they make a wonderful foundation for a main-dish salad. The most versatile way to prepare them is to grill them plain and let the dressing and accent ingredients do the heavy lifting. All of the components can be prepared earlier in the day (including grilling the chicken), covered, and refrigerated separately, then tossed together right before serving. To adapt either the main recipe or the variations for a crowd, increase the chicken to 2 pounds, add 1 pound pasta, cooked, or 3 cups cooked whole grains, and double the dressing.

1½ pounds boneless, skinless chicken breasts

¼ cup good-quality olive oil, plus more for brushing

Salt and pepper

Grated zest of 1 lime

2 tablespoons fresh lime juice

1 head Boston lettuce, torn into pieces

½ cup whole fresh mint leaves

1 ripe mango, peeled, pitted, and cut into 1-inch pieces

1 Start the coals or heat a gas grill for medium direct cooking. Make sure the grates are clean.

2 Pat the chicken dry with paper towels, then pound to an even thickness if necessary. Brush with oil and sprinkle with salt and pepper on both sides.

3 Put the chicken on the grill directly over the fire. Close the lid and cook, turning once, until the breasts are no longer pink in the center, 3 to 8 minutes per side depending on their size. (Nick with a small knife and peek inside.) Transfer the chicken to a plate and let rest while you put the rest of the salad together.

4 Make the dressing: Put the ¼ cup oil in a small bowl with the lime zest and juice and a pinch of salt. Whisk until the dressing thickens; taste and adjust the seasoning.

5 Put the lettuce and mint in a salad bowl and toss to mix. Cut the chicken across the grain into ½-inch slices and put over the greens. Top with the mango pieces, then drizzle with the dressing and serve (or toss before serving if you like).

Chicken Salad with Kale, Feta, Pine Nuts, and Dried Cranberries	In the dressing, substitute 2 tablespoons warm water and 1 tablespoon pomegranate molasses for the lime zest and juice and add 2 teaspoons honey. Instead of the lettuce and mint, remove the stems from 12 ounces kale and cut the leaves across into thin ribbons; reserve the stems for another use or slice them very thinly and add with the ribbons. Instead of the mango, finish the salad with ½ cup each dried cranberries and crumbled feta cheese and ¼ cup toasted pine nuts.
Chicken Salad with Tomato and Arugula	In the dressing, substitute 3 tablespoons red wine vinegar, 1 teaspoon chopped capers, and 3 mashed anchovy fillets for the lime zest and juice. Substitute 5 ounces baby arugula (about 6 cups) for the lettuce and mint and 1 cup quartered cherry tomatoes for the mango. Drizzle with the dressing, top with shavings of Parmesan cheese, and serve.
Chicken Salad with Grapes, Spinach, and Pecans	Replace the lime juice in the dressing with 3 tablespoons sherry vinegar, 1 tablespoon honey, and 2 teaspoons Dijon mustard. Substitute 5 ounces baby spinach (about 6 cups) for the lettuce and mint. Substitute 1 cup halved grapes and ½ cup toasted pecan halves for the mango.

---

7 MORE POULTRY RECIPES FOR THE GRILL ELSEWHERE IN THE BOOK

1. Chicken Skewers with Peanut Sauce (page 81)
2. Chicken Negimaki Bites (page 79) and its variations
3. Chipotle Chicken Wings with Lime Crema Dipping Sauce (page 82) and its variations
4. Rosemary-Garlic Chicken Liver and Onion Skewers (page 85)
5. Paella (page 149)
6. Jambalaya with Chicken, Shrimp, and Sausage (page 151)
7. Char Siu Chicken Wings (page 293)

Caesar Salad Poultry Burgers

Makes: 4 burgers or 8 to 10 sliders	Time: 30 minutes, plus chilling time	Ⓓ Ⓜ

To avoid the biggest challenge of chicken or turkey burgers—dryness—you need to compensate for the leanness of the meat. In this case, I incorporate a shortcut Caesar dressing that is also used for serving. Some tips: Be sure to chill the burgers until they're firm before grilling. If the outside browns too much before the inside cooks through, move them to a cooler side of the grill to finish. And finally, make sure to coat the grate well with oil before putting the burgers on.

¼ cup mayonnaise (to make your own, see page 460)

2 cloves garlic, 1 minced, 1 peeled and left whole

2 oil-packed anchovy fillets, drained and mashed

2 tablespoons freshly grated Parmesan cheese

1 tablespoon fresh lemon juice

½ teaspoon Worcestershire sauce

1½ pounds ground chicken or turkey (preferably all dark meat; to grind your own, see below)

Good-quality vegetable oil for oiling the grates

4 ciabatta rolls, split, or 8–10 slider buns (like potato or dinner rolls)

Good-quality olive oil for brushing the rolls

4 leaves heart of romaine, trimmed

1 Line a baking sheet with wax paper. Whisk the mayonnaise, minced garlic, anchovies, Parmesan, lemon juice, and Worcestershire together in a small bowl until smooth. Put the chicken in a medium bowl and add 2 tablespoons of the dressing. Cover and refrigerate the remaining dressing. Work the dressing into the chicken with your hands gently but completely. Form the mixture into 4 burgers ¾ to 1 inch thick (or 8 to 10 sliders). Put them on the prepared pan, cover, and refrigerate until firm, at least 1 hour.

2 Start the coals or heat a gas grill for medium direct cooking. Make sure the grates are clean, then rub them with vegetable oil–soaked paper towels held in long tongs.

3 Brush the cut sides of the rolls with olive oil. Put the burgers on the grill directly over the fire. Close the lid and cook, carefully turning once with two spatulas, until browned on the outside and no longer pink in the center, 5 to 7 minutes per side, and a minute or two less per side for sliders. (Nick with a small knife and peek inside.)

GRINDING YOUR OWN CHICKEN OR TURKEY

I almost always grind meat for burgers, especially for those made with poultry. I recommend using boneless thighs. For best results, make sure the meat is cold—a few minutes in the freezer does the trick—and cut it into pieces of relatively the same size. Then pulse it in a food processor or run it through a meat grinder until coarsely ground. It should just hold together when you gently squeeze a pinch in your palm.

4 For the last couple of minutes, toast the rolls on the grill, cut side down. To serve, rub the cut side of the top of each roll with the whole garlic clove.

Put a burger on the bottom half, add a dollop of the remaining dressing, a leaf of romaine, and the top of the roll.

Dilled Poultry Burgers with Lemony Feta-Yogurt Drizzle	Reduce the mayonnaise to 2 tablespoons and omit the garlic, anchovies, Parmesan, lemon juice, and Worcestershire. Mix the mayonnaise and 2 tablespoons chopped fresh dill, add to the chicken, sprinkle with salt and pepper, mix, and shape. Combine ½ cup Greek yogurt, ¼ cup crumbled feta cheese, and 2 tablespoons fresh lemon juice in a small bowl; add more chopped dill if you like. Replace the rolls with pita breads, warmed until pliable. Fold the grilled burgers into the pitas with the romaine and top with the sauce.
Chicken Satay Burgers with Creamy Peanut Sauce	Here coconut milk and peanut butter provide the extra fat and flavor: Omit the mayonnaise, garlic, anchovies, Parmesan, lemon juice, and Worcestershire. In Step 1, warm ¼ cup peanut butter in the microwave a few seconds to soften. Whisk in 2 tablespoons coconut milk; add 1 tablespoon each fresh lime juice, soy sauce, minced garlic, and minced fresh ginger, and ½ teaspoon red chile flakes. Use sesame hamburger buns instead of ciabatta rolls. Add 2 tablespoons of the peanut sauce to the chicken in Step 1 and proceed with the recipe. Add ¼ cup coconut milk to the remaining peanut sauce and whisk until smooth. Serve the burgers on toasted buns with the lettuce, the remaining peanut sauce, and lime wedges.
Turkey Burgers with Orange-Mint Aïoli and Pomegranate Seeds	Use ground dark meat turkey and have ¼ cup pomegranate seeds handy. Instead of the Caesar dressing, whisk together 6 tablespoons mayonnaise, 2 tablespoons chopped fresh mint, the grated zest of 1 orange, 1 tablespoon orange juice, and the minced garlic. In Step 1, mix 2 tablespoons mayonnaise with the turkey. Proceed with the recipe. Top the burgers with the aïoli and sprinkle with pomegranate seeds before closing up.

---

6 MAYONNAISES TO ADD FLAVOR TO YOUR POULTRY BURGERS

Mix 2 tablespoons of any of these sauces into 1½ pounds ground chicken or turkey and follow the directions, opposite, for forming and grilling the burgers.

1. Lemon Aïoli (page 38)
2. Garlic Mayonnaise (Aïoli; page 461)
3. Rouille (page 461)

4. Basil Mayonnaise (page 461)
5. Scallion Mayo (page 256)
6. Pepper Jelly Mayo (page 271)

D direct fire   I indirect fire   M make ahead   V vegetarian option

Chicken and Vegetable Kebabs

Makes: 4 servings	Time: 25 to 30 minutes	Ⓓ Ⓜ

The trick to combination kebabs is choosing vegetables that will be done in the time it takes the chicken to finish. You can also make these kebabs with boneless turkey breast or turkey tenderloins, as well as boneless turkey thigh meat. If you like, assemble the skewers several hours ahead, cover, and refrigerate until you're ready to grill.

1½ to 2 pounds boneless, skinless chicken breasts or thighs

2 cups cherry or grape tomatoes

3 tablespoons good-quality olive oil

Salt and pepper

1 If you're using bamboo or wooden skewers, soak them in water for 30 minutes. Meanwhile, start the coals or heat a gas grill for medium direct cooking. Make sure the grates are clean.

2 Cut the chicken into 1- to 1½-inch pieces, depending on the size of the tomatoes. Toss the chicken and tomatoes with the oil in a medium bowl and sprinkle with some salt and pepper. Alternate the chicken and tomatoes on the skewers.

3 Put the skewers on the grill directly over the fire. Close the lid and cook, turning the skewers several times to cook evenly, until the chicken is no longer pink in the center, 10 to 15 minutes total. (Nick with a small knife and peek inside.) Transfer to a platter and serve hot or at room temperature.

Chicken Kebabs with Tomatoes, Croutons, and Olives	Serve on a bed of baby spinach or arugula for a meal-size salad: Increase the oil to ½ cup. Cut about 4 ounces crusty bread into 1-inch cubes; put it in a bowl, drizzle with the extra oil, and toss to coat. Alternate on the skewers with pitted kalamata olives and the chicken and tomatoes.
Chicken and Cauliflower Kebabs with Yogurt and Cumin	Cauliflower florets cook through in minutes, making them a great pairing for chicken kebabs: Substitute 1 head cauliflower for the tomatoes and cut into florets big enough that you'll be able to run a skewer through them without their coming apart. Instead of the oil, whisk ½ cup yogurt together with 1 tablespoon ground cumin and ½ teaspoon red chile flakes; omit the salt and pepper. Toss the chicken pieces and cauliflower with the yogurt mixture to coat before skewering and grilling.
Balsamic Chicken and Kale Kebabs	This sounds crazy, but the kale gets perfectly crisp and charred: Substitute 12 ounces lacinato kale (also called Tuscan kale) for the tomatoes. Remove the stems (save them for another use, if you like) and cut each leaf in half lengthwise. Increase the oil to 6 tablespoons and whisk it with 1 tablespoon balsamic vinegar, 2 teaspoons Dijon mustard, and some salt and pepper. Toss the chicken and kale separately with the dressing until coated. Roll up the kale leaves before piercing them. Grill as directed.

Chicken Skewers with Italian Sausage and Lemon Wedges

Makes: **4 to 6 servings**	Time: **25 to 30 minutes**	Ⓓ Ⓜ

The perfect companions for a skewer: The fat from the sausage bastes the chicken as they grill together, leaving behind a pleasantly chewy texture and terrific flavor. Turkey thighs are a great option instead of chicken. Keep the sausage pieces to about 1 inch so they'll cook at the same pace as the chicken. Serve the skewers as is, or slide everything on top of a bed of rice or another grain, squeezing the lemon wedges over the top.

1 pound boneless, skinless chicken thighs

1 tablespoon good-quality olive oil

Salt and pepper

1 pound sweet or hot Italian sausage, cut into 1-inch pieces

2 lemons, cut into 8 wedges each

1 If you're using bamboo or wooden skewers, soak them in water for 30 minutes. Meanwhile, start the coals or heat a gas grill for medium direct cooking. Make sure the grates are clean.

2 Cut the chicken into 1-inch pieces, toss with the oil, and sprinkle with salt and pepper. Alternate the chicken, sausage, and lemon on the skewers, packing the food fairly tightly. (You can assemble the skewers several hours ahead, cover, and refrigerate until ready to grill.)

3 Put the skewers on the grill directly over the fire. Close the lid and cook, turning the skewers several times, until the chicken and sausage are no longer pink in the center, 8 to 12 minutes total. (Nick with a small knife and peek inside.) Transfer to a platter and serve.

Smoky Chicken Skewers with Chorizo and Lemon Wedges	Instead of Italian sausage, use fresh Mexican chorizo. Cured Spanish chorizo works too, and will get crisp as the chicken cooks through. Sprinkle the chicken with 1 teaspoon smoked paprika (pimentón) along with the salt and pepper before skewering.
Hoisin Chicken-Sausage Skewers with Lime Wedges	If you can find it, substitute Chinese sausage (*lap cheong*) for the Italian sausage. Toss the pieces of chicken with 2 tablespoons hoisin sauce before skewering. Substitute 3 limes for the lemons.
Za'atar Chicken Skewers with Lamb Sausage and Orange Wedges	Substitute merguez for the Italian sausage and 1 seeded orange for the lemons. Sprinkle the chicken with 1 tablespoon za'atar (page 456) before skewering.

Ⓓ direct fire   Ⓘ indirect fire   Ⓜ make ahead   Ⓥ vegetarian option

Double-Stuffed Bone-In Chicken Breasts

| Makes: **4 servings** | Time: **50 to 60 minutes** | |

If you like white meat chicken, then you've got to cook bone-in, skin-on breasts more often. It's fun to cut a slit into the middle and stuff it with something flavorful and then double-down with more seasoning under the skin. Choose whatever herb you like; you'll need less of intense leaves like rosemary, more of milder ones like basil or chives. So taste the butter mixture before stuffing if you're unsure. Since any escaping filling will cause flare-ups, I keep the heat a little lower for this recipe. Without the stuffing, bone-in breasts can be cooked over a medium direct fire.

1 lemon

6 tablespoons (¾ stick) butter, softened

1–2 tablespoons any chopped fresh herb

Salt and pepper

4 bone-in, skin-on chicken breast halves (1¾ to 2 pounds total)

1 Finely grate the zest of the lemon, then cut the lemon into thin slices. Mash the butter, zest, and herb together in a small bowl with some salt and pepper. Taste and adjust the seasoning.

2 Working with the skin side up, cut a slit into the thickest part of the breast with the tip of a small sharp knife. Keeping the opening slit just large enough for your finger (this will help the filling stay in the pocket), work the knife back and forth to create as big a pocket as possible inside the breast; be careful not to cut through to the other side. Divide the compound butter evenly between the breasts, pushing it into the slit and massaging it to fill the pocket.

3 Still using your fingers, separate the skin from the meat on one edge so you can work 2 lemon slices underneath to cover as much of the breast as possible. Sprinkle the breasts with salt and pepper and refrigerate them while you start the fire. (You can make these to this point up to several hours ahead.)

4 Start the coals or heat a gas grill for medium-low direct cooking. Make sure the grates are clean.

5 Put the chicken on the grill directly over the fire, skin side up. Close the lid and cook until firm when pressed and browned on top, 15 to 20 minutes. Turn to crisp the skin; cook for another 5 minutes. If the chicken is still pink at the bone at the thickest point, turn skin side up again to finish cooking. (Nick with a small knife and peek inside.) Transfer the chicken to a platter and let rest for 5 minutes.

Double-Stuffed Bone-In Dijon Chicken Breasts with Parmesan Butter	Omit the lemon, decrease the butter to 4 tablespoons (½ stick), and substitute ¼ cup freshly grated Parmesan for the herb. Add 2 teaspoons minced garlic. Spread 1 teaspoon Dijon mustard under the skin of each breast half.
Double-Stuffed Bone-In Chicken Breasts with Honey-Ginger Goat Cheese	Omit the lemon, butter, and herb. Cut an orange into thin slices and remove the seeds. In Step 1, mash 4 ounces goat cheese with 1 tablespoon each honey and minced fresh ginger; use this mixture for the stuffing. Slip 1 or 2 slices orange under the skin of each breast and brush the top with a little honey before grilling.
Double-Stuffed Bone-In Chicken Breasts with Cotija Cheese	Omit the lemon, butter, and herb. Grate the zest of 1 lime and cut the lime into thin slices (enough for 3 slices per breast half). In Step 1, combine ½ cup grated Cotija cheese, 2 tablespoons chopped fresh cilantro, the lime zest, and 2 teaspoons minced garlic; use this for the stuffing. Slip 3 thin lime slices under the skin of each breast and brush the top with olive oil before grilling.

Smoked Chicken Breasts

Makes: **4 servings**	Time: **60 to 70 minutes**	Ⓘ Ⓜ

Juicy bone-in chicken breasts flavored with a touch of smoke are wonderful as is; just hit the chicken with salt and pepper before putting it on the grill. They also are the foundation for a fantastic chicken salad and the inspiration for two different-but-similar smoky variations.

2 pounds bone-in, skin-on chicken breasts

Salt and pepper

1 Start the coals or heat a gas grill for medium-high indirect cooking. If using charcoal, position the coals so that the smoke will be pulled over the breasts and out the top vent, and put a drip pan under the indirect side of the grill. Make sure the grates are clean. If using gas, empty, clean, and replace the fat trap. When the grill is ready, add wood to the grill (see "Smoking," pages 10–12).

2 Trim excess fat and skin from the chicken without exposing the meat. Sprinkle the chicken with salt and pepper on both sides.

3 When the grill fills with smoke, put the breasts on the indirect side of the grill, skin side up. Close the lid. Keep the grill filled with smoke for about 30 minutes, replenishing the wood as needed. (You might like more or less smokiness.) Smoke the chicken for 30 minutes, then turn and rotate the pieces 180 degrees for even browning. Cook until the meat is no longer pink at the bone, about an hour total. (Nick with a small knife and peek inside.) Transfer the chicken to a plate and serve right away, at room temperature, or cover with plastic wrap and refrigerate for up to 3 days.

Smoked Chicken Salad	Lovely either on a bed of spinach leaves or in a sandwich: Remove the skin and bones from 2 smoked breast halves and shred or dice the meat. Put ¼ cup mayonnaise, the grated zest of 1 lemon, ¼ cup chopped red onion, and 1 teaspoon Dijon mustard (or more to taste) in a medium bowl and whisk to combine. Add the chicken and ½ cup chopped pecans; stir until the chicken is evenly coated with the dressing. Taste and season with salt and pepper as needed.
Smoked Turkey Wings	Keep these on hand in the freezer to add smoke flavor to dishes like you would a smoked ham hock; they'll keep for months: Salt and pepper as many turkey wings as you like and smoke as directed in the main recipe, using a medium to medium-low indirect fire. Because they're used to pass their smoke flavor on, you might want to keep the smoke going a bit longer. One-and-a-half- to 2-pound wings will take 1 to 1½ hours.
Smoked Chicken Livers	The trick here is to cook them slowly so they have time to absorb enough smoke: Remove any membranes or hard pieces from a 1-pound container of chicken livers; no need to rinse or pat them dry. Smoke as directed, using medium to medium-low indirect heat, until they are just lightly pink in the center, 20 to 30 minutes total. (Nick with a small knife and peek inside.) You can put them right on the grill or use a perforated grill pan. These are delicious in Creamy Chicken Liver Spread (page 86).

Bone-In Chicken Thighs with Caramelized Fish Sauce

| Makes: 4 servings | Time: 60 to 70 minutes, largely unattended | ⓘ |

I've found the easiest—and often the best—technique for getting moist-yet-crisp bone-in thighs with popping flavor is the same as for wings (see page 155): Season them with nothing more than salt and pepper and grill over indirect heat almost the entire time, with the lid down. Once they're cooked through, toss them—hot off the grill—into the sauce or glaze, then finish over direct heat to brown on both sides.

3 pounds bone-in, skin-on chicken thighs

Salt and pepper

¼ cup fish sauce

2 tablespoons turbinado sugar

1 tablespoon minced garlic

2 dried red chiles

1 Start the coals or heat a gas grill for medium-high indirect cooking (see "Cooking Bone-In Poultry Parts," page 156). Make sure the grates are clean. If using charcoal, put a drip pan under the indirect portion of the grill; for gas, empty, clean, and replace the fat trap.

2 Trim excess fat and skin from the chicken without exposing the meat. Pat the chicken dry with paper towels, then sprinkle with salt and pepper on both sides.

3 Put the thighs on the indirect side of the grill, skin side up, as close to the fire as possible without any danger of fat dripping onto the flames or pilot lights. Close the lid and cook for about 20 minutes, then turn the pieces and rotate them 180 degrees for even browning. Cook until the meat is no longer pink at the bone, 40 to 55 minutes total, depending on the size of the pieces. (Nick with a small knife and peek inside.)

4 While the thighs cook, put the fish sauce, sugar, garlic, and chiles in a small saucepan over low heat. Stir until the sugar dissolves completely. Let cool a few minutes before pouring into a large heatproof bowl; remove the chiles. When the thighs are done, transfer them to the bowl and toss to coat evenly with the glaze, using tongs. If using gas, turn the heat down to medium. Remove the thighs from the glaze, let any excess glaze drip off, then arrange the thighs skin side up on the grill directly over the fire. Cook, turning once, until crisp and brown, 1 to 3 minutes per side; move the thighs away from the flames if the glaze starts to burn. Transfer to a platter and serve.

> **4 MORE GLAZES TO USE WITH BONE-IN THIGHS**
>
> **1.** Maple-Mustard Glaze (page 300)
> **2.** Honey Dijon Glaze (page 277)
> **3.** Spicy Miso Glaze (page 126)
> **4.** Balsamic-Honey Glaze (page 279)

Ⓓ direct fire　ⓘ indirect fire　Ⓜ make ahead　Ⓥ vegetarian option

Bone-In Chicken Thighs with Honey-Lime Glaze	Replace the fish sauce, sugar, garlic, and chiles with 3 tablespoons each honey and soy sauce and the juice and grated zest of a lime. Simmer in a small saucepan over medium heat, stirring, until it becomes syrupy, just a few minutes. Add the grilled thighs and proceed with finishing the thighs.
Bone-In Chicken Thighs with Sweet Rosemary-Orange Glaze	Replace the fish sauce, sugar, garlic, and chiles with ½ cup orange juice and 2 tablespoons each honey and balsamic vinegar. Simmer in a small saucepan over medium heat, stirring, until it becomes syrupy, 5 to 10 minutes. Let cool a few minutes before pouring into a large bowl. Stir in 2 teaspoons chopped fresh rosemary and a generous pinch of black pepper and add the grilled thighs. Proceed with finishing the thighs.
Chaat Masala Bone-In Chicken Thighs	Omit the fish sauce, sugar, garlic, and chiles. Melt 4 tablespoons butter in a small saucepan over low heat, then stir in 1 tablespoon minced fresh ginger and 1 teaspoon (or more) chaat masala until fragrant. Remove from the heat and stir in 1 tablespoon fresh lemon juice. Pour into a large bowl, stir in ¼ cup chopped fresh cilantro, and add the grilled thighs. Proceed with finishing the thighs.

Piri-Piri Chicken

| Makes: 4 servings | Time: 60 to 80 minutes, plus marinating time, largely unattended | Ⓘ Ⓜ |

Piri-piri is both a fiery chile and the African hot sauce named for it, which is commonly used as a table condiment, ingredient—or marinade, as in this recipe. Heat isn't the only attraction; the sauce is loaded with garlic and lemon juice. Since piri-piri chiles can be tough to get your hands on, make the marinade with the hottest red chiles you can find. Or dial down the heat by using a mix of mild and hot chiles—or even all mild, like poblano or New Mexico green chiles. (Removing the seeds and white ribs will also help tame the heat; wear rubber gloves, please.) I make this with a cut-up chicken, but you can use a spatchcocked chicken (see page 196) or any combo of chicken parts.

10 red habanero chiles, stemmed (see the headnote)

½ cup fresh lemon juice

2 tablespoons good-quality olive oil

4 cloves garlic, peeled

½ teaspoon salt

1 whole chicken (3–4 pounds), cut into 8 pieces

Lemon wedges for serving

1 Put the chiles, lemon juice, oil, garlic, and salt in a blender or food processor and purée. Trim excess fat and skin from the chicken without exposing the meat. Put the chicken in a zipper bag or large bowl. Pour the marinade over the chicken and turn the pieces until coated. Cover and refrigerate for at least 8 hours or overnight.

2 Start the coals or heat a gas grill for medium-high indirect cooking (see "Cooking Bone-In Poultry Parts," page 155). Make sure the grates are clean. If using charcoal, put a drip pan under the indirect side of the grill; for gas, empty, clean, and replace the fat trap.

3 Put the chicken on the indirect side of the grill, skin side up, so the dark meat pieces are as close to the fire as possible without any danger of fat dripping onto the flames or pilot lights. Put the breasts farther away from the fire. Close the lid and cook, turning the pieces and rotating them 180 degrees for even browning after 15 to 20 minutes for breasts, 20 to 30 minutes for dark meat. Cook until the meat is no longer pink at the bone; depending on the size of the pieces, this can take 25 to 40 minutes total for the breasts and 40 to 60 minutes for dark meat. (Nick with a small knife and peek inside.)

4 Move the chicken directly over the fire, skin side down, to crisp for 1 to 3 minutes; if using gas, first turn the heat down to medium. Transfer to a platter and serve with lemon wedges.

recipe continues →

Piri-Piri Chicken with Lime and Ginger	Substitute lime juice for the lemon juice and add 2 tablespoons chopped fresh ginger before blending. Substitute lime wedges for the lemon.
Piri-Piri Chicken with Coconut and Smoked Paprika	Add 1 cup coconut milk—or if you can find it, coconut cream—*not* cream of coconut—and 2 teaspoons smoked paprika (pimentón) to the marinade before blending. Use just enough marinade to coat the chicken; reserve the rest. When the chicken is almost ready, simmer the remaining marinade in a small saucepan until hot and thickened, 5 to 10 minutes; don't let it come to a rolling boil or the coconut milk could break. After taking the chicken off the grill, pour over the sauce and serve.
Piri-Piri Shrimp	Popular in coastal Africa: Substitute 1½ to 2 pounds peeled large or jumbo shrimp (deveined if you like) for the chicken. Reduce the marinating time to 1 hour. In Step 2, prepare a medium-high direct fire. Put the shrimp on the grill directly over the fire (see "Grilling Shrimp," page 125). Close the lid and cook, turning once, until they're opaque all the way through, 2 to 5 minutes per side, depending on their size and how hot the fire is.

D direct fire   I indirect fire   M make ahead   V vegetarian option

Jerk Chicken

Makes: 4 servings	Time: 70 to 80 minutes, largely unattended	

The tradition of jerk cooking comes out of the Caribbean, originating in Jamaica. After a potent marinade, the food is smoked—traditionally with green pimento wood, the tree that produces allspice berries. The wood is available online, or you can use apple wood instead. For an even more authentic experience, see "Spatchcocking for Flavorful, Even Cooking" (page 196) and "Top-Shelf Grilling" (page 194), which describe how to cut a whole bird so it lies flat and then grill it long-distance over the fire. The good news is that you're in for a treat even without doing anything more than following this recipe.

4 scallions, cut into chunks

1 or 2 habanero or Scotch bonnet chiles, or to taste, stemmed (remove the seeds and pith if you want it a bit milder)

3 cloves garlic, peeled

1 small shallot, peeled

1 1-inch piece fresh ginger, peeled and sliced

2 tablespoons good-quality vegetable oil

2 tablespoons fresh lime juice

1 tablespoon brown sugar

1 tablespoon fresh thyme leaves

1 teaspoon ground allspice

1 teaspoon salt

1 teaspoon black pepper

½ teaspoon freshly grated nutmeg

3 pounds bone-in, skin-on chicken thighs, drumsticks, or a mix

1 Put the scallions, chiles, garlic, shallot, ginger, oil, lime juice, sugar, thyme, allspice, salt, pepper, and nutmeg in a blender or food processor and purée to a rough paste. Trim excess skin and fat from the chicken without exposing the meat. Pat the chicken dry with paper towels, then rub the jerk paste all over the pieces. Let the chicken sit at room temperature while you prepare the fire.

2 Start the coals or heat a gas grill for medium-high indirect cooking (see "Cooking Bone-In Poultry Parts," page 155). Make sure the grates are clean. If using charcoal, put a drip pan under the indirect side of the grill; for gas, empty, clean, and replace the fat trap.

3 Put the chicken on the indirect side of the grill, skin side up, as close to the fire as possible without any danger of fat dripping onto the flames or pilot lights. Close the lid and cook, turning the pieces and rotating them 180 degrees for even browning after 20 to 25 minutes. Cook until the meat is no longer pink at the bone, 40 to 50 minutes total, depending on the size of the pieces. (Nick with a small knife and peek inside.)

4 When the chicken is done, put it skin side up directly over the fire and cook, turning once, 1 to 3 minutes per side to crisp up; if cooking over gas, first turn the heat down to medium. Transfer to a platter and serve.

• recipe continues →

Jerk Pork	Substitute 2 pounds boneless pork shoulder, cut into 2-inch chunks, for the chicken. Prepare a medium indirect fire. Cook until the pork is tender and no longer pink in the center, 45 to 60 minutes.
Jerk Whole Fish	Substitute two 2-pound cleaned and scaled whole fish, like bass or red snapper. Cut several slashes into both sides of each fish and spread the jerk paste inside and out, working it into the cuts. Prepare a medium direct fire. Put the fish on the grill directly over the fire, at an angle or perpendicular to the grate. Close the lid and cook until the skin is charred and the fish releases easily, 10 to 12 minutes. Carefully turn the fish over using two spatulas. Close the lid and cook until the flesh on the bottom is fully opaque, another 4 to 5 minutes. Transfer to a platter and serve.
Rummed-Up Jerk Chicken	Add ½ cup dark rum to the jerk paste. And if you can find sugar cane (available at some Hispanic and Asian markets), put a few pieces on the fire to add smoke (see "Smoking," pages 10–12).

D direct fire I indirect fire M make ahead V vegetarian option

Chicken Adobo

| Makes: **4 servings** | Time: **1¼ to 1½ hours, largely unattended** | Ⓓ Ⓜ |

Adobo, the national dish of the Philippines, starts by simmering chicken, meat, or seafood in a vinegar–soy sauce brew, then crisps it by frying, broiling—or grilling. It's served over plain white rice with the reduced simmering liquid. For the most authentic results, use cane vinegar (available online and at specialty food stores). Sprinkling on a little sugar (as some Filipino cooks do) intensifies the glaze. This is a great choice for entertaining since you can precook the chicken on the stove up to a day before grilling.

¾ cup distilled white vinegar or rice vinegar

¼ cup soy sauce

8 cloves garlic, smashed

2 bay leaves

1 tablespoon black peppercorns

3 pounds bone-in, skin-on thighs or drumsticks, or a combination

Salt (optional)

1 to 2 tablespoons sugar (optional)

1 Put the vinegar, soy sauce, garlic, bay leaves, and peppercorns in a skillet or pot large enough to hold the chicken in a single layer; bring to a boil. Trim excess fat and skin from the chicken and add it to the liquid. Reduce the heat to low, cover, and cook, turning once or twice, until the chicken is cooked through and tender, 50 to 55 minutes. (At this point, you can let the chicken cool, then refrigerate it in the liquid for up to a day; skim the fat from the liquid before proceeding. The chicken will take longer to heat through on the grill.)

2 Start the coals or heat a gas grill for medium direct cooking. Make sure the grates are clean.

3 Remove the chicken from the cooking liquid. Return the pot to the stove over medium heat and let the liquid bubble and reduce until it's as thick and intense as you like, 10 to 15 minutes; taste and adjust the seasoning with salt if necessary.

4 While the liquid simmers, sprinkle the chicken on both sides with the sugar, if you're using it. Put the chicken skin side up on the grill directly over the fire. Close the lid and cook, turning once, until the chicken is browned and crisp in places, 5 to 8 minutes per side.

5 Return the chicken to the simmering liquid, turn several times to coat well, and serve with the sauce.

• recipe continues →

Chicken Adobo with Coconut Milk and Chiles	Add 2 hot green chiles (like jalapeño or Thai) along with the bay leaves. In Step 3, stir in ½ cup coconut milk before simmering.
Squid Adobo	Make either the main recipe or first variation with 2 pounds cleaned whole squid (buy it cleaned from your fishmonger, or for directions on cleaning squid, see page 137). In Step 1, simmer the whole squid tubes and tentacles until tender, 30 to 40 minutes. In Step 4, reduce the grill time to 3 to 4 minutes per side. In Step 5, cut the grilled squid into rings before returning it to the pot with the tentacles to coat with the sauce.
Pork Adobo	Make either the main recipe or the first variation using 2 pounds boneless pork shoulder or country-style ribs hacked into 2-inch pieces. In Step 1, simmer until the pork is tender, 30 to 40 minutes.

D direct fire   **I** indirect fire   **M** make ahead   **V** vegetarian option

Tandoori Chicken

| Makes: 4 servings | Time: 40 to 70 minutes, plus marinating time, largely unattended | Ⓘ Ⓜ |

A tandoor is a cylindrical wood- or charcoal-fired oven common in India. Since it's unlikely that you have access to one, you can get very good results on the grill. Tandoor cooking is extremely fast and hot (900°F), but for tender and juicy chicken without the special oven, I start with indirect heat and finish over direct heat to char the outside. Leaving the skin on helps protect the meat as it cooks.

1 cup yogurt

¼ cup fresh lemon juice

1 tablespoon minced garlic

1 tablespoon minced fresh ginger

1 tablespoon ground cumin

1 tablespoon ground coriander

2 teaspoons smoked paprika (pimentón)

2 teaspoons salt

1 whole chicken (3–4 pounds), cut into pieces, or 3 pounds bone-in, skin-on chicken parts

1 medium onion, cut into wedges

Good-quality olive oil for brushing

1 lemon, halved

1 Whisk the yogurt, lemon juice, garlic, ginger, cumin, coriander, paprika, and salt together in a large bowl to combine. Trim excess fat and skin from the chicken without exposing the meat. Add the chicken pieces to the marinade, turning to coat them completely. Cover with plastic wrap and refrigerate for 2 to 4 hours.

2 If you're using bamboo or wooden skewers, soak them in water for 30 minutes. Meanwhile, start the coals or heat a gas grill for medium-high indirect cooking (see "Cooking Bone-In Poultry Parts," page 155). Make sure the grates are clean. If using charcoal, put a drip pan under the indirect side of the grill; for gas, empty, clean, and replace the fat trap.

3 Thread the onion wedges onto 2 skewers, then brush with oil. Remove the chicken from the marinade, letting any excess drip off.

4 Put the chicken on the indirect side of the grill, skin side up, so the dark meat pieces are as close to the fire as possible without any danger of fat dripping onto the flames or pilot lights. Put the breasts farther away from the fire. Close the lid and cook, turning the pieces and rotating them 180 degrees for even browning after 15 to 20 minutes (breasts) and 20 to 25 minutes (dark meat). When you turn the chicken, put the onion skewers on the indirect side. Cook the chicken until the meat is no longer pink at the bone; depending on the size of the pieces, this can take 25 to 40 minutes total for the breasts and 40 to 50 minutes for the dark meat. (Nick with a small knife and peek inside.)

5 When the chicken is done, move everything skin side up directly over the fire and cook, turning once, 1 to 3 minutes per side to crisp up; if using gas, first turn the heat down to medium. At the same time, put the lemon halves cut side down directly over the fire. As the chicken and onions char, transfer them to a platter, squeeze the lemon halves over all, and serve.

● recipe continues →

Tandoori Cornish Hens	Substitute four 1- to 1½-pound Cornish hens for the chicken; spatch-cock them (see page 196). In Step 2, make a medium direct fire. Put the birds, breast up on the grill directly over the fire. Close the lid and cook until the meat is no longer pink at the bone at the breast and thigh/drumstick joint, 20 to 30 minutes. Turn the birds over and crisp the skin even more, 2 to 3 minutes.
Persian-Style Saffron Chicken	Loosely based on the Iranian dish *jujeh* kebabs: Substitute ½ cup lime juice for the lemon juice. Omit the ginger, coriander, and paprika. Add 2 tablespoons good-quality olive oil, the grated zest of 1 large orange, 2 teaspoons black pepper, and 1 teaspoon crushed saffron threads to the marinade. Put some of the marinade in a small bowl for the onion and the rest in a larger bowl for the chicken. Slice the onion across into rings instead of into wedges and add it to the marinade in the small bowl. Marinate the chicken in the larger bowl. Grill the chicken and onion separately as described. In Step 4, thread 16–20 cherry tomatoes onto skewers, brush them with olive oil, and cook directly over the fire until charred in spots and beginning to collapse, turning several times. Substitute 1 lime for the lemon.
Greek-Style Yogurt Chicken with Lemon and Oregano	Increase the garlic to 2 tablespoons and substitute 2 tablespoons chopped fresh oregano for the cumin, coriander, and paprika.

GETTING MORE FLAVOR FROM YOUR MARINADE

When you order tandoori chicken in an Indian restaurant, the skin is usually removed and the flesh is slashed in places. These cuts are made to increase the surface area of the meat before marinating and to deliver more flavor. Whether you leave the skin on or not—I like to leave it on to protect the surface from overcooking and getting chewy—this technique gives marinades, glazes, and flavor pastes better coverage, so go ahead and try it sometime. Scoring like this can decrease the cooking time a bit, so check on the progress 5 to 10 minutes earlier than you normally would.

North Alabama Chicken with White BBQ Sauce

Makes: 4 servings	Time: 40 to 70 minutes, largely unattended	

Big Bob Gibson Bar-B-Q in Decatur, Alabama, is dubbed "home of white barbecue sauce"—a tangy concoction based on mayonnaise and cider vinegar with a healthy dose of black pepper. Here's my take with a cut-up chicken, so there are plenty of nooks and crannies for the sauce to season. If you're using charcoal, you can throw a couple of chunks of hickory wood on the fire when you put the chicken on the grill, but it's not necessary for delicious results.

1 whole chicken (3–4 pounds), cut into 8 pieces

Salt and pepper

½ cup mayonnaise (to make your own, see page 460)

¼ cup cider vinegar

2 tablespoons apple juice

1 Start the coals or heat a gas grill for medium-high indirect cooking (see "Cooking Bone-In Poultry Pieces," page 155). Make sure the grates are clean. If using charcoal, put a drip pan under the indirect side of the grill; for gas, empty, clean, and replace the fat trap.

2 Trim excess fat and skin from the chicken without exposing the meat. Pat the chicken dry with paper towels, then season on all sides with salt and pepper.

3 Whisk the mayonnaise, vinegar, apple juice, a sprinkle of salt, and a generous pinch of pepper together in a large bowl until smooth. Let sit at room temperature while the chicken cooks.

4 Put the chicken on the indirect side of the grill skin side up, so the dark meat is as close to the fire as possible without any danger of fat dripping onto the flames or pilot lights. Put the breasts farther away from the fire. Close the lid and cook, turning the pieces and rotating them 180 degrees for even browning after 15 to 20 minutes for breasts, 20 to 30 minutes for dark meat. Cook until the meat is no longer pink at the bone; depending on the size of the pieces, this can take 25 to 40 minutes total for the breasts and 40 to 50 minutes for dark meat. (Nick with a small knife and peek inside.)

5 Fit a rimmed baking sheet with a wire rack. Move the chicken directly over the fire, skin side down, to crisp up for 1 to 3 minutes; if using gas, first turn the heat down to medium. Whisk the sauce briefly, and as the pieces of chicken finish, add them to the sauce and turn to coat. Transfer the pieces to the rack to let any excess sauce drip off, then serve.

• recipe continues →

North Alabama Chicken with White BBQ Sauce and
Buttermilk Angel Biscuits (page 483)

Chicken with Horseradish White BBQ Sauce	Horseradish adds even more kick: Decrease the cider vinegar to 2 tablespoons; substitute 4 teaspoons prepared horseradish for the apple juice. You can omit the black pepper from the sauce if you like.
Chicken with Chipotle White BBQ Sauce	Actually, it's pinkish, and delivers deep, smoky heat: Substitute 2 tablespoons rice vinegar for the cider vinegar and lime juice for the apple juice, and add 1 teaspoon ground chipotle chile powder, or to taste. Omit the black pepper from the sauce.
Chicken with Dijon White BBQ Sauce	The mellowest of these variations: Substitute 2 tablespoons red wine vinegar for the cider vinegar and 2 teaspoons Dijon mustard for the apple juice. Omit the black pepper from the sauce if you like.

Huli Huli Chicken

Makes: **4 servings**	Time: **70 to 80 minutes, largely unattended**	Ⓘ Ⓜ

The inspiration for huli huli chicken is the somewhat tamer teriyaki; I've been making this popular Hawaiian marinade different ways for decades (and so have others!). All versions share the umami of soy sauce offset by sweetness from some combination of sugar, ketchup, pineapple, and maybe some honey. In Hawaiian, *huli* means "to turn"—that should remind you to check on the chicken occasionally as it cooks to make sure it's not scorching. The main recipe and the variations are fantastic with pork—try it with ribs, chops, tenderloin, or belly. And all meats huli huli style are good candidates for grilling on the warming rack; if you have one, see "Top Shelf Grilling," page 194.

½ cup soy sauce

6 tablespoons sugar

3 cloves garlic, chopped

2 tablespoons chopped fresh ginger

1 teaspoon sesame oil

Salt and pepper (optional)

1 whole chicken (3–4 pounds), cut into 8 pieces or spatchcocked (see page 196)

2 tablespoons or more chopped fresh cilantro

1 Whisk the soy sauce, sugar, garlic, ginger, and oil together in a large bowl until the sugar dissolves. Taste and add salt and pepper if you like.

2 Trim excess fat and skin from the chicken without exposing the meat. Add the chicken to the marinade and turn the pieces to coat. Let sit at room temperature while you prepare the grill. Or cover and refrigerate for up to 4 hours.

3 Start the coals or heat a gas grill for medium-high indirect cooking (see "Cooking Bone-In Poultry Parts," page 155). Make sure the grates are clean. If using charcoal, put a drip pan under the indirect portion of the grill; for gas, empty, clean, and replace the fat trap.

4 Put the chicken on the indirect side of the grill skin side up, so the dark meat is as close to the fire as possible without any danger of fat dripping onto the flames or pilot lights. Put the breasts farther from the fire. Close the lid and cook, turning the pieces and rotating them 180 degrees for even browning after 15 to 20 minutes for breasts, 20 to 30 minutes for dark meat. Cook until the meat is no longer pink at the bone; depending on the size of the pieces, this can take 25 to 40 minutes total for the breasts and 40 to 50 minutes for dark meat. (Nick with a small knife and peek inside.)

5 Move the chicken directly over the fire, skin side down, to crisp up for 1 to 3 minutes; if using gas, first turn the heat down to medium. Transfer the chicken to a platter, sprinkle with the cilantro, and serve.

• recipe continues →

Ⓓ direct fire   Ⓘ indirect fire   Ⓜ make ahead   Ⓥ vegetarian option

**Huli Huli Chicken
with Hawaiian-Style
Potato Mac Salad
(page 432)**

Huli Huli Chicken with Pineapple and Honey	Sweeter and tangier, with a little heat: Omit the sugar and reduce the soy sauce to ¼ cup. Add ¼ cup ketchup, 2 tablespoons each pineapple juice and rice vinegar, 1 tablespoon honey, 1 teaspoon Worcestershire sauce, and as much sriracha or other hot sauce to the marinade as you like.
Sesame Huli Huli Chicken	For a richer, nuttier marinade: Whisk 3 tablespoons tahini into the marinade.
Teriyaki Chicken	Also delicious with beef and pork sirloin: Instead of making the huli huli marinade, put ¼ cup each soy sauce and mirin (or 2 tablespoons each honey and water) in a small saucepan over medium-low heat and warm until bubbling, 3 to 4 minutes. Remove from the heat and stir in 2 scallions, chopped, and 2 teaspoons each minced garlic and ginger. Don't marinate the chicken in the mixture; instead, in Step 4 brush the chicken with the sauce just before moving it over direct heat. Warm the remaining sauce to pass at the table.

TOP-SHELF GRILLING

Many charcoal and gas grills include a removable top warming rack that extends partway over the cooking grates. It's intended for keeping cooked food warm, or gently heating or toasting things like bread, but I've discovered this rack is even more useful for cooking, especially finicky poultry. Lots of slow-grilled chicken is traditionally put as much as a foot away from direct fire. So "long-distance grilling" lets you develop that same deep charred flavor while keeping the meat safe from flare-ups.

Cooking on the warming rack is also a real boon to gas grillers in search of extra smokiness. I've had exceptional results with chicken and turkey parts (try Caveman Turkey Legs, page 203). Even spatchcocked chicken (see page 196) can work; if your rack is a tad shallow, it's fine for the legs to extend out over the edge. Closer to the fire, they'll cook faster than the breasts, and leave you with perfectly cooked white and dark meat at about the same time.

5 OTHER RECIPES TO TRY ON THE WARMING RACK

1. Jerk Chicken (page 183)
2. Piri-Piri Chicken (page 181)
3. North Alabama Chicken with White BBQ Sauce (page 189)
4. Rosemary-Garlic Spatchcocked Chicken (page 217)
5. Salt-and-Pepper Duck Breasts (page 208); you'll have less worries about flare-ups!

D direct fire   I indirect fire   M make ahead   V vegetarian option

Spatchcocked Chicken with Garlic, Parsley, and Orange

Makes: **4 servings**	Time: **75 to 95 minutes, largely unattended**	Ⓘ Ⓜ

Remove the backbone from a whole bird and it will lie flat, instantly doubling the surface area—and the flavor and crisping potential. This easy technique is called spatchcocking or butterflying (see page 196). I almost always do chicken like this now, and it's also perfect for turkey and small birds like pheasants and guinea hens. Figure a 3- to 3½-pound pheasant will take about an hour; a 10- to 14-pound turkey—triple the flavor paste or marinade from any chicken recipe—will take 2 to 2½ hours.

1 whole chicken (3–4 pounds)

4 cloves garlic (or more), peeled

1 teaspoon salt, plus more as needed

2 tablespoons minced fresh parsley

1 tablespoon good-quality olive oil

Pepper

1 medium navel orange, halved

1 Spatchcock the chicken (see page 196). With the bird breast up, push down with the heel of your hand to crack the breastbone so the bird will lie flat. Trim excess fat and skin without exposing the meat. Pat the chicken dry with paper towels.

2 Mash the garlic with the salt into a paste, then mix with the parsley and oil in a small bowl. Taste and add more salt if necessary and some pepper. Rub the paste all over the chicken. Let the chicken sit at room temperature while you prepare the grill. Or cover and refrigerate for up to 12 hours.

3 Start the coals or heat a gas grill for medium-high indirect cooking, preferably for a three-zone fire (see "Cooking Whole Birds," page 155). Make sure the grates are clean. If using charcoal, put a drip pan under the indirect side of the grill; for gas, empty, clean, and replace the fat trap.

4 Put the chicken on the indirect side of the grill, skin side up, so the thighs are as close to the fire as possible without any danger of fat dripping onto the flames or pilot lights. Close the lid and cook until the internal temperature at the thigh, away from the bone, is 165°–170°F, 50 to 70 minutes, depending on the bird's size. Also check the temperature at the breast; if it's below 155°F, you can turn the chicken skin side down and move it closer to the fire, or if cooking with gas, turn up the heat on the closest burner.

5 When the breast is 155°F, turn the bird and put it directly over the fire until the skin is crisp, 1 to 3 minutes; if using gas, first turn the heat down to medium. At the same time, put the orange halves, cut side down, over the fire. Close the lid and cook until the orange is heated through, just another minute or 2. Transfer the chicken to a cutting board. Let it rest for 5 to 10 minutes, until the internal temperature at the breast comes up to 160°F. Cut into pieces, squeeze the orange over all, and serve.

• recipe continues →

Ginger-Cilantro Chicken	Replace the garlic with 2 tablespoons minced fresh ginger and substitute fresh cilantro for the parsley. Substitute two limes for the orange.
Devil's Chicken	Substitute 1 tablespoon minced rosemary for the parsley and add 2 teaspoons red chile flakes. Substitute a lemon for the orange.
Cambodian-Style Blackened Chicken	Traditionally, the spatchcocked bird would be wrapped and cooked in banana leaves, which are removed to crisp the skin before serving: Omit the garlic, parsley, oil, and salt and pepper. Put the grated zest and juice of 1 lime in a blender or food processor with 3 scallions, chopped, 4 peeled cloves garlic, 2 tablespoons good-quality vegetable oil, and 1 tablespoon each soy sauce, fish sauce, honey, and crushed black peppercorns. Purée, then rub the mixture all over the chicken. Substitute two limes for the orange.

SPATCHCOCKING FOR FLAVORFUL, EVEN COOKING

To spatchcock means to butterfly any poultry by cutting out the backbone to open the bird and allow it to lie flat. Since the heat and smoke will get to a spatchcocked bird on all sides, it cooks faster and develops more smokiness. Invest in a pair of sharp, sturdy kitchen shears to make short work of the process. As to the word itself, "spatchcock" is of Irish derivation, and thought to be a mash-up of the words "dispatch" and "cock," as in, "dispatch the cock."

STEP 1 With the bird breast down, use kitchen shears or a sharp knife to cut along one side of the backbone.

STEP 2 Cut along the other side of the backbone and remove it.

STEP 3 Flip the bird over, then push down on the breastbone with the heel of your hand to crack it so the bird will lie flat on the grill.

D direct fire   **I** indirect fire   **M** make ahead   **V** vegetarian option

Grill-Roasted Chicken with Classic BBQ Sauce

Makes: 4 servings	Time: 1¼ to 1½ hours, largely unattended	Ⓘ Ⓜ

Praise for spatchcocking aside (see page 196), a grilled whole chicken also makes a beautiful presentation when it's done right. The secret to keeping it juicy is cooking over indirect heat with the breast up most of the time and the back end closest to the fire. That way the dark meat will cook faster than the white meat. The simple ketchup-based sauce is sweet and tangy, and easy to change up (see variations opposite). It also pairs well with pork.

1 whole chicken (3–4 pounds)

Salt and pepper

1 tablespoon butter

2 tablespoons minced onion

1 tablespoon minced garlic

½ cup ketchup (to make your own, see page 462)

2 tablespoons cider vinegar

2 tablespoons brown sugar

1½ teaspoons Worcestershire or soy sauce

1 Start the coals or heat a gas grill for medium-high indirect cooking, preferably a three-zone fire (see "Cooking Whole Birds," page 155). Make sure the grates are clean. If using charcoal, put a drip pan under the indirect side of the grill; for gas, empty, clean, and replace the fat trap.

2 Trim excess fat and skin from the chicken without exposing the meat. Pat the chicken dry with paper towels, then season on all sides with salt and pepper.

3 Put the chicken on the indirect side of the grill, breast up, so the thighs are as close to the fire as possible without any danger of fat dripping onto the flames or pilot lights. Close the lid and cook until the internal temperature at the thigh, away from the bone, is 165°–170°F, 1 to 1½ hours, depending on the size of the bird. Also check the temperature at the breast; if it's below 155°F, you can turn the chicken breast down, move it closer to the fire, or if cooking with gas, turn up the heat on the closest burner.

4 While the chicken cooks, make the barbecue sauce: Melt the butter in a small saucepan over medium heat. Add the onion and garlic and cook, stirring a few times, until softened, 2 to 3 minutes. Add the ketchup, vinegar, brown sugar, and Worcestershire; whisk to combine. Simmer over low heat for 10 minutes to let the flavors develop. Taste and adjust the seasoning, adding salt and pepper if necessary. Remove from the heat and set aside until the chicken

---

4 OTHER BARBECUE SAUCES FOR GRILL-ROASTED CHICKEN

1. Char Siu (see Char Siu Baby Back Ribs, page 291)
2. Lexington-Style BBQ Sauce (see Pulled Pork with Lexington-Style BBQ Sauce, page 288)
3. Kansas City–Style BBQ Sauce (page 457)
4. Cola Barbecue Sauce (page 459)

Ⓓ direct fire   Ⓘ indirect fire   Ⓜ make ahead   Ⓥ vegetarian option

is ready. (You can make it up to a day ahead and refrigerate until ready to use.)

5 When the breast is at about 150°F, brush the bird all over with the barbecue sauce. Brush again when it is at 155°F. Move the chicken directly over the fire and close the lid; if using gas, first turn the heat down to medium or medium-low. Roll the bird over direct heat on one side for a couple minutes to char the skin in places and repeat with the other side. Keep a close eye on it, moving it to the cooler side if the sauce starts to color too much. Transfer the chicken to a cutting board and let it rest for 5 to 10 minutes, until the internal temperature at the breast comes up to 160°F. Cut into pieces and serve.

Grill-Roasted Chicken with Fired-Up BBQ Sauce	Add ½ teaspoon ground chipotle or other hot dried chile powder (or more to taste) to the sauce.
Grill-Roasted Chicken with Pomegranate BBQ Sauce	Omit the brown sugar and Worcestershire, substitute red wine vinegar for the cider vinegar, and add 1 tablespoon pomegranate molasses.
Grill-Roasted Chicken with Hoisin BBQ Sauce	Use soy sauce, not Worcestershire. Substitute hoisin sauce for ¼ cup of the ketchup, rice vinegar for the cider vinegar, and omit the brown sugar. Add 1 tablespoon minced fresh ginger to the onion and garlic as they soften.

Porchetta-Style Turkey Roulade

Makes: 4 to 6 servings	Time: 3 to 3½ hours, largely unattended	Ⓘ Ⓜ

Pork is the meat used in traditional Roman porchetta—sometimes an entire pig, more often a combination of roasts and fatty cuts. (See the first variation.) It's seasoned with a blend of fennel, rosemary, sage, and garlic, rolled up in its skin, and roasted to insane tenderness, with a crust you cannot believe. The approach works beautifully with leaner turkey and can be done a couple ways. One, using a thick piece of boneless turkey breast sometimes sold as "turkey London broil," is described here. The other is to buy a turkey "roast," which is usually several pieces wrapped in netting. Open it up to reveal the sections, work the flavor paste between them, and use kitchen twine to secure the rig again.

1 boneless, skinless turkey breast (2½–4 pounds)

Salt and pepper

4 ounces thinly sliced pancetta

½ cup fresh fennel fronds

¼ cup fresh rosemary leaves

12 fresh sage leaves

6 cloves garlic, peeled

1 tablespoon grated lemon zest

½ teaspoon red chile flakes

5 tablespoons good-quality olive oil

1 Start the coals or heat a gas grill for medium indirect cooking, preferably a three-zone fire (see page 8). Make sure the grates are clean. If using charcoal, put a drip pan under the indirect side of the grill; for gas, empty and clean the fat trap.

2 Slice into a long side of the turkey breast with a chef's knife, starting at the thicker end and cutting no closer than ½ inch to the other side. Open the breast like a book. Put plastic wrap or waxed paper on top and pound to an even thickness with a meat mallet, rolling pin, or heavy skillet. Sprinkle the meat on both sides with salt and pepper.

3 Spread the pancetta out in a single layer on the work surface so it's roughly the same size as the turkey and put the turkey on top.

4 Put the fennel fronds, rosemary, sage, garlic, lemon zest, and red pepper in a food processor or blender and pour in the oil. Purée to a paste, scraping down the sides of the container as needed. Scrape the flavor paste on top of the turkey and rub it evenly into every crevice. Roll up the turkey and pancetta lengthwise and tie with kitchen twine at about 2-inch intervals. (You can prepare the roulade and refrigerate it up to 12 hours or so in advance; let it sit out while the grill heats.)

5 Put the roulade on the indirect side of the grill, with a long side facing the fire. Close the lid and cook, turning and rotating the roast 180 degrees every 30 minutes for even browning, until the internal temperature in the center is 155°F, 2 to 3 hours, depending on its size and how hot the fire is. Start checking it regularly after 1 hour. If necessary, when the roulade is ready, you can crisp the pancetta more by putting it directly over the fire for a few minutes per side; just keep an eye on it.

Ⓓ direct fire　Ⓘ indirect fire　Ⓜ make ahead　Ⓥ vegetarian option

6 Transfer to a cutting board and let rest for 5 to 10 minutes, until the internal temperature at the center comes up to 160°F. Slice, transfer to a platter, pour over any accumulated juices, and serve.

Almost True Porchetta	To get the decadence of classic porchetta without roasting a whole pig, here are two options: Substitute the same size boneless pork shoulder roast for the turkey. To get it into one flat piece, you will probably need to make the first cut down the middle and then make two cuts outward in both directions; stop at least ½ inch from the edges. Alternatively, you can use the flavor paste to prepare and cook a bone-in pork shoulder as for Pernil (page 286).
Prosciutto-Wrapped Turkey Roll-Ups	Use turkey cutlets to make individual servings: Substitute 4 to 6 turkey cutlets for the turkey breast, pounding them to an even thickness. Replace the pancetta with prosciutto. Divide the flavor paste between the turkey cutlets and wrap each with 1 or 2 slices prosciutto. Secure with kitchen twine and reduce the grill time to 30 to 40 minutes.
Porchetta-Style Stuffed Leg of Lamb	These flavors also work perfectly with lamb: Substitute a 2- to 2½-pound butterflied boneless leg of lamb for the turkey and omit the pancetta. Remove as much of the surface fat as you can, then coat the lamb with the flavor paste, roll lengthwise, and tie it. Prepare a medium-high to medium indirect fire. Grill directly over the fire to brown it, turning a few times, 2 to 3 minutes per side. Then move the roast to the indirect side and cook until the internal temperature at the thickest point is 5°F below your desired doneness (see page 220), 45 to 60 minutes. Transfer to a cutting board and let rest 5 to 10 minutes before slicing and serving.

Caveman Turkey Legs

Makes: 4 servings	Time: 80 to 100 minutes, largely unattended	

State fair food at its finest, and I get why: First is the smoky flavor and pleasant chewiness of the darkest, richest part of the bird; it's also fun to indulge in your primal appetites and gnaw on a super-sized drumstick. Wonderful hot off the grill, at room temperature, or even cold, these turkey legs are a perfect choice for potlucks and picnics.

4 turkey legs (3–3½ pounds total)

Salt and pepper

6 tablespoons honey

2 tablespoons whole grain mustard

1 Start the coals or heat a gas grill for medium-high indirect cooking (see "Cooking Bone-In Poultry Parts," page 155). Make sure the grates are clean. If using charcoal, put a drip pan under the indirect side of the grill; for gas, empty, clean, and replace the fat trap.

2 Pat the turkey legs dry with paper towels, then sprinkle with salt and pepper on all sides. Put the legs on the indirect side the grill, so the top of the drumstick is as close to the fire as possible without any danger of fat dripping onto the flames or pilot lights. Close the lid and cook, turning and rotating the legs 180 degrees for even browning after about 30 minutes, until no longer pink at the bone, 60 to 70 minutes total. (Nick with a small knife and peek inside.) When done, the meat should be fork-tender.

3 While the legs cook, make the glaze: Whisk the honey and mustard together in a small bowl. After the legs have been on the grill for 45 minutes, brush them with the glaze; repeat about 10 minutes later. When they're done, brush once again and move them directly over the fire, turning as necessary until crisp, 1 to 3 minutes; if using gas, first turn the heat down to medium. Transfer to a platter and serve.

Honey-Lime Caveman Turkey Legs	Substitute 1 tablespoon grated lime zest and 2 tablespoons fresh lime juice for the mustard.
Bacon-Wrapped Caveman Turkey Legs	Smokier, and no longer sweet: Omit the honey and mustard. Have 8 slices bacon handy. Go easy on the salt in Step 2, then wrap each turkey leg with 2 slices bacon. The bacon should stick to itself but if it doesn't, secure the ends with a toothpick. Grill as directed until the bacon is crisp all over.
Hot and Savory Turkey Thighs	Though not always easy to find, turkey thighs are meaty and stay juicy on the grill; they're sold boneless or bone-in, and they can vary greatly in size, from 1 to 2½ pounds. Use this flavor variation with them, or any of the drumstick options: Substitute turkey thighs for the legs. Decrease the honey to 2 tablespoons and omit the mustard. Whisk together 2 tablespoons each gochujang, soy sauce, balsamic vinegar, and the honey. Cooking time will range from 1 to 1¾ hours, the smaller boneless thighs cooking more quickly than larger bone-in pieces.

Roast Turkey with Smoky Cumin Grill Salt

Makes: **8 to 10 servings**	Time: **2½ to 3½ hours, largely unattended**	Ⓘ Ⓜ

Grilling a whole turkey for Thanksgiving is a wonderful break with tradition, with the added benefit of freeing up the oven. Trussing or stuffing the turkey will impede the airflow into the cavity and mess with the results so please do neither. But do consider trying this with a spatchcocked turkey (see page 196); figure the cooking time will drop to between 2 and 2½ hours.

2 tablespoons salt

2 teaspoons ground cumin

2 teaspoons smoked paprika

2 teaspoons black pepper

1 whole turkey (10–14 pounds)

1 Start the coals or heat a gas grill for medium-high indirect cooking, preferably a three-zone fire (see "Cooking Whole Birds," page 155). Make sure the grates are clean. If using charcoal, put a drip pan under the indirect side of the grill; for gas, empty and clean the fat trap.

2 Stir the salt, cumin, paprika, and pepper together in a small bowl. Trim the excess fat and skin from the turkey without exposing any meat. Sprinkle as much of the cumin salt as you prefer evenly over and inside the turkey, patting gently so it sticks. (You can prepare the turkey to this point, cover and refrigerate it up to a day in advance; then let it sit while you heat the grill.)

3 Put the turkey on the indirect side of the grill, breast up, so the thighs are as close to the fire as possible without any danger of fat dripping onto the flames or pilot lights.

Close the lid and cook until the internal temperature at the thigh, away from the bone, is 165°–170°F, 2 to 2½ hours. Also check the temperature at the breast; if it is below 155°F, you can reposition the bird so the breast is closer to the fire, or turn up the heat on the burner closest to the breast if using gas. Keep checking the breast every 5 to 10 minutes until it registers 155°F at its thickest point.

4 Transfer the turkey to a cutting board and let rest for 5 to 10 minutes, until the internal temperature at the breast comes up to 160°F. Cut the breast halves off, then across into slices. Slice the rest of the meat off the bone and serve.

TO BRINE OR NOT TO BRINE?

If you want to brine poultry to add some flavor and try to seal in moisture, be my guest. But there are easier, less messy ways to get those results without taking up lots of refrigerator space or requiring a cooler and bags of ice. Grill salts and last-minute glazes are two options. And proper cooking always helps. My recipes provide lots of visual and temperature cues, and "Cooking Whole Birds" on page 155 gives more general guidance.

• recipe continues →

Ⓓ direct fire   Ⓘ indirect fire   Ⓜ make ahead   Ⓥ vegetarian option

Roast Turkey with Oniony Thyme Grill Salt	Substitute dried thyme and onion powder for the cumin and paprika.
Roast Turkey with Sweet Spice Grill Salt	Omit the paprika; add ½ teaspoon each ground cinnamon, cloves, and freshly grated nutmeg.
Roast Turkey with Lemon-Oregano Grill Salt	Omit the cumin and paprika; add the grated zest of 1 lemon and 2 teaspoons dried oregano.

Cornish Hens, Yucatan Style

Makes: 4 servings	Time: 65 to 85 minutes, largely unattended	Ⓓ Ⓜ

The diminutive size of Cornish hens makes them ideal for grilling over moderate direct heat. Just like chicken over indirect fire, they cook breast up and then are turned to crisp the skin. For hens 2 pounds and up, plan on two servings per hen; figure smaller birds serve one. In many supermarkets, Cornish hens are only available frozen. If that's the case, make sure they have thawed entirely before grilling.

6 cloves garlic, peeled

1 medium onion, quartered

1 tablespoon chopped fresh oregano or 1 teaspoon dried oregano

2 teaspoons ground cumin

2 teaspoons ancho chile powder

Pinch ground cloves

2 tablespoons good-quality vegetable oil

Salt and pepper

¼ cup orange juice (preferably fresh)

2 tablespoons fresh lime juice

2 or 4 Cornish hens, spatchcocked (see page 196)

2 limes, halved

1 Make the marinade: Put the garlic, onion, oregano, cumin, ancho, cloves, and oil in a blender or food processor with some salt and pepper and pulse until chopped and combined. Add the orange and lime juices; purée. Taste and adjust the flavors as you like.

2 Put the hens in a large baking dish and rub the marinade all over them, working it under the skin where you can. Let sit at room temperature as you heat the grill. (Or marinate in the refrigerator for up to several hours.)

3 Start the coals or heat a gas grill for medium direct cooking. Make sure the grates are clean.

4 Coat the hens once more with the marinade and put on the grill directly over the fire, skin side up. Close the lid and cook until the meat is no longer pink at the bone at the breast and thigh/drumstick joint, 20 to 40 minutes, depending on the size of the birds. (Nick with a small knife and peek inside.) When the birds are just done, turn them to crisp the skin, watching closely, for a minute or 2.

5 Transfer the hens skin side up to a cutting board and let rest for 5 minutes. Put the lime halves on the grill, cut side down. Cut the birds in half and serve on a platter, with the grilled lime halves to squeeze over them.

Cornish Hens Peruvian Style	This is usually prepared with chicken but works wonderfully with Cornish hens: For the marinade, mash 2 tablespoons minced garlic in a bowl with ¼ cup each fresh lime juice and soy sauce, 1 teaspoon each ground cumin and paprika, and salt and pepper to taste. Or use a mini processor if you've got one.
Cornish Hens with Cilantro and Scallions	This marinade is often used in Colombia with roast chicken: For the marinade, put 6 cloves garlic, peeled; 4 scallions, trimmed and chopped; ¼ cup roughly chopped fresh cilantro; 2 tablespoons fresh lime juice; 1 tablespoon chopped fresh oregano or 1 teaspoon dried; 2 teaspoons ground cumin; 1 tablespoon chopped fresh thyme or 1 teaspoon dried; and salt and pepper in a food processor and pulse to a purée.
Cornish Hens with Gingery Honey Glaze	Omit the marinade ingredients. Put 2 tablespoons each minced fresh ginger, fish sauce, and honey in a small bowl with a pinch salt and mash until combined; stir in ¼ cup fresh lime juice. Or use a mini processor if you've got one. Since the honey can burn, instead of using this paste as a marinade, brush it on the hens for the last 5 to 10 minutes of cooking, and don't turn them skin side down over the fire.

Salt-and-Pepper Duck Breasts

Makes: 4 to 6 servings	Time: 25 to 30 minutes	Ⓓ Ⓜ

Grilled duck can be terrific once you accommodate the fact that fire and rendering fat don't mix. Even just a couple of minutes over direct heat is enough to cause flare-ups. The solution is to release most of the fat in a skillet—slowly, so you can still cook the breast to medium-rare if you like—before the duck hits the grill. Why bother? Because duck kissed by fire and smoke is worth the trouble. Plus you can do the inside step up to a day in advance. And you'll have at least ¼ cup precious duck fat in the fridge for roasting potatoes later.

4 skin-on duck breasts (about 8 ounces each)

Salt and pepper

1 Start the coals or heat a gas grill for medium direct cooking. Make sure the grates are clean.

2 Trim the excess fat and skin from the duck without exposing the meat; reserve the scraps. With a sharp knife, cut slashes into the skin without slicing all the way down to the flesh; this will help render the fat as the duck cooks. Pat the duck dry with paper towels, then sprinkle both sides with salt and pepper.

3 Put the breasts in a cold large, heavy skillet, skin side down, along with the trimmings, and turn the heat to low. Let the breasts cook, rendering their fat, until the skin is golden brown and dry, 13 to 15 minutes; the flesh side of the breast should still be cool or room temperature to the touch. Remove the breasts from the skillet. (At this point, you can let the breasts cool, cover them, and refrigerate for up to a day.)

4 Put the duck on the grill directly over the fire, skin side up. Close the lid and cook until the breasts are one stage less done than you eventually want them, 3 to 10 minutes; nick the thickest places with a small knife and peek inside. Turn the breasts over to let the skin crisp, just 1 to 2 minutes. (Be aware that even though you've rendered most of the fat, some will still cause the fire to flare, perhaps spectacularly so. But it's okay; just keep clear of the flames.) Transfer the duck breasts to a platter, let rest for 5 minutes, slice, and serve with any accumulated juices.

Duck Breasts with Chipotle-Cumin Grill Salt	Instead of salt and pepper, rub the breasts with a mixture of 2 teaspoons salt, 1 teaspoon each ground cumin and dried oregano, and ½ teaspoon each black pepper and chipotle chile powder.
Duck Breasts with Sweet Miso Glaze	Sprinkle the duck only lightly with salt and omit the pepper if you like. In a small bowl, whisk together 6 tablespoons any miso and 3 tablespoons mirin or 1½ tablespoons each honey and water. To keep the glaze from burning, brush it on at the very end of cooking.
Salt-and-Pepper Goose Breasts	Unless you're a hunter, goose breasts are tough to find, but they are available online and elsewhere if you're willing to search. And they're also worth it. Goose breasts can be twice as heavy as duck breasts, with the potential for a greater percentage of fat. You may need only 2 goose breasts for 4 people. In Step 3, monitor the amount of rendered fat in the pan so you can carefully transfer it to a heatproof container whenever it threatens to submerge the meat. When you transfer the goose to the grill, it will probably take several minutes longer to cook; not only is it thicker, but it's better cooked until no pink remains.

LIQUID GOLD: DUCK AND GOOSE FATS

One of the benefits of fussing with whole ducks and geese is that you get to harvest the fat—nothing is better for browning potatoes. Over charcoal: Put a drip pan under the grates where the bird will cook; with a gas grill, catch the fat in a cleaned trap, checking frequently if the trap is small. Or if your grill is designed in such a way, remove the trap and stick a drip pan under the drain.

After collecting the fat, immediately pour it through a fine-meshed strainer to remove any bits and pieces, let it cool a bit, then refrigerate. It will firm up to the consistency of vegetable shortening and keep for months in an airtight container. If you cooked the bird with charcoal or added smoke, the fat will have a lovely smoky taste.

Don't forget about the trimmings from your duck or goose: Put them in a baking pan in a 300°F oven and let them render until you have liquid fat and crisp cracklings of skin, 20 to 30 minutes. From a 5-pound duck, you can expect a total of at least 1 cup fat; from a 12-pound goose, there could be more than 4 cups.

Grill-Roasted Duck with Hoisin Dipping Sauce

| Makes: **4 servings** | Time: **2½ to 3 hours, largely unattended** | ◐ |

Whole duck roasted on the grill is a revelation; when done correctly, the meat—even the breast—has the rich, silken texture of confit. Forget about medium-rare; this is a different kind of experience. To make this happen, the fire configuration and placement of the duck on the grill are key. You want the duck flanked on both sides by the fire, if possible; this will yield even cooking.

1 whole duck (4¾–6 pounds)

Salt and pepper

½ cup hoisin sauce

1 teaspoon sesame oil

1 teaspoon dry sherry

1 teaspoon sugar

1 Start the coals or heat a gas grill for medium-high indirect cooking; a three-zone fire is preferable if you are using a gas grill (see "Cooking Whole Birds," page 155). Make sure the grates are clean. If using charcoal, put a deep drip pan under the indirect side of the grill; for gas, empty, clean, and replace the fat trap.

2 Trim excess fat and skin from the duck (there will be lots of it; freeze it to render later). Avoid exposing the meat. With a sharp knife, cut slashes into the skin (particularly across the breast and around where the thigh and leg meet) without slicing all the way down to the flesh; this will help render the fat as the duck cooks. Pat the duck dry with paper towels, then sprinkle on all sides with salt and pepper.

3 Put the duck, breast side up, on the indirect side of the grill parallel to the fire; make sure it is positioned entirely over the drip pan if using charcoal, or clear of the flames and pilot lights on a gas grill. Close the lid and cook until the internal temperature at the thigh, away from the bone, is 170°F, 2 to 2½ hours, depending on the size of the duck. If you are using a two-zone fire, after about 1 hour rotate the duck 180 degrees for even cooking.

4 Transfer the duck to a cutting board and let rest for 5 to 10 minutes before carving. While the duck rests, whisk the hoisin sauce, oil, sherry, and sugar together in a small bowl.

5 To carve the duck, first cut the breast halves from the breastbone, then slice them across into several pieces so everyone can have a taste. Then cut off the wings, legs, and thighs as you would a chicken, locating the joints and cutting through them. Cut away and discard the rib cage of the duck, then cut across the back in three or four pieces. (There are some succulent tidbits tucked in there.) Serve the dipping sauce with the duck.

• recipe continues →

Grill-Roasted Duck with Star Anise Grill Salt	So aromatic: Combine 1 tablespoon salt and 1 teaspoon ground star anise in a small bowl. After slashing the duck skin in Step 2, sprinkle it with the grill salt on all sides, patting to help it stick.
Grill-Roasted Duck Legs	I'll take these over a roast duck or seared duck breast any day: Substitute 4 whole duck legs (the drumstick and thigh) for the whole duck (consider doubling that number; these are so good, you'll regret you didn't). Use plain salt and pepper or the Star Anise Grill Salt. Sprinkle the seasoning over both sides of the legs. Put on the indirect side of the grill, skin side up, and cook as directed, until you can almost flake the meat off at the thigh with a fork, 1¼ to 1½ hours, depending on their size. The fat should be fully rendered and the skin totally crisp; no need to move the legs over the fire. To serve, cut the thigh and drumstick apart.
Grill-Roasted Goose	Duck writ large in every way: First, a goose is larger than a duck, 8 to 12 pounds. Second, it has *way* more fat than a duck (see "Liquid Gold: Duck and Goose Fats," page 209, and "Safely Grilling Your Goose or Duck," below). Because of all the fat, it seems to cook hotter and faster; for that reason, it's a good idea to lower the heat of the fire to medium and to use a two-zone instead of a three-zone fire. Start checking the temperature at 1½ hours, even for a large goose. Keep your eyes open and adjust the heat as needed.

SAFELY GRILLING YOUR GOOSE OR DUCK

A whole goose can render up to 4 cups fat—a duck much less—so it's important to plan ahead. If you're using a gas grill, put a pan under the spot where the trap drains, if you can; otherwise, check and empty your fat trap early and often.

With charcoal, build a two-zone rather than three-zone fire, even if you have the room (I don't like having a pan full of goose or duck fat flanked by hot coals on both sides). Put a drip pan under the grate where the bird will go before you light the coals and make sure you have room to keep the fire away from

the fat. In either case, use something large, deep, and heavy-duty to catch the fat; double or triple up disposable foil pans.

When grilling a goose or duck, it's a good idea to have a fire extinguisher on hand. If the fat does catch fire—or even flares up—DO NOT spray or pour water on it. Doing so will send flaming oil droplets shooting in all directions. Rather, turn the gas grill burners off and close the gas line, if you can; for both gas and charcoal grills, close the lid and wait for the fire to subside.

D direct fire **I** indirect fire **M** make ahead **V** vegetarian option

Quail with Finadene Dipping Sauce

Makes: **4 servings**	Time: **23 to 25 minutes**	Ⓓ

Farm-raised quail are delicious little birds, only about 4 ounces each, but every bit of the meat is packed with flavor. They are sold whole and semiboneless; an additional benefit of buying semiboneless is that they are already spatchcocked. They're always best opened up to lie flat, and cook fast directly over a hot fire. The dark meat of quail pairs wonderfully with finadene, a dipping sauce of soy sauce, vinegar, and what are called "boonie peppers" on Guam, where this salsa-like sauce originates. Thai bird chiles are a good substitute, or use something milder to fine-tune the intensity. Finadene also makes a tasty dipping sauce for fish, shrimp, scallops, and even chicken breasts.

8 semiboneless quail

Salt and pepper

½ cup soy sauce

¼ cup distilled white vinegar (if you can find it, use coconut vinegar)

2 scallions, trimmed and thinly sliced

3 red Thai bird chiles, or to taste, thinly sliced

1 Start the coals or heat a gas grill for hot direct cooking. Make sure the grates are clean.

2 Season the quail on both sides with salt and pepper. Stir the soy sauce, vinegar, scallions, and chiles together in a small bowl.

3 Put the quail on the grill directly over the fire, skin side up. Close the lid and cook, turning once, until the quail are crisp on the outside and still pink inside, 2 to 5 minutes per side depending on their size. Transfer the quail to a platter. Serve 2 birds per serving, with the dipping sauce on the side.

• recipe continues →

Chicken Thighs with Finadene Dipping Sauce	Here the sauce does double duty as a marinade and dipping sauce: Double the sauce ingredients. Substitute 3 pounds bone-in, skin-on chicken thighs for the quail. Pour half the sauce into a large bowl and reserve the rest for dipping. Put the chicken in the large bowl and turn to coat completely. Prepare a medium-high indirect fire and grill the thighs, skin side up, over the indirect side with the lid down, until no longer pink at the bone, 40 to 50 minutes. (Nick with a small knife and peek inside.) Put the thighs skin side down directly over the fire to crisp up the skin for 1 to 3 minutes; if using gas, first turn the heat down to medium. Transfer to a platter and serve with the reserved sauce.
Quail with Lemon Finadene Dipping Sauce	The vibrant lemon flavor balances the richness of the dark quail meat: Omit the soy sauce and vinegar. Add 1 cup chopped fresh tomatoes, 6 cloves garlic, minced, ½ cup fresh lemon juice, and salt to taste.
Quail with Sherry-Honey Glaze	Omit the soy sauce, vinegar, scallions, and chiles. Instead, combine ¼ cup honey, 2 tablespoons sherry vinegar, and 1 tablespoon Dijon mustard. When the quail are cooked, brush both sides with the glaze. Put them directly over the fire, skin side up, for 1 to 3 minutes, then turn and let the glaze caramelize for another 1 to 3 minutes; if using gas, first turn the heat down to medium.

Five-Spice Squab

Makes: **4 servings**	Time: **25 to 27 minutes**	Ⓓ Ⓜ

Squab isn't popular in the United States, which I wish would change. It's young domesticated pigeon—a dark-meated bird, like quail and duck, with a fantastic rich, deep flavor. Look for them online or in specialty stores. They're sold whole or semiboneless, 10 to 18 ounces per bird. They're best spatchcocked (see page 196; if you can buy them semiboneless, they will already have the backbone removed). I recommend that you cook them to medium-rare or even rare.

3 tablespoons hoisin sauce

2 tablespoons rice wine or dry sherry

1 tablespoon soy sauce (preferably Chinese dark soy)

1 tablespoon rice vinegar

2 teaspoons sugar

1 teaspoon five-spice powder (to make your own, see page 456)

4 squabs (10–18 ounces each, semiboneless or spatchcocked)

1 Start the coals or heat a gas grill for medium direct cooking. Make sure the grates are clean.

2 Whisk the hoisin sauce, rice wine, soy sauce, vinegar, sugar, and five-spice powder together in a small bowl. Brush the mixture evenly over both sides of the squabs. (You can marinate the squabs for several hours in the refrigerator before grilling.)

3 Let excess marinade drip off the squabs and put them on the grill directly over the fire, skin side up. Close the lid and cook, turning once, until they are crisp on the outside and rosy pink inside, 5 to 10 minutes per side depending on their size. Carve into pieces if you like, transfer to a platter, and serve.

Chile-Lime Squab	Use a flavor paste instead of a marinade: Put 2 seeded jalapeño chiles, 4 cloves garlic, ½ inch peeled fresh ginger, 1 small onion, quartered, the juice of 1 lime, a pinch freshly grated nutmeg, and some salt and pepper in a mini food processor and process to a paste. Or mince and mix everything by hand. Rub the squab with the paste, then grill as directed.
Vietnamese-Style Squab	For the marinade, whisk together ¼ fish sauce and 2 tablespoons minced shallot with 1 tablespoon each peanut oil, sugar, and minced garlic, and 1 teaspoon sesame oil.
Curried Squab	Omit the marinade. Instead, combine 1 tablespoon curry powder, 1½ teaspoons salt, and a little pepper if you like. Stir in 2 tablespoons vegetable oil, then rub the mixture all over the squab, getting it into the nooks and crannies and working it under the skin, then grill as directed.

Ⓓ direct fire   Ⓘ indirect fire   Ⓜ make ahead   Ⓥ vegetarian option

Rosemary-Garlic Rabbit with Lemon Zest

Makes: 2 servings	Times: 50 to 55 minutes	Ⓓ Ⓜ

Rabbit is incredibly lean, with no fat layer to protect and baste the meat as it cooks. So to keep things moving quickly on the grill before it has a chance to dry out, I cut rabbit into serving pieces that brown evenly and can be taken off the grill as they finish.

1 whole dressed rabbit (2½ to 4 pounds)

6 cloves garlic, peeled

2 teaspoons salt

2 tablespoons minced fresh rosemary

Grated zest of 1 lemon

1 tablespoon good-quality olive oil, plus more for the grates

Lemon wedges for serving

1 Cut the rabbit into serving pieces: First, to cut the back legs off, feel for the hip socket, pop it, then wedge the knife in between the joints. There is no ball-and-socket for the front legs like for the back legs, so feel around for where the leg completely separates from the body, where there is just flesh attaching them; slice to separate. Remove and discard both sides of the rib cage. Then you'll see the belly flap; cut it off and put with the other pieces. What is left is the loin, or saddle, of the rabbit, wrapped around the backbone. Hack the backbone into 2 or 4 pieces.

2 Smash the garlic into a paste with the salt, then mix with the rosemary, lemon zest, and 1 tablespoon oil in a small bowl. Rub this paste into the rabbit and let it sit at room temperature while you get the grill ready. Or cover and refrigerate for up to several hours.

3 Start the coals or heat a gas grill for medium direct cooking. Make sure the grates are clean.

4 Put the rabbit pieces on the grill directly over the fire. Close the lid and cook, turning and moving the pieces to cook evenly, just until the meat is no longer pink at the bone; for the belly flaps, this will take 4 to 5 minutes per side. (Nick with a small knife and peek inside.) The hind legs will take the longest, 30 to 35 minutes total. As the pieces finish, transfer them to a platter. Serve with lemon wedges.

Marjoram-Garlic Rabbit with Lemon Zest	Marjoram is a wonderfully fragrant herb, somewhat similar to oregano, only more floral and underrated: Substitute chopped marjoram for the rosemary.
Thyme-Garlic Rabbit with Maple Syrup and Dijon	A bit of sweetness and heat added: Substitute chopped fresh thyme for the rosemary and add 1 tablespoon maple syrup and 1 teaspoon Dijon mustard to the paste.
Rosemary-Garlic Spatchcocked Chicken	This flavor paste is a delicious partner for chicken: Instead of rabbit, use a spatchcocked chicken (see page 195; a 3- to 4-pound bird will feed 4). Follow the directions for spatchcocked chicken on page 196. Figure it will take 50 to 70 minutes total.

Meat

Grilling beef, pork, and lamb is a heady, campfire-like experience that plays on all the senses: the hiss of fat as it hits the fire, the changing color of the flickering flames, the incomparable aroma of browning meat. Even on a gas grill, it's the ultimate call to dinner.

In this chapter you'll find recipes for beef (and veal), lamb (plus a nod to goat), and all kinds of pork. There are steaks here, to be sure, as well as everything from super-quick-cooking lamb rib chops (worked over a hot fire for a couple of minutes per side) to classic smoked brisket. I've also included some unexpected nose-to-tail cooking—those "nasty bits" that are completely transformed by fire and smoke.

And, of course, the burgers—recipes for beef, lamb, and pork, each with treatments tailored to spotlight the natural flavor of the particular meat—along with meatloaf, which is fabulous cooked on the grill.

The Basics of Grilling Meat

As with chicken, the cut dictates how to grill it. Only it's easier to make generalities: Tender pieces like chops and steaks are cooked directly over a medium-to-hot fire; tougher cuts like brisket benefit from indirect heat, usually at a lower temperature over a long period of time.

The rare exceptions are large, tender roasts like a whole beef tenderloin, which should be first seared over direct heat, then finished on the indirect portion of the grill to allow the interior to cook without the exterior overcharring. Some chewier cuts, like chuck or beef short ribs, can go either way, depending on how you treat them. Thinly sliced, these crossovers are terrific quickly charred directly over a hot fire. Or with the bones intact, smoked or grilled indirectly over low heat for hours, their meat eventually becomes melt-in-your-mouth tender.

And perhaps the most important key to successful grilling is this: You can always return something to the grill if it's not quite ready, but you can't undo overcooking.

Checking Doneness for Beef, Lamb, and Veal

A good-quality digital instant-read thermometer is almost always the most reliable way to judge doneness, especially with large, slowly cooked cuts. You can certainly nick a steak open to check on its progress in broad daylight or with good lighting—or a headlamp—at night. But you can really tear up a piece of meat trying to anticipate doneness (see "Carryover Heat," opposite).

An instant-read thermometer makes checking a snap. Be sure to insert the tip up to its sensor—you'll see it, usually less than ½ inch from the point—into the thickest place, avoiding any bones. Here are the temperature ranges for beef and lamb.

120°–130°F	Rare	Still quite red
130°–140°F	Medium-rare	Pinkish red
140°–145°F	Medium	Pink
145°–155°F	Medium-well	Little bit of pink
160°F	Well-done	No pink

The United States Department of Agriculture recommends slightly higher temperatures in each category when cooking steaks and other cuts. And I prefer veal done to medium, just lightly pink.

Checking Doneness for Pork

Until recently, the USDA guidelines directed to cook pork until no longer pink at the center—usually 160°F—to kill the parasite *Trichinella spiralis*, which causes trichinosis; this resulted in years of overdone, dry pork. Trichinosis is now extremely rare, and is actually killed when exposed to 140°F for one minute. As a result, the minimum temperature has been lowered to 145°F, ever so slightly pink inside after resting.

Checking Doneness for Ground Meat

Across the board, the USDA calls for ground meats to be cooked to 160°F (except ground poultry, which should be 165°F) to ensure that any *E. coli* or salmonella bacteria are killed. I pull beef and lamb burgers off at a lower temperature, so they're still pink. But I understand the regard for public safety that is behind the recommendation. Since a lot of bacterial contamination occurs during processing huge batches of meat from different animals through large commercial grinders that are hard to clean properly, two ways to minimize the risk are to buy the best-quality meat you can afford, and to grind it yourself (see page 260).

Carryover Heat

Meat continues to cook after you take it off the grill. Carryover—or residual—heat is the energy stored in a whole piece of meat or a burger during cooking that will continue to raise the internal temperature as it rests. The thermometer will bump up another 5° to 10°F, depending on the size of the cut, the cooking time, and how long you let it rest.

You want to let meat rest for a few minutes after cooking and before slicing in order to hold in the juices and improve the texture. So to capture your ultimate desired doneness, take it off the grill at 5° to 10°F less than your sweet spot; continue to monitor its temperature until you get the hang of the timing. If you take a steak off the grill cooked just the way you like it, by the time to take your first bite, it'll be overcooked.

For lean and tender pork cuts like chops, loin roast, or tenderloin, overcooking even a little will dry out the meat and make it chewy. So I take them off the fire at 135°F or maybe 140°F and let them sit until the internal temperature comes up to 145°F. For marbled cuts like shoulder, I poke the thermometer in a few different places and take it off when the lowest reading is 140°F. It's okay if some the fat and collagen hits 150°F or even 160°F; the meat will still be moist after resting.

WHAT DOES "GRASS-FED BEEF" MEAN?

Beef labeled as "grass-fed" should ideally indicate that the cow ate nothing but pasture grasses. In this country, most cattle eat grass for a while after weaning; then they're typically finished on a diet of soy, corn, and other grains (none of which are in the cow's natural diet) to marble the meat with fat and deliver the beefy flavor Americans expect.

Grass-fed beef has a different texture and flavor from grain-finished beef and is less damaging to the environment. In my experience grass-fed beef varies from one producer to the next and it can be quite appealing when it's good.

If you want to try grass-fed beef, be sure you're getting the real deal, which means buying from a trusted source or directly from the farmer. At this writing, there is still no grass-fed label standard that has USDA endorsement. And until there is, you don't know for sure whether the animal actually grazed in a field for its whole life or not.

The Perfect Steak

| Makes: 4 to 6 servings | Time: 25 to 30 minutes | Ⓓ |

I like to grill large steaks, then serve them sliced. The presentation is dramatic, and it's fun for everyone to feed from the same communal platter. If your idea of the perfect steak is a juicy slab all to yourself, no problem; just cut the steaks into portions before grilling.

1½–2 pounds boneless beef strip, sirloin, rib-eye, or other steaks (about 1 inch thick)

Salt and pepper

1 Start the coals or heat a gas grill for hot direct cooking. Make sure the grates are clean.

2 Pat the steaks dry with paper towels. Sprinkle with salt and pepper on both sides.

3 Put the steaks on the grill directly over the fire. Close the lid and cook, turning once, until 5° to 10°F shy of your desired doneness (see page 220), 2 to 4 minutes per side for medium-rare.

4 Transfer to a cutting board and let rest 5 to 10 minutes, continuing to check if you like. Cut into ½- to 1-inch slices, transfer to a platter, pour over any accumulated juices, and serve.

The Perfect Porterhouse or T-Bone Steak	These are best cut 1½ inches thick and weighing about 2 pounds. For medium-rare, cook for 4 to 5 minutes per side, taking care not to burn the outside; the leaner tenderloin (the smaller of the two pieces on either side of the bone) is best rare, so position it at the outer edge of the fire. After 5 minutes per side, if it is not done and is developing too much char, move the steak to a cooler part of the grill and cook for another 2 to 3 minutes before checking again.
The Perfect Bone-In Rib-Eye	This treat has become one of my favorite cuts to grill: Look for 1 or 2 big steaks, 2 to 3 inches thick, which will clock in at 2½ or more pounds each. Heat the grill for hot indirect cooking. Start the steak directly over the fire, with the bone positioned over the hottest point. Close the lid and cook, turning once, for 5 minutes per side. Move to the indirect side, with the bone positioned closest to the fire, and check the internal temperature. Close the lid and cook until 5° to 10°F shy of the desired doneness, 20 to 40 minutes, checking every 10 minutes or so initially, then more frequently as you get closer to your target temperature; reposition the steak as needed for even cooking. Transfer to a cutting board, let rest, cut away the bone, slice across the eye, and serve with the accumulated juices.

• recipe continues→

BUYING AND GRILLING STEAKS

The cut, how much you like it done, and the best way to cook it are all related. The supermarket meat counter—I mean a good one with an in-store butcher—offers many different steaks. Understanding where they come from on the cow goes a long way to choosing the right one for different occasions. Those cut from muscles on the back and backbone (like the rib-eye, strip, tenderloin, and porterhouse) get less of a workout and are the most tender and mild tasting. Those from active abdomen and hind sections (like flank, skirt, and sirloin) have more chew and can be more flavorful.

Most steak lovers want marbling—that interior lacework of fat that melts during cooking to deliver the rich, silky, beefy experience you expect from steak. Strip and rib-eye—from the same section of the cow as prime rib, only cut between the ribs and sold with or without the bones—are both tender and well marbled. Tenderloin has next to no marbling but its texture is super-soft (some say too much so) and puts up little resistance when you take a bite. Not surprisingly, these are the most expensive steaks.

Other cuts offer more value and excellent eating, so I urge you to venture out of your comfort zone. Try less familiar cuts like hanger steak (the classic cut for making *steak frites*), flat iron steak (with its unique geometric shape), tri-tip (cut from one of the sirloin roasts popular for regional California barbecue; see page 245), and cap steak (a somewhat hard-to-find by-product of cutting boneless rib-eyes). You can even have success with oddball arm and blade steaks as long as you cut around the inconvenient strips of gristle. But some cuts—like chuck and round steaks—are deceiving and won't be tender after quick grilling. Instead they require lots of cooking time or pounding (or both); or they can work cut in small pieces and skewered.

For some grillers, a perfect steak is "black and blue": charred on the outside and raw enough on the inside to slightly blue-tinged and still cold from the refrigerator. For others, it's medium-well done—not a trace of pink inside but ideally still fairly moist. I won't acknowledge well-done steaks as desirable; if you think that's what you like, try pulling them from the fire just a couple minutes earlier and see if they aren't better. And everyone else falls somewhere within that spectrum from red to pinkish gray.

If you're grilling black-and-blue steaks, they should be at least an inch thick, and go from fridge to fire interrupted only by a sprinkle of salt and pepper. (Better yet, put them in the freezer for 30 minutes or so right before grilling.) That initial chill provides a bit of protection against overcooking. Other than that, the temperature of steak when it hits the grill doesn't make a ton of difference: Inch-thick pieces of meat cook quickly no matter what, and thicker pieces require both direct and indirect fire.

About that fire: Get it as hot as your equipment can manage—500°F or above if possible. For 1-inch-thick black-and-blue, rare, or medium-rare steaks, make a direct fire. For thicker cuts or cooking beyond that doneness, you need both hot and cool zones (see page 8).

A true black-and-blue steak is a challenge met only with a screaming hot fire. When cooking with charcoal, if you can, shorten the distance between the grates and the coals. With gas, let the grill fully heat. When the grill hits peak temperature, take the steaks out of the fridge, blot them with paper towels, season on both sides with salt and pepper, and get them over the hottest spot of the fire. With gas, put the lid down since the heat will dissipate and the inside won't cook too fast; for charcoal, keep the lid off for the opposite reason. To keep the inside from cooking, sear the steaks for no more than 2 minutes per side then get them off the grill and check; they should be eaten before carryover heat cooks the meat further (see page 221).

For rare and medium-rare steaks, start a direct fire—anything over 450°F will do the trick. The idea is to develop a crusty exterior on the steaks, without burning, in the time it takes the interior to cook the way you want it (see page 220 for checking doneness).

Steaks taken beyond medium-rare require searing over direct fire, then finishing over indirect heat. This gives you more control of both the internal temperature and the exterior charring so that the meat is still moist even when there's little or no pink at the center. You can and should be prepared to move the steaks around and check frequently. For 1-inch-thick cuts, start with 3 minutes searing per side before moving the steaks to the indirect portion of the grill; thicker pieces will require more time.

The Perfect Steak with Black-and-Blue Butter

A spin on the steakhouse favorite that works for any of the recipes here: Earlier in the day, cream together 6 tablespoons softened butter, 4 ounces blue cheese, and 1 tablespoon cracked black peppercorns in a small bowl. Roll into a log, wrap in plastic wrap, and refrigerate until firm, at least 1 hour. Cut into 1-inch slices and leave them at room temperature while you heat the grill. Immediately after slicing and plating the steak, scatter the pats on top to melt.

Into-the-Fire Steaks

Makes: 4 to 6 servings	Time: 25 to 35 minutes	(D)

I'm serious: You're going to put meat directly on the coals. And instead of getting burnt bricks, the results are a sublime balance of charred crust and juicy interior. The best cuts for this are porterhouse, rib-eye, and strip; bone-in or boneless—it's your choice.

2 or more thick steaks (1–1½ inches thick; about 2 pounds total)

Salt and pepper

1 Prepare a hot direct fire using hardwood charcoal; make sure to use enough so you can spread the coals out thickly and still lay the steaks fully on top.

2 Pat the steaks dry with paper towels and sprinkle with salt and pepper on both sides.

3 When the coals are blazing hot, spread them out into an even bed. Put the steaks directly on the coals so they're not touching each other. Cook until 5° to 10°F shy of the desired doneness (see page 220), turning and moving them as needed. Timing will be extremely variable, depending on the thickness of the steaks and temperature of the fire, but figure boneless cuts release with few coals stuck to them at 3 to 4 minutes before the first turn. Then start checking with an instant-read thermometer after a couple more minutes. (Bone-in or thicker cuts will take a little longer.)

4 Pull or shake any embers off the meat above the fire and transfer the steaks to a cutting board. Let rest for 5 to 10 minutes, continuing to check the internal temperature. (Or nick with a small knife and peek inside.) Cut across into ½-inch slices, transfer to a platter, pour over any accumulated juices, and serve.

• recipe continues →

TIPS FOR INTO-THE-FIRE COOKING

1. Use untreated hardwood charcoal. The food will be sitting right on the fuel.
2. Dab away any moisture on the steaks with paper towels and season them with salt and pepper; you want to taste the fire and the food.
3. A pair of long-handled tongs is essential when working this close to a super-hot fire.
4. The steaks should lie flat on the coals, so make sure the fire is big enough to accommodate all of them with an inch or so in between.
5. The fire must be hot, with flaming red embers. Moisture from the meat can tamp down the fire. If you let the fire get past its prime or haven't made it big enough, the steaks may take longer to cook and not develop as much crust.
6. An instant-read thermometer will make determining doneness so much easier. Remember that the meat closest to the bone will cook the slowest, so take that into consideration when you take readings. To check, transfer the steak to a plate and insert the thermometer.
7. When turning the steaks, pieces of charcoal tend to stick. Pull them off with tongs and be sure not to take one into the house with you by mistake or drop one into dry grass.

Into-the-Fire Double-Cut Pork Rib Chops	Two ribs cut from a bone-in pork loin (or crown roast) take to this technique perfectly and the presentation is impressive: Substitute 2 double-cut pork rib chops for the steaks (3 to 3½ pounds total). Season and grill as directed until the internal temperature at the thickest point close the bone registers 135°F, 25 to 45 minutes total. Start checking after 20 minutes; the meat closest to the bone cooks the slowest. Transfer to a cutting board and let rest until the temperature rises to 145°F. Cut the chops from the bones, then across into ¼-inch slices. Cut the ribs apart. Transfer everything to a platter, pour over any accumulated juices, and serve with the bones.
Into-the-Fire Leg of Lamb	Fire and lamb are an unbeatable combination, and miraculously I've never burned the string off the roast: Substitute a 2-pound tied boneless leg of lamb roast for the steaks. Season and grill as directed until 5° to 10°F shy of the desired doneness. For rare, start checking the temperature at 20 minutes. Transfer to a cutting board and let rest 5 to 10 minutes, monitoring the internal temperature. Remove the string, slice as thickly as you like, and serve with the juices.
Into-the-Fire Whole Fish	You don't have to catch your own to cook fish like on a campfire: I like to use 1 small fish per person, ¾ to 1 pound each. Make sure they're cleaned and scaled. Grill as directed, turning once, until you can push a skewer or thin knife through the thickest point of the flesh with no resistance, 3 to 10 minutes per side; start checking after 5 minutes. Transfer to a platter and serve whole, or cut and lift the fillets from the frames and plate without the bones.

D direct fire   I indirect fire   M make ahead   V vegetarian option

Steak with Green Chimichurri

Makes: 4 to 6 servings	Time: 35 to 45 minutes	Ⓓ Ⓜ

Skewered beef steak cooked over a live wood fire is a classic offering of the South American barbecue or *asado* (also known as a *churrasco* in Brazil). Traditionally, the meat is cooked seasoned with nothing more than salt and pepper—some cooks insist on not seasoning until it comes off the grill—then sliced and served with chimichurri, a potent parsley-vinegar sauce. Flank steak is often used but you can use your choice of steak.

2 cups packed fresh parsley leaves

3 cloves garlic, peeled

¼ cup good-quality olive oil

2 tablespoons red wine vinegar

½ teaspoon red chile flakes, or more to taste

Salt and pepper

1½ to 2 pounds flank or skirt steak

1 Start the coals or heat a gas grill for hot direct cooking. Make sure the grates are clean.

2 Put the parsley, garlic, oil, vinegar, red pepper, and a sprinkle of salt in a blender or food processor and purée. Taste and adjust the seasonings as needed. Transfer to a small serving bowl. (You can prepare the sauce several hours ahead; cover and refrigerate.)

3 Pat the meat dry with paper towels and sprinkle with salt and pepper on both sides.

4 Put the steak on the grill directly over the fire. Close the lid and cook, turning once, until 5° to 10°F shy of the desired doneness (see page 220), 3 to 5 minutes per side for medium-rare flank steak, or 2 to 3 minutes per side for skirt steak.

5 Transfer to a cutting board and let rest 5 to 10 minutes, checking the internal temperature. (Or nick with a small knife and peek inside.) Slice thinly across the grain, transfer to a platter, pour over any accumulated juices, and serve with the chimichurri on the side.

Steak with Red Chimichurri	This less-famous cousin of green chimichurri adds layers of heat and smoke flavor: Add ½ teaspoon smoked paprika (pimentón) along with ¼ teaspoon chipotle chile powder or 1 teaspoon minced canned chipotle chile in adobo sauce, or more to taste, before puréeing.
Steak with Mixed Herb Chimichurri	Substitute up to 1 cup fresh mint and up to ½ cup fresh oregano for 1½ cups of the parsley. For some brightness, substitute fresh lemon or lime juice for up to half the vinegar.
Steak with Salsa Verde	Green sauce—as in the Italian version—is another way to add contrast to the smokiness of the steak: Substitute Salsa Verde (page 475) for the chimichurri.

Stuffed Flank Steak

| Makes: 4 to 6 servings | Time: 35 to 45 minutes | Ⓓ Ⓜ |

More work than a steak seasoned on the outside, but the only tricky part is slicing the steak in half with a very sharp knife along its length into two thin pieces. After spreading the filling over the steak, roll it so the grain runs from open end to open end. That way, it slices into tender spirals. If you can't find the Mexican cheese queso asadero, substitute another like queso Oaxaca or crumbled queso fresco; each will have a slightly different flavor.

1 1½- to 2-pound flank steak

Salt and pepper

1 cup grated queso asadero

½ cup chopped fresh oregano

4 cloves garlic, minced

1 Start the coals or heat a gas grill for medium-high direct cooking. Make sure the grates are clean. Cut at least ten 8-inch pieces of kitchen twine.

2 With a very sharp knife, slice the steak lengthwise into two pieces. With a meat mallet, rolling pin, or the bottom of a cast-iron skillet, pound the two thin steaks evenly to no more than ½-inch thick. Pat them dry with paper towels and sprinkle with salt and pepper on both sides.

3 Combine the cheese, oregano, and garlic in a small bowl. Divide the mixture between the steaks and spread it out almost to the edges. Roll the steaks up so that the grain of the meat runs the length of the roll, so you'll be slicing them across the grain. Tie the steaks closed with the twine every 2 inches or so. (You can prepare the recipe to this point up to several hours in advance and refrigerate.)

4 Put the stuffed steaks on the grill directly over the fire. Close the lid and cook, turning the rolls every 2 to 3 minutes for even browning, until 5° to 10°F shy of the desired doneness (see page 220); start checking them with an instant-read thermometer after 10 minutes. Depending on the thickness of the rolls, they should take 15 to 20 minutes total for medium-rare.

5 Transfer to a cutting board and let rest 5 to 10 minutes, checking the internal temperature. (Or nick with a small knife and peek inside.) Cut the rolls into 1-inch slices, transfer them spiral side up to a platter, pour over any accumulated juices, and serve.

• recipe continues →

Stuffed Flank Steak with Mozzarella and Basil	Substitute shredded mozzarella for the queso asadero and omit the oregano. Top the cheese with a layer of fresh basil leaves before rolling; you'll need 1 cup or more.
Stuffed Flank Steak with Prosciutto and Rosemary	Substitute Parmesan cheese for the queso asadero and 2 tablespoons chopped rosemary for the oregano. In Step 3, layer 4 ounces thinly sliced prosciutto over the cheese before rolling.
Stuffed Flank Steak with Peppery Greens and Goat Cheese	Replace the cheese, oregano, and garlic with 8 ounces goat cheese, 1 tablespoon minced garlic, the grated zest of 1 lemon, 1 tablespoon fresh lemon juice (or more to taste), and lots of black pepper, mashed together in a small bowl. Spread the mixture over one side of each of the steaks. Layer 2 cups roughly chopped watercress or arugula over the top before rolling.

D direct fire   I indirect fire   M make ahead   V vegetarian option

Breaded Steaks with Parmesan and Garlic

| Makes: 4 servings | Time: 25 to 30 minutes | Ⓓ |

Long before Southerners cooked up chicken-fried steak, Sicilians dredged beef in seasoned bread crumbs to crisp over an open fire. To keep the crumbs from sticking, well-oiled grates are essential, as is working over a medium fire. You can also use this recipe for chicken breasts or paillards, thin pork chops, or pork sirloin cutlets. Adjust the cooking times as needed.

Good-quality vegetable oil for the grates

1 cup dry bread crumbs

½ cup freshly grated Parmesan cheese

¼ cup chopped fresh parsley

2 tablespoons minced garlic

½ teaspoon salt

½ teaspoon black pepper

1½ pounds boneless strip, rib-eye, or sirloin steaks (½ to ¾ inch thick)

2 tablespoons good-quality olive oil

Lemon wedges for serving

1 Start the coals or heat a gas grill for medium direct cooking. Make sure the grates are clean, then rub them with oil-soaked paper towels held in tongs.

2 Combine the bread crumbs, Parmesan, parsley, garlic, salt, and pepper on a large plate.

3 Using a meat mallet or rolling pin, pound the steaks to a thickness of ½ inch or less. Brush both sides with the olive oil, then dredge in the bread crumbs, pressing to coat them completely.

4 Put the steaks on the grill directly over the fire. Close the lid and cook, turning once, until 5° to 10°F shy of the desired doneness (see page 220), 3 to 4 minutes per side for medium-rare.

5 Transfer to a cutting board and let rest 5 to 10 minutes, continuing to check the temperature with an instant-read thermometer. (Or nick with a small knife and peek inside.) Cut into ½- to 1-inch slices, transfer to a platter, pour over any accumulated juices, and serve with lemon wedges.

Breaded Steaks with Rosemary and Pecorino	Substitute pecorino Romano for the Parmesan and 1 tablespoon minced fresh rosemary for the parsley; omit the salt.
Breaded Steaks with Manchego and Oregano	Substitute Manchego cheese for the Parmesan and 2 tablespoons minced fresh oregano for the parsley.
Breaded Steaks with Ginger and Five-Spice Powder	Give it a Pan-Asian spin: Omit the cheese. Substitute panko for the bread crumbs and ¼ cup chopped fresh cilantro for the parsley, and add 2 tablespoons minced fresh ginger and 1 teaspoon five-spice powder. Replace the olive oil with good-quality vegetable oil. Grill as directed and serve with soy sauce and the lemon or lime wedges.

Romanian Garlic Steak

Makes: 4 to 6 servings	Time: 40 to 45 minutes	Ⓓ Ⓜ

For garlic lovers, steak doesn't get any better than this dish, called *fleica* in Romanian. And you even have my blessing if you want to double the amount of garlic. As for the cut, flank steak is most common in Romania, but some steakhouses in the United States prepare it with boneless or bone-in rib-eye. It also works with skirt steak or thick top round, which is often sold as London broil. All should be sliced thinly before serving (see "Going Against the Grain," below). Try giving this garlic treatment to lamb chops, a butterflied boneless leg of lamb, or lamb kebabs.

8 cloves garlic, minced

1 teaspoon salt

Juice of 1 lemon

1½ to 2 pounds flank steak

¼ cup good-quality olive oil

1 To make the marinade, combine half the garlic with the salt and lemon juice in a small bowl.

2 Put the steak in a large shallow baking dish and work the marinade into it on both sides, using your hands to massage it evenly all over the steak. Let sit at room temperature while you prepare the fire. Or cover and refrigerate for several hours or overnight.

3 Start the coals or heat a gas grill for hot direct cooking. Make sure the grates are clean. Whisk the remainder of the garlic and the oil together in another small bowl with a fork, pressing down on the garlic as you work.

4 Remove the steak from the marinade and let any excess drip off. Put the steak on the grill directly over the fire. Close the lid and cook, turning once, until 5° to 10°F shy of the desired doneness (see page 220), 4 to 5 minutes per side for medium-rare.

5 Transfer to a cutting board and let rest for 5 to 10 minutes, checking the internal temperature. (Or nick with a small knife and peek inside.) Slice thinly across the grain, transfer to a platter, pour over any accumulated juices, and serve with the garlic oil on the side to drizzle over.

GOING AGAINST THE GRAIN

When slicing meat, particularly tougher cuts, for the tenderest result, cut against the grain. In meat, the "grain" refers to the muscle fibers, which, when cooked, can be chewy. If you cut with the grain, or parallel to the fiber, you'll get the full effect of that chewiness. If you slice against, or perpendicular to, the grain, you'll end up with a tender mouthful.

Brisket is a prime example of a cut that should be sliced across the grain, as should boneless short ribs, tri-tip roast, and flank and skirt steaks.

Ⓓ direct fire   Ⓘ indirect fire   Ⓜ make ahead   Ⓥ vegetarian option

Cuban-Style Garlic Steak	Turn the garlic marinade and oil into a mojo marinade and sauce: For the marinade, combine all the garlic with ¼ cup each orange juice and good-quality olive oil, 2 tablespoons each fresh lime and lemon juices, and chopped fresh oregano, and the salt. Transfer ¼ cup of the marinade to another small bowl and let it sit for up to an hour, or cover and refrigerate. Use the rest to marinate the meat as directed. After grilling and slicing the steak, drizzle with the reserved ¼ cup mojo and serve.
Marinated Steak with Jalapeño and Orange	For the marinade, combine all the garlic with ¼ cup each orange juice and good-quality olive oil, 2 tablespoons soy sauce, and 2 thinly sliced jalapeño chiles. Transfer ¼ cup of the marinade to another small bowl and stir in 2 teaspoons grated orange zest. Use the rest to marinate the meat as directed. After grilling and slicing the steak, drizzle with the reserved sauce and serve.
Worcestershire Steak	Use 4 cloves garlic for the marinade and add 1 tablespoon Worcestershire sauce. Omit the remaining garlic and the olive oil.

Beef Salad with Fresh Mint

Makes: 4 servings	Time: 35 to 45 minutes	

A simple, light salad with both bright and hearty flavor. You can make this with any boneless steak, like flank, skirt, sirloin, rib-eye, strip, or tenderloin. Just be sure to cut the meat across the grain for the most tender and attractive slices. The salad is also delicious served with sliced grilled chicken breasts or paillards, boneless pork cutlets, or shrimp.

4 cups torn Boston or romaine lettuce leaves, mesclun, or any salad greens mixture

1 cup torn fresh mint leaves

½ small red onion, cut into thin julienne

1 cucumber, peeled, seeded if necessary, and cut into thin julienne

1 carrot, peeled and cut into thin julienne

Juice of 2 limes

2 tablespoons soy sauce

2 tablespoons rice vinegar

1 tablespoon sugar

1 jalapeño chile, seeded if you like, thinly sliced

Salt and pepper

1½ pounds boneless steak (see the headnote)

1 Start the coals or heat a gas grill for medium-high direct cooking. Make sure the grates are clean.

2 Put the lettuce, mint, onion, cucumber, and carrot in a large bowl. Whisk the lime juice, soy sauce, vinegar, sugar, jalapeño, and 1 tablespoon water together in a small bowl; the mixture will be thin. Taste and add salt and pepper if you like. (You can prepare the salad and dressing up to several hours in advance; refrigerate both until you're ready to serve; drape a damp kitchen towel over the vegetables to keep them fresh.)

3 Pat the steak dry with paper towels, then sprinkle with salt and pepper on both sides. Put the steak on the grill directly over the fire. Close the lid and cook, turning once, until 5° to 10°F shy of the desired doneness (see page 220), 2 to 3 minutes per side for skirt steak or 3 to 5 minutes per side for a 1-inch steak (medium-rare).

4 Transfer to a cutting board and let rest while you dress the salad; check the temperature of the meat occasionally. (Or nick with a small knife and peek inside.)

5 Transfer 2 tablespoons of the dressing to a medium-sized bowl. Drizzle the rest of the dressing over the salad and toss to coat. Transfer the salad to a platter if you like.

6 Thinly slice the steak across the grain. Put the beef and any accumulated juices in the bowl with the reserved dressing and toss to combine. Scatter the steak slices over the salad, drizzle with the juices, and serve.

D direct fire   **I** indirect fire   **M** make ahead   **V** vegetarian option

Vietnamese-Style Beef and Noodle Salad with Fresh Herbs	Substitute 1 cup each torn fresh Thai (or Italian) basil and cilantro leaves for half the lettuce, and fish sauce for the soy sauce. Before preparing the fire, steep 6 ounces rice vermicelli in boiling water until soft; drain, rinse until cold water, and let sit in a bowl cold water. After transferring the salad to the platter, drain the noodles and toss them in the reserved dressing first; scatter them over the salad. Repeat with the beef. Garnish the salad with ½ cup chopped roasted peanuts.
Beef Salad with Fingerlings, Green Beans, and Basil	A few hours before serving, bring 8 ounces fingerling or baby potatoes in salted water to cover to a boil and cook until fork-tender, 15 to 20 minutes. Transfer the potatoes to a bowl of ice water to stop the cooking. Add 8 ounces trimmed green beans to the boiling water and cook until crisp-tender, 2 to 3 minutes; drain and rinse under cold water. Drain and refrigerate both vegetables. Substitute basil for the mint, and omit the cucumber and carrot. For the dressing, replace the lime juice, soy sauce, vinegar, sugar, and jalapeño with ½ cup good-quality olive oil, 3 tablespoons red wine vinegar, and some salt and pepper. Stir in 1 fresh tomato, chopped, and the red onion. Toss the lettuce and basil with half the dressing and transfer to the platter. Scatter the potatoes and green beans over the top, then the steak, and drizzle with the remaining dressing.
Beef Salad with Mint and Chickpeas	Omit the cucumber and carrot. Put the lettuce on a platter. Toss the mint leaves and onion with 2 cups cooked chickpeas. For the dressing, replace the lime juice, soy sauce, vinegar, sugar, and jalapeño with ½ cup good-quality olive oil, ¼ cup fresh lemon juice, 1 tablespoon honey, and salt and Aleppo pepper or red chile flakes to taste. Toss half of the dressing with the chickpea mixture, scatter it over the lettuce, and top with the sliced steak. Drizzle with the remaining dressing and serve.

Steak and Scallions Yakiniku Style with Tare Sauce

Makes: 4 to 6 servings	Time: 25 to 30 minutes	Ⓓ Ⓜ

Yakiniku means "grilled meat" in Japanese, and also refers to specific do-it-yourself barbecue restaurants where the tables have built-in grills. Guests order a choice of raw ingredients—beef, pork belly, chicken, shrimp, squid, and vegetables are all traditional—to cook and eat leisurely with a dipping (*tare*) sauce. For even more adventure, try this with sliced beef heart.

2 pounds boneless strip or rib-eye steak (1–1½ inches thick)

¼ cup soy sauce

2 tablespoons sake

2 tablespoons mirin (or substitute 1 tablespoon each honey and water mixed together)

1 tablespoon sugar

1 tablespoon apple juice

1 teaspoon any miso

1 teaspoon minced garlic

1 teaspoon minced fresh ginger

2 bunches scallions, trimmed

2 teaspoons toasted sesame seeds

1 Start the coals or heat a gas grill for medium-high direct cooking. Make sure the grates are clean.

2 Pat the steak dry with paper towels, then cut across into ½-inch slices.

3 Whisk the soy sauce, sake, mirin, sugar, apple juice, miso, garlic, and ginger together in a small bowl until the sugar dissolves. (You can prepare the sauce several hours ahead and refrigerate.)

4 Put the scallions on the grill directly over the fire. Close the lid and cook, turning once, until they are pliable and browned, 3 to 4 minutes per side. Transfer to a cutting board.

5 Working rapidly, put the sliced beef on the grill, each slice flat down on the grate. Cook for 1 minute, then turn. By the time you finish turning them all, start transferring the meat to a platter in the order they went onto the grill. Cut the scallions into pieces and add to the platter. Divide the sauce among 4 small serving bowls, scatter the sesame seeds on top, and serve.

Ⓓ direct fire　Ⓘ indirect fire　Ⓜ make ahead　Ⓥ vegetarian option

Beef Tongue Yakiniku Style with Tare Sauce	Tongue is a traditional yakiniku offering: Follow the directions for Smoked Tongue (page 268) through Step 2. When you're ready to grill, slice the chilled tongue, then cook and serve as directed.
Bulgogi	This Korean specialty is akin to *kalbi*, only with thinly sliced steak instead of short ribs. The timing is different from yakiniku but the process is similar: Omit the tare sauce. Make the kalbi marinade on page 249. After slicing the steak, toss it with the marinade and let it sit while you prepare the fire. Grill as directed and serve with Boston lettuce leaves to wrap the pieces of beef; top with gochujang.
Thai-Style Sliced Steak with Crying Tiger Dipping Sauce	The name comes from the heat of chile—in this case cayenne. After marinating the steak, you can grill sliced as directed in Step 5, or grill it whole, then slice it: Replace the dipping sauce with 6 tablespoons fresh lime juice, ¼ cup fish sauce, and 1 tablespoon sugar in a small bowl, plus 1 tablespoon chopped fresh cilantro and ¾ teaspoon cayenne, or more or less to taste. Make a marinade with 2 tablespoons soy sauce and 1 tablespoon each oyster sauce and fish sauce. Turn the steak in the marinade several times until coated; let sit while you prepare the fire. Grill whole or sliced, as you prefer.

BISON AND VENISON

I've grilled bison and venison, both burgers and steaks, with excellent results. Both are much lower in fat than beef. The ground bison in supermarkets is generally 90% lean; the percentage of fat should be marked on the package. So if you cook these meats much beyond medium-rare, they will dry out.

Keep an eye on them and you'll be fine, even the first time. Venison burgers cook up fast over medium-high heat; I like them about an inch thick and on the fire for 2 to 3 minutes per side.

Since the flavor of bison and venison steaks is unique—and the price of these cuts high—keep the seasonings simple so you can get the full effect of the grill. If you're a hunter or lucky enough to be friends with one, be prepared for a pronounced flavor. Farm raised is milder. Either way, season the meat with some salt and pepper, grill it to medium-rare, and dig in.

Balsamic-Marinated Whole Beef Tenderloin with Herbs

Makes: 10 or more servings	Time: 45 to 60 minutes, plus marinating time	D I M

Since tenderloin lacks the marbling essential to great beef flavor and chew, it's not one of my favorite cuts. But it's undeniably tender, and I'm outnumbered by the folks who love it. Marinating it in balsamic vinegar makes me like it more.

The tenderloin is unevenly shaped in a pretty pronounced way. You can either grill it as is, which will yield beef cooked from well done to rare, which may be a good thing if your guests like their steak cooked to different degrees of doneness. Or, you can fold the thinner end of the tenderloin under the thicker part and use kitchen twine to tie it every 1 to 2 inches to create an evenly shaped roast (you can also ask the butcher to do this for you).

½ cup good-quality olive oil

¼ cup roughly chopped fresh parsley

2 tablespoons balsamic or sherry vinegar

1 tablespoon coarsely ground or cracked black peppercorns

1 teaspoon fresh thyme leaves, several thyme sprigs, or ½ teaspoon dried thyme

1 bay leaf

4 cloves garlic, lightly smashed

1 beef tenderloin (5–6 pounds), trimmed of fat and silverskin (see page 245)

Salt and pepper

1 Combine the oil, parsley, vinegar, peppercorns, thyme, bay leaf, and garlic in a large bowl and whisk. Pat the tenderloin dry with paper towels, then put it in the bowl and turn to coat completely with the marinade. Marinate the roast for up to an hour at room temperature, turning it every 15 minutes or so. Or cover and refrigerate it for several hours or overnight, turning it occasionally.

2 Start the coals or heat a gas grill for hot indirect cooking. Make sure the grates are clean.

3 Remove the tenderloin from the marinade and put it on the indirect side of the grill, with one of the long sides closest to the fire. Close the lid and cook until 10°F shy of the desired doneness (see page 220), rotating and turning the roast as necessary. Start checking it after about 20 minutes; medium-rare will take 25 to 30 minutes.

4 Move the tenderloin directly over the fire and sear until well browned, 2 to 3 minutes per side.

5 Transfer to a cutting board and let rest 5 to 10 minutes, checking the internal temperature. (Or nick with a small knife and peek inside.) Cut the roast into ½-inch or thicker slices, transfer to a platter, pour over any accumulated juices, and serve.

Grill-Roasted Boneless Prime Rib Roast	Unlike the tenderloin, the rib roast (where rib-eyes come from) has beautiful marbling and just the right balance of tenderness to chew. So use the marinade as a finishing sauce if you like and hit the roast with just salt and pepper before grilling (or try a grill salt or rub from page 455). A roast can range from 3 to 6 pounds. Like the tenderloin, prime rib is somewhat irregularly shaped and benefits from being tied to ensure even cooking. Cook as directed in Steps 3–5; start checking the temperature at 30 minutes.
Grill-Roasted Standing Rib Roast	This is a prime rib roast with the bones. A full rib roast includes seven ribs and can weigh more than 15 pounds. But you can buy smaller ones, with just three ribs, weighing around 5 pounds. Figure two servings per rib. Omit the marinade. I prefer to simply season it well on all sides with salt and pepper, or you could use any herb or spice mix you prefer. Cook as directed in Steps 3–5. Because the meat closest to the bone cooks slower, position the bone side closest to the fire and when you sear it at the end, put the bone side over the hottest part of the fire. Cook times will range from 1½ to 4 hours, depending on size and how hot the fire is. For a smaller roast, start checking the internal temperature at 30 minutes; largest roasts, at 1 hour. Repeat frequently thereafter, always in multiple places near and away from the bones.
Grill-Roasted Strip Loin	Like a prime rib roast, the strip loin (where strip steaks are cut) has terrific marbling and is much less expensive per pound than beef tenderloin. It's also evenly shaped, so there is no need to tie it. A whole boneless strip loin weighs 10 to 12 pounds and will take about 1½ hours to get to medium-rare. You can also ask to have it cut into smaller roasts. A whole loin will come with a thick layer of hard fat along one side; trim that down so it is no more than ⅛ inch thick. Omit the marinade. Like for a standing rib roast, I prefer to simply season it well on all sides with salt and pepper, or to use an herb or spice mix. Cook as directed in Steps 3–5, starting to check the temperature after 30 minutes for a smaller roast, after 1 hour for a full strip loin.

Carne Asada Tacos

| Makes: **4 servings** | Time: **20 to 30 minutes** | **D** |

Carne asada translates simply to "grilled meat" in Spanish, but when uttered with tacos you're probably talking about skirt steak. It's a chewy cut and must be cooked quickly and sliced across the grain to guarantee tenderness, but the evenly distributed fat makes for rich and satisfying eating. You don't have to season the meat much but you can; feel free to tinker with the spices and herbs according to what you like and what you have: Ground cumin, chili powder, ground coriander, and/or dried thyme are all good.

Corn tortillas are traditional for tacos, as is serving the tortillas doubled up. If you like flour tortillas, go for it; the same goes for using one tortilla per taco instead of two.

1 teaspoon salt

2 teaspoons dried oregano (preferably Mexican)

½ teaspoon chipotle chile powder

½ teaspoon ancho chile powder

1½ pounds skirt steak

1 large ripe avocado

2 or 3 limes

Hot sauce of your choice

1 small red onion, halved, thinly sliced, and separated

½ cup chopped fresh cilantro

½ cup sour cream or Mexican *crema*

2 cups salsa of your choice
(see list on page 96)

12–18 6-inch corn tortillas for serving

1 Combine the salt, oregano, and chipotle and ancho powders in a small bowl. Pat the steak dry with paper towels, then sprinkle the rub evenly over both sides, gently patting to help it stick.

2 Start the coals or heat a gas grill for hot direct cooking. Make sure the grates are clean.

3 While the grill is heating, halve the avocado and remove the pit; scoop the flesh into a bowl and mash, leaving it a bit chunky. Squeeze in the juice of 1 of the limes (or more or less to taste) and add a few dashes hot sauce. Stir gently to combine. Cut the remaining lime(s) into 8 wedges. Put the onion, cilantro, sour cream, and salsa into small serving bowls.

4 Put the steak on the grill directly over the fire. Close the lid and cook, turning once, until medium-rare, 2 to 3 minutes per side. (Nick with a small knife and peek inside.)

5 Transfer to a cutting board, let rest 5 minutes, and slice thinly across the grain (or chop it if you like). Transfer to a platter and pour over any accumulated juices. Quickly heat the tortillas on the grill (see "Heating Tortillas," page 100), then put the steak, tortillas, and accompaniments on the table for everyone to assemble their own tacos.

• recipe continues →

Carne Asada Quesadillas	These are great for lunch, dinner, appetizers: Grate 8 ounces queso asadero, Chihuahua, or Oaxaca. Use eight 8-inch flour tortillas. Brush one side of each tortilla with a good-quality vegetable oil. After cooking the meat, adjust the grill to a medium direct fire (for charcoal, wait for the coals to die down to medium or work on the outer edges of the fire). Spread the guacamole on the dry side of 4 of the tortillas, then sprinkle with the cheese, onion, and cilantro. Top with the steak and the remaining tortillas, oiled side up. Put the quesadillas directly over the fire, close the lid, and cook, carefully turning once until the bottoms are golden brown and the cheese has melted, 3 to 4 minutes per side. Transfer to a cutting board and let sit 1 to 2 minutes before slicing each into wedges. Serve with the sour cream and salsa.
Carne Asada Tlayuda	Open-face quesadillas to fold and hold or eat with a knife and fork: Drain and rinse a 15-ounce can black beans. Put the beans in a blender or food processor with 2 tablespoons chopped garlic and some salt and pepper and purée, adding a small amount of water to get the machine going. Heat in a small saucepan until bubbling. Grate 8 ounces queso asadero, Chihuahua, or Oaxaca. Dice 2 avocados and toss with the lime juice. Chop 2 fresh tomatoes. Brush one side of 6 to 8 corn tortillas with a good-quality vegetable oil. Turn and spread with the bean purée and top with cheese. After cooking the meat, adjust the grill to a medium direct fire (for charcoal, wait for the coals to die down to medium or work on the outer edges of the fire). Grill the tortillas with the lid closed until the cheese has melted, 1 to 2 minutes. Transfer to a large platter and top with the diced avocado, tomatoes, red onion, and cilantro. Pass the salsa at the table.
Carne Asada Fries	You'll never go back to nachos: Omit the onion and cilantro. Make a half-recipe of Grill Fries (page 427); if you like, add some chili powder to the seasoning. Grate 8 ounces queso asadero, Chihuahua, or Oaxaca. Turn on the broiler and move the rack about 4 inches from the heat. Chop the grilled steak. Put the fries in a 10-inch cast-iron skillet, followed by the steak and cheese. Broil until the cheese is completely melted and browned in spots. Serve this as a communal appetizer or dinner. Dollop with the sour cream and guacamole and pass the salsa on the side.

D direct fire   I indirect fire   M make ahead   V vegetarian option

Santa Maria–Style Tri-Tip Roast

Makes: 6 to 8 servings	Time: 45 to 65 minutes, largely unattended	**D** **I**

Tri-tip, true to its name, is a large triangular cut from the bottom sirloin. Until recently it was largely unknown outside of California, where it's the focal point of barbecue in Santa Maria. But instead of the slow-and-low smoked meats of the South, the tradition calls for grilling this well-marbled roast hot and fast—at some distance—over red oak. Unless the grates are adjustable, the best way to simulate the style is to cook tri-tip with indirect heat for the lion's share of the time, with a final sear before taking it off the grill. Sirloin has wonderful beefy flavor best when cooked to medium-rare.

2 teaspoons salt

2 teaspoons garlic powder

1 teaspoon black pepper

1 tri-tip roast (2–2½ pounds), trimmed of excess fat and silverskin (see below)

1 Start the coals or heat a gas grill for medium-high indirect cooking. Makes sure the grates are clean. If cooking with charcoal, put a drip pan under the indirect side of the grill. If cooking with gas, empty, clean, and replace the fat trap.

2 Combine the salt, garlic powder, and pepper in a small bowl. Sprinkle the roast evenly all over with the rub, lightly patting to help it stick.

3 Put the tri-tip on the indirect side of the grill, with one of the longer sides closest to the fire. Close the lid and cook until 10°F shy of the desired doneness (see page 220). Start checking after about 20 minutes; for medium-rare it will take 25 to 45 minutes.

4 Move the roast directly over the fire and sear, turning once, until well browned, 2 to 3 minutes per side.

5 Transfer to a cutting board and let rest 5 to 10 minutes, checking the internal temperature. (Or nick with a small knife and peek inside.) Cut across the grain into ½-inch or thinner slices and serve, drizzled with any accumulated juices.

REMOVING SILVERSKIN

Silverskin is an inelastic silvery membrane that needs to be removed before cooking. You most often come across it when prepping beef or pork tenderloin. To remove it, get a very sharp, thin knife under one end of it and then shave down along its underside, pulling it up and away as you do, so you remove only silverskin, not meat.

● recipe continues →

Tri-Tip Roast with Onion Rub	I don't usually use onion powder but a good granulated kind can taste like caramelized onions: Substitute onion powder for the garlic powder.
Miso-Marinated Tri-Tip Roast	Up to 24 hours before you start the fire, whisk together ½ cup red miso and 1 tablespoon each minced fresh ginger, minced garlic, and Dijon mustard. Whisk in enough mirin or sake to make the mixture spreadable. Coat the tri-tip with the paste, then marinate at room temperature for up to an hour, otherwise in the refrigerator, until you're ready to grill.
Baltimore Pit Beef Sandwiches with Horseradish Sauce	These sandwiches are traditionally made with eye of round or bottom round, but I find tri-tip works great: To make the sauce, put ½ cup mayonnaise, ¼ cup prepared horseradish sauce, 1 tablespoon fresh lemon juice, and some salt and pepper in a small bowl; whisk, then refrigerate. A really crusty exterior is key to Baltimore pit beef, so start the tri-tip over direct heat, searing it well on all sides before moving it to indirect heat, then cook it to 5° to 10°F shy of the desired doneness and transfer to a cutting board. After resting, slice the beef as thinly as you can across the grain; if it ends up in shards, all the better. Pile it on kaiser rolls (toast them on the grill, if you like), dollop with the horseradish sauce, top with a slice of tomato and sweet onion, cap with the top of the roll, and chow down.

Ⓓ direct fire　Ⓘ indirect fire　Ⓜ make ahead　Ⓥ vegetarian option

Madeira-Style Beef Skewers

| Makes: **4 to 6 servings** | Time: **25 to 30 minutes** | **D** **M** |

Also known as *espetada,* these skewers are ubiquitous at Portuguese American festivals in the United States, where they're frequently called "meat on a stick." The scent of bay leaves on the grill is intoxicating. If you can source branches to use as the skewers, soak them first, and definitely use fresh bay leaves if available. For the beef, all sorts of thick cuts work, including tenderloin, sirloin, and top round (often sold as London broil). I love these served with grilled cherry tomatoes (page 443) and onions (page 433).

1½ to 2 pounds boneless beef steak

6 cloves garlic, peeled

1 tablespoon sea salt

2 tablespoons good-quality olive oil

30–35 bay leaves (preferably fresh)

1 Trim any excess fat from the steak, then cut it into 1- to 1½-inch chunks. Put in a large bowl.

2 With a mortar and pestle or in a blender or mini food processor, mash or process the garlic and salt to a paste, then stir in the oil. Pour over the beef and work into the meat with your hands until the chunks are completely coated. (You can do this up to several hours in advance; if more than an hour, cover and refrigerate until you're ready to grill.)

3 If you're using bamboo or wooden skewers, soak them in water for 30 minutes. Meanwhile, start the coals or heat a gas grill for medium-high direct cooking. Make sure the grates are clean.

4 When the fire is ready, thread the beef onto skewers, alternating the chunks with bay leaves; if any leaves break, wedge them between meat chunks.

5 Put the skewers on the grill directly over the fire. Close the lid and cook, turning once or twice, 4 to 5 minutes per side total, depending on the desired doneness (see page 220). Transfer to a platter and serve.

• recipe continues →

Afghan-Style Beef Kebabs	Here the marinade is a purée of spiced green papaya (available in Asian food stores and some supermarkets), which contains a powerful tenderizing enzyme. That makes it a great choice for less tender steak cuts, like flank or top round. However, overmarinating can turn the beef to mush: Omit the garlic salt, oil, and bay leaves. Put ½ cup chopped green papaya, ¼ cup yogurt, 2 tablespoons each chopped fresh mint and cilantro, 1 tablespoon each chopped garlic and chopped jalapeño, and 1 teaspoon each ground cumin and salt in a blender or food processor and pulse to a paste. Use that to coat the meat and let it marinate in the refrigerator for at least 1 or up to 4 hours.
Dijon-Tarragon Beef Kebabs	Omit the garlic cloves, salt, oil, and bay leaves. Whisk together ¼ cup Dijon mustard, 1 tablespoon each red wine vinegar, good-quality olive oil, minced garlic, and chopped fresh tarragon. Use this to marinate the meat.
Mexican-Style Beef Kebabs	Omit the bay leaves. Reduce the salt to 1½ teaspoons and add ¼ cup fresh oregano leaves, the juice of 1 lime, and 1 teaspoon each ground cumin and ancho chile powder to the garlic; process to a paste and use to coat the meat.

D direct fire   I indirect fire   M make ahead   V vegetarian option

Korean-Style Short Ribs

Makes: 4 servings	Time: 50 to 60 minutes	Ⓓ Ⓜ

To make these delectable short ribs, called *kalbi* or *galbi* in Korean, you take a cut of beef that's usually braised, slice it thin, hit it with a powerful marinade, then grill it fast over as hot a fire as you can summon. The results are spectacular. Fold the meat and some bonus seasonings into a lettuce leaf and you've got something incredible in your hands.

A couple ingredients are worth highlighting. First is gochujang, a fermented Korean chili paste with a unique interplay of sweet, hot, and savory flavors. It's now widely available in the United States, and worth finding. Perilla is an herb from the mint family with an anisey flavor; shiso is a close relative. If you can't find perilla or shiso, substitute basil leaves, though it won't quite be the same.

The rib cut preferred for kalbi is flanken: Three or more meaty ribs, still attached to one another, are thinly sliced across the bone. You end up with thin slices that have little ovals of bone on one side. Depending on where you live, this cut may not be easy to find. Substitute boneless short ribs and fillet them into long, thin strips (see the photos on page 252).

1 small onion, quartered

½ Asian or regular pear, peeled, cored, and quartered

6 cloves garlic, peeled

½ cup soy sauce

¼ cup sugar

2 tablespoons rice wine or sake

1 tablespoon sesame oil

2½ pounds flanken-cut bone-in short ribs, or 2 pounds boneless short ribs, each cut into a single thin strip (see page 253)

1 head Boston lettuce, pulled apart into leaves

12 or so fresh perilla leaves (optional)

1 or 2 hot green chiles (like jalapeño), thinly sliced

Gochujang for serving

2 tablespoons toasted sesame seeds

2 scallions, trimmed and chopped

1 Put the onion, pear, garlic, soy sauce, sugar, rice wine, and sesame oil in a blender or food processor and purée. Put the short ribs in a large baking dish or rimmed baking sheet. Pour the marinade over them, turning them several times to completely coat. Let sit at room temperature while you prepare the fire. Or cover and refrigerate for several hours or overnight, turning the beef several times.

2 Start the coals or heat a gas grill for hot direct cooking. Make sure the grates are clean.

3 Put the lettuce, perilla leaves if you're using them, and sliced chiles on a large platter, leaving room for the grilled short ribs. Put some gochujang in a small bowl.

4 Remove the beef from the marinade, scraping any solids from the purée off the strips.

• recipe continues →

5 Put the strips on the grill directly over the fire. Close the lid and cook, turning once, until the meat chars in places and is medium-rare in the center; this will only take 1 to 2 minutes per side.

6 Transfer to a cutting board and slice into pieces. Put on the platter, garnish with the sesame seeds and scallions, and serve family style.

L.A.-Style Short Rib Tacos	This popular West Coast street food substitutes kalbi for carne asada in a delicious mash-up of Korean and Mexican flavors: Chop the remaining half of the Asian pear and combine it in a small bowl with 1 fresh tomato, chopped; ½ cup chopped fresh cilantro; and the chopped scallions. Omit the sesame seeds, lettuce, and perilla leaves. Slice the grilled kalbi thinly across the grain and serve in hot corn or flour tortillas, topped with the Asian pear salsa, sliced chiles, gochujang, and a generous squeeze of lime juice.
Korean-Style Whole Boneless Short Ribs	If you can't find flanken-cut short ribs and don't feel handy enough with a knife to cut boneless short ribs into thin strips, you can still enjoy the flavors of kalbi. These are best not cooked beyond medium-rare: Substitute whole boneless short ribs for the thin strips. Let them marinate for several hours before grilling, turning them every half hour or so. Reduce the grill heat to medium-high and cook the ribs to 5° to 10°F shy of rare or medium-rare (see page 220), turning them on all sides every 3 minutes; this will take 15 to 20 minutes total. Let rest until they hit the desired temperature, then slice the meat thinly across the grain.
Korean-Style Short Ribs with Pineapple and Ginger	Substitute ½ cup pineapple juice for the Asian pear and honey for the sugar, and add a 1-inch piece fresh ginger, peeled and cut into thin slices, before puréeing.

• recipe continues →

CUTTING BONELESS SHORT RIBS FOR KALBI

If your butcher can't get flanken-cut bone-in short ribs, buy boneless short ribs instead. For 4 servings, three meaty ribs should be enough, which will be in excess of 2 pounds. To cut the ribs successfully, you need a very sharp knife. First, trim off any fat or silverskin (see page 245) remaining on the surface of the ribs. To cut the rib into a single strip, you're essentially going to cut it in a spiral.

STEP 1 Set a rib on a cutting board and cut across the top of the rib as if you mean to take a thin slice off it.

STEP 2 But when you get almost to the edge, change the angle of your knife and start cutting downward.

STEP 3 Cut downward, continuing to slice thinly.

STEP 4 Change the angle of your knife and slice in the other direction, then downward again.

STEP 5 Keep doing this, rotating the rib and unrolling the growing strip as you do.

STEP 6 When you're done, you can leave it in a single strip, but it's easier to grill cut into a couple of large pieces.

D direct fire   **I** indirect fire   **M** make ahead   **V** vegetarian option

Smoked Brisket

Makes: 12 or more servings	Time: about 7 hours, intermittently attended	Ⓘ Ⓜ

You can't rush brisket. The cut comes from the hard-working pectoral muscles and is interwoven with collagen-rich connective tissue. A full brisket is composed of two muscles known as the flat and the point. The point sits on top of the flat at the thicker, more irregularly shaped end of the brisket. The point has very nice fat marbling, while the flat is leaner; a band of fat separates the two. For the optimal balance of tenderness and flavor, brisket needs to cook beyond well done.

To get there, conventional wisdom dictates slow-and-low smoking on the grill—at 225° to 250°F—which puts a whole brisket at 12 hours, with you carrying coals to replenish the fire most of the time. I prefer to cook the brisket at 300°F using a combination of outdoor and indoor cooking that delivers incredible results in almost half the time (it's a technique well known to smokers, called the "Texas crutch"). The technique works the same on a 2-pound piece of brisket as it does on a 12-pounder. It also yields a generous amount of delicious meat juice that you can pour over the sliced brisket to serve.

Most barbecue brisket is smoked with oak, but use whatever wood you like. Two hours on a grill filled with smoke delivers just the right amount.

1 whole beef brisket (8–12 pounds)

2 tablespoons salt

2 tablespoons black pepper

1 Start the coals or heat a gas grill for medium-low indirect cooking. If cooking with charcoal, position the coals so the smoke will be pulled over the brisket and out the top vent; put a drip pan under the indirect side of the grill. For gas, empty, clean, and replace the fat trap. When the grill temperature is at 300°F, add wood to the fire (see "Smoking," pages 10–12).

2 While the grill heats, trim the external fat on the brisket to a layer ¼ inch thick. Combine the salt and pepper in a small bowl, then sprinkle it evenly all over the brisket, gently patting to help it stick. (You can do this up to the day before, cover, and refrigerate; take the meat out when you start the fire.)

3 When the grill fills with smoke, put the brisket on the indirect side with the thicker point end closest to the fire. Close the lid and cook, keeping the temperature in the grill at 300°F (if it sinks a bit lower or goes a bit higher at times, that's okay, but try to keep it right around 300°F) and replenishing the wood as needed to keep the grill filled with smoke. After about an hour, start checking the internal temperature of the brisket in multiple spots; reposition the meat as necessary to ensure even cooking. Replenish the wood for another hour. When the internal temperature of the brisket is at least 160°F when you test it in multiple spots, transfer it to a baking sheet; depending on the size of the brisket, this will take 4 to 5 hours.

4 Heat the oven to 300°F. Wrap the brisket tightly in foil; save and refrigerate the flavorful juices in the pan. Put the wrapped brisket on a

• recipe continues →

clean baking sheet and bake until it's is fork-tender, 1½ to 2½ hours, depending on the size of the brisket. Checking the temperature occasionally is helpful but the only way to know when it's done is to taste it. Once it hits 200°F, take a slice and see what you think. If it's not quite tender enough, rewrap it tightly and let it bake a bit longer. Don't let the internal temperature go much above 210°F, though.

5 Transfer the brisket to a cutting board and let it rest for 15 minutes. Warm the drippings captured in the foil wrapping, along with the reserved juices from Step 4, in a small saucepan until bubbling. Slice the brisket thinly across the grain. Put the slices on a platter, pour over the warm juices, and serve right away. (If you like, you can let it cool, cover, refrigerate, and reheat it the next day, but nothing really beats the flavor and texture of fresh cooked brisket.)

Hot and Smoky Brisket	This triples up on the smoke flavor; it's a nice choice for gas grillers having a hard time maintaining good smoke in their grill: Substitute 1 tablespoon smoked paprika (pimentón) for the black pepper in the rub and add 1 teaspoon chipotle chile powder.
Smoked Brisket with Baharat Rub	This Middle Eastern spice mix is outstanding with beef: For the rub, mix 1 tablespoon salt with 3 tablespoons baharat (page 456).
Smoked Bone-in Beef Short Ribs	You can do these with any of the three brisket rub treatments. Also, because short ribs have much more marbling than brisket, you can let the grill temperature sit between 300° and 350°F. For each serving plan on two 8- to 12-ounce bone-in ribs: Remove any excessive surface fat from the meaty side of the ribs, but leave the connective tissue on the bone side or the meat will fall off. Start with the bones closest to the fire and turn, move, and rotate them every 30 minutes or so for even cooking. Figure on 1½ to 2 hours total cooking time, leaving them on the grill the entire time.

MAKING BURNT ENDS

Though you can happily make "burnt ends" from smoked pork shoulder, ham, and even lamb, classic Kansas City–style burnt ends come from the point end of brisket. After smoking the whole thing, the fatty and perfectly charred tip is removed from the flat and cut into chunks of about 1 inch.

Toss the chunks with barbecue sauce (see page 457 for a list of sauces in the book). Some cooks make them quite saucy, then put them in a foil pan and back on the grill to smoke for an hour or more, until dark and caramelized. But you can also lightly coat them, throw them into a perforated grill pan, and set them right over the fire. Close the lid, stay nearby, and turn them as needed to let them develop a crust without drying out. Any way you burn 'em, they're amazing—on their own, on a bun, in a taco, scrambled with eggs, turned into hash, or added to a pot with beans (see Smoked Beans with Burnt Ends and Drippings, page 391).

D direct fire   I indirect fire   M make ahead   V vegetarian option

The Real Deal Burger with Fiery Ketchup

Makes: 4 burgers or 8 to 10 sliders	Time: 25 to 30 minutes	Ⓓ Ⓜ

A burger needs only three things: good and slightly fatty meat, gentle handling, and quick cooking. For more about grinding your own meat—which is easy and allows you to use better-quality cuts—see " Do-It-Yourself Ground Meat" on page 260. I suppose a burger also needs something to eat it on and with, and for that you're on your own, though a hot sauce–spiked ketchup is a good place to start.

1½ pounds not-too-lean sirloin or chuck, cut into 1-inch chunks, or good-quality preground beef

½ white onion, cut into chunks (optional)

Salt and pepper

½ cup ketchup (to make your own, see page 462)

1 tablespoon hot sauce, or to taste

4 hamburger buns or 8–10 slider buns (like potato or dinner rolls), split

Sliced red onion for serving (optional)

Sliced tomatoes for serving (optional)

1 Start the coals or heat a gas grill for hot direct cooking. Make sure the grates are clean.

2 If grinding your own, put the meat and white onion, if you're using it, in a food processor; work in batches if your machine is small. Sprinkle with salt and pepper and pulse until coarsely ground—finer than chopped, but not much. If you're starting with preground meat, mince the onion and incorporate it into the meat.

3 Cook up a spoonful in a small skillet to taste it; adjust the seasoning. Handling the meat as little as possible to avoid compressing it, shape it lightly into 4 burgers, 1 to 1½ inches thick, or 8 to 10 sliders. Whisk the ketchup and hot sauce together in a small bowl. (You can form the burgers and prepare the ketchup several hours in advance; cover and refrigerate until you're ready to grill.)

4 Put the burgers on the grill directly over the fire. Close the lid and cook until one stage shy of the doneness you want, 3 to 7 minutes per side, depending on their size and how well done you want them; the carryover heat will finish the job. Nick with a small knife and peek inside to check.

5 Transfer to a platter. Put the buns cut side down on the grill to toast. Serve the burgers on the toasted buns with the ketchup, red onion, and tomato on the side for topping.

● recipe continues →

Guac Burger	Avocado makes everything better: Omit the ketchup. In Step 3, halve and pit 1 large ripe avocado, scoop the flesh from the skin into a bowl, and mash. Add 2 tablespoons chopped red onion, the juice of ½ lemon or more, and some hot sauce; stir to mix. To serve, top each grilled burger with guacamole and garnish with a dollop of sour cream.
Pancetta Burger with Easy Onion Jam	Forgo the traditional bacon burger for pancetta—thinly sliced, it'll cook up fast on the grill: Omit the ketchup and hot sauce. Make a recipe of Easy Onion Jam (page 433). While the burgers are grilling, put 8 thin slices pancetta around the edge of the fire and grill, turning occasionally until they are crisp. To serve, top each burger with 2 slices pancetta and a spoonful of jam.
Hoisin Burger with Scallion Mayo	Savory and cooling all at once: Substitute mayonnaise for the ketchup and 3 scallions, trimmed and minced, for the hot sauce; stir in 1 tablespoon fresh lime juice. Sear the burgers for 2 minutes on one side, turn, brush the tops with hoisin sauce, and sear for another 2 minutes. Turn and brush with hoisin twice more as you finish cooking the burgers to your preferred doneness.

10 WAYS TO FLAVOR KETCHUP

Good-quality store-bought ketchup pairs amazingly well with lots of different flavors. Add any of these to ¼ cup ketchup. And you can certainly try mixing and matching.

1. 1 tablespoon pesto (it sounds bizarre but it is so good)
2. 1 tablespoon soy sauce
3. 1 tablespoon hoisin sauce
4. Grated zest of 1 lemon or lime
5. 1 tablespoon minced garlic, fresh ginger, or pickled ginger
6. Any kind of hot sauce, minced fresh chile, or pure chile powder to taste
7. Mustard to taste; try hot Chinese mustard—the sweetness of the ketchup is a great foil for the searing heat of the mustard
8. Grated fresh or prepared horseradish to taste; add lemon juice to taste and you have cocktail sauce
9. 1 tablespoon each peanut butter or tahini and water: instant sweet satay sauce
10. 2 tablespoons mayonnaise and 1 tablespoon chopped pickles: Thousand Island!

D direct fire **I** indirect fire **M** make ahead **V** vegetarian option

Green Chile Cheeseburgers

Makes: 4 burgers or 8 to 10 sliders	Time: 20 to 25 minutes	Ⓓ Ⓜ

In New Mexico, where this burger is ubiquitous, flat green chiles from the Hatch Valley are the first choice. They're flavorful with mellow, herbal heat, not blow-your-head-off hot. Anaheim and poblano chiles are common replacements, though they can be milder—Hatch chiles are increasingly easy to find. But use whatever heat level you like.

Put the chiles on the grill while it heats so that they're roasted by the time you're ready to cook the burgers. Though it's not traditional, I like to also add extra chili flavor to the meat. As for the cheese, American is the most common on this burger in Southwestern restaurants. But I just can't. A sharp white cheddar, or a Mexican melting cheese like asadero or Chihuahua, is so much better.

2 Anaheim chiles

2 poblano chiles

1½ pounds not-too-lean sirloin or chuck, cut into 1-inch chunks, or good-quality preground beef

½ white onion, cut into chunks (optional)

Salt and pepper

1 teaspoon chili powder

4 ounces grated or thinly sliced cheese (see the headnote)

4 hamburger buns, split, or 8–10 slider buns (like potato or dinner rolls)

1 Start the coals or heat a gas grill for hot direct cooking. Make sure the grates are clean. Put the chiles on the grill directly over the fire as it heats up. Roast the chiles until they are blackened on all sides. Transfer to a bowl and put a plate or lid over it.

2 If grinding your own, put the meat and white onion, if you're using it, in a food processor; work in batches if your machine is small. Sprinkle with salt, pepper, and the chili powder and pulse until coarsely ground—finer than chopped, but not much. (If you're starting with preground meat, mince the onion and incorporate it into the meat.)

3 Cook up a spoonful in a small skillet to taste it; adjust the seasoning. Handling the meat as little as possible to avoid compressing it, shape it lightly into 4 burgers, 1 to 1½ inches thick, or 8 to 10 sliders.

4 When the chiles are cool enough to handle, remove the skins and cut off the stems. You can seed them or leave the seeds in for some extra heat. Chop the chiles. (You can form the burgers and prepare the chiles several hours in advance; keep separate, cover, and refrigerate.)

5 Put the burgers on the grill directly over the fire. Close the lid and cook, turning once, until one stage shy of the doneness you want them, 3 to 7 minutes per side, depending on their size and how well done you want them; the carryover heat will finish the job. (Nick with a small knife and peek inside.) For the last minute or so, divide the chiles between the burgers and top with cheese.

6 Transfer to a platter. Put the buns cut side down on the grill to toast. Serve the burgers on the toasted buns.

• recipe continues →

Molten Blue Cheese Burger	Get your cheese fix from the inside out: Omit the chiles and chili powder. In Step 3, form each burger around a 1-inch chunk of blue cheese.
Make-Your-Own-Pimento-Cheese Burger	Take your burger for a Southern stroll: Omit the chiles and chili powder. Instead of the grated or sliced cheese, combine ½ cup grated extra sharp cheddar cheese and ¼ cup mayonnaise. Drain half of a 4-ounce jar of pimentos and add them along with ¼ teaspoon Worcestershire sauce and a little salt and pepper. Top each burger with a dollop of pimento cheese when it comes off the grill.
Reuben Burger	A decadent mess: Omit the chiles and chili powder, and use thinly sliced Swiss cheese. Whisk together 6 tablespoons mayonnaise, 2 tablespoons each ketchup and chopped dill pickle, and 1 tablespoon Dijon mustard in a small bowl. Drain about 1 cup sauerkraut. After you turn the burgers, top each with several tablespoons of the sauerkraut, then a slice of Swiss. Finish the burgers with a dollop of the dressing.

12 MIX-AND-MATCH IDEAS FOR FLAVORING BURGERS

Burgers don't need more than salt and pepper, but they'll respond enthusiastically to all sorts of flavors. Try incorporating some of the following into the ground meat mixture, combining them as you like.

1. 2 tablespoons minced fresh parsley, basil, chives, chervil, or other herbs
2. 1 teaspoon minced garlic or 2 cloves Grill-Roasted Garlic (page 464), mashed, or to taste
3. 1 tablespoon minced anchovies
4. 1 tablespoon minced fresh ginger or 1 teaspoon ground ginger
5. 1 tablespoon soy sauce, Worcestershire, steak, or other flavored sauce
6. ¼ cup minced shallot or scallions
7. 1 teaspoon Tabasco or other hot sauce, or to taste
8. 1 teaspoon curry powder, chili powder, or other spice mixture, or to taste
9. Up to ½ cup grated or crumbled cheese (like Parmesan, cheddar, blue, or feta)
10. 1 cup cooked spinach or other greens, squeezed dry and chopped
11. 1 tablespoon ground dried porcini mushrooms (do this in a spice grinder; it's about equivalent to a 3.5-ounce packet of dried mushrooms) or ½ cup reconstituted porcini, chopped
12. 1 tablespoon freshly grated horseradish or prepared horseradish, or more to taste

D direct fire   I indirect fire   M make ahead   V vegetarian option

DO-IT-YOURSELF GROUND MEAT

I'm a longtime advocate of grinding your own meat—beef, pork, lamb, as well as seafood and poultry. When you buy commercially raised and sold meat labeled "ground beef," you have no idea what you're getting. Huge quantities are ground from anonymous cuts from different animals. If that doesn't give you pause, consider the health concerns: Preground meat carries the risk of salmonella and *E. coli* contamination, which has caused many authorities to recommend cooking burgers to the well-done stage. And to that I say: Why bother?

Labels like "Ground sirloin, 85% lean" and "Ground chuck, 90% lean" are one notch improved: At least you know the cut and the fat content, absolutely crucial for a juicy burger or meat loaf. And I can't argue much with ground meat bought directly from a reliable farmer, meat locker, or butcher.

Still, when you grind your own you know exactly what you're getting. You don't even need a meat grinder—though if you have one, use it! A food processor makes quick work of grinding: Start with a nice-looking chuck roast, or a couple well-marbled sirloin steaks, some pork or lamb shoulder, or boneless chicken thighs. Cut the meat into 1- to 2-inch chunks and pulse in the food processor until chopped. A 12-cup food processor can handle a pound or so at a time; if you have a smaller machine, work in batches. You can do extra and freeze what you won't use immediately, or you can grind the meat as you need it.

Buy relatively fatty meat; you're going to have to eyeball the percentages (unless you trim and weigh fat and lean separately and do the math). If you start with meat that's 95 percent lean—that's hardly any fat at all—you are going to get the filet mignon of burgers: tender but not especially tasty. Typical chuck or sirloin, with 15 to 20 percent fat, will deliver flavorful meat with good texture and moisture. More than that veers into decadence. For pork and lamb choose naturally fatty cuts like shoulder. Boneless thighs and legs are the only sensible choices for ground poultry; include a little of the skin if you like (and be sure to cook the meat all the way through).

Stick to short bursts of pulsing or you'll overprocess; you want chopped meat, not a purée. The finer the grind, the grainier the texture and the more likely you'll be to pack it together too tightly and make the burger tough.

For the same reason, handle the meat minimally and gently when shaping burgers: With a light hand, form about 6 ounces meat into one burger, 1 to 1½ inches thick. At no time—before, during, or after cooking—should you press down on a burger with a spatula like a short-order cook.

Finally, season aggressively: I'd start with a large pinch of salt and work up from there. To taste, you can cook up a spoonful of the raw meat in a skillet, then make adjustments as necessary. For some ideas about how to season and flavor your burger (or meat loaf) meat, see the list on page 258.

Bacon-Wrapped Chipotle Meat Loaf

| Makes: 6 to 8 servings | Time: 1½ to 2 hours, largely unattended | Ⓘ Ⓜ |

Everything changes when you cook meat loaf on the grill. It develops a crust all over, stays tender and juicy all the way through, and takes on that signature grilled flavor. If you're cooking on a charcoal grill, add wood if you like but it's not necessary; for gas grillers, I recommend an hour or so of smoke at the beginning of the cook time (see "Smoking," pages 10–12). Equal parts beef, pork, and veal is the classic meat combination. Over the years I've also used all lamb, all beef, all pork, and a mix of beef and pork; to grind your own, see opposite. You can change the flavor of the meat mixture using the ideas in "12 Mix-and-Match Ideas for Flavoring Burgers" on page 258.

½ cup bread crumbs (preferably fresh)

½ cup milk

1 egg, lightly beaten

2 tablespoons canned chipotle chiles mashed with some of the adobo, or to taste

1 tablespoon minced garlic

2 pounds ground meat (see the headnote)

½ cup minced onion

½ cup minced carrot

Salt and pepper

3 or 4 slices bacon

1 Start the coals or heat a gas grill for medium-high indirect cooking. If using charcoal, put a drip pan under the indirect side of the grill; for gas, empty, clean, and replace the fat trap.

2 Line a baking sheet with a piece of tin foil. Put the bread crumbs and milk in a large bowl; let sit until the crumbs have absorbed the milk, about 5 minutes. Stir in the egg, mashed chipotles, and garlic. Add the meat, onion, carrot, and some salt and pepper and mix gently with your hands until just combined.

3 Transfer the meat to the center of the prepared pan and shape into a loaf shorter and narrower than the drip pan, 1½ to 2 inches high. Top with the bacon, placing the strips so they run the length of the loaf. (You can prepare the loaf up to several hours in advance; cover and refrigerate until you're ready to grill; cook time will be 10 to 15 minutes longer.)

4 Slide the foil sheet with the meat loaf onto the indirect side of the grill; if using charcoal and a drip pan, make sure the drippings will land in the pan. Close the lid and cook until the internal temperature in the center of the loaf registers 160°F, 1 to 2 hours. About halfway through, use two spatulas to turn the loaf; move or rotate it if needed for even cooking. Start checking the temperature at 1 hour.

5 Transfer to a platter or cutting board and let rest 5 to 10 minutes before slicing.

• recipe continues →

Eat Your Greens Meat Loaf	Omit the chipotles. Bring a large pot of water to a boil and salt it. Trim away the thick stems and rinse 10 ounces fresh spinach; blanch for 30 seconds, then drain, rinse under cold running water, squeeze completely dry, and chop; sprinkle with salt, pepper, and a little freshly grated nutmeg. Increase the bread crumbs to 1 cup. Add the spinach along with the meat.
Meat Loaf with Ginger, Garlic, and Cilantro	Omit the chipotles. Increase the garlic to 2 tablespoons and add 1 tablespoon each soy sauce, sriracha, and minced fresh ginger with the garlic. Substitute minced scallions for the onion and add ¼ cup minced fresh cilantro.
Chipotle Turkey or Chicken Loaf	Substitute ground dark meat turkey or chicken for the meat and turkey bacon for the regular bacon. Since turkey bacon is shorter than pork bacon, you may find it works better to put the strips across the loaf instead of along its length; it might take a couple extra pieces to cover the loaf.

D direct fire I indirect fire M make ahead V vegetarian option

Balkan-Style Beef Sausages with Kajmak

Makes: 4 servings	Time: 50 to 60 minutes	Ⓓ Ⓜ

In the Balkans, these popular grilled finger-shaped sausages are called *ćevapi*, from the Persian word for "kebab." Made from minced meat, they're the Eastern European evolution of the skewered meat tradition and have subregional variations. They're usually served with flatbread, a refreshing, creamy spread known as *kajmak*, and *ajvar*, a delicious purée of grill-roasted red peppers and eggplant.

I've simplified this so you can assemble all the components easily: Grilling the sausages right on the grate saves putting them on and off skewers. (Use flat metal skewers if you decide to be more authentic; spinning sausages on round ones will drive you nuts.) The sauce is a shortcut. If you don't have time to make *ajvar*, it's not the end of the world. But don't skip the baking soda and lemon juice—important for a juicy sausage.

You can serve these with buttered bulgur or rice, or spend the time you saved making Naan (page 488) or Lebanese Flatbread (page 490), spread them with *kajmak* and *ajvar*, top with the sliced *ćevapi*, and fold to eat.

4 ounces cream cheese, softened

2 tablespoons butter, softened

¼ cup sour cream

Salt and pepper

Ajvar (page 35; optional)

1 teaspoon baking soda

1 teaspoon fresh lemon juice

1½ pounds ground beef (to grind your own, see page 260; or use preground)

½ cup minced onion

1 tablespoon minced garlic

1 teaspoon smoked paprika (pimentón)

1 Earlier in the day or even a day or two before, make the *kajmak:* Stir the cream cheese and butter together in a small bowl until smooth, then stir in the sour cream and a sprinkle of salt. Refrigerate in an airtight container until you're ready to serve. Make the *ajvar* if you're using it.

2 Put the baking soda and lemon juice in a large bowl and let it bubble for a minute or 2. Add the beef, onion, garlic, paprika, at least 1 teaspoon pepper, and some salt and work gently with your hands until just combined.

3 Pinch a golf ball–sized piece of the meat mixture in your hand and gently squeeze it into a sausage 3 to 3½ inches long and about 1 inch thick. Repeat with the remaining meat, putting them on a platter without touching. Cover with plastic wrap and refrigerate while you prepare the grill, or for up to a day.

4 Start the coals or heat a gas grill for medium-high direct cooking. Make sure the grates are clean.

recipe continues →

5 Put the sausages on the grill directly over the fire, on an angle or perpendicular to the grate. Close the lid and cook, turning them every 1 to 2 minutes for even browning, until crusty and just cooked through; this can take at least 5 and up to 15 minutes total, depending on their size.

6 Transfer to a clean platter and serve, passing the *kajmak* and *ajvar* at the table.

Balkan-Style Beef and Lamb Sausages	I heartily endorse this common alternative combination: Substitute ground lamb (ideally from the shoulder or leg) for half the ground beef.
Romanian Beef Sausages (*Mici* or *Mititei*)	This popular street food is traditionally served with mustard and crusty bread, with French fries on the side: Omit the *kajmak*, *ajvar*, and onion. Increase the garlic to 2 tablespoons, use sweet paprika instead of smoked, and add 1 teaspoon dried summer savory and ½ teaspoon each ground allspice, cumin, and coriander to the meat mixture; season with salt and pepper.
Italian-Style Beef Spiedini with Pecorino and Prosciutto	Omit the *kajmak*, *ajvar*, onion, and paprika. Add 4 ounces minced prosciutto (or grind it with the meat if you're going that route), ¼ cup grated pecorino Romano cheese, and 2 tablespoons minced fresh rosemary.

Grilled Beef or Calf's Liver

| Makes: **4 servings** | Time: **20 to 25 minutes** | Ⓓ |

I'm guessing more people would like liver if they tried it grilled medium-rare and not dry and overcooked. Cooked with restraint it's delicious, rich, dense, and as tender as any meat there is. Serve with grilled onions (page 433) or scallions (page 437). You can also use this recipe for lamb's or pig's liver.

1–1½ pounds beef or calf's liver

Salt and pepper

Lemon wedges for serving

1 Start the coals or heat a gas grill for medium direct cooking. Make sure the grates are clean.

2 If necessary, slice the liver lengthwise into slices about ½ inch thick. Pat the slices dry with paper towels, then sprinkle with salt and pepper on both sides.

3 Put the liver on the grill directly over the fire. Close the lid and cook, turning when the slices release easily, until the outside browns on both sides and the center is cooked to one stage shy of the preferred doneness, 1 to 4 minutes per side, depending on how well done you like it.

4 Transfer to a platter, let rest for 5 minutes, then cut across into slices and serve with lemon wedges.

Lamb's Liver with Cumin and Smoked Paprika	Lamb's liver is more strongly flavored than beef or calf's liver. You're likely to find it sold whole, not in slices like calf's liver: Peel away any remaining membranes and cut out any veins, then cut in half lengthwise. Stir 1 teaspoon each smoked paprika (pimentón), ground cumin, and salt and ¼ teaspoon black pepper together in a small bowl. Sprinkle the slices on both sides with the spice mix, then grill as directed.
Soy-Lime Marinated Liver	Whisk ¼ cup each soy sauce and fresh lime juice, 2 tablespoons each chopped garlic and turbinado sugar, and 1 tablespoon chopped fresh ginger in a large, shallow bowl. Add the liver slices and turn them in the marinade to coat. Refrigerate for at least 1 hour or overnight before grilling as directed. Garnish with chopped fresh cilantro and serve with lime wedges.
Liver Kebabs	This is a popular way to prepare liver and other offal cuts in South America and Asia. In Morocco they're made from lamb and the pieces are wrapped in caul fat before skewering and grilling: Cut the liver into 1- to 1½-inch cubes and season or marinate using one of the variations above. Thread onto skewers and grill 2 to 4 minutes total, turning as often as you can. Serve with lemon or lime wedges.

Smoked Tongue

| Makes: 3 to 4 servings | Time: 4½ hours, largely unattended, plus overnight chilling | Ⓘ Ⓜ |

Maybe you don't think tongue is for you, but done this way it's truly amazing. It's not labor free but the work is intermittent, leaving you free to cook sides or entertain guests. I like hickory smoke for this, and an hour is plenty of time to make a meaningful contribution to the flavor. Enjoy the tongue thinly sliced on a baguette, with mustard and cornichons.

1 beef tongue (1½–2 pounds)

1 onion, quartered

4 cloves garlic, peeled

10 black peppercorns

2 bay leaves

1 tablespoon salt

1 Put all the ingredients in a large pot and cover generously with water. Bring to a boil, lower the heat to a gentle bubble, and cook until a knife inserted in the thickest part of the tongue goes in with little or no resistance, 2 to 3 hours. Add more water if needed to keep the tongue covered.

2 Drain, let cool to the point you can handle it, and remove the skin; it should peel off easily. Cool to room temperature, then cover and refrigerate overnight.

3 Start the coals or heat a gas grill for medium-low to low indirect cooking. If using a charcoal grill, position the coals so the smoke will be pulled over the tongue and out the top vent. Make sure the grates are clean. When the grill is ready, add wood to the fire (see "Smoking," pages 10–12).

4 When the grill fills with smoke, put the tongue on the indirect side of the grill. Close the lid and cook until the internal temperature at the thickest point registers 135° to 140°F, 2 to 2½ hours, keeping the grill temperature between 225° and 275°F. Replenish the wood as needed to keep the grill filled with smoke for the first hour.

5 Transfer the tongue to a cutting board. You can slice it and enjoy warm, or let it cool to room temperature and slice or refrigerate to eat cold.

Smoked Tongue Sandwich with Caper-Dijon Mayo and Pickled Red Onions	Better than any deli sandwich! In Step 1, while the tongue is cooking, put ½ cup rice vinegar, 3 tablespoons sugar, and ½ teaspoon salt in a small saucepan; bring to a simmer, stirring until the sugar dissolves. Remove from the heat. Cut a small red onion in half, then into thin half-moons. Pull the pieces apart into a heatproof bowl. Pour over the hot vinegar mixture and stir to coat fully. Let cool, then refrigerate overnight. In Step 3, while the tongue smokes, whisk together ½ cup mayonnaise, 2 tablespoons chopped capers, 1 tablespoon Dijon mustard, and salt and pepper to taste in a small bowl. Spread slices of rye bread with the mayo, pile on the sliced tongue, top with drained red onions, and serve.
Sliced Tongue with Ponzu Sauce	Grilled, not smoked: Make Ponzu Sauce (page 468). After simmering and chilling the tongue overnight, slice it as thinly as you can and layer it in a large baking dish. As you layer the slices, pour over about ½ cup of the ponzu sauce, making sure the slices are coated on both sides. Let the tongue marinate while you prepare a hot direct fire. Put the tongue on the grill directly over the fire. Even if you're grilling with gas, don't bother to close the lid. By the time you get all the slices on, it will be time to turn the first slices; cook them for only 1 to 2 minutes per side. Transfer to a platter as they finish. Serve with lettuce leaves for wrapping and the remaining ponzu sauce for dipping.
Tacos de Lengua	No need to smoke the tongue, though you certainly can and use it like that. Or after simmering and chilling, cut it into ½-inch slices, brush them lightly with a good-quality vegetable oil, and season with salt and pepper. Sear the slices over a hot direct fire, turning once, until they get crusty, 3 to 4 minutes per side. Transfer to a cutting board and roughly chop. Serve in warm corn tortillas with lots of chopped fresh cilantro, fresh salsa, guacamole, and lime wedges.

Smoked Bologna

Makes: 4 to 6 servings	Time: 1 to 1½ hours, largely unattended	Ⓘ Ⓜ

No joke—this is good. In places like Nashville, this is a common sight: a chub of bologna scored in a crosshatch pattern, hit with a powerful seasoning, and smoked with hickory or oak until the color of black coffee. Since the bologna is already cooked, the idea is to just heat it through and infuse it with smoke. And there is no need to invest in an entire stick of bologna if you don't want to; you can have the counterperson at the deli cut a big chunk.

1 1½-pound chunk beef bologna

2 tablespoons golden mustard

1 tablespoon honey

1 Start the coals or heat a gas grill for medium-low indirect cooking. If using a charcoal grill, position the coals so the smoke will be pulled over the bologna and out the top vent. Make sure the grates are clean. When the grill temperature is at 300°F, add wood to the fire (see "Smoking," pages 10–12).

2 While the grill comes to temperature, peel off the outer protective skin of the bologna (if it has one; not all do). With a sharp knife, score the bologna on all sides about ½ to 1 inch deep in a crosshatch pattern. (This will increase the surface area exposed to the mustard glaze and the smoke.) Combine the mustard and honey in a small bowl and stir until smooth, then spread all over the bologna, being sure to work it down into all the cuts.

3 When the grill fills with smoke, put the bologna on the indirect side of the grill. Close the lid and cook until the bologna darkens considerably from the smoke and it has the strength of smoke flavor you want, rotating it after 30 minutes to cook evenly. Once it's been on the grill 30 minutes, brush it with the glaze again, then every 15 minutes or so. An hour of smoke is usually sufficient; cut a piece off to test it. To get the glaze crusty, you can move the bologna directly over the fire before taking it off the grill, turning it every 1 to 2 minutes as needed. Transfer to a cutting board and enjoy hot, warm, or at room temperature cut into pieces or slices. Or let cool entirely, cover with plastic wrap, and refrigerate for up to 5 days.

Ⓓ direct fire Ⓘ indirect fire Ⓜ make ahead Ⓥ vegetarian option

Crispy Smoked Bologna Sandwich	The classic way to eat smoked bologna is to cut it into ½-inch slices, put them back on the grill directly over the fire to char at the edges, then enjoy between two slices of white bread slathered with more mustard. But after going to the trouble of smoking it, I want a little more: For each sandwich, grill 2 slices bologna. Spread a slice of country bread with equal amounts of mayonnaise and mustard, add a slice of Gruyère cheese, the bologna, and 1 or 2 thin tomato slices; top with the other slice of bread. Butter the bread on the outside and pop back on the grill over medium direct heat, turning once, until the sandwich crisps and browns and the cheese has melted, 2 to 4 minutes per side.
Smoked Bologna Bits with Pepper Jelly Mayo	Mouths will hang open in disbelief until they taste these babies. I like to serve this while the bologna is still warm: After smoking the bologna, cut it into 1-inch cubes. Whisk together ¼ cup mayonnaise and 3 tablespoons (or to taste) pepper jelly in a small bowl. Put the cubes on a serving plate along with the mayonnaise and toothpicks.
Smoked Bologna Salad with Red Onion and Tomatoes	Cut the smoked bologna into ½-inch slices, then into 2-inch strips; you want about 2 cups. Halve and thinly slice a small red onion. Cut 2 fresh tomatoes into wedges. Tear ½ cup fresh mint leaves. Whisk ¼ cup good-quality olive oil, 2 tablespoons fresh lime juice, and a little salt and pepper together in a salad bowl. Add the bologna, onion, tomatoes, and mint. Toss, taste, and adjust the seasonings. Serve over iceberg wedges if you like.

Veal Chops with
Grill-Fried Sage Leaves and
Crisp Broccoli (page 394)

Simply Seared Veal Chops

Makes: 4 servings	Time: 25 to 30 minutes	Ⓓ

Excellent veal chops are an indulgence, so keep it simple with salt and pepper and savor the meat. A last-minute squeeze of lemon is a perfect foil to the flavor from the grill. If you aren't prepared to eat veal chops medium-rare to medium, then you're probably better off trying this using bone-in center-cut pork chops, cooked until faintly pink in the middle—the final internal temperature in the center when it hits your plate should be 145°F—or veal shoulder chops. Shoulder chops are thinner and chewier (and much less expensive than loin or rib chops) but still very tasty. They are quite large, up a pound, and one is enough for 2 people. They can be cut apart into two pieces—one boneless, one bone-in—and only take 1 to 2 minutes per side on a hot grill.

4 veal loin or rib chops (about 1 inch thick, 12–16 ounces each)

Salt and pepper

Lemon wedges for serving

1 Start the coals or heat a gas grill for hot direct cooking. Make sure the grates are clean.

2 Pat the chops dry with paper towels. Sprinkle with salt and pepper on both sides.

3 Put the chops on the grill directly over the fire. Close the lid and cook, turning once, to one stage shy of the desired doneness (see page 220). For medium-rare, 4 to 5 minutes per side; an instant-read thermometer should register 135°F.

4 Transfer to a platter and let sit about 5 minutes, checking the temperature occasionally. When the chops are ready, serve right away with lemon wedges.

Veal Chops with Grill-Fried Sage Leaves	Super simple but adds so much flavor and looks beautiful: Brush both sides of the chops with good-quality olive oil; you'll need about 1 tablespoon per chop. Cover the meaty part of each chop on both sides with fresh sage leaves in a single layer, pressing them so they stick to the oil; depending on the size of the chop and the leaves, for each side you could need 3 to 8 leaves. Brush the leaves with oil. When you turn the chops, do it carefully so the sage leaves come along with the chops.
Veal Chops with Rosemary and Sherry Vinegar	Right before you prepare the fire, whisk together ½ cup good-quality olive oil and 2 tablespoons each sherry vinegar and fresh rosemary leaves in a small bowl. Put the chops in a large, shallow baking dish and pour the oil over them; turn to coat them completely. Proceed with the recipe.
Veal Chops with Classic Gremolata	The traditional accompaniment to braised veal shanks is a tasty topper for grilled chops: Omit the lemon wedges and instead serve the chops garnished with Classic Gremolata (page 476) and a drizzle of olive oil.

Pomegranate-Honey Pork Tenderloin

Makes: **4 servings**	Time: **25 to 35 minutes**	Ⓓ

Pork tenderloin is lower in fat than any other cut of pork, and is not the most flavorful, so an assertive glaze can work wonders. The cooking time is extremely short—and the leftovers make fantastic sandwiches. This glaze works for any cut of pork, and is also nice with lamb, chicken, and salmon. If you can't find pomegranate molasses, simmer 1 cup unsweetened pomegranate juice until it becomes syrupy and use a tablespoon or two of that instead.

1½ pounds pork tenderloin, trimmed of excess fat and silverskin (see page 245)

Salt and pepper

2 tablespoons honey

1 tablespoon pomegranate molasses

2 teaspoons soy sauce

1 teaspoon sugar

Juice of ½ lime

1 Start the coals or heat a gas grill for medium-high direct cooking. Make sure the grates are clean.

2 Pat the meat dry with paper towels. Sprinkle with salt and pepper on all sides. Whisk the honey, pomegranate molasses, soy sauce, sugar, and lime juice in a small bowl, taste, and adjust the seasoning with salt.

3 Put the tenderloin on the grill directly over the fire. Close the lid and sear for 3 minutes. Turn the pork, brush the seared side with the glaze, close the lid, and let the other side sear for 3 minutes. Turn and brush with the glaze. Continue to turn and brush with the glaze every few minutes until the internal temperature at the thickest point is 135° to 140°F, another 10 to 20 minutes, depending on its thickness and how hot the fire is. If the glaze browns too much, move the tenderloin to the outside edge of the fire or turn the heat down.

4 When the pork is done, transfer it to a cutting board, and let rest until the internal temperature rises to 145°F. Cut across into slices and serve.

Sesame-Honey Pork Tenderloin	Substitute sesame oil for the pomegranate molasses and use the juice from the entire lime. Garnish with toasted sesame seeds and chopped chives if you like.
Mustard-Curry Pork Tenderloin	For the glaze, replace the honey, pomegranate molasses, soy sauce, sugar, and lime juice with 2 tablespoons Dijon mustard and 1 tablespoon curry powder.
Miso-Rubbed Pork Tenderloin	Omit the glaze. Instead, rub the tenderloin with ¼ cup white, yellow, or red miso.

Ⓓ direct fire　　Ⓘ indirect fire　　Ⓜ make ahead　　Ⓥ vegetarian option

Bacon-Wrapped Pork Medallions

Makes: 4 servings	Time: 25 to 30 minutes	D M

Grilling pork tenderloin as medallions increases the surface area you can expose to seasoning or glaze and to the fire. Another strategy is to take a cue from filet mignon—the corresponding cut of beef—and wrap the side of each medallion with a strip of bacon. To give the bacon some time to crisp, it's best to cook these over a slightly cooler fire than I normally use for pork tenderloin. These are fantastic the next day, eaten cold straight from the refrigerator or brought to room temperature.

1½ pounds pork tenderloin, trimmed of excess fat and silverskin (see page 245)

Salt and pepper

8 ounces sliced bacon

1 Start the coals or heat a gas grill for medium direct cooking. Make sure the grates are clean.

2 Pat the meat dry with paper towels. Sprinkle with salt and pepper on all sides.

3 Cut the tenderloin across into medallions so that their thickness matches the width of the bacon slices. Pat dry with paper towels and sprinkle with salt and pepper on both sides. Wrap a piece of bacon around the outside of the medallion and secure it with a toothpick. Repeat for the remaining medallions. Or you can secure the bacon by running two skewers parallel through the medallions, with several medallions on each pair of skewers.

4 Put the medallions on the grill directly over the fire. Close the lid and cook until the bacon has browned and the pork is slightly pink in the center (an internal temperature of 140°F), 10 to 15 minutes total, turning the medallions every few minutes so the bacon cooks evenly. If the bacon starts to darken too quickly, move the medallions to the outside edge of the fire.

5 Transfer to a platter, let rest about 5 minutes, until the internal temperature rises to 145°F. Serve.

Prosciutto-Wrapped Pork Medallions	An Italian twist on the pork-on-pork theme: Substitute thinly sliced prosciutto for the bacon (you'll need much less, just 3 or 4 ounces) and cut the slices in half lengthwise. Since the prosciutto is already cooked, you can use a hotter fire if you like, up to medium-high. If you do, the medallions will cook through a couple of minutes faster. And no need to turn the medallions as often; once is fine.
Bacon-Wrapped Pork Medallions with Honey-Dijon Glaze	These are hot, sweet, and spicy all at once: Whisk ¼ cup each Dijon mustard and honey together in a small bowl. Use this to brush the outsides before wrapping. Sear the first side for 3 minutes, then turn and brush the top with the glaze. Sear the other side for 3 minutes, then turn and brush with the glaze. Cook each side another 2 minutes, turn, and glaze one more time, then finish cooking as directed.
Lemon-Pepper Bacon-Wrapped Pork Medallions	Kick it up by marinating the medallions and using a seasoned bacon: Before you prepare the fire, toss the medallions in a mixture of ¼ cup lemon juice, 1 teaspoon each lemon zest and black pepper, and a little salt. Marinate at room temperature while the grill heats. Lightly pat dry with paper towels and wrap each with a strip of pepper bacon. Proceed with the recipe.

Grill-Roasted Pork Loin

Makes: 4 servings	Time: 60 to 85 minutes, largely unattended	Ⓘ

Pork roasts of all kinds are terrific on the grill, and the loin is a good example of how less can be more. If you get one that's relatively evenly shaped, you don't even have to tie it.

1 boneless pork loin (2½–3 pounds)

Salt and pepper

1 Start the coals or heat a gas grill for medium to medium-high indirect cooking. Make sure the grates are clean. If using charcoal, put a drip pan under the indirect portion of the grill; for gas, empty, clean, and replace the fat trap.

2 Trim excess surface fat from the pork if you like; if you like the fat a little on the thick side, slash it in a crosshatch pattern almost to the meat so the fat can melt faster. Sprinkle with salt and pepper on all sides.

3 Put the loin, fat side up, on the indirect side of the grill with the long side facing the fire. Close the lid. Start checking the temperature after about 30 minutes, and turn, move, and rotate the loin as needed for even cooking. Cook until the internal temperature at the center is 135° to 140°F, 45 to 70 minutes total depending on the diameter of the roast and how hot the fire is. If it hasn't browned by the time the inside is ready, move it directly over the fire and let it brown for a minute or 2 on all sides.

4 Transfer to a cutting board and let rest until the internal temperature reaches 145°F, then cut into ½-inch or thicker slices and serve.

Pork Loin with Balsamic-Honey Glaze	You can glaze larger roasts, too, just later in the game so the glaze doesn't burn: Whisk together 2 tablespoons each balsamic vinegar and honey in a small bowl. Season and cook the pork as directed. When the internal temperature hits 125°F, start brushing the loin on all sides with glaze every 5 minutes or so.
Tarragon-Lemon Pork Loin with Dijon	Another way to flavor pork loin is to work an herb paste into the meat, then glaze: Mince together 1/4 cup fresh tarragon leaves, 3 cloves garlic, and the grated zest of 1 lemon until a paste forms. Use a paring knife to cut slits all over the pork loin. Stuff the paste into the slits, then brush the loin with a mixture of 2 tablespoons Dijon mustard and 1 tablespoon mayonnaise. Grill as directed.
Rack of Pork with Lime-Ancho Grill Salt	Also known as a pork rib roast, this is the equivalent of a standing beef rib roast. And it's spectacular grilled: Substitute 1 rack of pork with 4 ribs (about 4 pounds) for the boneless pork loin; have the butcher cut through the chine bone so you will be able to cut between the ribs when it is done. Instead of seasoning with salt and pepper, rub the roast all over with a mixture of 1 teaspoon each salt and ancho chile powder and the grated zest of 1 lime. Put the rack on the grill with the bone side facing the fire (the meat closest the bone takes longer to cook, so doing this will help even out the cooking time). Cook time will be longer, 1 to 1 1/2 hours; toward the end check the temperature in multiple spots. After resting, cut the loin from the ribs and slice. Cut the ribs apart. Serve the sliced pork and ribs with lime wedges.

Thin-Cut Coconut Pork Chops with Pickled Vegetables

Makes: 4 to 6 servings	Time: 50 to 55 minutes, plus chilling time	Ⓓ Ⓜ

In Cambodia, there's a popular breakfast dish called *bai sach chrouk,* traditionally prepared over charcoal fires by roadside vendors. It's served with rice and a bird's nest of pickled shredded vegetables, and stands at the intersection of sweet, sour, savory, and spicy. This takes you there, any time of day.

You can use this recipe with pork sirloin steaks, too. I also like to use this marinade for pork kebabs and boneless chicken. And chopped leftover pickles are delicious on burgers or stirred into tuna salad.

¾ cup rice vinegar

¼ cup sugar

1 teaspoon salt

1 4-inch piece daikon radish, peeled

2 Kirby or other small cucumbers

1 carrot, peeled

½ to 1 jalapeño or other hot green or red chile, to taste, seeded

1 tablespoon fresh ginger cut into thin julienne

½ cup coconut milk

2 tablespoons soy sauce

2 tablespoons honey

2 tablespoons fish sauce

1 tablespoon fresh lime juice

4 cloves garlic, smashed to a paste

1½ to 2 pounds thin-cut bone-in pork chops

1 Put the vinegar, sugar, and salt in a small saucepan. Bring to a boil, stirring until the sugar and salt dissolve. Remove from the heat; let cool completely.

2 Cut the daikon, cucumber, carrot, and jalapeño into thin strips about 2 inches long. Put them in a bowl, add the ginger, and toss to combine. Pour the cooled vinegar mixture over, cover, and refrigerate for at least 3 hours to let the flavors develop. If storing longer, transfer to an airtight container. The pickles will keep their crunch for 4 to 5 days.

3 Put the coconut milk, soy sauce, honey, fish sauce, lime juice, and garlic in a small bowl and stir to combine. Put the pork chops in a zipper bag or large baking dish, pour the marinade over, and turn the chops until completely coated. Refrigerate until you're ready to grill, for up to several hours.

4 Start the coals or heat a gas grill for hot direct cooking. Make sure the grates are clean.

5 Remove the pork chops from the marinade and put on the grill directly over the fire. Close the lid and cook, turning once, until no longer pink in the center, 3 to 5 minutes per side. (Nick with a small knife to peek inside.) Transfer to a platter and serve with the pickled vegetables on the side.

• recipe continues →

Ⓓ direct fire   Ⓘ indirect fire   Ⓜ make ahead   Ⓥ vegetarian option

Hot and Sweet Coconut-Pineapple Pork Chops	Substitute ¼ cup pineapple juice for the honey and add 1 tablespoon sriracha or other hot sauce.
Braised-and-Grilled Coconut Baby Backs or Spareribs	Fantastic make-ahead party food: Substitute 3–4 pounds baby back ribs or spareribs, cut into individual ribs, for the pork chops. Put the marinade in a baking dish large enough to hold the ribs in a single layer. Add the ribs and cook in a 350°F oven until a knife slides easily through the meat, about 1 hour. Transfer the ribs to a platter. Or refrigerate them for up to 24 hours. Grill as directed over a medium-high direct fire until browned and crisp in places and heated through, 3 to 7 minutes per side.
Sweet Soy Pork Chops with Garlic and Ginger	Omit the coconut milk and lime juice, increase the soy sauce and fish sauce to ¼ cup each, and substitute ¼ cup sugar for the honey. Add 2 tablespoons minced fresh ginger. Stir the marinade until the sugar dissolves.

D direct fire　I indirect fire　M make ahead　V vegetarian option

Thick-Cut Pork Chops with Quick Orange-Sage Drizzle

| Makes: **4 servings** | Time: **40 to 45 minutes** | **D** **I** |

The trick to a juicy, beautifully browned thick pork chop is to cook it with a combination of direct and indirect heat. Sear it well over the fire, then move it off the heat to finish cooking. You can put the drizzle sauce together in five minutes; it's a wonderful way to finish the pork. Also feel free to leave it off entirely and serve the chops simply with lemon wedges.

4 boneless loin pork chops (1–2 inches thick each)

Salt and pepper

4 tablespoons (½ stick) butter

1 tablespoon minced shallot

2 tablespoons fresh orange juice

1 tablespoon grated orange zest

2 teaspoons minced fresh sage

1 Start the coals or heat a gas grill for medium-high indirect cooking. Make sure the grates are clean.

2 Pat the chops dry with paper towels and sprinkle with salt and pepper on all sides.

3 Put the chops on the grill directly over the fire. Close the lid and sear, turning once, until well browned, 2 to 3 minutes per side. Move the chops to the indirect side of the grill and cook until the internal temperature at the thickest point is 135° to 140°F, another 10 to 20 minutes.

4 Transfer the chops to a platter and let rest until the internal temperature rises to 145°F. While the chops rest, melt the butter in a small saucepan over medium-low heat; you can also do this on the grill, if you prefer. Add the shallot and cook until it softens, 1 to 2 minutes. Add 2 tablespoons water and the orange juice and let bubble for a minute or 2. Stir in the orange zest and sage and season with salt and pepper. Drizzle over the pork chops and serve.

Bone-In Thick-Cut Pork Chops with Quick Orange-Sage Drizzle	Since bone doesn't conduct heat as well as meat, the area nearest the bone is going to cook more slowly. When you put the chops on the grill to sear, position them so the bone is over the hottest part of the fire. When you move the chops to the indirect portion of the grill, position them so the bone is closest to the fire without being over it. Proceed with the recipe as directed.
Thick-Cut Pork Chops with Quick Ginger-Lime-Basil Drizzle	Substitute fresh ginger for the shallot, lime juice and zest for the orange, and 2 tablespoons chopped fresh basil for the sage.
Thick-Cut Pork Chops with Quick Lemon-Rosemary Drizzle	Substitute good-quality olive oil for the butter, garlic for the shallot, lemon juice and zest for the orange, and rosemary for the sage.

Filipino-Style Pork Skewers

Makes: 4 servings	Time: 50 to 60 minutes	Ⓓ Ⓜ

Sweet caramelized morsels of pork are ubiquitous party food throughout the Philippines. Instead of the typical lemon-lime soda or ginger ale for the marinade, I go with ginger beer. For a more authentic flavor, get your hands on some banana ketchup to use instead of the regular kind. Also known as "banana sauce," the popular Filipino condiment is made from mashed bananas, vinegar, sugar, ginger, and other spices.

You can also make these with pork tenderloin; because it's leaner, you can use higher heat if you like and cook the skewers faster. And this marinade is also delicious with chicken and tofu.

2 pounds boneless pork shoulder

½ cup ginger beer

2 tablespoons soy sauce

2 tablespoons ketchup

2 tablespoons brown sugar

1 tablespoon minced garlic

1 tablespoon fresh lime juice

Salt and pepper

1 Trim the pork of excess fat and cut into 1- to 1½-inch pieces.

2 Put the ginger beer, soy sauce, ketchup, sugar, garlic, lime juice, and some salt and pepper in a large bowl and whisk to combine. Add the pork and stir to coat. Let sit at room temperature while you prepare the fire or up to 1 hour. Or refrigerate up to overnight.

3 If you're using bamboo or wooden skewers, soak them in water for 30 minutes. Meanwhile, start the coals or heat a gas grill for medium to medium-low direct cooking. Make sure the grates are clean.

4 Skewer the pork; you can push the pieces close together. Put the skewers on the grill directly over the fire. Close the lid and cook until crusty brown and no longer pink in the center; turn the skewers every 2 minutes or so. Total cooking time will be about 20 minutes. Transfer the skewers to a platter and serve.

Spanish-Style Pork Skewers	Also known as *pinchos morunos,* these kebabs have a deep, complex flavor from the North African spice blend ras el hanout: Omit the marinade. Instead whisk together 3 tablespoons good-quality olive oil, 2 tablespoons sherry vinegar, 2 teaspoons ras el hanout (page 456), and 3 cloves garlic, smashed. Use this to marinate the pork.
Lemongrass Pork Skewers	Omit the marinade. Remove the tough outer layers from 2 stalks lemongrass, chop the tender insides, and put them in a blender or mini food processor with 2 large chopped shallots, 3 cloves garlic, 2 tablespoons fish sauce, and 1 tablespoon each fresh lime juice, sugar, and toasted sesame seeds. Season with salt, black pepper, and red chile flakes and purée to a paste. Taste and adjust the seasonings; use this to marinate the pork.
West Indian–Style Pork Skewers	Omit the marinade. Cut 4 scallions into pieces and put them in a blender or mini food processor with 4 cloves garlic, ¼ cup fresh lime juice, 2 tablespoons good-quality vegetable oil, 1 teaspoon each ground allspice and dried thyme, and ¼ teaspoon freshly grated nutmeg; add some salt and pepper and purée to a paste. Taste and adjust the seasonings; use this to marinate the pork.

---

12 MORE KEBABS TO MAKE

1. Chicken Skewers with Peanut Sauce (page 81)
2. Chicken and Vegetable Kebabs (page 170) and its variations
3. Chicken Skewers with Italian Sausage and Lemon Wedges (page 171) and its variations
4. Rosemary-Garlic Chicken Liver and Onion Skewers (page 85)
5. Seafood Skewers with Croutons and Orange (page 120) and its variations
6. Coconut-Rum Shrimp and Pineapple Skewers (page 129) and its variations
7. Madeira-Style Beef Skewers (page 247) and its variations
8. Sweetbread Skewers with Lemon (page 87) and its variations
9. Liver Kebabs (page 267)
10. Shashlik with Onions and Grapes (page 318) and its variations
11. Lamb or Veal Kidney Skewers with Sherry Vinegar (page 86)
12. Adana Kebabs (page 320) and its variations

Pernil

| Makes: 6 to 10 servings | Time: 4½ to 7½ hours, plus marinating time, largely unattended | Ⓘ Ⓜ |

I'm constantly tinkering with this iconic Puerto Rican roast pork, but it always has the spirit of the recipe generously shared with me more than 30 years ago by the family of my friend Peter Blasini. Traditionally prepared in a low oven, it translates beautifully to the grill. If you are a fan of cracklings, bone-in pork shoulder or a picnic ham is the way to go; at the end of the cook time, the skin—which traps the juices and seasonings—will be a gorgeous hickory brown.

You've got leeway on the grill temperature; anywhere between 225° and 350°F is fine. The higher temp will get it done faster, with more surface browning. And with so much fat and connective tissue, even though these cuts cook notoriously unevenly, they're so forgiving it's almost impossible to overcook them. If you're cooking with gas, adding smoke will create another layer of flavor (see "Smoking," pages 10–12), but it's not necessary.

4 cloves garlic, peeled

1 onion, quartered

2 tablespoons chopped fresh oregano or 1 tablespoon dried oregano

1 mild fresh chile, stemmed and seeded (optional)

1 small dried hot red chile (optional)

1 tablespoon salt

2 teaspoons black pepper

2 tablespoons peanut or other good-quality vegetable oil

2 tablespoons white or red wine vinegar, orange juice, or lime juice

1 bone-in pork shoulder or picnic ham (4–7 pounds)

1 Make the flavor paste: Put the garlic, onion, oregano, chiles, salt, and pepper in a blender or mini food processor and purée into a paste, adding the oil in a drizzle through the lid as the machine runs, and scraping down the sides as necessary. Or mince everything together on a cutting board, put in a bowl, and mix in the oil. Add the vinegar and pulse or stir to combine.

2 Leave the skin on the pork if it has it. With a sharp knife, cut incisions into the pork on all sides. Rub the flavor paste all over, pushing it down into the cuts and getting it into every nook and cranny. Let it sit at room temperature for up to an hour, or cover and refrigerate up to 24 hours.

3 Start the coals or heat a gas grill for medium to medium-low indirect cooking. Make sure the grates are clean. If using charcoal, place a drip pan under the indirect portion of the grill; for gas, empty, clean, and replace the fat trap.

4 Put the pork, skin side down, on the indirect side of the grill. Close the lid and cook until the internal temperature in the meatiest portion of the pork is at least 150°F, 4 to 7 hours, depending on its weight and how hot the fire is. Start checking the temperature in multiple places in the shoulder after 1 hour, and more frequently as it gets closer to being done. Turn, rotate, and move the pork as needed so that the least done part of the pork is closest to the fire.

5 Transfer to a cutting board and let it rest for 10 to 15 minutes. Cut off the skin. Cut the meat into chunks, trimming away any big pieces of fat. If you like, scrape the fat off the skin, then cut it into pieces and serve the cracklings with the pork.

Colombian-Style Pernil	Omit the oregano and chiles in the flavor paste. Double the garlic and add 1 bunch scallions, 1 seeded red bell pepper, and 1 tablespoon each ground cumin and paprika or achiote powder. Purée and use as directed.
Pernil with Cilantro and Lime	Double the garlic, substitute 1 cup fresh cilantro sprigs for the oregano, omit the onion and chiles, and use ¼ cup lime juice instead of the vinegar. After processing, this is more liquid than paste. Work it into the pork everywhere you can. If you have any left, reserve it and brush the pork several times with it after it browns until it's gone.
Pernil with Sazón	The simplest way to season pork roast: Omit the flavor paste. Instead, rub the pork with a mixture of 1 teaspoon each salt, black pepper, dried oregano, garlic powder, ground cumin, ground coriander, and paprika or achiote powder.

Pulled Pork with Lexington-Style BBQ Sauce

Makes: **8 or more servings**	Time: **10 or more hours, largely unattended**	Ⓘ Ⓜ

It's true what they say: To get pork so tender you can tease it apart with a fork, you've got to go slow-and-low. Start with a piece from the shoulder, hard-working muscles laced with lots of fat and collagen—the same protein that gives us gelatin. When the meat is 170°F, all that stuff melts, leaving behind meat that comes apart at the seams.

I like an hour of smoke; definitely don't go beyond two hours or you'll mask the taste of the pork. If you're cooking with a charcoal grill, have an extra bag of coals on hand. This is not the time to run out of fuel. If you've got a gas grill, read "Smoking in a Gas Grill," page 11.

The matter of seasoning is serious business in states that pride themselves on barbecue. The main techniques are rubs (a mix of dry ingredients massaged into the meat before smoking), mops (usually flavorful vinegar- or juice-based sauces used to baste the meat as it cooks), and sauces (which may be brushed on during or after smoking and are served as a condiment). The "proper" method and sauce can vary from state to region to cook. There are many iconic examples throughout the book including this recipe and the first two variations on page 290, three different contributions from the Carolinas.

To make the pork ahead, cook it the day before you want to serve it, pull the meat, toss it with the sauce, and then cover and refrigerate. The next day, reheat it gently, covered with foil, in a 300°F oven just until hot. Or just make the sauce up to a couple of days ahead; refrigerate in a covered jar. The classic way to eat pulled pork is on a hamburger bun (don't bother toasting it), topped with coleslaw—what type is a whole 'nuther story but there's a great option here.

1 bone-in pork shoulder, Boston butt, or picnic ham (6–10 pounds)

Salt and pepper

1½ cups distilled white vinegar

½ cup ketchup

2 tablespoons brown sugar

½ teaspoon red chile flakes, or to taste

Pinch cayenne

Creamy Cabbage and Carrot Slaw (page 398) for serving

8 or more hamburger buns, split

1 Start the coals or heat a gas grill for medium-low indirect cooking. If using a charcoal grill, position the coals so the smoke will be pulled over the pork and out the top vent. Make sure the grates are clean. If using charcoal, put a drip pan under the indirect side of the grill; for gas, empty, clean, and replace the fat trap. When the grill temperature is 300°F, add wood to the fire (see "Smoking," pages 10–12).

2 While the grill comes to temperature, trim the external fat on the pork to about ¼ inch thick. If

• recipe continues →

it's partially covered with skin, slice off as much of it as possible so the smoke can penetrate the meat. Season the pork generously all over with salt and pepper. (You can prepare the pork up to a day before and refrigerate it.)

3 When the grill fills with smoke, put the pork on the indirect side of the grill, with the thicker end closest to the fire; the temperature will immediately drop. Close the lid. Every hour or so, turn, move, and rotate the pork for even cooking. Cook, keeping the temperature in the grill between 250° and 300°F, until you can stick a fork in the meat and turn it with little or no resistance; this can take 8 to 12 hours, depending on the size of the pork and how hot the fire is.

4 While the pork cooks, make the sauce: Combine the vinegar, ketchup, brown sugar, pepper flakes, cayenne, and a sprinkle of salt and pepper in a saucepan over medium heat; whisk and bring to a gentle bubble. Taste and adjust the seasonings. Remove from the heat.

5 Transfer the pork to a cutting board or platter. To "pull" the pork, break it apart into manageable pieces and rake 2 forks in opposite directions to shred the pork. Discard any bones or skin. Put the pork in a large serving bowl. Toss the pork with just enough sauce to lightly coat it and serve, passing the remaining sauce, the slaw, and buns at the table.

Pulled Pork with North Carolina Vinegar Sauce	This sauce hails from the eastern part of the state, versus the western North Carolina Lexington version. It's strong stuff, hot and puckery, with just a little bit of sweetness from the brown sugar: Use cider vinegar and increase it to 2 cups. Omit the ketchup. Increase the red pepper flakes to 2 teaspoons and the cayenne to 1 teaspoon. No need to heat the sauce; just whisk it all together in a bowl.
Pulled Pork with South Carolina Mustard Sauce	A completely different take: For the sauce, whisk together 1 cup yellow mustard (no Dijon here; use the ballpark stuff), 2/3 cup brown sugar, 1/3 cup distilled white vinegar, 1 tablespoon Worcestershire sauce, 2 teaspoons hot sauce, and salt and pepper to taste.
Pulled Pork Deviled Eggs	No matter how much you love pulled pork, you're going to have leftovers, even a little bit, which is all you need for these babies: Hard-boil 6 eggs; cool, peel, and cut them in half lengthwise. Pop the yolks into a bowl, add 1/4 cup mayonnaise and 1 tablespoon barbecue sauce and mash until smooth. Fold in 1/2 cup chopped pulled pork. Taste and adjust the flavors and texture with salt and pepper, or more mayonnaise and sauce. Stuff the mixture back into the egg halves.

D direct fire   I indirect fire   M make ahead   V vegetarian option

Char Siu Baby Back Ribs

Makes: 4 to 6 servings	Time: 2½ to 3 hours, largely unattended	

If you've never cooked ribs start to finish on the grill, try it first with baby back ribs. The racks take less time and space than spare ribs and they're super tender and meaty. This iconic Chinese sauce is also easier than messing with smoke. It pairs wonderfully with chicken as well, or try it brushed over slices of eggplant or tofu.

4 pounds baby back ribs

Salt and pepper

¼ cup hoisin sauce

¼ cup honey

¼ cup soy sauce (preferably dark)

2 tablespoons rice wine or dry sherry

1 tablespoon minced fresh ginger

¼ teaspoon five-spice powder (to make your own, see page 456), or more to taste

1 Start the coals or heat a gas grill for medium to medium-low indirect cooking. Make sure the grates are clean. If using charcoal, put a drip pan under the indirect side of the grill; for gas, empty, clean, and replace the fat trap.

2 Season the ribs with salt and pepper on both sides. Put the hoisin sauce, honey, soy sauce, wine, ginger, and five-spice powder in a small bowl and whisk to combine.

3 Put the ribs, meaty side up, on the indirect side of the grill, long side facing the fire. Close the lid and maintain the temperature at 250° and 300°F, though 300°F the whole time is fine. Cook for 1 hour, then brush the sauce over both sides of the ribs. Every half hour from then on, turn, move, and rotate the racks for even cooking; when the glaze looks baked on, brush with more. Cook until you can easily cut between two ribs with a sharp knife, 2 to 2½ hours total; start to check for doneness at 1½ hours.

A QUICK SURVEY OF PORK RIBS

Baby back ribs. The leanest and smallest of all ribs. Cut from near the backbone, a rack will weigh 1½ to 2 pounds; they cook up fastest on the grill. When you go to buy them, look closely to avoid "shiners"— racks where you can clearly see the bones showing through on both sides. Shiners cheat you of meat.

Spare ribs. These are cut from closer to the breastbone and are much fattier (largely in the form of marbling, which will melt and deliver delicious flavor) than baby backs. A full slab of spare ribs weighs between 3 and 4 pounds and is irregularly shaped, somewhat like a fan.

Center-cut ribs. Also known as St. Louis–style ribs, this is a squared-off slab of spare ribs. You'll know you have center-cut ribs (it's not always marked on the package) if you find an odd flap of meat included underneath the rack. Grill it along with the ribs, although it tends to remain chewy.

• recipe continues →

4 Give the ribs a final brush of sauce, then put them directly over the fire, turning once, until the sauce is brown and crusty, 3 to 5 minutes per side depending on how hot the fire is at that point.

5 Transfer to a cutting board, cut the ribs apart, put on a platter, and serve with plenty of napkins.

Char Siu Pork Kebabs	When you can't wait for ribs: Heat the grill for a medium to medium-low direct fire; soak bamboo or wooden skewers if you're using them. Cut 1½ to 2 pounds boneless pork shoulder or boneless country-style ribs into 1- to 1½-inch pieces. Toss with the sauce, then skewer. Cook directly over the fire, turning the skewers every few minutes for even cooking, until the pork is cooked through and crusty, about 20 minutes total.
Char Siu Pork Belly	These glazed pork belly slices make the richest sliders ever: Substitute one 2-pound piece pork belly for the ribs. Cook as for the ribs (you can let the grill temperature go as high as 350°F) until the internal temperature is at least 140°F (check in multiple places), 1½ to 2 hours. Transfer to a cutting board; let rest for 5 to 10 minutes, then cut into 1-inch-thick slices. Put the slices directly over the fire and cook until they start to brown, 2 to 5 minutes per side. Brush with the sauce and cook until crusty, another 2 to 3 minutes per side, brushing a second time with the sauce if you like. Transfer to a platter and serve as is, or in slider buns, or cut up and add to a pot of beans (page 390).
Char Siu Chicken Wings	Heat the grill for medium to medium-hot indirect cooking. Substitute 2½ pounds chicken wings for the ribs. With a chef's knife, cut the wings at each joint into 3 sections; save the wing tips for stock if you like. Cook the wingettes and drumettes on the indirect side of the grill until tender and cooked through, 20 to 30 minutes. Toss the wings with the sauce until completed coated. Put on the grill directly over the fire and cook, turning once, until the glaze gets crusty, 2 to 5 minutes per side depending on how hot the fire is. Transfer to a platter and serve.

Spare Ribs with Sweet Ancho-Cumin Rub

Makes: 4 to 6 servings	Time: 3 to 4½ hours, largely unattended	I M

Spare ribs are most tender when cooked slowly the entire time on the grill, so they require some patience. They'll make you happy simply roasted with fire. If you want to add smoke (see page 10), do it at the beginning and for not more than an hour or so; otherwise the smoke flavor starts to overshadow the rich taste of the pork. This style of ribs, served without sauce, is known as "dry" ribs. If you want to make a sauce available at the table, see the list on page 457.

1 tablespoon sugar

2 teaspoons salt

2 teaspoons black pepper

2 teaspoons ground cumin

2 teaspoons ancho chile powder

2 teaspoons paprika

About 4 pounds spare ribs

1 Start the coals or heat a gas grill for medium to medium-low indirect cooking. Make sure the grates are clean. If using charcoal, put a drip pan under the indirect side of the grill; for gas, empty, clean, and replace the fat trap.

2 To make the rub, stir the sugar, salt, pepper, cumin, ancho powder, and paprika together in a small bowl. Rub into the ribs on both sides. (You can do this up to several hours ahead of cooking.)

3 When the grill is ready, put the ribs, meaty side up, on the indirect side of the grill, with one of the long sides closest to the fire. Close the lid. Maintain the temperature between 250° and 300°F, though 300°F the whole time is fine. Every half hour, turn, move, and rotate the racks for even cooking. Cook until the meat is tender enough that you can easily cut between the ribs, 2 to 4 hours total, depending on how hot the fire is.

4 Transfer to a cutting board and let rest until cool enough to handle, then cut between the ribs, put on a platter, and serve.

Memphis-Style Ribs	Two choices—either give them a double blast of seasoning before and after grilling ("dry ribs"), or cook them "wet," brushing them with Memphis-Style Barbecue Sauce (page 459) several times during cooking without a final dose of vinegar and seasoning: For the rub, stir together 1 tablespoon brown sugar, 1½ teaspoons each salt, paprika, garlic powder, and celery salt, 1 teaspoon each black pepper, onion powder, dry mustard, dried thyme, and cayenne, and ½ teaspoon ground cumin. Reserve 1½ tablespoons of the rub in a small bowl. Work the rest of the rub into the rack(s) on both sides. Grill as directed. When they come off the grill, brush on both sides with about ⅓ cup cider vinegar and sprinkle evenly with the reserved rub. Let rest, then cut into individual ribs and serve.
Kansas City–Style Ribs	For the rub, stir together 1 tablespoon each brown and white sugar, 1½ teaspoons each salt, paprika, garlic powder, chili powder, and celery salt, and 1 teaspoon each black pepper and onion powder. During the last half hour of cooking, brush the ribs several times with Kansas City–Style BBQ Sauce (page 457).
Unsmoked Smoky Spare Ribs	If you want your ribs to have smoke flavor without the bother of feeding the fire with wood, this is your recipe: For the rub, use Best Ever Rub with Smoked Paprika (page 455).

Pork Belly Bites

Makes: 6 to 8 servings	Time: 3 to 4 hours, largely unattended	Ⓘ Ⓜ

You know this cut: Bacon comes from pork belly. It's almost all fat, but wrapped around the most tender meat of the pig. Smoke it, don't smoke it—your choice (see page 10 if you decide to). Look for a piece with a good meat-to-fat ratio; avoid pieces that are way more fat than meat. If you're a fan of cracklings, look for one with the skin still on. For more seasoning oomph, you can rub the belly with any of the spice blends on page 456.

1 piece pork belly (2–4 pounds)

Salt and pepper

1 Start the coals or heat a gas grill for medium indirect cooking. Make sure the grates are clean. If using charcoal, put a drip pan under the indirect side of the grill; for gas, empty, clean, and replace the fat trap.

2 If the pork belly has the skin, cut it away or leave it on for cracklings as you like. Trim away some fat, leaving about a ½-inch layer covering the meat, or more if that's what you're after. Sprinkle with salt and pepper on all sides.

3 Put the pork belly on the indirect side of the grill, long side facing the fire. Close the lid. Maintain the temperature in the grill at 300° to 350°F. Reposition the pork belly every 30 minutes or so to ensure even cooking. Start checking the internal temperature of the meat (not the fat) after 1 hour. Cook until the internal temperature is at least 140°F at any point (check in multiple places with an instant read thermometer), 1½ to 3 hours total, depending on the size and how hot the fire is.

4 Transfer to a cutting board and let it rest until the internal temperature reaches 145°F. (You can let it cool to room temperature, cover, and refrigerate for up to 5 days before proceeding.) If you left the skin on and want cracklings, cut the skin away from the belly as soon as it is cool enough to handle. Put it back on the indirect side of the grill to render for another 30 minutes or so. If using charcoal, you can let it do that as the fire dies. Then move it directly over the fire to get it super crisp, turning it several times; it should only take a few minutes. Keep a close eye on it; you don't want it to char at all. Transfer to a cutting board and cut into bite-size pieces.

5 Trim away any large pieces of fat away from the pork belly, then cut the meat into bite-size pieces to eat right away or slice or dice to use in another dish.

Ⓓ direct fire   Ⓘ indirect fire   Ⓜ make ahead   Ⓥ vegetarian option

Korean-Style Pork Belly Wraps	My take on the Korean dish *samgyeopsal*, grilled pieces of pork belly wrapped in lettuce with *ssamjang*, a hot and savory sauce: Peel and cut 1 carrot and 1 Kirby or other small cucumber into thin 2-inch sticks. Cut 2 scallions into 2-inch lengths, then slice thinly lengthwise. Cut 1 green chile of your choice into thin rounds. For the sauce, stir together ¼ cup any miso, 2 tablespoons gochujang, 1 tablespoon sesame oil, 2 teaspoons sesame seeds, and 1 clove garlic, minced, in a small bowl. In Step 5, cut the cooked pork belly into slices about 1 inch thick and 2 inches square; cook over a medium direct fire, turning once, until browned and crisp, 2 to 5 minutes per side. Stay close to the grill and move the pieces as necessary to avoid flare-ups. To serve, put slices of pork belly on a leaf of butter lettuce, add a few carrot and cucumber sticks, fresh mint or perilla (shiso) leaves, sliced chile, and scallion shreds, and smear with a bit of the sauce. Roll up, eat, repeat.
Korean-Style Pork Belly or Jowl Sliders	Oh, these are good: Grill slices of pork belly or pork jowl (see the following variation) as directed for the wraps variation. Stir 2 tablespoons of the *ssamjang* (or to taste) from the wraps variation into ½ cup mayonnaise. Serve the slices on Hawaiian slider rolls topped with several pieces of scallion and a dollop of the *ssamjang* mayo.
Smoked Pork Jowl	This is a real treat—just as tender, more succulent, and there's a better meat-to-fat ratio. The jowl might come tied up like a roast in an effort to make it an even shape; if it does, leave it that way. And it will likely come with the skin still on. Like pork belly, you can smoke it if you like; I stop at an hour of smoke so it doesn't overwhelm the pork flavor. For a 2-pound pork jowl, cook time will be about 2½ hours; follow as directed for pork belly. After cooking, you can cut the jowl up and use the bits as a seasoning meat. Or slice and fry or grill over direct heat for the one of the tastiest breakfast meats ever.

Smoked Hocks or Shanks

| Makes: as many as you would like | Time: 2½ to 7 hours, intermittently attended | Ⓘ Ⓜ |

Hocks are basically the same thing as shanks, only a little less so—hocks are 2- to 3-inch crosscuts from the shank. Shanks run from 1½ to 2 pounds each, hocks between about ½ to 1 pound each. Smoked ham hocks are commonplace in supermarkets, though they tend to look less than appetizing. You will likely need to special order shanks from a butcher, ditto unsmoked hocks; the good news is they're not expensive. Invest a couple of hours in nearly effortless smoking and you'll be rewarded with a deep smoke flavor that will transfer to anything the hocks or shanks touch. Cook them further, until the meat is so tender you can pick it apart, and you can enjoy them for dinner. If you're smoking hocks to use as seasoning, you might as well do a grill full of them, then cool and freeze the extras; they'll last for months.

Pork hocks and/or shanks

Salt and pepper

1 Start the coals or heat a gas grill for medium to medium-low cooking. If using a charcoal grill, position the coals so the smoke will be pulled over the pork and out the top vent. Make sure the grates are clean. If using charcoal, put a drip pan under the indirect side of the grill; for gas, empty, clean, and replace the fat trap. When the grill is ready, add wood to the fire (see "Smoking," pages 10–12).

2 While the grill comes to temperature, prepare the shanks and/or hocks: Both come with the skin on. If you like cracklings, leave it on but cut through the skin every couple of inches down to the fat to allow the fat to render and the smoke to penetrate the meat. If you don't want cracklings, use a sharp, thin knife to remove the skin, leaving a thin layer of fat covering the meat. Sprinkle all over with salt and pepper.

3 When the grill fills with smoke, put the hocks or shanks on the indirect side of the grill. Close the lid; figure on 2 hours of smoke. After that point,

stop adding smoking wood but maintain the grill temperature between 250° and 300°F. If you're cooking hocks or shanks with the intent of using them as seasoning in a long-simmering dish, take them off the grill when you can insert a skewer or thin knife through the meaty portion with just a little resistance; this will take 2 to 3 hours (including the smoking time), depending on their size. The meat will get totally tender when it simmers in the dish. If not using right away, let cool, wrap well, and refrigerate or freeze.

4 If you intend to serve them whole or add the smoked meat to a shorter-cooking dish, continue to cook until the skewer goes in with no resistance and you can pull the pork away from the bone with a fork; depending on their size, this can take 4 to 5½ hours for hocks, 5 to 6½ hours for shanks (including the smoking time). Transfer them to a platter and serve.

Ⓓ direct fire   Ⓘ indirect fire   Ⓜ make ahead   Ⓥ vegetarian option

Smoked Pig's Trotters	Pig's feet or trotters are generally used for seasoning; there's not much meat on that bone. Pig's feet also include the hooves, which contain lots of gelatin-forming collagen, making them a great addition to stock, as well as all sorts of braises and soups: Don't bother cutting slits into the skin. Smoke and continue to cook as directed opposite until you can insert a skewer with no resistance into the little bit of meat at the top of the trotter, and the skin at the top starts to pull away from the meat, 3 to 4 hours total.
Smoked Pork and Beans	Follow the directions for the Smoked Beans with Burnt Ends and Drippings (page 391), putting the beans under a pork shank or 2 hocks as they smoke. When the hocks or shank are done, move the beans to a 350°F oven to finish cooking. When the hocks or shanks are cool enough to handle, remove and shred the meat and stir it into the beans. If you like, cut the cracklings into small pieces and stir those into the beans right before serving to keep them crunchy.
Collards with Smoked Ham Hocks	A delicious side for any barbecue: Put 2 smoked hocks in a saucepan and add 2 cups water. Bring to a boil, reduce the heat to a simmer, and let gently bubble until the pork is very tender, 30 to 40 minutes; reserve the water. Transfer the hocks to a cutting board. Cut the tough stems out of 1½ pounds well-washed collards, then chop the leaves. Heat 2 tablespoons good-quality olive oil in large pot over medium heat. Add the collards, 1 teaspoon sugar, and salt and pepper to taste. Stir until the collards wilt, then add the reserved water, bring to a boil, reduce the heat to a gentle but steady bubble, and simmer until the collards are silky and tender, 30 to 45 minutes. Meanwhile, remove the meat from the hocks and chop or shred into small pieces. Stir into the collards, let heat through, and serve.

Ham Steak with Spicy Pineapple Glaze

Makes: **4 to 6 servings**	Time: **30 to 40 minutes**	Ⓓ Ⓜ

Ham steak takes ham from special occasion to weekday cooking. Work it on the grill with a sweet-and-hot glaze and it'll deliciously caramelize, just like the tastiest bits on a full-size ham but in a fraction of the time. I like sriracha or something similarly garlicky here, but use what you like—smoky or habanero sauces are good, too. You can make the glaze earlier in the day.

¼ cup pineapple preserves

2 tablespoons brown sugar

1 tablespoon hot sauce, or to taste

1 or 2 center-cut bone-in ham steaks (1–1½ inches thick; about 2 pounds)

1 Start the coals or heat a gas grill for medium direct cooking. Make sure the grates are clean.

2 To make the glaze, stir the preserves, brown sugar, and hot sauce together in a small bowl.

3 Put the ham steak(s) on the grill directly over the fire. Close the lid, cook for 5 minutes, then turn. Close the lid and cook for another 5 minutes. Brush the top with the glaze and turn again; brush the top with glaze as well. Cook until the glaze on the bottom starts to brown (this will only take a minute or 2, depending on how hot the fire is), then turn. Brush the top with glaze again and cook until the other side starts to brown. Continue building up the glaze until the steak is hot throughout and browned and crusted on both sides.

4 Transfer to a cutting board, slice, and serve.

Ham Steak with Marmalade-Mustard Glaze	For the glaze, whisk together 6 tablespoons marmalade and 2 tablespoons each brown sugar and Dijon mustard.
Ham Steak with Maple-Mustard Glaze	For the glaze, whisk together ¼ cup each maple syrup and Dijon mustard.
Ham Steak with Hoisin-Ginger Glaze	For the glaze, put ¼ cup hoisin sauce, 2 tablespoons soy sauce, 1 inch sliced peeled fresh ginger, 1 tablespoon fresh lime juice, and 1 teaspoon sesame oil in a mini food processor and process until smooth.

Sheboygan-Style Bratwursts

Makes: **4 servings**	Time: **35 to 40 minutes**	Ⓓ

Sheboygan, Wisconsin, considers itself the bratwurst capital of the world. Its residents are champions of the fresh pork or pork-and-beef sausage brought over by the German immigrants who settled in the city. This is the classic way to serve them at a brat fry (locals say they are "frying" brats when they grill them)—one brat per roll, or make them "doubles" with two. Wherever you live, seek out the best sausage in your town.

4 or 8 fresh bratwursts

4 hard rolls (preferably semmel rolls)

Coarse brown mustard for serving

Ketchup for serving

Thinly sliced onion for serving

Dill pickle slices for serving

1 Start the coals or heat a gas grill for medium-low to low direct cooking. Make sure the grates are clean.

2 Put the brats on the grill directly over the fire. Close the lid and cook, turning them every few minutes, until cooked through and crusted on all

---

8 WAYS TO EAT HOTDOGS, AMERICAN STYLE

No, I haven't included a recipe for how to grill hotdogs, since all you do is just roll them around over a medium-hot direct fire for a few minutes. But here's a list of some of the things you can do with them when you do make 'em.

1. **Sonoran Dog.** Popular in Arizona: Wrap with bacon before grilling, then top with grilled peppers and onions, pinto beans, salsa, tomatoes, mustard, mayo, and cheese

2. **Michigan Coney Island or Coney Dog.** Dress with yellow mustard, top with a meat sauce made from ground beef heart (you can use chili instead, if you like) and then chopped onion

3. **Kansas City Dog.** Like a Reuben: Smother in sauerkraut, and melt Swiss cheese over the top. Serve in a sesame seed bun

4. **Polish Boy.** A Cleveland creation: Top with French fries, barbecue sauce, and coleslaw

5. **Chicago Dog.** Dress with chopped onions, pickled sport peppers, sliced fresh tomatoes, piccalilli relish, and a dill pickle spear; serve on a poppy seed bun

6. **Texas Wiener.** Actually hails from New Jersey: Serve with spicy mustard, chili, and chopped onions

7. **North Carolina Dog.** Not surprisingly, North Carolinians top their dogs the way they do their pulled pork: with coleslaw

8. **Seattle Dog.** Toast the bun and spread with cream cheese, then dress the dog with grilled onions, jalapeños if you like, and your choice of barbecue sauce, sriracha, or mustard

• recipe continues →

sides, 20 to 25 minutes total. If they're browning too fast, move them to the outside edge of the fire or turn the heat down so they can cook through slowly, developing a deep brown color without bursting or burning.

3 Transfer the brats to a platter. Split the rolls and put 1 or 2 bratwurst in each. Serve, passing the condiments at the table.

Beer-Braised Brats with Onions	An extended beer bath keeps the brats plump on the grill and infuses them with flavor: Melt 4 tablespoons (½ stick) butter in a large pot over medium heat. Add 2 onions, sliced, and cook until softened, 8 to 10 minutes, stirring occasionally. Add the brats, nestling them down into the onions, and pour in two 12-ounce bottles or cans of beer, whatever kind you prefer. Bring to a boil, reduce the heat to a simmer, and let it bubble away, turning the brats occasionally, until most of the beer has evaporated, 40 to 60 minutes. Transfer the brats to a medium direct fire and grill until deeply browned on all sides, turning frequently, 4 to 6 minutes total. Serve on hard, hotdog, Portuguese, or other rolls as you prefer, topped with the braised onions.
Cider-Braised Brats with Sauerkraut	Same principle as above: Put 2 cups cider and 1 pound drained and rinsed fresh sauerkraut in a large skillet. Bring to a boil, reduce the heat to a simmer, and nestle in the brats. Cook as in the variation above, except the cider will reduce faster, in 30 to 40 minutes. Top the grilled brats with the sauerkraut.
Beer-Braised Italian Sausage with Onions and Peppers	Substitute sweet and/or hot Italian sausage links for the brats. Follow the directions for Beer-Braised Brats with Onions, but use olive oil instead of butter and add 2 green bell peppers, stemmed, seeded, and sliced, to the onions.

D direct fire   I indirect fire   M make ahead   V vegetarian option

Garlicky Pork Burgers

Makes: 4 burgers or 8 to 10 sliders	Time: 45 minutes	(D) (M)

Pork makes such a juicy, satisfying burger, all you need is a good bun. I prefer to grind my own mixture but if your store sells good-quality, preferably locally raised ground pork, go for that. Don't manhandle the meat or the burgers will be tough. If you like cheese on your burgers, mozzarella, provolone, and Emmental are good choices with pork.

1½ pounds fatty boneless pork shoulder or 18 ounces lean pork and 6 ounces pork fat, cut into chunks, or 1½ pounds good-quality preground pork

1 teaspoon salt

1 teaspoon black pepper

4 cloves garlic, chopped

4 hard rolls, split, or 8–10 slider buns

1 Start the coals or heat a gas grill for medium direct cooking. Make sure the grates are clean.

2 Working in batches if necessary, put the meat, salt, pepper, and garlic in a food processor and pulse until coarsely ground—finer than chopped, but not much. (If using preground meat, put it in a bowl with the salt, pepper, and garlic and work them together gently with your hands.) If you like, take a bit of the mixture and fry it up until brown on both sides and cooked through; taste it and adjust the seasonings if necessary. Handling the meat as little as possible to avoid compressing it, shape it lightly into 4 burgers, 1 to 1½ inches thick, or 8 to 10 sliders. (You can do this several hours in advance; cover with plastic wrap and refrigerate until you're ready to grill.)

3 Put the burgers on the grill directly over the fire. Close the lid and cook until the burgers release from the grates easily, 5 to 10 minutes, then turn and cook the other side until the burgers are no longer pink in the center; the internal temperature should be 160°F (check with an instant-read thermometer, or nick with a small knife and peek inside).

4 Transfer to a platter. Toast the rolls. Serve the burgers on the rolls.

Gingery Pork Burgers	One small switch, one huge difference: Instead of the garlic, peel a 2-inch piece fresh ginger and slice into thin coins (or chop if using preground pork).
Pork Burgers with Onions and Peppers	Cut 2 small green or red bell peppers in half and pull out the stems and seeds. With the palm of your hand, flatten each half. Cut four ½-inch-thick slices from a large onion. Brush the peppers and onion slices on both sides with good-quality olive oil. Put the peppers and onions on to grill at the same time as the burgers (or first if you don't have enough space). Grill the peppers and onions until tender and charred, 4 to 5 minutes per side. Remove the skin from the peppers if you like. To serve, put half a pepper and an onion slice on top of each burger and slip it into the roll—or not.
Five-Spice Pork Burgers with Peaches	Halve 2 peaches and remove the pits. Instead of the garlic, add 2 teaspoons five-spice powder to the pork. When you put the burgers on the grill, add the peaches cut side down. Cook, turning once or twice, until they're soft and develop grill marks, 3 to 5 minutes per side. Serve each burger topped with a peach half.

Italian-Style Sweet Pork Sausage with Fennel Seeds

Makes: 8 or more sausage patties	Time: 30 minutes	Ⓓ Ⓜ

All sausages follow the same basic principle: Grind together pork, fat, and spices. I use the food processor, but an old-fashioned meat grinder is just as good, if not better (see "Do-It-Yourself Ground Meat," page 260). The best sausages usually contain about 30 percent fat. It might seem like a lot but it's distributed throughout, and lets you crisp the outside without drying out the inside. Keep this in mind when you choose and trim the pork shoulder. You can stuff the meat into casings if you like, but it's easier to cook patties—which you can also serve as burgers or sliders.

2½ pounds fatty boneless pork shoulder (see the headnote), cut into 1-inch cubes

3 cloves garlic, minced

1 tablespoon fennel seeds

1 teaspoon salt

1 teaspoon black pepper

Sausage casings (optional)

1 Working in batches if necessary, put the meat in a food processor and pulse until coarsely ground—finer than chopped, but not much. Take your time and be careful not to pulverize the meat. As you finish each batch, transfer it to a bowl. Add the garlic, fennel seeds, salt, and pepper and work the mixture gently with your hands to incorporate them into the meat; add a little water if the mixture seems dry and crumbly. Cook up a spoonful in a small skillet to taste it; adjust the seasoning. Shape into 8 or more patties, or stuff into casings if you prefer. (You can freeze some or all of them, wrapped well, for up to several months.)

2 Start the coals or heat a gas grill for medium direct cooking. Make sure the grates are clean.

3 Put the sausages on the grill directly over the fire. Close the lid and cook until they release from the grates easily, 5 to 10 minutes, then turn and cook the other side until the sausages are no longer pink in the center; the internal temperature should be 160°F (check with an instant-read thermometer, or nick with a small knife and peek inside). Transfer to a platter and serve.

Italian-Style Hot Pork Sausage	Add 1 tablespoon each paprika and red chile flakes and increase the black pepper to 1½ teaspoons.
Mexican-Style Chorizo	The chorizo sold in Mexico is distinctly different from its cured Spanish and Portuguese cousins, and is always sold fresh: Omit the fennel seeds. Add ¼ cup distilled white vinegar, 2 tablespoons ground ancho chile powder, 2 teaspoons dried Mexican oregano, 1 teaspoon ground cumin, ½ teaspoon ground coriander, and ¼ teaspoon each ground cloves and allspice.
Pork Sausage with Ginger and Scallions	My take on a style of sausage popular with the Hmong people of Southeast Asia: Omit the fennel seeds. Add ½ cup minced scallions, ¼ cup minced fresh ginger, the grated zest and juice of 1 lime, and 1 tablespoon fish sauce.

Rack of Lamb with Sesame Dipping Sauce

| Makes: **4 servings** | Time: **40 to 60 minutes** | Ⓓ Ⓘ |

Lamb rack is expensive and luxurious, delicious, and virtually foolproof on the grill—and it stands up to an assertive sauce. There are eight ribs per rack, with only a couple of bites per rib, so you'll need two racks for four people. Remove the chine bone (or ask the butcher to do it) so you can easily cut through the ribs to separate them at the table. Trim the racks of as much surface fat as you can without losing any meat; rendering lamb fat really flares.

¼ cup rice vinegar

¼ cup soy sauce

2 teaspoons sesame oil

2 racks of lamb (1½–2 pounds each), trimmed of surface fat

Salt and pepper

1 Start the coals or heat a gas grill for medium to medium-high indirect cooking. Make sure the grates are clean.

2 To make the dipping sauce, whisk the vinegar, soy sauce, and sesame oil together in a small bowl. Divide the sauce between 4 small dipping bowls.

3 Pat the lamb racks dry with paper towels and sprinkle with salt and pepper on all sides.

4 When the grill is between 400° and 500°F, put the lamb directly over the fire with the thick ends of the racks over the hottest part. Close the lid and cook, turning once, until well browned, 4 to 5 minutes per side. Move the racks to the indirect side of the grill, with the thick ends positioned closest to the fire. Close the lid and cook until they are 5° to 10°F shy of the desired doneness (see page 220), 10 to 30 minutes total, depending on the size of the racks, how you like them done, and how hot the fire is.

5 Transfer to a cutting board and let rest 5 to 10 minutes, checking the internal temperature occasionally. (Or nick with a small knife and peek inside.) Cut the racks between the ribs into chops and serve with the dipping sauce.

---

8 MORE SAUCES TO SERVE WITH RACK OF LAMB

1. Cilantro-Mint Chutney (page 474)

2. Lime Dipping Sauce (page 117)

3. Lemon-Dill Oil (page 103)

4. Tare Sauce (page 238)

5. Salmoriglio (page 119)

6. Mojo Sauce (page 423)

7. Green Chimichurri (page 229)

8. Crying Tiger Dipping Sauce (page 239)

• recipe continues →

Ⓓ direct fire   Ⓘ indirect fire   Ⓜ make ahead   Ⓥ vegetarian option

Rack of Lamb with Harissa Yogurt	For the dipping sauce, whisk together 6 tablespoons yogurt, 1 generous tablespoon harissa (or to taste), and 1 teaspoon minced garlic. Add salt and pepper if you like.
Rack of Lamb with Honey Mustard Dipping Sauce	For the dipping sauce, whisk together 2 tablespoons each good-quality olive oil and white balsamic vinegar, 1 tablespoon each stoneground mustard and honey, and 1 teaspoon minced garlic.
Rack of Lamb with Smoked Paprika Rub	This easy rub adds a little bit of sweet and smoke: Omit the dipping sauce. Stir together 1 tablespoon brown sugar, 2 teaspoons smoked paprika (pimentón), and 1 teaspoon each salt and pepper. Don't pat the lamb dry or season it; sprinkle the rub evenly over the racks or chops on all sides, gently patting to help it stick.

SUBSTITUTING GOAT FOR LAMB

Americans are finally catching on to what the rest of the world has known for centuries: Goat is good, especially on the grill. The meat—which cooks and tastes a lot like lamb—is becoming easier to find: in farmers markets and specialty butchers, sure; but also in natural food stores and grocers that specialize in Indian, Hispanic, Mediterranean, and Middle Eastern ingredients.

Grilling is an excellent way to try cooking and eating goat. Here's how: The lamb recipes in this chapter will all work for goat, too, with a couple minor adjustments. When the recipe calls for a cut of lamb (like the leg or shoulder), figure you'll need two of the same goat cuts; otherwise just go by the pounds given in the ingredient list. If a recipe calls for a cut you can't find and it's boneless shoulder or leg, then get goat stew meat. If you can't find anything called rack of goat, ask for the saddle or rib roast or bone-in loin cut; you can cook it whole or ask the butcher to cut between the ribs for chops (or do it yourself). Goat will cook faster than lamb, sometimes in half the time, so check it early and often. The same visual cues and tests for doneness apply. And all the seasonings that go with lamb work just as well with goat. All you have to do is follow the recipe and divide the rubs, marinades, or sauces among whatever pieces you have.

D direct fire I indirect fire M make ahead V vegetarian option

Burnt-Fingers Lamb Chops

Makes: 4 servings	Time: 30 to 35 minutes, plus marinating time	Ⓓ Ⓜ

This is a classic way to grill lamb chops in Rome, where they're called *scottaditi* or "burnt fingers"—so delicious, you'll burn yourself grabbing them right off the grill. They're traditionally made with rib chops, which make a luxe appetizer. You can use loin chops, though you'll be missing the convenient handle for eating them.

½ cup good-quality olive oil

2 tablespoons minced fresh rosemary

4 cloves garlic, minced

Salt and pepper

4 bay leaves, torn

12 rib or 8 loin lamb chops

Lemon wedges for serving

1 To make the marinade, whisk together the oil, rosemary, garlic, and some salt and pepper in a small bowl. Add the bay leaves. Put the chops in a large baking dish in a single layer or in a zippered bag. Add the marinade and turn the chops until they are entirely coated. Let marinate for up to an hour at room temperature. Or cover and refrigerate for several hours, turning the chops at least once.

2 Start the coals or heat a gas grill for hot indirect cooking. Make sure the grates are clean.

3 Take the chops out of the marinade and let any excess drip off. Put the chops on the grill directly over the fire. Close the lid and cook, turning once, to the desired doneness: for medium-rare, 3 to 4 minutes per side for loin chops and about 2 minutes per side for rib chops. Or if they're going to rest at all before you serve, pull the chops one stage shy of the desired doneness (see page 220: nick with a small knife and peek inside). To prevent over-charring, moving them back and forth between the hot and cool sides of the grill.

4 Transfer the chops to a platter and serve with lemon wedges.

Lamb Chops with Oregano	Instead of rosemary, use up to ¼ cup minced fresh oregano, depending on how intense you want it.
Tandoor-Style Lamb Chops	Nothing beats the flavor and crust of yogurt-marinated lamb: For the marinade, whisk together 1 cup yogurt, ½ cup fresh lemon juice, ¼ cup each minced garlic and fresh ginger, 2 tablespoons garam masala, and salt and pepper to taste. Refrigerate the chops in the marinade for several hours; scrape most of it off before grilling.
Lamb Chops with Shallot-Ginger-Lemongrass Paste	Instead of the marinade, make a flavor paste: Put 2 shallots; a 1-inch piece fresh ginger, cut into slices; the tender inner core of 2 stalks lemongrass cut into pieces; 2 cloves garlic; 1 tablespoon fish sauce; and the grated zest and juice of 1 lime in a blender and purée to a paste. Rub this over the chops and let marinate as directed in Step 1 before grilling.

Meat

Lamb Ribs with Maple-Dijon Dipping Sauce

| Makes: 4 to 6 servings | Time: 1½ to 2 hours, largely unattended | Ⓘ Ⓓ |

The pork belly of lamb, only with bones for gnawing. It's hard to believe this extraordinary eating experience used to be sold for scrap. Lamb ribs are attached to the breast; they require slow cooking to tenderize the meat and melt away as much fat as possible. Give what's left the chop treatment and serve with a dipping sauce and you won't be able to stop eating. If you're cooking with charcoal, I recommend starting with a big, hot fire and not stoking it. To avoid a total fireball when you crisp up the ribs, you want the fire to be pretty mellow. Even so there will be flare-ups, so don't walk away. Give the ribs 1 to 3 minutes per side, then get them off.

5 pounds lamb breast

Salt and pepper

¼ cup maple syrup

¼ cup Dijon mustard

2 tablespoons brown sugar

1 tablespoon red wine vinegar or sherry vinegar

1 Start the coals or heat a gas grill for high to medium-high indirect cooking. Make sure the grates are clean. If using charcoal, put a drip pan under the indirect side of the grill; for gas, empty, clean, and replace the fat trap.

2 Pat the ribs dry with paper towels and sprinkle with salt and pepper on both sides. To make the dipping sauce, whisk the maple syrup, mustard, brown sugar, and vinegar together in a small bowl.

3 Put the ribs on the indirect side of the grill, bone side up, with a long side facing the fire. Close the lid. Move and rotate the breast after 30 minutes for even cooking. Cook until the meat is tender. Test it by trying to cut apart two ribs; you should be able to do it with no resistance. This will take 1 to 1½ hours, depending on how hot the fire is.

4 Transfer the breast pieces to a cutting board, cut between the bones into individual ribs, and return them to the grill, directly over the fire. (If cooking with gas, turn the burners down as low as they will go.) Close the lid and let them crisp up, turning once, for 1 to 3 minutes per side. Serve with the dipping sauce.

Lamb Ribs with Sweet Chili Dipping Sauce	For the dipping sauce, whisk together 6 tablespoons Thai sweet chili sauce and 3 tablespoons each fish sauce and fresh lime juice.
Lamb Ribs with Ginger-Garlic Dipping Sauce	For the dipping sauce, whisk together ¼ cup each soy sauce and orange juice and 2 tablespoons each minced fresh ginger and garlic.
Lamb Ribs with Cranberry–Black Pepper Dipping Sauce	For the dipping sauce, simmer 1 cup unsweetened cranberry juice over medium heat until it's reduced to ½ cup. Whisk in 2 tablespoons each balsamic vinegar and turbinado sugar and 2 teaspoons coarsely ground black pepper.

Ⓓ direct fire   Ⓘ indirect fire   Ⓜ make ahead   Ⓥ vegetarian option

Dilled Leg of Lamb

Makes: 6 to 8 servings	Time: 2 to 3 hours, largely unattended	Ⓘ Ⓜ

Grilling a bone-in leg of lamb yields dramatic results with very little effort. Cooked the entire time over indirect heat, it will develop a beautifully browned—and delectable—crust. Since it's impossible to cook this funky-shaped cut to the same doneness throughout, your best bet is to take it off the grill when the lowest temperature is about 5°F shy of the doneness you prefer for lamb; that way, you'll end up with lamb at pretty much all levels of doneness, all of it juicy.

If you have a choice, buy the leg without the shank, which doesn't take that well to grilling and adds expense. You can also buy half-legs of lamb; the butt half is preferable. Plan on cooking times for a 3- to 4-pound half-leg to be about two-thirds of what they are for a whole leg.

1 bone-in leg of lamb (7–9 pounds)

¼ cup chopped fresh dill

¼ cup minced garlic

1 tablespoon good-quality olive oil

1 lemon, zest grated and lemon cut in half

1 teaspoon salt

1 Start the coals or heat a gas grill for medium to medium-high indirect cooking. Make sure the grates are clean. If using charcoal, put a drip pan under the indirect side of the grill; for gas, empty, clean, and replace the fat trap.

2 Trim the leg of as much surface fat as you can without losing any of the meat, then cut 1-inch incisions all around the leg. Work the dill, garlic, oil, lemon zest, and salt together into a paste in a small bowl with your fingers. Stuff the flavor paste into all the incisions, folds, and crevices. Rub any remaining paste over the meat. (You can prepare the lamb up to a day ahead and refrigerate; take it out when you start the grill.)

3 Put the leg on the indirect side of the grill with the long, thick side closest to the fire. Close the lid. Check the internal temperature of the leg in multiple places after 45 minutes and change the position of the leg so the portion with the lowest temperature is closest to the fire. Continue to monitor and adjust the position every 15 to 20 minutes until the lowest reading is 5° to 10°F shy of the desired doneness (see page 220). This will take 1½ to 2½ hours, depending on the size of the leg, how hot the fire is, and how you like your lamb.

4 Transfer the leg to a cutting board and let rest for 5 minutes, checking the internal temperature occasionally. (Or nick with a small knife and peek inside.) Slice thinly off the bone, squeeze the lemon halves over the sliced meat, and serve.

• recipe continues →

North African–Style Leg of Lamb	*Mechoui* lamb is traditionally slow-and-low spit-roasted and basted with butter until it falls apart. It's even better when the lamb is cooked to medium-rare: Instead of the flavor paste, combine 1 teaspoon each ground cumin, smoked paprika (pimentón), and salt; add ½ teaspoon each ground allspice, coriander, and turmeric. Slice 6 cloves garlic and insert them into the incisions. Melt 4 tablespoons butter. Sprinkle the spice mix all over the leg, patting to help it stick. Grill as directed; after 45 minutes, begin basting the leg on all sides with the butter. Continue to do this every time you check on the lamb's progress, until the butter is used up or the lamb is ready.
Roman-Style Leg of Lamb	Substitute rosemary for the dill and add 1 tablespoon red wine vinegar and 6 oil-packed anchovy fillets. Put the mixture in a mortar and crush into a paste with a pestle, or mash it in a small bowl with a fork.
Leg of Lamb with Lavender and Garlic	More floral than rosemary with the same woodsy aroma: Substitute 2 tablespoons chopped fresh lavender leaves for the dill; make sure the lavender is unsprayed.

Butterflied Leg of Lamb, Shawarma Style

Makes: **4 servings**	Time: **50 to 60 minutes, plus marinating time**	Ⓓ Ⓜ

Traditional shawarma as prepared in the Middle East is a large hunk of meat that's slowly spit-roasted and served in thin slices shaved from the outside first. Quickly grilling a butterflied leg seasoned with the flavorings of shawarma is a surprisingly close approximation. Serve the meat to eat with a knife and fork or turn into a pita sandwich with fresh tomatoes and thin slices of cucumber and onion, drizzled with a little yogurt and a squeeze of lemon. (To make your own pitas, see page 492.) You can use this flavor paste or any of the variations with bone-in leg of lamb, lamb chops, or boneless chicken thighs.

The challenge with butterflied leg is that it is somewhat held together by the fat on one side. Rendering lamb fat can cause big flare-ups, resulting in the lamb burning, not browning. If you find that happening, move the lamb to the outer edge of the fire; the cook time may increase.

2 to 2½ pounds butterflied leg of lamb (about half a leg)

½ cup packed fresh cilantro leaves

2 cloves garlic, peeled

2 teaspoons paprika

2 teaspoons ground cumin

1 teaspoon black pepper

1 teaspoon salt

½ teaspoon ground cinnamon

½ teaspoon ground ginger

½ teaspoon freshly grated nutmeg

¼ teaspoon ground cloves

2 tablespoons good-quality olive oil, or as needed

1 Trim as much surface fat as possible from all sides of the lamb without causing it to fall apart.

2 To make the flavor paste, put the cilantro, garlic, paprika, cumin, pepper, sault, cinnamon, ginger, nutmeg, and cloves in a blender or mini food processor with the oil and process into a smooth paste, adding more oil, 1 tablespoon at a time, as needed to purée the mixture. Rub the paste over the lamb into all the nooks and crannies. Let sit at room temperature while you prepare the fire. (You can prepare the lamb to this point up to a day in advance; cover or put in a zipper bag and refrigerate. Take it out when you fire up the grill.)

3 Start the coals or heat a gas grill for medium direct cooking. Make sure the grates are clean.

4 Put the lamb on the grill directly over the fire. Close the lid and cook, turning once, until the internal temperature at the thickest point is 5° to 10°F shy of the desired doneness (see page 220), 10 to 20 minutes per side, depending on the thickness of the lamb, how hot the fire is, and how you like your lamb.

5 Transfer to a cutting board and let rest 5 to 10 minutes, checking the internal temperature occasionally. (Or nick with a small knife and peek inside.) Slice thinly across the grain and serve.

Ⓓ direct fire   Ⓘ indirect fire   Ⓜ make ahead   Ⓥ vegetarian option

Butterflied Lamb with Orange and Mint	For the flavor paste, purée ½ cup packed fresh mint leaves, 2 tablespoons each good-quality olive oil and grated orange zest, 1 teaspoon each ground cardamom and black pepper, and salt to taste. Add more olive oil during puréeing if necessary.
Butterflied Lamb with Persillade	For the flavor paste, purée ½ cup packed fresh parsley leaves, 2 tablespoons good-quality olive oil, 2 cloves garlic, the grated zest of 1 lemon, and salt and pepper to taste. Add more olive oil during puréeing if necessary.
Sichuan Pepper Butterflied Leg of Lamb	Butterflied leg of lamb is also wonderful marinated, especially with this amazing spice more closely related to roses than peppers: Instead of the flavor paste, put ¼ cup good-quality vegetable oil in a blender with 3 tablespoons rice vinegar, 2 tablespoons each soy sauce, sesame oil, and Sichuan peppercorns, and 2 cloves garlic, minced; purée. Pour into a large baking dish, add the lamb, and turn to coat well on both sides. Marinate at room temperature while you prepare the fire or in the refrigerator for up to 4 hours, turning it several times.

Shashlik with Onions and Grapes

| Makes: **4 to 6 servings** | Time: **40 to 50 minutes, plus marinating time,** largely unattended | Ⓓ Ⓜ |

Shashlik comes from the Turkish word *şiş*—as in "shish kebab"—and means skewered food. Lamb is a very popular meat for kebabs throughout Eastern Europe; this recipe is based on a Georgian version. Don't be afraid of all the vinegar—the flavor after grilling is fantastic.

2 pounds boneless lamb (from the leg or shoulder)

1 small onion, cut into small wedges

4 bay leaves

1 cup red wine vinegar

24 large seedless red and/or green grapes, or as needed

1 Trim any excess fat from the lamb, then cut into 1½-inch chunks (you need about 24 pieces). Put the meat in a large bowl. Add the onion, bay leaves, and vinegar and toss to combine. Cover and marinate in the refrigerator for at least 4 hours and up to 12 hours, but no more or the acid in the vinegar will soften the fibers of the meat too much.

2 If you're using bamboo or wooden skewers, soak them in water for 30 minutes. Meanwhile, start the coals or heat a gas grill for medium-high direct cooking. Make sure the grates are clean.

3 When the fire is just about ready, drain the lamb and discard the marinade. Thread the lamb onto skewers, alternating the chunks with a few layers of onion and a grape.

4 Put the skewers on the grill directly over the fire. Close the lid and cook, turning once, 4 to 10 minutes per side, depending on how well done you like your lamb. (Nick with a small knife and peek inside.) Transfer to a platter and serve.

Carrot-Ginger Lamb Kebabs with Cherry Tomatoes	Omit the onion, bay leaves, and vinegar. Marinate the lamb in a mixture of 1 cup carrot juice, ¼ cup fresh lime juice, and ¼ cup minced fresh ginger. Substitute cherry tomatoes for the grapes.
Sherried Lamb Kebabs with Figs	Omit the onion, bay leaves, and vinegar. Marinate the lamb in a mixture of ½ cup sherry vinegar, ¼ cup good-quality olive oil, and 2 tablespoons chopped garlic. Substitute 12 or more fresh figs for the grapes, brushing them with the marinade before putting the skewers on the grill.
Zinfandel Lamb Kebabs with Watermelon	Omit the onion and vinegar. Marinate the lamb and bay leaves in a mixture of ½ cup each zinfandel and good-quality olive oil. Replace the grapes with enough watermelon cut into 1½-inch cubes to alternate on the skewers. Brush the watermelon with marinade before putting the skewers on the grill.

Ⓓ direct fire   Ⓘ indirect fire   Ⓜ make ahead   Ⓥ vegetarian option

Adana Kebabs

Makes: 4 servings	Time: 50 to 60 minutes	Ⓓ Ⓜ

These minced lamb kebabs, which are more like sausages, originate in Turkey. For the best flavor and texture, the lamb should be at least 20% fat. So if you're grinding your own, lamb shoulder or leg of lamb works best; be sure to include some fatty pieces as well. Here the kebabs are grilled right on the grates, but you can skewer them lengthwise and give them a bit of a squeeze to make sure they are firmly attached. Use flat metal skewers so the kebabs don't spin when you turn them.

These are traditionally served on flatbread with a salad of grilled red peppers and tomatoes, sliced onion, parsley, and a good sprinkle of sumac.

1½ pounds ground lamb shoulder or leg (to grind your own, see page 260)

½ cup minced red bell pepper

½ cup minced onion

2 tablespoons ground sumac

4 teaspoons ground cumin

2 teaspoons ground coriander

2 teaspoons red chile flakes or Aleppo pepper

Salt

1 Put the lamb, bell pepper, onion, sumac, cumin, coriander, red pepper, and some salt in a large bowl and work everything together with your hands until combined. Pinch off golf ball–sized pieces of the mixture and with one hand, squeeze them into sausages 3 to 3½ inches long and about 1 inch thick. Put them on a platter without touching, cover with plastic wrap, and refrigerate while you prepare the fire, or for up to 12 hours.

2 Start the coals or heat a gas grill for medium-high direct cooking. Make sure the grates are clean.

3 Put the sausages on the grill directly over the fire. Close the lid and cook, turning them every 1 to 2 minutes for even browning, until crusty and just cooked through. (Nick with a small knife and peek inside.) Depending on how hot the fire is, this will take 6 to 15 minutes total. Transfer to a clean platter and serve.

Lamb and Bulgur Kebabs	Put ½ cup each bulgur and boiling water in a large heatproof bowl. Stir and cover. Let sit until all the water is absorbed and the bulgur has cooled. Decrease the lamb to 1 pound, the onion to ¼ cup, and the cumin to 2 teaspoons. If you're using red chile flakes, only use 1 teaspoon; use the full 2 teaspoons Aleppo pepper. Add the lamb, onion, cumin, and red bell pepper to the bulgur, along with ½ cup finely chopped pistachios, ¼ cup minced fresh parsley, 2 tablespoons minced garlic, ½ teaspoon ground allspice, and some salt and pepper. Stir gently to combine.
Syrian-Style Kebabs	Omit the cumin and coriander. Replace the bell pepper and onion with 1 cup minced fresh parsley, and add 1 tablespoon minced garlic.
Lyulya-Style Lamb Kebabs	This seasoning is common in Central Asia: Omit the red bell pepper. Increase the onion to 1 cup. Add ¼ cup chopped fresh parsley and 2 tablespoons minced garlic, substitute paprika for the coriander, and omit the sumac. Serve sprinkled with ¼ cup chopped fresh mint.

KEBAB-FRIENDLY RICE

The best way to serve kebabs—no matter what kind—is over a bed of rice to soak up the delicious juices. You can change up the flavorings in the rice to match or complement the kebabs you'll be serving. Here are three versions I mix and match with kebabs.

Coconut Rice. Combine 1½ cups each coconut milk, water, and jasmine rice in a medium-sized saucepan. Bring to a boil, reduce the heat so the liquid bubbles gently, cover, and cook until holes form in the surface of the rice, about 10 minutes. Turn the heat off and let sit until all the liquid is absorbed, 10 to 15 minutes. Fluff the rice before serving.

Curried Rice with Chickpeas. Heat 1 tablespoon good-quality vegetable oil in a medium-sized saucepan over medium heat, add ½ cup chopped onion and 1 tablespoon each minced garlic and fresh ginger, and cook, stirring occasionally, until softened, 3 to 5 minutes. Stir in 1 tablespoon curry powder until fragrant. Add 1½ cups basmati rice, stirring to coat the grains with the flavored oil. Add 1½ cups each chopped tomatoes and water, 1 cup cooked chickpeas, and some salt and pepper. Stir to combine, then cook as directed for Coconut Rice.

Rice Pilaf with Peas and Mint. Melt 2 tablespoons butter in a medium-sized saucepan over medium heat. Add 1 cup chopped onion and cook, stirring occasionally, until softened, 3 to 5 minutes. Add 1½ cups long-grain rice and 1 cup fresh or frozen peas and stir to coat the grains. Add 3 cups water and some salt and stir to combine. Cook as directed for Coconut Rice. Sprinkle with ½ cup or more chopped fresh mint before serving.

Tzatziki Lamb Burgers

Makes: 4 or 5 burgers or 8 to 10 sliders	Time: 40 to 50 minutes	Ⓓ Ⓜ

Given the chance, I'll choose a lamb burger over beef, hands down. Made with good-quality meat, they taste just fine with nothing more than salt and pepper. Up the ante and you have something extraordinary. If you can't get excellent preground lamb that's locally raised and super-fresh, grind your own (see "Do-It-Yourself Ground Meat," page 260). That stuff sold in hermetically sealed plastic containers has no flavor.

1½ pounds boneless lamb shoulder or leg or good-quality ground lamb

1 tablespoon chopped fresh oregano

1 teaspoon salt

1 teaspoon black pepper

1 tablespoon minced garlic

½ cup Greek yogurt

1 tablespoon good-quality olive oil, plus more for brushing

1 tablespoon red wine vinegar

2 tablespoons crumbled feta cheese

4 or 5 ciabatta rolls, split, or 8–10 slider buns (like potato or dinner rolls)

Thinly sliced cucumbers for serving

1 Working in batches if necessary, put the lamb, oregano, salt, pepper, and garlic in a food processor and pulse until coarsely ground—finer than chopped, but not much. (If you're using preground meat, put it in a bowl with the seasonings and work them together gently with your hands.) Take a bit of the mixture and fry it up to taste for seasoning; adjust if necessary. Handling the meat as little as possible to avoid compressing it, shape the mixture lightly into 4 or 5 burgers or 8 to 10 sliders. Refrigerate the burgers until you're ready to grill; if you make them several hours in advance, cover with plastic wrap.

2 Start the coals or heat a gas grill for medium-high direct cooking. Make sure the grates are clean.

3 Whisk the yogurt, oil, and vinegar together in a small bowl until smooth. Stir in the feta. Taste and adjust the seasoning with salt and pepper.

4 Put the burgers on the grill directly over the fire. Close the lid and cook, turning once, until just shy of the desired doneness, 4 to 10 minutes per side (the carryover heat will finish the job). Nick with a small knife and peek inside to check.

5 Transfer the burgers to a plate. Brush the cut sides of the rolls lightly with oil and toast directly over the fire, 1 to 2 minutes. Top with a burger, then several slices of cucumber, a dollop of the sauce, and the other half of the roll. Serve with the remaining sauce on the side.

Ⓓ direct fire   Ⓘ indirect fire   Ⓜ make ahead   Ⓥ vegetarian option

Persian-Style Lamb Burgers with Minted Yogurt	Omit the oregano and garlic. In addition to the salt and pepper, add 1 teaspoon each ground cumin and coriander, ½ teaspoon each ground cinnamon and allspice, and ¼ teaspoon ground cardamom to the lamb. Replace the vinegar and feta with 2 tablespoons chopped fresh mint and 1 tablespoon grated orange zest. Omit the cucumber slices, if you like.
Curry Lamb Burgers with Lime Yogurt	Replace the oregano with 2½ tablespoons curry powder and add 2 tablespoons minced fresh ginger. Replace the vinegar and feta with the grated zest and juice of 1 lime and 2 tablespoons chopped fresh cilantro. If you like, top each burger with a thin slice of ripe mango instead of cucumber.
Garlic-Rosemary Burgers	Substitute rosemary for the oregano. Omit the sauce. After toasting the rolls, rub the cut side of the rolls with a garlic clove, and replace the cucumber with sliced tomato.

Merguez

| Makes: 8 large sausages | Time: 1 to 1½ hours | Ⓓ Ⓜ |

Merguez is a spicy lamb or lamb-and-beef sausage popular throughout North Africa and parts of Europe. It's gaining traction in the United States, too. The same three-to-one meat-to-fat ratio of other sausages is the goal. (For more on grinding your own meat, see "Do-It-Yourself Ground Meat," page 260.) You can stuff the meat into casings if you like, but it's easier to cook these as patties. You can also serve these sausages as burgers or sliders or form them into Middle Eastern–style kebabs, on skewers or not; see page 320. Or try a merguez frites sandwich, popular street food in France: Cut open a piece of baguette, smear with mustard or mayo, and fill with grilled merguez and a handful of French fries.

This makes 8 large sausages, so you might want to freeze half if you're serving only 4 people; shape or stuff the sausages before freezing them.

2½ pounds boneless lamb shoulder or leg, with fat

2 tablespoons minced garlic

2 tablespoons harissa

1½ teaspoons paprika

1½ teaspoons fennel seeds

1½ teaspoons cumin seeds

1½ teaspoons coriander seeds, crushed

1½ teaspoons salt

1½ teaspoons black pepper

Ice water (optional)

Sausage casings (optional)

1 Cut the lamb and fat into 1-inch cubes. Put about 2 cups of the mixture in a food processor and pulse until finely chopped. Take your time and be careful not to pulverize the meat. As you finish each batch, transfer it to a bowl.

2 Add the garlic, harissa, paprika, fennel, cumin, coriander seeds, salt, and pepper and work them into the meat with your hands until evenly distributed; add ice water 1 tablespoon at a time if the mixture seems very dry. Cook up a spoonful in a small skillet to taste it; adjust the seasoning. Shape into patties, or stuff into casings if you prefer.

3 Start the coals or heat a gas grill for medium direct cooking. Make sure the grates are clean.

4 Put the sausages on the grill directly over the fire. Close the lid and cook, turning once, until barely pink inside (the internal temperature in the center should be 145°F), 5 to 10 minutes per side, depending on how thick they are and how hot the fire is. Check often with an instant-read thermometer, or nick with a small knife and peek inside. If there are a lot of flare-ups, move the sausages to the edge of the fire. Transfer to a platter and serve.

Lamb Sausage with Chives	Not as strong as onions and with a pleasant herbaceousness: Omit the harissa. Add ½ cup chopped fresh chives when grinding the meat, or add to the ground lamb along with the other seasonings.
Lamb Sausage with Pecorino and Parsley	Omit the harissa, paprika, cumin, and coriander. Add ¾ cup grated pecorino Romano cheese and ⅓ cup chopped fresh parsley.
Venison Sausage with Caraway and Rosemary	Venison sausage is a real treat, but unless you're a hunter or friend of a hunter, it's unlikely you'll be able to get a piece with the fat ratio you need, so supplement the meat with pork fat: Replace the lamb with 1¾ pounds lean venison and ¾ pound pork fat. Omit the harissa, paprika, fennel, cumin, and coriander. After grinding, add the garlic, ¼ cup red wine, 2 tablespoons chopped fresh rosemary, 1 tablespoon caraway seeds, the salt, and pepper.

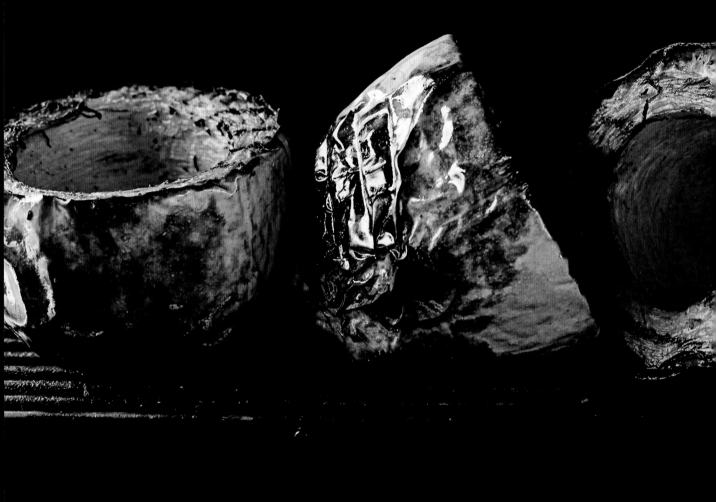

Vegetarian Mains

I don't have a meat-or-bust approach to grilling. Vegetables can and should get prime real estate over the fire. Their variety of colors, tastes, and textures always adds excitement to outdoor cooking. And since vegetables are more popular than ever you may as well have plenty of mains—and sides, which start on page 378—in your repertoire.

The hearty dishes in this chapter will wow vegetarians and everyone else with satisfying grilled alternatives for weeknight dinners, party spreads, and celebrations.

Many are inspired by age-old vegetable cooking traditions. Others are utterly modern. There are even surprising and delicious vegan options here and elsewhere in the book; see the list below.

Tofu and tempeh—two very different soy foods—are important vegetable proteins for vegetarians and vegans, and they're easy to love when they're seasoned well and cooked over fire. I've got lots of recipes here for grilling and smoking both of them as a centerpiece, as well as many dishes where they play a supporting role.

The other two big ingredients in this chapter are eggplant and mushrooms. Personal bias, yes—they're two of my favorite vegetables—but they also happen to work perfectly on the grill, take to many different flavor spins, and are hearty and satisfying.

So from burgers and composed salads to stuffed or layered vegetables, the bulk of these recipes qualify as stand-alone vegetarian mains. To build more into the meal, like a salad, some bread, a side, or even some meat, be sure to browse the Appetizers and Snacks, Breads and Desserts, and Vegetables and Sides chapters.

---

21 VEGETARIAN APPETIZERS AND SNACKS

Those marked with an asterisk are also vegan or have a vegan variation.

1. *Baba Ghanoush (page 23)
2. *Smoky Guacamole (page 26)
3. *Fire-Roasted Tomatillo Salsa with Grilled Tortilla Wedges (page 27)
4. *Ancho-Dusted Jícama Sticks with Lime (page 29)
5. *Radishes with Butter and Sea Salt (page 30)
6. *Rosemary and Garlic Olives (page 31)
7. *Quick-Pickled Charred Vegetables (page 32)
8. *Smoked Nuts (page 56)
9. *Roasted Peppers (page 34)
10. Jalapeño Poppers with Smoked Gouda (page 37)
11. *Crisp Baby Artichokes with Lemon Aïoli (page 38)
12. *Brussels Sprout Skewers with Green Olive Dipping Sauce (page 41)
13. Mushrooms with Herbed Goat Cheese and Toasted Walnuts (page 43)
14. Smoked Cheese (page 45)
15. Provoleta (page 47)
16. Real Grilled Cheese Bites (page 50)
17. Cheesy Jalapeño Quesadillas (page 51)
18. *Bruschetta (page 21)
19. Pizza Bianca (page 52)
20. Rosemary Polenta Squares with Orange Crème Fraîche and Olives (page 60)
21. *Tofu Skewers with Peanut Sauce (page 81)

D direct fire   I indirect fire   M make ahead   V vegetarian option

Tofu Steaks

Makes: 2 to 4 servings	Time: 20 to 30 minutes	Ⓓ Ⓥ

Tofu is transformed on the grill—and there's no need to freeze or press it first to get that pleasant chew. The outside develops a crust and chars in spots while the inside becomes warm and custardy. For center-of-the-plate steaks, figure one block per two people; as part of a larger meal, one can stretch into more servings. You can also cook tofu kebabs the same way, cutting the steaks into 24 or so 1- to 1½-inch cubes, then threading them on skewers. (To minimize spinning, use flat metal skewer.) The cook time will be about the same.

1 block firm or extra-firm tofu (14–16 ounces)

Good-quality olive oil for brushing

Salt

Pepper (optional)

1 Start the coals or heat a gas grill for medium direct cooking. Make sure the grates are clean.

2 Cut the tofu across into 1-inch-thick steaks. Pat dry with paper towels, then brush with oil and sprinkle with salt on both sides.

3 Put the tofu on the grill directly over the fire. Close the lid and cook, turning once, until the slices develop a crust and release easily from the grate, about 5 minutes per side. Sprinkle with more salt and some pepper if you like and serve.

Miso Tofu Steaks	You can use any miso, but robust red or brown miso are the best: Warm ½ cup red miso and 2 tablespoons each sake or white wine and mirin in a small saucepan over low heat. Whisk until smooth; taste and add a little sugar if you like. Once the first side has released from the grate, brush the tofu liberally with the miso glaze and continue to cook, turning and basting, until the tofu is dark brown.
Crisp and Chewy Tofu Steaks	For a steak with a denser texture and some crunch, or for cottage fry–like sticks, you've got two options: Cut the tofu into thinner pieces, about ½ inch thick, or keep the slices 1 inch thick but cook them longer over a medium-low fire, until they dry out a little more and become mostly crust, 10 to 20 minutes total, turning them several times.
Marinated Tofu Steaks	Marinating can also add flavor to tofu's crust during grilling. Let it go anywhere from 30 minutes to overnight; refrigerate if it's any longer than an hour: Put ¼ cup good-quality olive oil in a shallow baking dish with 3 tablespoons fresh lemon juice, 2 tablespoons minced onion, 1 tablespoon minced garlic, and some salt and pepper. Add the tofu steaks, turning them to coat and continue to turn them occasionally as they marinate.

Grilled Tempeh

Makes: 2 servings	Time: 20 to 25 minutes	D V

Like tofu, tempeh is terrific on the grill. But unlike tofu, it's fermented and has a pronounced tanginess; it's also denser and chewier, with whole beans—and sometimes rice or grains—visible. So I often use grilled tempeh as a component—cubed or crumbled in salads, in a pita or taco, and so on. It's usually sold in eight-ounce pieces about an inch thick, which you can brush with oil and put straight on the grill, or cut into 16 or so cubes for kebabs; cook time will be about the same.

1 8-ounce piece tempeh

Good-quality olive oil for brushing

Salt

Pepper (optional)

1 Start the coals or heat a gas grill for medium direct cooking. Make sure the grates are clean.

2 Brush the tempeh with oil and sprinkle with salt on both sides.

3 Put the tempeh on the grill directly over the fire. Close the lid and cook, turning once, until it develops a crust and releases easily from the grates, about 3 minutes per side. Sprinkle with more salt and some pepper if you like, and serve.

---

9 MARINADES FOR TOFU OR TEMPEH

All of these will add fantastic flavor. Marinate for as little as 30 minutes or up to overnight in the refrigerator.

1. Sweet Soy-Lime marinade (page 111)
2. Finadene Dipping Sauce (page 213)
3. Crying Tiger Dipping Sauce (page 239)
4. Vinaigrette from Boneless Chicken Breasts and Red Onion en Escabeche (page 160)
5. Dijon-Orange Vinaigrette (page 382)
6. Tare Sauce (page 238)
7. Salmoriglio (page 119)
8. Mojo Sauce (page 423)
9. Sherry Vinaigrette (page 395)

D direct fire   I indirect fire   M make ahead   V vegetarian option

Crunchy Tempeh	This is perfect for when you want to crumble the tempeh into another dish: Cut the tempeh across into ½-inch slices, sprinkle with salt, and cook over a medium-low fire, turning frequently, until browned and crisp, 10 to 20 minutes total.
Barbecued Tempeh	Wonderful crumbled into Vegetarian or Vegan Baked Beans (page 391): Once the tempeh has been grilled, brush it with your choice of barbecue sauce (see page 457 for a list) and let it caramelize over the fire for a minute or so per side.
Ponzu-Marinated Tempeh	Make Ponzu Sauce (page 468). Use about ½ cup to marinate 8 ounces tempeh slices or cubes as described in the tofu variation on page 329.

---

16 SATISFYING VEGAN MAINS

1. Tofu Steaks (page 329)
2. Grilled Tempeh (opposite)
3. Smoked Tofu (page 332)
4. Chana Chaat Burgers (page 338)
5. Beet Burgers with Dates and Ginger (page 340)
6. Design-Your-Own Nut Burgers (page 341)
7. Portobello Caprese Stacks (page 345)
8. Curry-Coconut Cauliflower Steaks with Pistachios (page 347)
9. Eggplant with Tomatoes and Peanuts (page 349)
10. Quinoa Salad with Apples, Brussels Sprouts, and Walnuts (page 373)
11. Spaghetti Squash with Fresh Tomato Sauce (page 361)
12. Tomatoes Stuffed with Chickpeas and Rice (page 352)
13. Stuffed Winter Squash with Quinoa, Green Beans, and Tomatoes (page 358)
14. Stuffed Cabbage with Summer Vegetables (page 356)
15. Vegetarian Paella with Artichokes, Red Peppers, and White Beans (page 366)
16. Tofu Masala (page 370)

Smoked Tofu

Makes: 2 main dish servings, or more as a component	Time: 35 to 50 minutes, largely unattended	Ⓘ Ⓜ Ⓥ

Smoked tofu adds so much flavor to any dish (see "9 Ways to Enjoy Grilled or Smoked Tofu or Tempeh," opposite) and it's a snap to do. The smoke works to evaporate the water in tofu so the results are smaller, denser pieces. To me the sweet spot is 30 minutes of smoking but try more or less; with such a short window, wood chips are the best choice. If you keep the grill temp below 350°F, you'll end up with smoky—but not dry—slices perfect on a toasted bun with lettuce and tomato. Change up the flavors with marinades or spice rubs; see the marinade options in other recipes and "9 Spice Mixes You Can Make Yourself," page 456.

1 block firm or extra-firm tofu (14–16 ounces)

Good-quality vegetable oil for brushing

Salt and pepper

1 Start the coals or heat a gas grill for medium indirect cooking. If using a charcoal grill, position the coals so that the smoke will be pulled over the tofu and out the top vent.

2 Drain the tofu and pat dry with a paper towel. Slice across 1 inch or thinner. Brush the slices with oil to help the smoke stick, and sprinkle with salt and pepper on both sides.

3 When the grill is ready, add wood chips to the fire (see "Smoking," pages 10–12) and close the lid. When the grill is full of smoke, put the tofu on the indirect side. Close the lid and cook until the surface has turned golden, 20 to 30 minutes (or darker and longer if you like). Depending on how close the slices are to the fire, the edges might get browner and the slices may develop grill marks. Make sure the grill is full of smoke the entire time; you may need to add another cup of wood chips.

4 Serve or use in something else right away, or let cool, cover, and refrigerate for up to 5 days.

Smoked Tofu Bites with Dipping Sauce	An easy appetizer: After smoking the tofu, cut it into 1-inch cubes and serve on toothpicks with Ponzu Sauce (page 468) or Peanut Sauce (page 469) or its variations.
Smoky Vegan Tofu Dip with Lemon	This has a consistency similar to hummus and you can use it in the same way: As soon as the tofu has enough smokiness, get it off the grill to retain as much moisture as possible. Cut 8 to 12 ounces smoked tofu (usually 1 block) into pieces, put in a food processor, and purée until first crumbled, then creamy. Add 2 tablespoons good-quality olive oil, 1 tablespoon fresh lemon juice, and 1 teaspoon grated lemon zest. Purée until smooth. Keep adding more oil, 1 tablespoon at a time, until you have a somewhat loose consistency, between a spread and a dip. Taste, sprinkle with salt and adjust the flavor with more lemon juice, if needed. Makes about 1 cup.
Smoked Tempeh	Tempeh is a lot drier and denser than tofu, so smoke doesn't penetrate it as deeply. Cutting it into smaller pieces—just big enough so they won't fall through the grates—helps: Cut two 8-ounce pieces of tempeh into 1- to 1½-inch cubes and toss with ¼ cup good-quality vegetable oil to coat. (To smoke the tempeh whole, brush the pieces with about 2 tablespoons oil.) Grill as directed; taste occasionally to make sure it's as smoky as you want. Time is the same for cubes and whole pieces. Use right away or refrigerate up to a week.

---

9 WAYS TO ENJOY GRILLED OR SMOKED TOFU OR TEMPEH

For all of these ideas, you can cube, chop, slice, or crumble the tofu or tempeh as you like.

1. Add to tacos or quesadillas, like Cheesy Jalapeño Quesadillas (page 51)
2. Include in all kinds of salads
3. Add to stuffing or savory bread pudding, like Main-Course Bread Pudding with Mushrooms and Rosemary (page 376)
4. Include in a stir-fry
5. Add to scrambled eggs
6. Stir into soups, stews, or curries
7. Enjoy as part of a wrap, like Tofu–Asian Pear Wraps with Green Goddess Dressing (page 334)
8. Add to the filling of stuffed vegetables like Tomatoes Stuffed with Chickpeas and Rice (page 352) or Stuffed Winter Squash with Quinoa, Green Beans, and Tomatoes (page 358)
9. Stir into Vegetarian or Vegan Baked Beans (page 391)

Tofu–Asian Pear Wraps with Green Goddess Dressing

Makes: 4 servings	Time: 45 to 50 minutes	Ⓓ Ⓜ Ⓥ

These well-balanced wraps are satisfying and bursting with fresh herb flavor. Asian pear—with the sweetness of pears and the crispness of apples—provides a refreshing crunch inside but you can use a regular pear or apple. You can prepare the dressing up to a few hours ahead and refrigerate.

½ cup mayonnaise

½ cup packed baby spinach

½ cup packed fresh parsley leaves

¼ cup packed fresh tarragon leaves

1 tablespoon fresh lemon juice, or more as needed

Salt and pepper

1 block firm tofu (14–16 ounces)

Good-quality olive oil for brushing

4 10-inch flour tortillas

1½ to 2 cups baby arugula

1 Asian pear, quartered, cored, and thinly sliced (no need to peel)

1 Start the coals or heat a gas grill for medium direct cooking. Make sure the grates are clean.

2 To make the dressing, put the mayonnaise, spinach, parsley, tarragon, and lemon juice in a blender or food processor with some salt and pepper and purée. Taste and adjust the seasoning, adding more lemon juice if you like.

3 Cut the tofu across into 1-inch slices. Pat dry with paper towels, then brush with oil and sprinkle with salt on both sides.

4 Put the tofu on the grill directly over the fire. Close the lid and cook, turning once, until it develops a crust and releases easily from the grate, about 5 minutes per side. Transfer to a cutting board and cut into 1-inch cubes.

5 To make the wraps, warm the tortillas directly over the fire without crisping them, less than a minute per side. Spread each tortilla with some dressing and add a handful of arugula. Divide the tofu cubes between the tortillas, top with sliced pear, roll up, cut in half, and serve with the remaining dressing on the side.

Tempeh–Asian Pear Wraps with Green Goddess Dressing	Substitute two 8-ounce pieces tempeh for the tofu, and thinly sliced kale for the arugula if you like. Grill as directed; the tempeh will only take about 3 minutes per side. Crumble the tempeh and finish the wraps as directed.
Tofu-Cauliflower Wraps with Parmesan Herb Dressing	Substitute basil for the tarragon in the dressing and add ½ cup grated Parmesan cheese. Season generously with pepper. Instead of the Asian pear, cut two 1- to 1½-inch-thick slices cauliflower, through the stem end. Brush with good-quality olive oil and grill with the tofu until tender and a bit charred in places, 10 to 15 minutes per side; move it to a cooler part of the grill as necessary to prevent burning. Roughly chop the cauliflower and finish the wraps as directed.
Barbecued Tofu Tacos with Spicy Lime Mayo	Sriracha or other garlicky hot sauce is perfect here. One serving is 3 tacos: Substitute twelve 6-inch corn tortillas for the flour tortillas and 2 cups shredded cabbage for the arugula; chop the Asian pear. Instead of the dressing, whisk together ½ cup mayonnaise, 1 tablespoon soy sauce, 2 teaspoons hot sauce (more or less to taste), and the grated zest of 1 lime. Heat ¾ cup barbecue sauce (see page 457 for a list). After grilling the tofu, cut it into cubes and toss with the barbecue sauce. Fill each taco with a little tofu; top with cabbage, pear, and a drizzle of the mayonnaise.

Scallion-Sesame Tofu Sliders

| Makes: 6 servings | Time: 45 to 50 minutes, plus chilling time | Ⓓ Ⓜ Ⓥ |

Sea greens add both taste and texture to tofu, which makes a perfect backdrop for a burger with Japanese flavors. Puréeing part of the tofu and adding an egg and some panko helps hold everything together, but since these are a bit on the fragile side, make them small and take care when turning them; if you have a perforated grill pan, this would be a perfect time to use it.

There are lots of ways to serve these burgers: On small buns with the usual condiments; on a bed of plain-cooked soba or udon noodles, drizzled with sesame oil and soy sauce; or as the centerpiece of a rice or grain bowl.

¼ cup dried arame or other dark sea green, like kombu

Boiling water

1½ pounds firm tofu

1 egg, beaten

12 scallions, trimmed and minced

½ cup panko

¼ cup sesame seeds

1 tablespoon soy sauce, or more to taste

2 teaspoons sesame oil

Salt and pepper

1 Cut the sea greens into small pieces with scissors and put in a heatproof bowl. Pour boiling water over them and soak for 1 or 2 minutes. Drain well.

2 Gently squeeze the tofu to remove excess water and pat dry with paper towels. Put about half the tofu and all the sea greens in a food processor and pulse until just crumbled. Transfer to a large bowl. Put the remaining tofu in the processor and purée until smooth. Add it to the bowl along with the egg, scallions, panko, sesame seeds, soy sauce, and oil. Sprinkle with a little salt and lots of pepper and stir well to combine. With wet hands, form the mixture into 12 sliders. Put them on a platter without touching, and refrigerate for at least 1 hour. (You can make the sliders up to a day or so in advance; cover tightly and refrigerate.)

3 Start the coals or heat a gas grill for medium-high direct cooking. Make sure the grates are clean.

4 Put the sliders on the grill directly over the fire. Close the lid and cook, turning once, until they start to brown and release easily from the grates, about 5 minutes per side. Transfer to a plate and serve as you like (see the headnote).

Tofu-Walnut Burgers	Rich and silky: Reduce the tofu to 1 pound and omit the sesame seeds. Add ½ cup chopped walnuts, cashews, almonds, or hazelnuts to the first batch of tofu and pulse until the mixture is crumbly. Add ¼ cup chopped walnuts to the second batch of the tofu and process until smooth. Proceed with the recipe.
Tofu Sesame Burgers with Adzuki Beans	Nice reddish brown color and meaty texture: Reduce the tofu to 1 pound. Add 1 cup well-drained adzuki beans to the processor with the sea greens and tofu and pulse a few times until crumbled. Proceed with the recipe.
Tofu-Tempeh Burger	Deeply flavored: Replace 8 ounces of the tofu with 8 ounces tempeh. Pulse the tempeh with the sea greens and a little bit of the tofu until crumbly. Proceed with the recipe.

11 TOPPERS FOR VEGETARIAN BURGERS

1. Scallion Mayo (page 256)
2. Garlic Mayonnaise (Aïoli; page 461)
3. Black Bean Ketchup (page 463)
4. Jamaican Jerk Ketchup (page 463)
5. Balsamic Syrup (page 467)
6. Peanut Sauce (page 469)
7. Romesco Sauce (page 470)
8. Fresh Mango Salsa with Basil (page 473)
9. Cilantro-Mint Chutney (page 474)
10. Baba Ghanoush (page 23)
11. Smoky Guacamole (page 26)

Chana Chaat Burgers

Makes: 4 to 8 servings	Time: 40 to 45 minutes, plus chilling time	Ⓓ Ⓜ Ⓥ

I love the flavors in *aloo chana chaat*, the saucy Indian appetizer of potatoes and chickpeas, and they happen to make a wonderful burger, too. No need for a bun; serve these with your favorite chutney (try Cilantro-Mint Chutney, page 474, or its variations). These can be a bit crumbly, so if you have a perforated grill pan, use it. Otherwise, just handle them gently. Look for chaat masala in Indian markets; its somewhat tangy taste is distinctive. If you can only find garam masala, go for it; you'll still be happy.

3½ cups cooked chickpeas, drained

1½ cups mashed potatoes

1 cup minced onion

½ cup chopped fresh cilantro

2 teaspoons chaat masala

2 teaspoons grated lime zest

1 teaspoon ground cumin

Salt and pepper

1 Put the chickpeas and potatoes in a large bowl and mash with a potato masher or fork until they come together. Add the onion, cilantro, chaat masala, lime zest, and cumin; work them in by mashing with a wooden spoon or the back of a fork. Taste and add some salt and pepper if needed. With wet hands, shape the mixture into 8 burgers. Put them on a platter without touching, and refrigerate for at least 1 hour. (You can make the burgers up to a day or so in advance. Cover tightly and refrigerate.)

2 Start the coals or heat a gas grill for medium direct cooking. Make sure the grates are clean.

3 Put the burgers on the grill directly over the fire. Close the lid and cook, turning once, until they develop a crust and release easily from the grates, about 8 minutes per side. Transfer to a platter and serve.

Cheesy Chana Chaat–Sweet Potato Burgers	The addition of the cheese is unconventional but deliciously gooey, and sweet potatoes partner beautifully with the chickpeas: Substitute mashed sweet potatoes for the regular potatoes and add ½ cup shredded mozzarella.
Smoky Black Bean–Sweet Potato Burgers	Substitute black beans for the chickpeas and mashed sweet potatoes for the regular potatoes. Replace the chaat masala with 1 teaspoon smoked paprika (pimentón).
Falafel Burgers	Use either chickpeas or cooked peeled fava beans. Substitute parsley for the cilantro. Replace the chaat masala and lime zest with 2 tablespoons minced garlic, 1 teaspoon ground coriander, and ¼ teaspoon cayenne, or to taste.

Ⓓ direct fire   Ⓘ indirect fire   Ⓜ make ahead   Ⓥ vegetarian option

Beet Burgers with Dates and Ginger

Makes: **6 servings**	Time: **40 to 45 minutes, plus chilling time**	Ⓓ Ⓜ Ⓥ

Dried fruit is the secret ingredient in these rich and gorgeous burgers. The flavor is sweet and slightly earthy. Like the other vegetable burgers in this section, they can be a tad fragile, so make them small, take care when turning them, and use a perforated grill pan if you have one. These are so burger-like, I suggest layering two of them on a crusty roll with the usual fixings.

1 pound beets, peeled and grated (about 5 cups)

½ cup packed pitted dates, broken into pieces

½ cup almonds

1 1-inch piece peeled fresh ginger, cut into coins

½ cup bulgur

Salt and pepper

¾ cup boiling red wine or water

1 tablespoon Dijon or other mustard

Cayenne or red chile flakes (optional)

1 Put the beets in a food processor with the dates, almonds, and ginger; pulse until everything is well chopped but not quite a paste. Transfer the mixture to a large bowl and add the bulgur and a sprinkle of salt and pepper. Stir in the boiling wine, mustard, and cayenne to taste if you're using it and cover the bowl with a plate. Let sit for 20 minutes for the bulgur to soften. Taste and adjust the seasonings. Shape into 12 burgers, put on a platter without touching, and refrigerate for at least 1 hour. (You can make the burgers up to a day or so in advance. Cover tightly and refrigerate.)

2 Start the coals or heat a gas grill for medium direct cooking. Make sure the grates are clean.

3 Put the burgers on the grill directly over the fire. Close the lid and cook, turning once, until they release easily from the grates, about 5 minutes per side. Serve with your preferred fixings or toppings.

Beet Burgers with Dried Plums	Substitute dried plums (prunes) for the dates.
Beet Burgers with Garlic and Rosemary	Substitute 1 tablespoon minced garlic for the ginger and 1 tablespoon minced fresh rosemary leaves for the cayenne.
Beet Burgers with Figs and Hoisin	Substitute dried figs for the dates and hoisin sauce for the mustard.

Ⓓ direct fire   Ⓘ indirect fire   Ⓜ make ahead   Ⓥ vegetarian option

Design-Your-Own Nut Burgers

Makes: 4 servings	Time: 40 to 45 minutes, plus chilling time	Ⓘ Ⓜ Ⓥ

It's so easy to change up the ingredients in these burgers simply by mixing and matching combinations of nuts, binders, and spices that I wrote the recipe to include all the options. The burgers are easier to handle on the grill when made smaller; figure two make one serving. They also tend to burn when grilled directly over the fire, so indirect is the way to go. I prefer to serve these as is over greens or in a pita rather than on a bun. Any leftovers are delicious broken up and added to pasta, pilaf, or salad.

1 medium onion, cut into pieces

1 cup walnuts, pecans, almonds, cashews, or other nuts (preferably raw)

1 cup raw rolled oats or cooked short-grain white or brown rice

2 tablespoons ketchup, miso, tomato paste, nut butter, or tahini

1 teaspoon chili powder (to make your own, see page 456) or any spice mix you like, or to taste

Salt and pepper

1 egg

Broth, soy sauce, wine, or other liquid if necessary

1 Put the onion in a food processor and pulse to a paste. Add the nuts and oats and pulse to chop, but not too finely. Add the ketchup, chili powder, some salt and pepper, and the egg. Process briefly; don't grind the mixture too finely.

2 Add a little liquid—water, broth, soy sauce, wine, whatever is handy—if necessary; the mixture should be moist enough to hold together without being wet. With damp hands, shape the mixture into 8 burgers; put on a platter without touching and refrigerate for at least 1 hour. (You can make the burgers up to a day or so in advance. Just cover tightly and refrigerate.)

3 Start the coals or heat a gas grill for medium indirect cooking. Make sure the grates are clean.

4 Put the burgers on the indirect side of the grill. Close the lid and cook, turning once, until they develop a crust and release easily from the grates, about 5 minutes per side. Transfer to a plate and serve.

Nuttier Nut Burgers	Use 1½ cups nuts and reduce the oats to ½ cup.
Nut-and-Seed Burgers	Substitute up to ½ cup of the nuts with sesame, sunflower, or pumpkin seeds.
Vegan Nut Burgers	These are so good: Omit the egg. Use miso or nut butter, not ketchup, and use soy sauce for the liquid. Hold 1 sheet nori over the fire with tongs and toast for a few seconds until crisp, then crumble and add to the food processor in Step 1.

Sweet Potato–Eggplant Stacks with Lime Ricotta

Makes: 4 servings	Time: 40 to 50 minutes	Ⓓ Ⓘ Ⓥ

You can be endlessly inventive with vegetable stacks, discovering your own favorite combinations. You want to cut the vegetables about ½ inch thick, and then layer twice—any higher than that and your stack is likely to topple. Before you start to grill, read through Step 3 to help you time the vegetables so they all finish together.

1 large sweet potato, peeled and cut into eight ½-inch rounds

1 eggplant, cut across into eight ½-inch rounds

3 red onions, cut across into ½-inch rounds

¼ cup good-quality olive oil

Salt and pepper

¾ cup ricotta cheese

Grated zest and juice of 1 lime

Chopped fresh basil for garnish

1 Start the coals or heat a gas grill for medium-high indirect cooking. Make sure the grates are clean.

2 Brush the vegetable slices with the oil, coating them completely; sprinkle with salt and pepper on both sides. Whisk the ricotta and lime zest and juice together in a small bowl with some salt and pepper. Taste and adjust the seasoning.

3 Put the onions on the grill first, directly over the fire. Close the lid and cook, turning once, until the slices brown and are soft all the way through, 8 to 10 minutes per side. Check them a few minutes after you put them on; if they're coloring too quickly, move them to a cooler part of the fire. Put the sweet potato on the indirect side of the grill and cook, turning once, until you can pierce them all the way through but they're not mushy, about 6 minutes per side, then move them directly over the fire and cook, turning once, until brown, about 2 minutes per side. Put the eggplant over direct heat and cook, turning once, for 5 to 8 minutes per side; it's done when brown and tender. Transfer everything to a platter as it finishes.

4 To make stacks, start with eggplant on the bottom, followed by onion, then sweet potato; repeat. Top each stack with a generous dollop of lime ricotta, garnish with basil, and serve with the remaining ricotta in a small bowl on the side.

● recipe continues →

Ⓓ direct fire　Ⓘ indirect fire　Ⓜ make ahead　Ⓥ vegetarian option

Sweet Potato–Eggplant Stacks with Burrata and Parlsey-Cilantro Pesto	This creamy cousin of mozzarella is a real indulgence: Omit the ricotta, lime zest and juice, and basil and make Parsley-Cilantro Pesto (page 42). Use 4 of the smallest burrata you can find; if you can only find large burrata, get one and quarter it. Put a burrata (or wedge of burrata) next to each stack along with a spoonful of the pesto.
Eggplant-Zucchini Stacks with Spiced Yogurt	An excellent use for big zucchini: Heat the grill for direct heat. Substitute 1 large zucchini for the sweet potato; don't peel. Replace the ricotta with yogurt and the lime zest and juice with 1 teaspoon ras el hanout (page 456) or more to taste. Substitute mint for the basil. Cook the zucchini slices over direct heat; they will only take a couple minutes on each side to cook through.
Portobello-Eggplant Stacks with Orange-Pepper Ricotta	The portobello adds real heartiness: Substitute 4 portobello mushrooms, caps brushed clean and stems removed, for the sweet potato (use only one per stack). Substitute the grated zest of 1 orange and 2 tablespoons orange juice for the lime zest and juice, and add 1 teaspoon black pepper. Omit the basil. Grill the portobellos over direct heat until they're juicy and tender throughout, 3 to 5 minutes per side. Start the stack with the portobello, then the onion and eggplant, then another layer of onion and eggplant.

D direct fire   I indirect fire   M make ahead   V vegetarian option

Portobello Caprese Stacks

| Makes: **4 servings** | Time: **30 to 35 minutes** | **D** **V** |

So simple to grill—especially with gas, which fires up quickly—and so satisfying. The recipe is easy to scale up for a crowd or down for a quiet weeknight dinner. And it's perfect to serve at cookouts alongside burgers. During peak tomato season, use a thick slice from a juicy, ripe heirloom fruit for truly memorable eating.

4 portobello mushrooms, stems removed and caps wiped clean

6 tablespoons good-quality olive oil

Salt and pepper

24 large fresh basil leaves

4 tomato slices (each about ¾ inch thick; 2 large tomatoes)

4 slices fresh mozzarella cheese (about 4 ounces)

Balsamic Syrup (page 467) for serving

1 Start the coals or heat a gas grill for medium-high direct cooking. Make sure the grates are clean.

2 Brush the mushrooms with the oil and sprinkle with salt and pepper on both sides.

3 Put the mushrooms on the grill directly over the fire. Close the lid and cook, turning once, until well browned and tender, 3 to 5 minutes per side.

4 Transfer the mushrooms to a platter, gill side up. Cover the top with the basil, then add the tomato slices, and finally the mozzarella. Return the stacks directly over the fire, close the lid, and cook until the cheese melts, 2 to 4 minutes. Serve hot or at room temperature, drizzled with balsamic syrup.

Portobello Caprese Burgers with Lemon Mayo	Whisk ¼ cup mayonnaise with 4 teaspoons grated lemon zest, or more to taste. Toast 4 split ciabatta rolls while you're melting the mozzarella on the mushrooms, then put each stack on a roll and dollop on the mayonnaise.
Portobello Stacks with Green Tomato and Smoked Cheddar	Substitute green tomato slices for the ripe; sprinkle with salt and pepper. Omit the basil and balsamic syrup and replace the mozzarella with smoked cheddar. When the mushrooms are cooked halfway through, put the tomato slices over direct heat, and cook, watching closely, until browned on both sides, 3 to 5 minutes per side. In Step 4, spread a dollop of mustard on the mushrooms if you like, then proceed with the recipe.
Portobello Cashew Stacks	Vegan—and you'll want to put the nut butter on other vegetables, too: Omit the cheese. Put 1 cup roasted cashews in a food processor and let the machine run; add water 1 tablespoon at a time until a spreadable paste forms. Taste and add salt if you like. In Step 4, top the mushrooms with the basil and tomato, then add a spoonful of the cashew butter and spread it around a little. Return it to the grill to heat through and serve with the balsamic syrup.

Lemon-Rosemary Cauliflower Steaks with Manchego

Makes: 4 servings	Time: 35 to 45 minutes	Ⓓ Ⓥ

Large cauliflower forms dense heads that make fun "steaks" for grilling. They take to all sort of seasonings and accompaniments, so it's easy to build a satisfying meal around them.

1 large head cauliflower (about 2 pounds)

6 tablespoons good-quality olive oil

1 tablespoon chopped fresh rosemary

Salt and pepper

Grated zest of 1 lemon

½ cup grated or crumbled Manchego cheese

1 Start the coals or heat a gas grill for medium direct cooking. Make sure the grates are clean.

2 Trim the bottom from the cauliflower so it lies flat. Cut downward, top to bottom, in 4 equally thick slices. Stir the oil and rosemary together in a small bowl with some salt and pepper; brush on the slices on both sides.

3 Put the slices on the grill directly over the fire. Close the lid and cook until the cauliflower is tender and a bit charred in places, 10 to 15 minutes per side; a skewer or thin knife inserted at the thickest point should go in with little resistance. If the slices start to brown too much, move them to a cooler part of the grill. Transfer to a platter, sprinkle with the lemon zest, then the Manchego, and serve.

Smoky Cauliflower Steaks with Orange and Manchego	Substitute 1 teaspoon smoked paprika (pimentón) for the rosemary and orange zest of the lemon zest.
Parmesan Cauliflower Steaks	Substitute oregano for the rosemary, omit the lemon zest, and add 1 tablespoon minced garlic to the oil. Substitute freshly grated Parmesan for the Manchego.
Curry-Coconut Cauliflower Steaks with Pistachios	Instead of the olive oil, use 1 cup coconut cream. (Don't confuse it with cream of coconut. If you can't find it, refrigerate two 14-ounce cans full-fat coconut milk without shaking them first. When they're chilled, open the cans and skim the thick cream off the top; freeze and use the rest of the milk later.) Replace the rosemary and lemon zest with 1 tablespoon curry powder and some salt and pepper; marinate the cauliflower in this for a few minutes, or up to a couple of hours, before grilling. Substitute chopped pistachios for the Manchego.

Eggplant Parmesan with Grill-Roasted Tomato Sauce

Makes: **4 servings**	Time: **40 to 50 minutes**	Ⓓ Ⓥ

For once, eggplant parm that actually tastes like eggplant, tomatoes, and cheese, not oil. And this is so easy and fast you'll never go back to breading and frying. The sauce is nothing more than chopped grill-roasted cherry tomatoes—all the seasoning they need is a little salt to heighten their natural flavor, concentrated as they gently hiss over a hot fire. You'll make them frequently, I bet.

2 eggplants (¾ to 1 pound each)

5 tablespoons good-quality olive oil

2 tablespoons balsamic vinegar

Salt and pepper

6 cups cherry or grape tomatoes

1 cup freshly grated Parmesan cheese

About 1 cup packed fresh basil leaves

8 ounces mozzarella cheese, thinly sliced

1 Start the coals or heat a gas grill for medium-high direct cooking. Make sure the grates are clean.

2 Peel the eggplant if you like, and cut each lengthwise into 4 slices not more than ¾ inch thick each. Whisk 4 tablespoons of the oil and the vinegar together with some salt and pepper in a small bowl. Brush the eggplant slices with the oil mixture on both sides. Put them on a baking sheet until you're ready to grill them.

3 Toss the tomatoes with the remaining 1 tablespoon oil and either skewer them or put them in a perforated grill pan and spread them into a single layer.

4 Put the tomatoes on the grill directly over the fire. Close the lid and cook, turning the skewers or

shaking the pan several times, until they start to look wrinkled and get a bit charred in places, 5 to 8 minutes total. Don't let them cook too long; they should be saucy when you cut them up. Transfer the tomatoes to a bowl.

5 Put the eggplant on the grill directly over the fire. Close the lid and cook until the slices are browned and tender, 5 to 8 minutes per side.

6 While the eggplant is cooking, chop the tomatoes by hand on a cutting board or in the bowl with an immersion blender, leaving the sauce somewhat chunky. If you chopped by hand, transfer the tomatoes and any juices back to the bowl. Sprinkle the sauce with salt and pepper; taste and adjust the seasoning.

7 As the eggplant is ready, transfer the slices to a platter. Top each slice with 2 tablespoons Parmesan, a layer of basil leaves, and a layer of mozzarella. Return the slices to direct heat, close the lid, and cook until the mozzarella melts, 4 to 5 minutes. Return the eggplant to the platter. Reheat the tomato sauce if you like, top the eggplant with the sauce, and serve.

Ⓓ direct fire   Ⓘ indirect fire   Ⓜ make ahead   Ⓥ vegetarian option

Eggplant with Grill-Roasted Tomato Raita	Here the eggplant is topped with a creamy, crunchy, smoky yogurt-based salad instead of cheese: Omit the Parmesan, basil, and mozzarella. Before grilling, brush the eggplant with a mixture of ¼ cup good-quality olive oil, 2 teaspoons ground cumin, and some salt and pepper. Peel and chop 1 Kirby or other small cucumber. Put the grilled tomatoes in a bowl with ½ cup yogurt and the cucumber; stir gently to combine. To serve, top the eggplant with the raita and garnish it with chopped fresh cilantro.
Glazed Eggplant with Feta and Mint	More of a Middle Eastern spin: Instead of the Parmesan and mozzarella, crumble 8 ounces feta cheese; chop ¼ cup fresh mint instead of the basil. Before grilling, brush the eggplant with a mixture of 2 tablespoons each pomegranate molasses (or honey) and good-quality olive oil. Stir in 1 tablespoon ground sumac, ¼ to ½ teaspoon Aleppo pepper or red chile flakes, and some salt into the tomatoes after chopping. Top the grilled eggplant with the warm tomato sauce and the feta, and garnish with the mint; no need to return it to the grill.
Eggplant with Tomatoes and Peanuts	A vegan option—and a shockingly good combination: Use Thai basil if you can find it, or cilantro, and chop it; juice 1 lime. Combine 3 tablespoons soy sauce and ¼ cup peanut butter in a small bowl with enough water to make a thick sauce. Before grilling, brush the eggplant with good-quality vegetable oil; after you turn the slices, spoon the peanut sauce on top. Stir the basil and lime juice into the chopped tomatoes. Top the eggplant with the sauce and garnish with chopped peanuts; no need to return it to the grill.

Eggplant Salad with Yogurt and Tomatoes

Makes: 4 servings	Time: 35 to 45 minutes	Ⓓ Ⓜ Ⓥ

A room-temperature salad at the intersection of savory, smoky, tart, and refreshing. Eat it as is, over a bed of baby spinach or steamed basmati rice, or stuffed into pitas (to make your own, see page 492). If cherry tomatoes look better, use them instead of the big guys. Skewer about a dozen—or toss them in a perforated grill pan—and grill them with the eggplant for a double dose of fire flavor.

1 large eggplant (1½ pounds)

¼ cup good-quality olive oil, plus more for brushing

Salt and pepper

1½ cups yogurt

1 or 2 cloves garlic, minced, to taste

¼ cup chopped scallions

¼ cup chopped fresh mint

1 tablespoon fresh lemon juice, or to taste

1 large or 2 medium fresh tomatoes, cut into bite-sized chunks

Ground sumac for garnish (optional)

1 Start the coals or heat a gas grill for medium-high direct cooking. Make sure the grates are clean.

2 Peel the eggplant if you like; cut it into ¾-inch slices. Brush with the oil and sprinkle with salt and pepper to taste on both sides.

3 Put the eggplant on the grill directly over the fire. Close the lid and cook, turning once, until the slices develop deep grill marks and are tender, 5 to 8 minutes per side; brush the eggplant with more oil if it starts to look dry. Transfer to a cutting board and chop into bite-sized pieces.

4 Put the yogurt, garlic, scallions, mint, and lemon juice in a large bowl and stir to combine. (You can prepare the recipe to this point up to a day before; cover and refrigerate the eggplant and yogurt mixture separately.)

5 Add the tomatoes and eggplant to the yogurt and stir to coat. Serve chilled or bring to room temperature and garnish with sumac if you like.

Eggplant Salad with Tomatoes and Tofu	Use a 1-pound eggplant. Cut ½ block firm tofu (7–8 ounces) into 1-inch slices and pat dry. Brush with good-quality olive oil and sprinkle lightly with smoked paprika (pimentón) on both sides. Put on the grill with the eggplant and cook, turning once, until the slices develop a crust and release easily from the grates, 3 to 5 minutes per side. Cut into cubes and add to the yogurt mixture along with the eggplant and tomatoes.
Eggplant Salad with Tomatoes and Tempeh	Brush 8 ounces tempeh with good-quality olive oil. Put on the grill with the eggplant and cook, turning once, until it develops a crust and releases easily from the grates, about 2 minutes per side. When cool enough to handle, crumble into the yogurt mixture before adding the eggplant and tomatoes.
Eggplant Salad with Sweet Onions and Tomatoes	Omit the scallions and sumac; substitute parsley for the mint and lime juice for the lemon juice. Cut a small-to-medium sweet onion (like a Vidalia or Walla Walla) into 1- to 1½-inch wedges. Skewer them and brush with good-quality olive oil. Grill with the eggplant and cook until softened and charred in spots, turning several times; the onion may need to stay on the grill a bit longer than the eggplant. Toss the vegetables with the yogurt mixture.

Tomatoes Stuffed with Chickpeas and Rice

Makes: 4 servings	Time: 60 to 70 minutes with cooked rice	I M V

Grilled tomatoes make a delicious edible container for all kinds of savory fillings. Once stuffed, they're cooked with indirect heat so the tomato won't burst while absorbing the flavor of the fire. For charcoal grillers, the smokiness will happen even if you don't add wood to the fire; with gas it's worth it to get a couple of handfuls of wood chips going (see page 11). Look for ripe but firm tomatoes—overly ripe tomatoes will not hold together when you hollow them out. And I often cook additional rice to serve as a bed for the tomatoes and catch all the juices as you cut into them.

4 large, firm fresh tomatoes
(12 ounces or more each)

Salt and pepper

2 tablespoons good-quality olive oil,
plus more for drizzling

2 tablespoons minced ginger

1½ cups cooked white rice

1 cup cooked chickpeas

½ cup chopped fresh mint

Lime wedges for serving

1 If any of the tomatoes don't sit squarely on the counter, cut a thin slice from the bottom to stabilize it. To core the tomatoes, slice across the top to make a 2- to 3-inch-wide opening. (You can save the tops to put back on after stuffing the tomatoes.) Use a spoon, serrated grapefruit spoon, or melon baller to scoop out the insides, leaving a wall about ¼ inch thick. Discard the woody core and seeds and chop the pulp and bottom slices, saving the juice. Sprinkle the insides of the tomatoes with salt and pepper.

2 Heat the oil in a medium-sized skillet over medium-high heat. Add the ginger and stir until fragrant, 1 to 2 minutes. Add the tomato pulp and juice, sprinkle with salt and pepper, and cook, stirring occasionally, until most of the liquid has evaporated, 10 to 20 minutes. Add the rice and chickpeas and stir with a fork until combined. Remove from the heat and stir in the mint; taste and adjust the seasoning. Carefully stuff the mixture into the tomatoes and drizzle the tops with oil. Set the tops back on if you like. (You can make the stuffed tomatoes to this point up to several hours in advance; cover and refrigerate.)

3 Start the coals or heat a gas grill for medium-high indirect cooking. Make sure the grates are clean. When the grill is ready, add wood to the fire if you're using it.

4 Put the tomatoes on the indirect portion of the grill. Close the lid and cook until the tomatoes begin to wrinkle a bit and the filling is hot, 15 to 25 minutes, carefully moving and rotating the tomatoes once for even cooking. Serve hot, warm, or at room temperature with lime wedges.

• recipe continues →

Dilled Stuffed Tomatoes with White Beans and Bulgur	Take it in a Mediterranean direction: Substitute garlic for the ginger, cooked bulgur for the rice, white beans for the chickpeas, and dill for the mint. Serve with lemon wedges or a final splash of red wine vinegar.
Cheesy Stuffed Tomatoes with Black Beans and Cilantro	A Southwestern spin: Substitute garlic for the ginger, black beans for the chickpeas, and cilantro for the mint. Sprinkle the top of each with a generous tablespoon of grated Chihuahua or Monterey Jack cheese about 2 minutes before you take them off the grill.
Coconutty Stuffed Tomatoes with Chickpeas and Rice	Toasted coconut adds just a bit of sweet and crunch to the filling: Stir in ¼ cup toasted unsweetened coconut along with the mint.

D direct fire   I indirect fire   M make ahead   V vegetarian option

Tomato Melts with Spinach Salad

Makes: 2 to 4 servings	Time: 20 to 25 minutes	Ⓓ Ⓥ

Forget the patty melt and make this simple combo for a light lunch or dinner for two. If you're making these with vine-ripened tomatoes from the farmers' market or your garden, you can cut them even thicker. Double the cheddar if you like 'em really cheesy. I serve the dressed salad on top, but you could also make sandwiches out of them.

1 or 2 large fresh tomatoes (enough for 4 thick slices across)

2 tablespoons good-quality olive oil, plus more for brushing

Salt and pepper

2 teaspoons white wine vinegar

1 teaspoon Dijon mustard

3 cups baby spinach

4 slices cheddar cheese (about 4 ounces)

1 Start the coals or heat a gas grill for medium direct cooking. Make sure the grates are clean.

2 Core the tomatoes and cut 4 thick slices (about 1 inch); save the trimmings. Brush them with oil and sprinkle with salt and pepper on both sides. Whisk the 2 tablespoons oil, vinegar, and mustard together in a bowl. Chop the trimmings from the tomatoes; add them to the dressing along with the spinach and toss until evenly coated.

3 Put the tomato slices on the grill directly over the fire. Close the lid and cook for 3 minutes. Turn the tomatoes and top each slice with a slice of cheddar. Close the lid and cook until the cheese is melted, 2 to 3 minutes. Transfer to plates and serve with the salad on top.

Tomato Melts with Kale Salad	These two swaps totally change the flavor: Substitute baby kale for the spinach (or large kale leaves, stemmed and cut into thin ribbons). Use Manchego cheese instead of the cheddar.
Tomato Melts with Arugula Salad	The mellow flavor of the mozzarella plays nicely with the peppery sharpness of the arugula: Substitute red wine vinegar for the white wine vinegar, baby arugula for the spinach, and fresh mozzarella for the cheddar.
Crunchy Green Tomato Melts with Spinach Salad	A great way to enjoy big late-season tomatoes: Wipe the grates well with good-quality vegetable oil before grilling to keep the crumbs from sticking. Combine ½ cup stoneground cornmeal with some salt and pepper. Substitute green tomatoes for the ripe tomatoes. Dip one side of each slice in ¼ cup buttermilk, then dredge that same side in the cornmeal. Grill dredged side down, until the slices are tender and crisp and release easily, 3 to 5 minutes; no need to turn. Omit the cheese. Put the tomatoes crumb side up on a platter and top with the salad.

Stuffed Cabbage with Summer Vegetables

Makes: 12 rolls, 4 to 6 servings	Time: About an hour	D I M V

Cabbage is amazing grilled: The leaves are sturdy enough to stand up to the fire without splitting, yet retain some crispness even when fully tender. The smoky flavor here complements the garden-fresh filling. Try these rolls topped with Grill-Roasted Tomato Sauce (page 348).

2 tablespoons good-quality olive oil, plus more for brushing and drizzling

1 onion, chopped

Salt and pepper

2 tablespoons minced garlic

1 cup thinly sliced snow peas

1 cup chopped summer squash

1 cup fresh or frozen corn kernels (no need to thaw them)

1 large head green or Savoy cabbage (about 4 pounds)

¼ cup chopped fresh basil

Grated zest of 1 lime

1 Put the oil in a large skillet over medium-high heat. When it's hot, add the onion, sprinkle with salt and pepper, and cook, stirring occasionally, until it's soft, about 5 minutes. Add the garlic and stir until fragrant, about another minute. Add the snow peas, squash, and corn and cook, stirring occasionally, until the squash is just tender, about 5 minutes. Season to taste with salt and pepper. Remove from the heat.

2 Use a thin-bladed sharp knife to cut a cone-shaped wedge out of the bottom of the cabbage, removing its core. Pull off 12 large, untorn, unblemished leaves and put in a steamer above a couple inches of salted water (you may need to work in batches). Cover and cook until the leaves are just flexible enough to bend, about 5 minutes. Drain and rinse under cold water to stop the cooking. (Reserve the remaining cabbage leaves for another use.)

3 Stir the basil and lime zest into the filling; taste and adjust the seasoning. To stuff the cabbage leaves, put the leaves, concave side up, on a work surface or cutting board. Make a V-cut in each leaf to remove the tough central stem. Put a heaping ¼ cup or so of filling in the center of a leaf, just above where you cut out the stem. Fold over the sides, then roll up from the stem end, making a little package (like a burrito). Don't roll too tightly; you'll quickly get the hang of it. Skewer the rolls with a toothpick or 2 to hold them together or just put them on a platter seam side down. (You can make the stuffed cabbage to this point up to a day or 2 in advance; cover and refrigerate.)

4 Start the coals or heat a gas grill for medium indirect cooking. Make sure the grates are clean.

5 Brush the rolls with oil on all sides and sprinkle with salt. Put the rolls on the indirect side of the grill, but close to the fire. Close the lid and cook 3 minutes per side, turning once, to heat the filling, then finish directly over the fire for 30 seconds or so per side to brown. Transfer to a platter, drizzle with a little more oil, and serve.

Stuffed Cabbage with Summer Vegetables and Grilled or Smoked Tofu	Make these even more substantial by adding tofu: Make Grilled or Smoked Tofu (page 329 or 332) and chop enough to measure 1 cup. Use a small onion and decrease the other vegetables to ¾ cup each. Stir the tofu in with the basil and zest.
Stuffed Cabbage with Parmesan Vegetables	Decrease the vegetables to ¾ cup each and stir ¾ cup freshly grated Parmesan into the filling along with the basil and zest.
Hoisin-Glazed Cabbage Rolls with Chickpeas, Cauliflower, and Rice	Substitute 1 shallot for the onion, drained cooked chickpeas for the snow peas, chopped cauliflower for the squash, and cilantro for the basil. Omit the corn. Add 1 tablespoon chopped fresh ginger and ¼ teaspoon (more or less) red chile flakes along with the garlic. Stir 1 cup cooked basmati rice into the filling along with the cilantro and zest. Brush the rolls with hoisin sauce; grill as directed, adjusting the rolls as needed to keep the glaze from burning.

Stuffed Winter Squash with Quinoa, Green Beans, and Tomatoes

Makes: 4 servings	Time: 60 to 75 minutes, largely unattended	Ⓓ Ⓜ Ⓥ

Acorn squash gets all the attention, but you can stuff lots of winter squashes, including kabocha, buttercup, and sweet dumpling, or small spaghetti squash and pumpkins. Sweet dumplings are quite small, less than a pound, so use one per serving, cutting the top off just enough so you can get to the seeds. For the other varieties, choose squash that weigh 1½ to 2 pounds. When halving them, do it horizontally through the equator or vertically through the stem, whichever makes more sense for the shape of that particular variety.

¾ cup quinoa

2 or 4 winter squash (see the headnote)

2 tablespoons good-quality olive oil, plus more for brushing and drizzling

Salt and pepper

1 cup chopped cherry or grape tomatoes

½ cup thinly sliced green beans (cut across into rounds)

2 tablespoons chopped fresh parsley

2 cloves garlic, minced

1 Start the coals or heat a gas grill for medium direct cooking. Make sure the grates are clean.

2 Put the quinoa in a saucepan with 1½ cups water, bring to a boil, reduce the heat so the water bubbles gently but steadily, cover, and cook undisturbed until the surface is dotted with holes and the water is almost all absorbed, about 15 minutes. Turn off the heat and let stand until the kernels are tender and fluffy, 5 to 10 minutes.

3 Cut the squash in half. If necessary, take a thin slice off the uncut side so the squash half sits on the work surface without rocking. Remove the seeds with a spoon, serrated grapefruit spoon, or melon baller. Brush the interior and cut surface with oil; for varieties with edible skin, also brush the skin. Sprinkle all over with salt and pepper.

4 Put the squash on the grill directly over the fire, skin side down. Close the lid and cook until the flesh is just fork tender, 25 to 45 minutes, depending on the size; start checking doneness at 20 minutes. Turn them cut side down to brown, about 5 minutes. Transfer to a plate, cut side up.

5 While the squash are on the grill, finish the filling. Put the quinoa, tomatoes, green beans, parsley, garlic, and 2 tablespoons oil in a bowl; sprinkle with salt and pepper and toss with a fork until combined. Cover to keep warm. (You can prepare the filling and partially cook the squash earlier in the day; cover and refrigerate until you're ready to grill; cooking time may be a bit longer.)

6 If necessary, heat the grill for medium direct cooking. Divide the filling between the squash halves. Return to the grill, directly over the fire, close the lid, and cook until the filling is hot, 10 to 15 minutes. Transfer to a platter, drizzle the tops with a little oil if you like, and serve.

Stuffed Winter Squash with Israeli Couscous, Tempeh, and Corn	Everything remains the same except the filling: Crumble or chop 4 ounces Grilled Tempeh (page 330). Substitute Israeli couscous for the quinoa and fresh or frozen corn kernels for the green beans; add the grated zest of 1 navel orange along with the parsley and garlic.
Curried Stuffed Winter Squash with Coconut Rice, Kale, and Tomatoes	For the filling, substitute 2 cups cooked Coconut Rice (page 321) for the quinoa; mint for the parsley; and instead of green beans chop 1 cup kale (stems in or not, your choice). Stir in 1 tablespoon each minced fresh ginger and curry powder along with the garlic.
Stuffed Winter Squash with Bulgur, Zucchini, and Red Pepper	For the filling, substitute cooked bulgur for the quinoa and basil for the parsley. Omit the green beans and tomatoes. Chop 1 small-to-medium zucchini and 1 red bell pepper; and add the grated zest of 1 lemon.

Spaghetti Squash with Fresh Tomato Sauce

Makes: 4 servings	Time: 75 to 80 minutes, largely unattended	D M V

A vegetable-forward, gluten-free alternative to pasta that hails from the '70s when none of that stuff mattered. Grilling the squash brings the idea into the twenty-first century. The strands inside this squash are fibrous and wrap from side to side, not top to bottom, so if you cut through the equator, you'll end up with longer strands. To make this when good tomatoes aren't in season, use Romas or one 28-ounce cans diced tomatoes with their juice. Hearty enough for a meal, but also a fantastic side dish.

1 large spaghetti squash (3½–4 pounds)

2 tablespoons good-quality olive oil, plus more for brushing the squash

Salt and pepper

2 tablespoons chopped garlic

2 pounds fresh tomatoes, chopped

¼ cup chopped fresh basil

Freshly grated Parmesan for serving (optional)

1 Start the coals or heat a gas grill for medium direct cooking. Make sure the grates are clean.

2 Cut the squash in half through the equator (not end to end). Remove the seeds with a spoon. Brush the cut sides and interior with oil and sprinkle with salt and pepper.

3 Put the squash on the grill directly over the fire, skin side down. Close the lid and cook, turning the squash every 10 minutes or so for even cooking, until the flesh is fork-tender, 40 to 50 minutes total; start checking it for doneness at 30 minutes. Turn the halves cut side down until browned, 5 to 10 minutes. Transfer to a plate. (The squash will stay hot in the skin for about 15 minutes.)

4 While the squash is on the grill, make the tomato sauce. Put the 2 tablespoons oil and the garlic in a large skillet over medium heat and cook until the garlic is fragrant and gently sizzling. Add the tomatoes, sprinkle with salt and pepper, and adjust the heat to a gentle bubble. Cook, stirring occasionally, until they cook down into a thickened sauce, 25 to 35 minutes; increase the heat to medium-high if your tomatoes throw off a lot of liquid. Taste and adjust the seasoning and keep warm. (Or you can make the tomato sauce up to a day or two ahead and gently reheat it when the squash goes on the grill.)

5 Stir the basil into the tomato sauce. Scrape a fork over the interior of the squash from bottom to top to remove the flesh from the skin and tease it apart into long strands. Put in a large serving bowl and toss with the tomato sauce to evenly coat the strands. Taste and adjust the seasoning. Serve hot, with Parmesan for sprinkling if you like.

• recipe continues →

Spaghetti Squash with Tomato Sauce and Snow Peas	So fresh tasting! Tossing the snow peas with the hot squash and sauce is enough to take the "raw" off: Trim 8 ounces snow peas and slice at an angle. Toss with the squash along with the tomato sauce. If you like, substitute mint for the basil.
Spaghetti Squash with Tempeh-Tomato Sauce	Grill 8 ounces tempeh (page 330) along with the squash, then crumble it into the cooked tomato sauce.
Spaghetti Squash with Parmesan and Butter	Omit the oil, garlic, tomatoes, and basil for the tomato sauce. Instead, toss the hot squash strands with 4 tablespoons (½ stick) melted butter and 1 cup freshly grated Parmesan. Season generously with black pepper. If you like, you can also add 1 cup cooked peas.

D direct fire I indirect fire M make ahead V vegetarian option

Chiles Rellenos with Charred Green Enchilada Sauce

| Makes: **4 servings** | Time: **About 1 hour** | Ⓓ Ⓜ Ⓥ |

You wouldn't think the classic Mexican stuffed chiles could get any better—but on the grill they do. For a double dose of smokiness, the tomatillos for the sauce also take a turn over the fire. If you can only find small chiles, get 10 and stuff 8. For the make-aheads: Prepare the sauce up to a day before, refrigerate, and let come to room temperature before serving. You can stuff the poblanos earlier in the day and refrigerate them until you're ready to grill.

1¼ pounds tomatillos, husked and rinsed

5 large poblano or other mild fresh green chiles

3 tablespoons good-quality olive oil

2 large onions, chopped

5 cloves garlic, minced

1 teaspoon dried oregano (preferably Mexican)

1 cup vegetable broth or water

Salt and pepper

3 cups grated or shredded Chihuahua or Monterey Jack cheese

½ cup chopped fresh cilantro

¼ cup fresh lime juice

Crumbled queso fresco for garnish

1 Start the coals or heat a gas grill for medium direct cooking. Make sure the grates are clean.

2 Put the tomatillos and 1 of the poblanos on the grill directly over the fire. Close the lid and cook the tomatillos, turning every few minutes, until the skins are lightly browned and blistered, 10 to 15 minutes. Cook the poblano until it's blackened, 15 to 20 minutes. When the vegetables are done, transfer them a bowl. (If you're using a charcoal grill and will continue with the recipe now, close the lid to conserve heat; you may want to add more fuel later to get the heat level back up. For gas, you can turn it off until you've finished making the sauce.) When the poblano is cool enough to handle, remove the skin, stem, and seeds. Chop by hand along with the tomatillos, saving the juices.

3 Put the oil in a large, deep skillet over medium heat, add the onions and garlic, and cook, stirring occasionally, until quite soft and golden, 10 to 15 minutes. Add the tomatillos and poblano, oregano, broth, and a large pinch of salt and pepper; stir and bring to a gentle bubble. Cook, stirring occasionally, until the mixture is slightly thickened, 10 to 15 minutes. Remove from the heat. Use an immersion blender to purée the sauce in the pan, or very carefully transfer it to a blender, purée, and return it to the pan.

4 Cut a slit into one side of each of the remaining poblanos, from the stem down to the tip. Carefully remove the seeds without ripping the chiles, then stuff them with the Chihuahua or Jack cheese.

5 Heat the grill for medium direct cooking, if necessary. Put the chiles on the grill, slit side facing up so the cheese doesn't melt out, directly over

● recipe continues →

the fire. Close the lid and cook until the skins have blistered and the flesh is tender, 10 to 15 minutes, depending on their size and how hot the fire is. Transfer to a platter.

6 Stir the cilantro and lime juice into the sauce; taste and adjust the seasonings. Spoon the sauce over the chiles, sprinkle with queso fresco, and serve.

Chiles Rellenos with Corn and Pumpkin Seeds	The corn and seeds provide great crunchy texture: Substitute ¾ cup each fresh or frozen corn kernels and pumpkin seeds (pepitas) for 1½ cups of the cheese. Before using them, toast the seeds in a dry skillet over medium heat, shaking the pan frequently, until they pop and brown, about 5 minutes.
Chiles Rellenos with Goat Cheese and Walnuts	Tangy from the goat cheese and almost meaty from the walnuts: Substitute 1½ cups each fresh goat cheese and finely chopped walnuts for the Chihuahua or Jack cheese. Combine the goat cheese and walnuts; use a piping bag or sturdy plastic bag with the corner cut off to fill the chiles.
Chiles Rellenos with Black Beans and Pepper Jack Cheese	When you can't get enough heat: Use pepper Jack cheese, decreasing the amount to 1 cup, and add 1 cup mashed black beans and 1 teaspoon minced garlic to the filling.

Vegetarian Paella with Artichokes, Red Peppers, and White Beans

Makes: 8 servings	Time: 80 to 90 minutes	Ⓓ Ⓜ Ⓥ

Similar to the meat-and-seafood version on page 149, I amp up this paella's smoke flavor by grilling some of the ingredients before adding them. The rice becomes more of a focus in this version, so use one that remains toothsome during cooking; even long-grain will work. No need for a special paella pan; a large cast-iron skillet works fine. For more details read "The Pace of Paella" on page 151.

6 tablespoons good-quality olive oil

1 large onion, chopped (2–2½ cups)

Salt and pepper

6 tablespoons minced garlic (9–10 cloves)

1 teaspoon smoked paprika (pimentón)

2 fresh tomatoes, grated (1½–2 cups)

2 tablespoons fresh lemon juice

6 baby artichokes

2 red bell peppers

2 bay leaves

2 cups short-grain rice (preferably Valencia/Bomba or Calasparra)

4 cups vegetable broth or water, plus more if needed

Generous pinch saffron threads, crushed (optional)

2 cups cooked cannellini beans

1 Put 4 tablespoons of the oil in a 12-inch or larger deep flameproof skillet or paella pan over medium heat. When it's hot, add the onion and some salt and pepper and cook, stirring occasionally, until very soft, 4 to 5 minutes. Add 4 tablespoons of the garlic and stir until fragrant, 2 to 3 minutes. Add the paprika and stir for 1 to 2 minutes. Add the tomatoes and cook, stirring occasionally, until they soften and most of their liquid evaporates, 15 to 20 minutes; adjust the heat so the mixture

bubbles gently as the sofrito thickens. Remove the pan from the heat if it is ready before you complete the next step. (You can make the sofrito earlier in the day, and refrigerate it; reheat before proceeding).

2 Meanwhile, whisk the remaining 2 tablespoons oil and the lemon juice together in a bowl with some salt. Peel away and discard the outer leaves of each artichoke until the leaves are half yellow and half green. With a sharp knife, cut across the top of the artichoke to remove the green tops. Leave 1 inch of stem and use a paring knife or vegetable peeler to trim the bottom so no green color remains. Cut the artichoke in half lengthwise from top to bottom. As each artichoke is trimmed, add it to the oil mixture and toss to coat evenly; this helps delay discoloring. (You can cover the bowl with a damp towel and refrigerate for up to several hours.)

3 Start the coals (use 2 chimney starters full of fuel, about 80 briquettes) or heat a gas grill for hot direct cooking. Make sure the grates are clean.

4 Put the red peppers on the grill directly over the fire while the grill is heating, close the lid, and cook, turning occasionally, until their skins are black and blistered all over, 15 to 25 minutes total. Transfer them to a bowl.

5 When the grill is ready, put the artichokes directly over the fire, cut side down. Close the lid and cook until crisp, 5 to 6 minutes. Transfer to a platter. Close the lid of the grill; if using gas, turn the burners down to medium. Cut the artichoke pieces in half. Remove the skins, seeds, and stems from the red peppers and cut them into 1-inch strips.

6 Return the sofrito to medium heat. When it's hot, add the rice and stir until the grains are fully coated. Add the broth and the saffron if you're using it; stir to combine. Increase the heat to high and cook, stirring occasionally, until steaming but not yet bubbling. Add the beans, then the artichokes and red pepper strips, tucking them into the rice. Taste some of the liquid and adjust the seasoning; if it's a little bland, add some more salt. Carefully transfer the pan to the grill, centering it over the fire. Close the lid.

7 After 20 minutes, check the paella's progress. At this point, the broth should have been absorbed by the rice to the point that the top of the paella is dry; stick a fork down into the rice by the edge of the pan; you should see bubbles. Close the lid.

8 Check again after another 10 minutes. Try a forkful of rice. If it's tender and the broth hasn't been fully absorbed, give it a little more time, but keep checking. It should not be soupy at all. In a perfect paella, a tasty crust will develop at the bottom without the rice sticking to the pan. If the rice isn't tender, check on its progress every 10 to 15 minutes; if it is dry and burning, drizzle with a little more stock.

9 When the rice is done, bring the pan to the table and let it sit for 5 to minutes before serving family style.

Paella with White Beans, Red Peppers, and Spinach	Omit the artichokes. Toss 1 pound chopped fresh spinach with 1 tablespoon good-quality olive oil and the juice and grated zest of 1 lemon. After adding the beans and red peppers, pile the spinach on top, covering the rice. It will soften and cook into the paella.
Paella with Eggplant, Red Peppers, and Zucchini	Omit the artichokes and beans. Cut 1 eggplant into 1-inch slices lengthwise and 1 zucchini in half lengthwise. Brush both with olive oil, then put on the grill after you've taken off the red peppers. Grill until deeply colored on one side, 3 to 5 minutes. Transfer to a cutting board and cut into bite-sized pieces. Add to the rice along with the red peppers in Step 6.
Paella with Smoky Sofrito	You can add an extra layer of flavor to any of these versions by first grilling the onion and tomatoes for the sofrito: Cut the onion into 1-inch slices and brush with good-quality olive oil. Replace the grated tomatoes with 4 cups cherry tomatoes. Toss them with 1 tablespoon olive oil and skewer them or put them on a perforated grill pan. Put them on the grill directly over the fire, close the lid, and cook until the onion browns (it doesn't need to cook through); cook the tomatoes until they blister. Transfer both to a cutting board and chop, then pick up with making the sofrito in Step 1.

Paneer Masala

Makes: **4 to 6 servings**	Time: **60 to 70 minutes**	Ⓓ Ⓜ Ⓥ

Traditionally the cheese in this Indian dish would be pan-fried, then added to the vegetable sauce. The grill changes everything. Look for paneer in natural food stores or Indian markets. If you can't find it, substitute halloumi or queso fresco, which also won't lose their shape when grilled directly over the fire. Serve this with basmati rice, Chapati (page 487), or Naan (page 488).

2 small red onions, cut into wedges

1 bell pepper, seeded and cut into 1- to 1½-inch pieces

1 tablespoon good-quality vegetable oil, plus more for brushing

4 cups cherry or grape tomatoes

1 or more thick pieces paneer (14–16 ounces)

1 large onion, cut into chunks

1 1-inch piece fresh ginger, peeled and thinly sliced

4 cloves garlic, peeled

2 tablespoons butter

2 teaspoons ground cumin

1 teaspoon ground turmeric

¼ teaspoon red chile flakes, or more to taste

Salt and pepper

½ cup yogurt

Chopped fresh cilantro for garnish

1 If you're using bamboo or wooden skewers, soak them in water for 30 minutes. Start the coals or heat a gas grill for medium-high direct cooking. Make sure the grates are clean.

2 Thread the red onion and bell pepper onto skewers. Brush with oil. Toss the tomatoes in a medium bowl with the 1 tablespoon oil until coated. Thread the tomatoes onto skewers or pour onto a perforated grill pan.

3 Put the paneer, onion and pepper skewers, and tomatoes on the grill directly over the fire. Close the lid. Cook the cheese, turning once, until it is browned in spots, 3 to 5 minutes per side. Transfer to a cutting board. Cook the tomatoes, turning the skewers or shaking the pan several times, until they wrinkle and brown or char in a few places, 5 to 10 minutes; transfer to a platter. Cook the onion and bell peppers, turning them occasionally, until softened and browned in places, 10 to 20 minutes. Transfer to the platter and remove from the skewers. Cut the paneer into 1-inch or smaller cubes. (You can grill the vegetables and paneer several hours or even the day before; let cool, cover, and refrigerate.)

4 Put the onion chunks in a blender or food processor along with the ginger and garlic and purée until smooth, scraping down the side of the container as needed.

5 Melt the butter in a large skillet over medium heat. Add the onion purée (no need to wash the blender or work bowl), cumin, turmeric, and red pepper and sprinkle with salt and pepper. Cook, stirring, until fragrant and golden, 8 to 10 minutes.

6 Purée the grilled tomatoes. Add to the onion mixture and cook, stirring a few times, until a lot of the liquid has evaporated, 5 to 10 minutes. Remove

• recipe continues →

Ⓓ direct fire   Ⓘ indirect fire   Ⓜ make ahead   Ⓥ vegetarian option

from the heat and stir in the yogurt, ½ cup water, and the grilled paneer and vegetables. Taste the sauce and adjust the seasoning, adding more red pepper if you like. Return the pan to the stove and adjust the heat to a gentle bubble. Cook until the paneer and vegetables are heated through. Garnish with the cilantro and serve.

Saag Paneer	My take on the classic: Omit the grilled onions and peppers. Substitute 1 tablespoon garam masala for the cumin and turmeric. In Step 6, after you add the tomatoes to the onion purée and it starts to bubble, add 10 ounces baby spinach or chopped regular spinach (or use half mustard greens and half spinach). Cover the pan until the spinach softens, just a few minutes. Uncover, stir, and let the sauce bubble until thickened; then add the yogurt, water, and paneer and finish as directed.
Paneer and Cauliflower Coconut Masala	Omit the grilled onions and peppers. Cut enough cauliflower to get about 2 cups small florets. Substitute 1 cup coconut milk for the yogurt and water. In Step 4, add 1 seeded jalapeño when you process the onion to a purée. After you add the tomatoes to the onion purée and it starts to bubble, add the cauliflower; cook and stir until it's crisp-tender, 5 to 10 minutes, stirring occasionally. Add the coconut milk, then the paneer, and simmer until it's hot and the cauliflower is fully tender, another 5 to 10 minutes.
Tofu Masala	Make either of these variations, only replace the paneer with 1 block firm or extra-firm tofu (14–16 ounces). Cut into ½- to ¾-inch slices and grill (page 329). Cut into cubes and add to the sauce as directed in Step 6.

D direct fire   I indirect fire   M make ahead   V vegetarian option

Calzones with Three Cheeses and Spinach

Makes: 4 calzones	Time: 2 to 3 hours, largely unattended, if you make your own dough	D M V

Cooked on the grill, calzones are out of this world. And since you can prepare the dough and filling ahead of time—and just assemble them at the last minute—they're perfect for entertaining. One calzone makes a hearty main course; add a small green salad and you're set. I often make half batches of two different fillings and form the dough into eight rounds instead of four; that way everyone gets a sampler. You could cut them up for appetizers or make them even smaller, as mini calzones.

1 recipe dough from Pizza Bianca (page 52; omit the olive oil for drizzling and the rosemary), mixed and risen

All-purpose flour as needed

1 cup chopped cooked spinach (start with about 1 pound raw, or you can use frozen; squeeze it dry before chopping)

1 clove garlic, chopped

2 cups ricotta cheese

1 cup shredded mozzarella cheese

½ cup freshly grated Parmesan cheese

Salt

Red chile flakes

1 Knead the dough lightly and cut it into 4 equal pieces. Form into balls and put them on a lightly floured work surface. Sprinkle with a little flour and cover with plastic wrap or a kitchen towel; let rest for 20 minutes.

2 Start the coals or heat a gas grill for medium to medium-high direct cooking. Make sure the grates are clean.

3 To make the filling, combine the spinach, garlic, and ricotta, mozzarella, and Parmesan cheeses in a bowl. Taste and adjust the seasoning, adding salt if necessary; add red pepper to taste.

4 Roll or lightly press each dough ball into a flat round, lightly flouring the work surface and the dough as necessary (do not use more flour than you need to). Let the dough sit for a few minutes so it relaxes and is easier to work. Roll or stretch the dough into thin 6- to 8-inch rounds, taking care not to tear it. Divide the filling between the rounds, putting it off center. Fold one edge over and onto the other, then fold the edges together back toward the filling to seal, pressing them closed with your fingertips. Transfer the calzones to a baking sheet.

5 Carefully put the calzones on the grill directly over the fire. Close the lid and cook, turning once, until the dough rises, develops a crust, and browns or even chars in spots, 4 to 5 minutes per side; you know they're ready to turn when the bottom releases easily from the grates. Transfer to a plate and let set for 5 minutes before serving.

• recipe continues →

Mixed Mushroom Calzones with Rosemary	Omit the spinach and red chile flakes; increase the garlic to 1 tablespoon. Chop 1 tablespoon fresh rosemary. Trim and slice 1½ pounds mixed mushrooms (button, cremini, portobello, shiitake, whatever you like). Heat 1 tablespoon good-quality olive oil in a large skillet over medium-high heat. Add the mushrooms and some salt and pepper. Cook, stirring occasionally, until the mushrooms release their liquid and it evaporates and they start to brown in spots, 5 to 15 minutes, depending on the assortment. Add the garlic and rosemary, Let cool a few minutes, then mix with the cheeses. Proceed as directed for filling and grilling the calzones.
Kale and Olive Calzones	Omit the garlic and red chile flakes. Substitute 1 pound lacinato (Tuscan) kale for the spinach. Remove the stems and slice the leaves across into thin ribbons, then chop. Toss with 2 tablespoons sherry vinegar and a sprinkle of salt and let sit for 15 minutes. Drain, squeezing to extract as much liquid as possible and add to the cheeses, along with ½ cup chopped pitted black olives. Proceed as directed for filling and grilling the calzones.
Calzones with Charred Broccoli Raab	The sweetness of the cheese and the bitterness of raab go together beautifully: Omit the garlic and red chile flakes. Grate the zest of 1 lemon. Substitute 1 pound broccoli raab for the spinach. Trim about ½ inch from the bottom of the stems and toss with 1 tablespoon good-quality olive oil. As soon as the grill is ready, put it directly over the fire in a single layer, close the lid, and cook until the stems are crisp-tender and the leaves wilted and blackened, 3 to 5 minutes total; no need to turn. Transfer to a cutting board and roughly chop. Combine with the cheeses along with the zest. Proceed as directed for filling and grilling the calzones.

---

6 GREAT GRILLED ADD-INS TO CALZONE FILLING

1. Substitute 2 cups Baba Ghanoush (page 23) for the spinach and garlic.
2. Increase the Parmesan to 1 cup and substitute 1 cup chopped Roasted Peppers (page 34; use red peppers) for the spinach.
3. Substitute 4 chopped grilled baby artichokes (see page 38) and the grated zest of 1 lemon for the spinach.
4. Smoke the ricotta cheese before adding it to the filling (page 46).
5. Substitute 1½ cups chopped Smoked Cauliflower (page 402) and ½ cup chopped pitted olives for the spinach and garlic.
6. Substitute 1 cup Easy Onion Jam (page 433) for the spinach and garlic.

D direct fire   I indirect fire   M make ahead   V vegetarian option

Quinoa Salad with Apples, Brussels Sprouts, and Walnuts

Makes: 4 to 6 servings	Time: 60 to 70 minutes	Ⓘ Ⓜ Ⓥ

In a world loaded with vegetable bowls, the grain salad remains the pioneer. And you can make almost all the components days ahead and assemble them for a hearty work lunch. The Brussels sprouts are easiest to grill in a perforated grill pan, but if you don't have one just buy sprouts large enough so they won't fall between the grates. The amount of dressing called for here very lightly coats all the components of the salad; if you like a moister salad—or want to add some greens—double the ingredients.

1 cup quinoa

Salt and pepper

1 pound Brussels sprouts, trimmed and any discolored leaves removed

8 tablespoons good-quality olive oil

2 apples

¾ cup chopped fresh parsley

2 tablespoons white wine vinegar

2 teaspoons Dijon mustard

Grated zest of 1 lemon

1 cup walnut halves, toasted (page 537)

1 Put the quinoa and ½ teaspoon salt in a saucepan with 1½ cups water, bring to a boil, reduce the heat so the water bubbles gently but steadily, cover, and cook undisturbed until the surface is dotted with holes and the water is almost all absorbed, about 15 minutes. Turn off the heat and let stand until the kernels are tender and fluffy, 5 to 10 minutes.

2 Start the coals or heat a gas grill for medium to medium-high indirect cooking. Make sure the grates are clean.

3 Toss the sprouts and 1 tablespoon of the oil together in a bowl. Sprinkle with salt and pepper to taste and toss again.

4 If you're using one, put the sprouts in a perforated grill pan. Put the sprouts on the indirect side of the grill. Close the lid and cook, turning them at least once, until they're fork-tender, 20 to 35 minutes. If you want a bit of char, finish them directly over the fire, turning them frequently, for 2 to 3 minutes. Transfer to a bowl. When cool enough to handle, quarter each through the stem.

5 Transfer the quinoa to a large serving bowl. Add the Brussels sprouts. Core the apples and cut them into cubes; add to the bowl along with the parsley. Whisk the remaining 6 tablespoons oil, the vinegar, mustard, and lemon zest together in a small bowl. Taste and season with salt and pepper. Pour over the salad and toss everything to combine. Right before serving, add the nuts. Serve at room temperature.

● recipe continues →

Quinoa Salad with Apples, Asparagus, and Tempeh	Substitute trimmed asparagus for the Brussels sprouts; grill directly over a medium fire until browned in spots and crisp-tender, 5 to 10 minutes, depending on their thickness. Grill 8 ounces tempeh (page 330). When cool enough to handle, cut the asparagus into 1½- to 2-inch lengths and chop the tempeh. Add both to the salad in Step 5.
Freekeh Salad with Apples, Brussels Sprouts, and Almonds	Replace the walnuts with chopped almonds. Toast 1 cup cracked freekeh in a saucepan over medium heat, shaking the pan, until fragrant, 3 to 5 minutes, then cook as for quinoa in Step 1, increasing the water to 2½ cups. Drain off any water that may remain before mixing it with the other ingredients.
Bulgur Salad with Escarole and Orange	Add grilled eggplant if you've got leftovers: Substitute bulgur for the quinoa and 2 sectioned peeled oranges for the apples. Omit the Brussels sprouts and walnuts. Substitute ½ cup chopped mint for the parsley and sherry vinegar for the white wine vinegar. Cut 2 trimmed heads escarole in half through the stem. Brush with good-quality olive oil and sprinkle with salt all over. Grill directly over the fire until the escarole is wilted and charred in spots, 3 to 5 minutes per side. Transfer to a cutting board and cut across into 1-inch strips. Serve within an hour after assembling or wait to assemble until you're ready to serve.

Bread Pudding with Mushrooms and Rosemary

Makes: 4 to 6 servings as a main course; 8 servings as a side	Time: About 1 hour, largely unattended	Ⓓ Ⓜ Ⓥ

Savory bread pudding is a lot like stuffing. And grilling the bread and vegetables before baking adds a huge amount of flavor.

5 tablespoons good-quality olive oil

2 pounds cremini mushrooms, trimmed

Salt and pepper

1 large onion, cut into ½-inch wedges

1 12-ounce loaf ciabatta bread, split lengthwise

3 eggs

4 cups milk

4 tablespoons (½ stick) butter, melted, plus more for the pan

2 tablespoons chopped fresh rosemary

2 cups grated Gruyère, Emmental, cheddar, or Jack cheese (about 8 ounces)

1 If you're using bamboo or wooden skewers, soak them in water for 30 minutes. Start the coals or heat a gas grill for medium direct cooking. Make sure the grates are clean.

2 Put 3 tablespoons of the oil in a large bowl. Add the mushrooms, sprinkle with salt and pepper, and toss until coated. Skewer the mushrooms through their sides. Thread the onion on skewers and brush with the remaining 2 tablespoons oil.

3 Put the skewers on the grill (put the mushrooms cap down, if possible) directly over the fire. Close the lid and cook until everything softens. The mushrooms will take about 5 minutes; there is no need to turn them. The onions will take 15 to 25 minutes; turn them several times. It's fine if they char a bit.

4 When you take the mushrooms off, put the bread on the grill cut side down, and let brown and crisp, about 5 minutes, then turn and grill another 3 to 4 minutes. Transfer the vegetables to a platter and the bread to a cutting board. When cool enough to handle, remove the vegetables from the skewers and cut the bread into 1½-inch cubes. Slice the mushrooms and cut the onions into pieces.

5 Whisk the eggs in a large bowl, then whisk in the milk and melted butter. Stir in the rosemary and some salt and pepper, then add the bread, pushing it down into the milk multiple times, if necessary, to make sure all if it gets coated. Let sit for 15 to 20 minutes at room temperature, pushing down on the bread every few minutes.

6 Coat a 9- × 13-inch baking pan with butter. Stir the mushrooms and onions into the bread custard, then add the cheese and stir until distributed evenly. Pour into the pan. (You can make the bread pudding to this point up to a day before; cover and refrigerate until you're ready to bake it.)

7 Heat the oven to 350°F. Put the pan on the center rack and bake until a thin knife inserted in the center comes out clean or nearly so, 45 to 60 minutes, or a bit longer if baking straight from the refrigerator. Serve hot.

Ratatouille Bread Pudding	Omit the mushrooms, substitute mozzarella for the Gruyère, and chop 4 cloves garlic. Skewer 20 cherry or grape tomatoes. Cut about 1 pound eggplant, 1 bell pepper, and 1 zucchini into 1½-inch pieces; skewer them separately. Brush all the vegetables with good-quality olive oil and sprinkle with salt and pepper. Grill the eggplant, pepper, and zucchini, turning the skewers several times to cook evenly, until the vegetables are soft and charred in spots and the tomatoes are wrinkled, 5 to 15 minutes. If you like, cut the grilled vegetables into smaller pieces. Add to the bread custard along with the onion and garlic.
Bread Pudding with Brussels Sprouts and Shallots	Heat the grill for medium to medium-high indirect cooking. Substitute 1½ pounds Brussels sprouts for the mushrooms and 1 pound small shallots for the onion. Substitute fresh thyme leaves for the rosemary. Use the Gruyère or substitute 1 cup crumbled Gorgonzola or another blue cheese. Toss the sprouts and shallots with ¼ cup good-quality olive oil and sprinkle with salt and pepper. Transfer to a perforated grill pan grill and cook on the indirect side until tender and brown, 20 to 35 minutes, stirring a few times. Cut the sprouts and shallots into quarters, then add to the bread custard. Top the pudding with ½ cup chopped hazelnuts for the last couple of minutes baking.
Bread Pudding with Asparagus	Substitute 1½ pounds asparagus for the mushrooms and use a red onion. Trim the asparagus and toss with 1 tablespoon good-quality olive oil; sprinkle with salt. Grill the asparagus, turning once or twice, until it's crisp-tender, 5 to 10 minutes; cut it into 1-inch lengths, In Step 6, add to the bread mixture along with the onion. Substitute Parmesan for the Gruyère. In Step 5, substitute ¼ cup chopped fresh tarragon for the rosemary.

Vegetables and Side Dishes

As long as you've got the fire blazing, you may as well stay outside and cook. Nothing is as easy to grill as vegetables. And even more in your favor: Almost every vegetable loves the fire just as much as burgers and chicken.

I can make a whole meal of the dishes in this chapter. They're simple and flavorful, and fall on a wide spectrum of textures, so it's fun to mix and match a few on a gorgeous platter. My hope is that you'll be similarly inspired. But the main purpose of these recipes is to provide colorful, bright-tasting companions for the fish, poultry, and meat you've

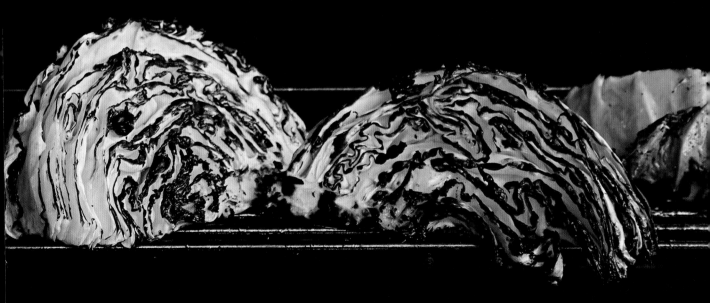

already got on the grill. That means I've also included the handful of classic nongrilled sides that scream cookout, like potato salad and baked beans.

The organization here is easy, too. The recipes are generally alphabetized by vegetable—including some killer beans and all sorts of potatoes—with a couple additional starchy sides that don't qualify as vegetables to round out the chapter.

The Basics of Grilling Vegetables

The guidelines for cooking vegetables with fire are virtually universal. As with other directions throughout the book, every recipe in this chapter that involves the grill tells you how to prepare it. But in reality, you've probably already got a fire going for the main course. There's bound to be a need to wing it a bit, and vegetables forgive you for that.

Take the heat levels as guidelines, factor in what else is going on the grill, and then use your good judgment. Coals too hot? Cook the vegetables on the outer edges. Cooler than the recipe directs? The vegetables might take a little longer to cook. (On gas you can just adjust the burners.) And if your main course needs to be over direct heat and the vegetable indirect—or vice versa—make a two- or three-zone indirect fire and use all parts of the grill. So maybe you'll add a few coals between cooking the different components of the meal, or you'll need to turn the burners on the gas grill up or down.

Some distinctions can be helpful, but these, too are general: Most vegetables cook quickly over a direct fire without burning. The ones that require slower, lower heat are those you'd expect: sturdy, hard vegetables like Brussels sprouts and roots and tubers. If the vegetable has a lot of water—like greens or mushrooms—it's more forgiving over high heat. The ones with sugar—carrots and sweet potatoes, for example—will blacken over a too-hot fire. The outcomes will be different if you grill them direct or indirect, or even right in the fire—and it's all good. And try smoking them, especially firm, porous vegetables like cauliflower, onions, and cabbage, which absorb a great deal of smoke flavor in just half an hour (see more about smoking on page 10).

The point is to be as flexible as the vegetables are. You can always build a moderately hot indirect fire and move food around. To me, this is outdoor cooking at its best. And when in doubt, just cook the vegetables first. They can be left at room temperature for about an hour—and are often even better that way. Or grill them earlier in the day, refrigerate, and take them out to take the chill off when you start the fire.

One bit of practical advice: Try to select produce that is about the same size when it is to be cooked whole (like fingerling potatoes, asparagus, green beans, or Brussels sprouts), or cut it into even-sized pieces or slices so that everything is done at about the same time. When that's not possible, just be prepared to move things around on the grill and have a platter ready to pull pieces as soon as they're ready.

Savory Applesauce on the Grill

Makes: 1¾ to 2 cups	Time: 40 to 45 minutes	Ⓓ Ⓜ Ⓥ

It turns out that the grill is a very efficient way to cook an apple, its skin serving as its own cooking vessel. In a matter of minutes, the apple's juices simmer and soon the fruit is soft all the way through. No need for fancy equipment—just cut the apple away from the core and use a food processor, blender, or immersion blender. The skins will disintegrate into—and intensify—the sauce. Sweetened only by the apple's natural sugars and cooked over fire, I consider this a savory side dish rather than a sauce; pick a variety of apple that has a pleasing balance of sweet to tart, or use a mix of apples.

1½ pounds whole apples

Salt

1 Start the coals or heat a gas grill for medium direct cooking. Make sure the grates are clean.

2 Put the apples on the grill directly over the fire. Close the lid and cook until the fruit feels soft when gently squeezed with tongs, 10 to 20 minutes total, depending on their size. Transfer to a cutting board and let sit until cool enough to touch.

3 Cut the flesh from around the core of each apple; discard the cores. Put the chunks in a blender or food processor and process until smooth, or put them in a bowl and purée with an immersion blender until as chunky or smooth as you like. Add a generous pinch of salt, then taste and adjust the seasoning. Serve or refrigerate in an airtight container for up to 3 days.

Applesauce with Ginger	You can add either fresh ginger or candied—both will give the sauce a nice kick, the latter also brings some sweetness: Add 2 tablespoons chopped fresh or candied ginger (or to taste) to the blender along with the apples.
Spicy Applesauce	Brings the heat in a different way from the first variation: Add part or all of a seeded jalapeño or other hot fresh chile to the blender along with the apples. Or add some ground dried chiles or cayenne to the sauce.
Pear Applesauce with Fresh Rosemary	A delicious partner for pork: Reduce the apples to 1 pound and add 8 ounces ripe pears. If the pears are still a little firm, they may take a bit longer to soften, 25 to 30 minutes total. Before or after puréeing, add 1 tablespoon chopped fresh rosemary.

Avocado with Lemon

Makes: 4 servings	Time: 20 to 25 minutes	D V

Don't relegate avocados to guacamole; half an avocado warmed on the grill is a rich, cooling side.

2 ripe avocados

Good-quality olive oil for brushing

1 lemon, halved

Salt and pepper

1 Start the coals or heat a gas grill for medium direct cooking. Make sure the grates are clean.

2 Cut the avocados in half lengthwise. Carefully strike a chef's knife into the pit, then wiggle it a bit to lift and remove it. Insert a spoon underneath the flesh against the skin and run it all the way around to separate the entire half of the avocado. Repeat with the other avocado. Brush with oil, then squeeze one of the lemon halves over them thoroughly on both sides so they don't discolor. Cut the other lemon half into 4 wedges.

3 Put the avocados on the grill directly over the fire, cut side down. Close the lid and cook, turning once, until browned in places, 5 to 10 minutes total. Serve the halved avocados as is, or slice and fan them for a prettier presentation. Sprinkle with salt and pepper and garnish with the lemon wedges.

Avocado with Chile and Cilantro	Add some flavorful confetti: Substitute 2 limes for the lemon; halve one to rub the avocado and cut the other into 4 wedges. Seed and chop a serrano chile; chop several sprigs cilantro. After sprinkling the avocados with salt and pepper, scatter the chiles and cilantro on top and serve with the lime wedges.
Sesame-Soy Avocado	Substitute sesame oil for the olive oil and a lime for the lemon. To serve, put the avocados cut side up, pour a bit of soy sauce into the "bowl," and sprinkle with toasted sesame seeds.
Avocado with Dijon-Orange Vinaigrette and Watercress	Substitute a small orange for the lemon. Juice the second orange half. Whisk it with ¼ cup good-quality olive oil, 1 teaspoon Dijon mustard, and a little salt and pepper. Top each avocado half with a small handful of watercress sprigs and drizzle with the dressing.

Simplest Grilled Asparagus

Makes: 4 servings	Time: 20 to 25 minutes	D V

If you've never tried asparagus blasted with high heat, you're in for a treat.

1½–2 pounds asparagus

1–2 tablespoons good-quality olive oil or melted butter

Salt

1 Start the coals or heat a gas grill for hot direct cooking. Make sure the grates are clean.

2 Cut the tough bottoms from the asparagus. If they're thick, trim the ends with a vegetable peeler. Toss with the oil and sprinkle with salt.

3 Put the asparagus on the grill directly over the fire, perpendicular to the grates so they don't fall through. Close the lid and cook, turning once, until the thick part of the stalks can barely be pierced with a skewer or thin knife, 5 to 10 minutes total. Transfer to a platter and serve.

Asparagus with Shaved Parmesan	Such a lovely presentation: Use a vegetable peeler to shave about 2 ounces Parmesan cheese into thin ribbons; you should have about ½ cup. Scatter over the asparagus when it's hot off the grill.
Asparagus and Green Beans with Lemon	Substitute ¾–1 pound green beans for half the asparagus; try to select beans about the same length and thickness as the asparagus. Trim the beans. If the beans are a bit thinner than the asparagus, wait a minute or 2 before putting them on the grill with the spears. They should cook in about the same amount of time. Serve with lemon wedges.
Asparagus with Sumac and Basil	When you toss the asparagus with the oil, add 1 teaspoon ground sumac. Sprinkle the grilled asparagus with 2 tablespoons chopped fresh basil.

---

6 CLASSIC WAYS TO SERVE SIMPLEST GRILLED ASPARAGUS

Finish grilled asparagus with any of these toppers. Many are good in combination.

1. Drizzle with more good-quality olive oil or melted butter—Beurre Blanc (page 132) is super—or top with several pats of your choice of Compound Butter (page 466)
2. Serve with lemon or lime wedges or a few drops of vinegar
3. Put a dollop of plain or flavored mayonnaise alongside for dipping
4. Top with minced or chopped hard-boiled eggs.
5. Garnish with chopped roasted red peppers (page 34)
6. Sprinkle with fresh herbs, especially tarragon

Beets and Greens with Lemon-Dill Vinaigrette

Makes: 4 servings	Time: 50 to 60 minutes, largely unattended	Ⓓ Ⓜ Ⓥ

My first choice for grilling beets are the small ones, not much more than 2 inches across. Cooked direct over a medium or slightly cooler fire, they're like warm candy in a little more than half an hour. Larger beets take much longer and need to be moved on and off direct heat to keep from burning. For that reason I prefer to first boil or roast them indoors until tender, peel, slice them thickly, brush with oil, and then put them directly over the fire for 2 minutes or so per side. In either case, buy beets with their greens still attached and in good shape. A few minutes over the fire tenderizes the leaves, tones down their bitterness, and infuses them with a pleasant toastiness. The stems cook up nicely, too; they're crisp-tender with an earthy, minerally flavor.

1½ pounds small beets, with fresh-looking greens still attached if possible

½ cup plus 2 tablespoons good-quality olive oil

Salt and pepper

3 tablespoons fresh lemon juice

2 tablespoons minced fresh dill

1 Start the coals or heat a gas grill for medium to medium-low direct cooking. Make sure the grates are clean.

2 Cut the greens off the beets. Throw away any wilted or discolored leaves; rinse the remainder well to remove any grit and drain. Trim the root ends of the beets and scrub well under running water. Pat the leaves and beets dry. Toss the beets with 2 tablespoons of the oil and a sprinkle of salt until evenly coated.

3 Put the beets on the grill directly over the fire. (No need to wash the bowl.) Close the lid and cook, turning them every 5 to 10 minutes, until a knife inserted in the center goes through with no resistance, 30 to 40 minutes total. Transfer to a plate and let sit until cool enough to handle.

4 Toss the beet greens in the reserved bowl to coat in oil. Put the greens on the grill directly over the fire. Close the lid and cook, tossing once or twice, until they're bright green and browned in spots, 2 to 5 minutes total. Keep a close eye on them; if they're on too long, they'll crisp up to the point where they'll shatter. Transfer to a plate.

5 Put the remaining ½ cup oil and the lemon juice in a serving bowl and whisk until thickened. Stir in the dill and some salt and pepper. Peel the skin from the beets and cut into halves or quarters. Cut the stems from the leaves in 1-inch lengths; cut the leaves across into ribbons. Put the beets, leaves, and stems in the bowl and toss with the vinaigrette until coated. Serve warm or at room temperature. Or make up to several hours ahead, cover, and refrigerate to serve chilled.

● recipe continues →

recipe continues →

Beets and Greens with Almonds and Parsley	Substitute sherry vinegar for the lemon juice and parsley for the dill, and add ¼ cup toasted sliced almonds and ½ teaspoon each ground cumin and coriander. If making this ahead, add the almonds right before serving so they stay crunchy.
Beet Salad with Avocado and Oranges	A fabulous interplay of ingredients, and gorgeous: Grill 1 pound beets as directed, including their greens. Substitute 1 teaspoon finely grated orange zest for the dill. Peel and section 2 small navel oranges. Cut a pitted, peeled ripe avocado into bite-sized chunks. Add the oranges and avocado to the vinaigrette along with the beets. If making this ahead, add the avocado just before serving so it doesn't discolor.
Beet Salad with Cabbage and Mango	Another beauty on the plate, with the added crunch of cabbage: Grill 1 pound beets as directed, including their greens. Substitute 2 tablespoons fresh lime juice and 1 tablespoon fish sauce for the lemon juice. Add the grated zest of 1 lime, and fresh mint for the dill. Quarter 1 small head cabbage, cut away the core, and cut into thin ribbons. (You can also grill the cabbage before slicing it; see page 397.) Cut a peeled and pitted ripe mango into bite-sized pieces. Add the cabbage and mango to the vinaigrette along with the beets.

GRILLING TURNIPS

You can use turnips—and their greens, if you've got them—the same way as beets in many recipes. It's kind of amazing how much smoke flavor they take on in the relatively short time they're on the grill if you're using a charcoal grill. As with beets, select small turnips, no more than about 2 inches across. Follow the technique for grilling beets, except peel them first, and cook over medium-low direct heat. (For large turnips, follow the directions in the headnote on page 399.) Check on them after about 2 minutes—if they're taking on color fast, move them to the edge of the fire or over indirect heat. Small turnips should be super-tender in 20 to 40 minutes.

You can substitute turnips in Beets and Greens with Lemon-Dill Vinaigrette and the Beets and Greens with Almonds and Parsley variation. You can also substitute them in Orange-Glazed Carrots or Parsnips (page 399) and all its variations, or serve turnips by themselves or in combination with other grilled roots and tubers like carrots, parsnips, and potatoes.

Green Beans with Sliced Garlic

Makes: 4 servings	Time: 35 to 40 minutes	Ⓓ Ⓜ Ⓥ

Two components—garlic sautéed in oil and beans charred on the grill—come together on the plate. I like to sauté the garlic before heating the grill so the oil has time to absorb the flavor; you can even do it earlier in the day, which will also save you time at the end. Try to select beans that are about the same size and no more than medium thickness—any thicker and the texture tends to be a bit woody and bland. A perforated grill pan makes this a snap.

3 tablespoons good-quality olive oil

4 cloves garlic, or more to taste, thinly sliced

Salt and pepper

1½ pounds green beans, trimmed

1 Put the oil and garlic in a large skillet over the lowest heat possible. Cook, shaking the pan occasionally and adjusting the heat if necessary, until the garlic is sizzling steadily. Keep a close eye on the garlic; it shouldn't color at all, but will puff and become quite fragrant. Remove from the heat, sprinkle with salt and pepper, and let sit at room temperature while you prepare the fire.

2 Start the coals or heat a gas grill for hot direct cooking. Make sure the grates are clean.

3 Put the green beans on the grill directly over the fire, perpendicular to the grates if you're not using a grill pan. Close the lid and cook until charred in places and a knife inserted into the center of a bean goes in without any resistance, 3 to 5 minutes depending on their thickness.

4 If the oil is no longer warm, while the beans are on the grill, put the skillet back over low to medium heat. Warm the oil just until the garlic starts to sizzle again, then remove from the heat. Transfer the beans directly to the skillet, toss to coat well, taste and adjust the seasoning, and serve.

Green Beans with Cherry Tomatoes, Garlic, and Basil	Cut fresh basil leaves across into thin ribbons; you want about ¼ cup. Skewer 16 to 20 cherry tomatoes and put them on the grill with the green beans. When they start to char and pucker, transfer them to the skillet. Add the beans, toss, and serve.
Sugar Snap Peas or Snow Peas with Sliced Garlic and Mint	The taste of springtime: Substitute sugar snap or snow peas for the green beans; trim them to remove the strings. Grill just until the peas turn bright green, 1 to 3 minutes. Add ¼ cup fresh mint leaves cut across into thin ribbons, toss with the oil and garlic, and serve.
Fava Beans with Sliced Garlic, Dill, and Lemon	No need to shell and peel fresh favas; every bit of them is edible after grilling, even the pods, though the smaller they are the less starchy they'll be: Substitute in-shell fava beans for the green beans. Grill as directed. Before you add them to the garlic oil, chop the beans across into pieces about ½ inch wide. Add 2 tablespoons chopped fresh dill, and the juice of ½ lemon (or more).

From-Scratch Baked Beans

Makes: 6 to 8 servings	Time: At least 4 hours, largely unattended, plus soaking time	Ⓜ Ⓥ

A barbecue isn't a barbecue without baked beans. The flavor of homemade is so much better than store-bought, no matter how much you doctor them. You can make these several days ahead, cover, refrigerate, and reheat before serving.

1 pound dried navy, great Northern, or other dried white beans (limas, pintos, and red beans also work), picked over, rinsed, and soaked for 6 to 12 hours in water to cover

8 ounces salt pork or slab bacon

½ cup molasses, or to taste

2 teaspoons dry mustard or 2 tablespoons Dijon mustard, or more to taste

Salt and pepper

1 Drain the beans, put in a large ovenproof pot, and add water to cover the beans by 2 inches. Bring to a boil, reduce the heat so the water is gently bubbling, partially cover the pot, and cook the beans just until they begin to become tender, 15 to 30 minutes depending on the bean. Drain the beans, reserving the cooking liquid; no need to rinse the pot.

2 Heat the oven to 300°F. Cube or slice the salt pork or bacon and put it in the bottom of the pot you used to cook the beans. Cover the meat with the beans and add the molasses and mustard. Add enough of the reserved liquid to cover the bean mixture by about an inch. (Add boiling water if there's not enough.) Stir to combine.

3 Bake, uncovered, for an hour. After that, check and stir every half hour or so, adding more water if necessary to keep everything covered. After about 3 hours, taste and adjust the seasoning with salt and pepper, as well as more mustard or molasses.

4 When the beans are very tender, fish out the meat and put it on top of the beans; raise the heat to 400°F. Bake until the pork browns a bit and the beans are bubbly, about 10 minutes. Serve hot.

Ⓓ direct fire   Ⓘ indirect fire   Ⓜ make ahead   Ⓥ vegetarian option

From-Scratch Baked Beans with Hoisin and Ginger	Substitute hoisin sauce for ¼ cup of the molasses and stir in ¼ cup chopped fresh ginger before baking.
Vegetarian or Vegan Baked Beans	No smokiness, less fat, but still really good: Omit the meat. Chop 1 large onion. After draining the beans, put 2 tablespoons butter or good-quality olive oil in the pot and cook the onion over medium heat until soft. Add the beans and 2 cups peeled, seeded, and chopped tomatoes (canned are fine; include the juices) along with the molasses and mustard.
Smoked Beans with Burnt Ends and Drippings	Save this for when you are smoking a brisket (see page 253): Omit the pork. Mix the beans with the molasses and mustard in a deep disposable foil pan. Put this pan under the brisket instead of a drip pan and cover the beans with an inch of the cooking liquid and boiling water if necessary. Cook the beans along with the brisket until the beans are very tender. Check the beans when you move the brisket into the oven; if they're not as tender as you want, move them into the oven as well and keep testing them every half-hour or so. When the brisket is done, cut the point from the brisket, cut it into 1-inch cubes, toss with barbecue sauce, and grill in a perforated grill pan as directed in "Making Burnt Ends" on page 254, then stir those into the beans before serving.

---

7 IDEAS FOR BAKED BEANS

Add any or a combination of these suggestions before baking the beans.

1. Add ketchup to taste, or substitute brown sugar or maple syrup (or a combination) for the molasses.
2. Add Worcestershire or soy sauce to taste.
3. Bring on the heat with sriracha, Vietnamese chili-garlic sauce, Korean gochujang, or your choice of hot sauce to taste.
4. Substitute sausage, cut into chunks, for the salt pork or bacon.
5. In Step 2, add 2 cups coconut milk and enough of the reserved liquid to cover the beans by an inch.
6. Add 1–2 tablespoons curry powder, chili powder, or any other spice mix you like (see page 456).
7. Increase the smokiness by stirring in up to 1 tablespoon smoked paprika (pimentón).

Baby Bok Choy with Lime-Miso Vinaigrette

Makes: **4 servings**	Time: **30 to 35 minutes**	Ⓓ Ⓜ Ⓥ

These bright green heads are a fraction of the heft of full-grown bok choy and have a mellower, sweeter taste. The resulting side dish is lovely with salmon or other full-flavored fatty fish. The size of baby bok choy can vary significantly. To ensure they're all the same size, leave the smallest whole, quarter the largest lengthwise, and halve the ones in between. You can cut the bok choy and make the vinaigrette several hours ahead; refrigerate until you're ready to grill.

¼ cup good-quality vegetable oil

Grated zest of 1 lime

2 tablespoons fresh lime juice

2 tablespoons white or light miso

1 tablespoon rice vinegar

Salt and pepper

1½ pounds baby bok choy

1 Start the coals or heat a gas grill for medium direct cooking. Make sure the grates are clean.

2 Whisk the oil, lime zest and juice, miso, and vinegar together in a small bowl until combined and thickened. Taste and adjust the seasoning with salt and pepper.

3 Trim the bottoms from the bok choy and cut into halves or quarters as needed. Pour half the vinaigrette into a large baking dish. Add the bok choy and turn in the vinaigrette until completely coated.

4 Put the bok choy on the grill directly over the fire. Close the lid and cook, turning once, until the leaves brown and you can insert a knife through the core with no resistance, 5 to 10 minutes per side, depending on their size. Transfer to a platter, drizzle with the reserved vinaigrette, and serve warm or at room temperature.

Baby Bok Choy with Sesame-Miso Vinaigrette	Omit the lime zest and add 1 teaspoon each sesame oil and red chile flakes.
Baby Bok Choy with Coconut-Chile Sauce	Omit the vinaigrette. Seed and chop 1 or more small red chiles (like Thai); whisk it together with ¼ cup coconut milk, 1 tablespoon each rice vinegar and fish sauce, the grated zest of 1 lime, and some salt and pepper. Use as directed for the vinaigrette.
Ginger-Garlic Baby Bok Choy with Black Vinegar	Sweet and smoky, Chinese black vinegar is available at most Asian markets; if you can't find it, balsamic vinegar approximates its flavor though it won't be the same: For the vinaigrette, whisk together ¼ cup good-quality vegetable oil, 3 tablespoons black vinegar, 1 tablespoon each minced fresh ginger and garlic, and 1 teaspoon soy sauce.

Ⓓ direct fire　Ⓘ indirect fire　Ⓜ make ahead　Ⓥ vegetarian option

Crisp Broccoli

Makes: 4 servings	Time: 25 to 30 minutes	Ⓓ Ⓥ

If you like roasting broccoli in a hot oven until it's browned and super-crunchy, you're going to love this. To make it with florets instead of large spears, you need a perforated grill pan to keep from losing them to the fire. (See the photo on page 272.)

1½ pounds broccoli

2 tablespoons good-quality olive oil

Salt and pepper

1 Start the coals or heat a gas grill for medium-high direct cooking. Make sure the grates are clean.

2 Cut the broccoli into florets or spears, as you like. Put on a baking sheet, pour over the oil, sprinkle with salt and pepper, and toss until the broccoli is evenly coated. If grilling florets, transfer to a perforated grill pan right before you take them out to the grill.

3 Put the broccoli on the grill directly over the fire. Close the lid and cook, turning often, until crisp tender, 5 to 15 minutes total, depending on how crunchy or charred you want it. Transfer to a platter, taste and adjust the seasoning, and serve.

Crisp Broccoli with Za'atar	When the broccoli comes off the grill, toss it with 1 tablespoon good-quality olive oil and 1 teaspoon za'atar (page 456), or more to taste. Serve with lemon wedges.
Crisp Broccoli with Orange-Mint-Ginger Gremolata	When the broccoli comes off the grill, toss it with 1 tablespoon good-quality olive oil and ¼ cup Orange-Mint-Ginger Gremolata (page 476).
Thai-Style Crisp Broccoli	When the broccoli comes off the grill, toss it with a mixture of 2 tablespoons each fresh lime juice and fish sauce, 2 teaspoons sugar, 1 teaspoon minced garlic (or more to taste), and ¼ teaspoon red chile flakes whisked together.

Ⓓ direct fire Ⓘ indirect fire Ⓜ make ahead Ⓥ vegetarian option

Brussels Sprouts with Thyme

Makes: **4 servings**	Time: **30 to 50 minutes**	Ⓘ Ⓥ

Since they're relatively dense, Brussels sprouts should be cooked over indirect heat, then finished over direct fire for additional browning if you like. Try to get sprouts of about the same size so they cook evenly. You shouldn't have any problem grilling large Brussels sprouts directly on the grate, but for ease of turning—or if you prefer smaller sprouts or like to cut the larger ones in half—use a perforated grill pan.

1½ pounds Brussels sprouts, trimmed and any discolored leaves removed

2 tablespoons good-quality olive oil

Salt and pepper

1 tablespoon fresh thyme leaves

1 Start the coals or heat a gas grill for medium to medium-high indirect cooking. Make sure the grates are clean.

2 If the Brussels sprouts are large, cut them in half through the stem. Put the sprouts and oil in a bowl; toss to coat the sprouts evenly with the oil. Sprinkle with salt and pepper to taste and toss again.

3 Put the sprouts on the indirect side of the grill. Close the lid and cook, turning them once, or shaking the grill pan, until they're tender enough for a fork or skewer to pierce the stem, 15 to 35 minutes, depending on how hot the fire is. If you want deeper color and a little char, move them directly over the fire, turning them frequently, for 2 to 3 minutes. Transfer to a serving dish, add the thyme, toss to coat evenly, and serve.

Sweet-and-Sour Brussels Sprouts	Before placing on the grill, toss the sprouts in a mixture of 1 tablespoon each good-quality olive oil, turbinado sugar, and cider vinegar, and lots of pepper.
Mustardy Brussels Sprouts with Walnuts	Walnuts are a perfect complement to the sprouts: Toast ½ cup or more walnut halves in a 350°F oven until fragrant, 10 to 12 minutes; chop. Before grilling, toss the sprouts with a mixture of 1 tablespoon each mayonnaise, Dijon mustard, and good-quality olive oil, and some salt and pepper. When the sprouts come off the grill, sprinkle with the toasted walnuts.
Brussels Sprouts with Pine Nuts, Dried Cranberries, and Sherry Vinaigrette	Colorful and so delicious: Toast ¼ cup or more pine nuts in a small dry skillet over medium-low heat, shaking and watching them carefully, until fragrant, 5 to 10 minutes. Whisk together ¼ cup good-quality olive oil, and 1 tablespoon (or more) sherry vinegar; add 1 teaspoon each Dijon mustard and smoked paprika (pimentón), and some salt and pepper. Toss the sprouts with 2 tablespoons of the vinaigrette before grilling. When they come off the grill, toss them with the remainder of it, along with the pine nuts and ½ cup dried cranberries.

Cabbage Wedges with Warm Pancetta Vinaigrette

Makes: **8 servings**	Time: **30 to 35 minutes**	D M V

Not that there's anything wrong with coleslaw and sauerkraut, but cabbage has so much more potential. It's phenomenal grilled. Cut into thin wedges and seared directly over the fire, it develops fantastic flavor and texture. Top it with a warm vinaigrette spiked with crisp bits of pancetta and everyone is happy.

1 small head red or green cabbage (2 pounds or less)

5 tablespoons good-quality olive oil

4 ounces thickly sliced pancetta, chopped

3 tablespoons sherry vinegar or white wine vinegar

Salt and pepper

1 Start the coals or heat a gas grill for medium direct cooking. Make sure the grates are clean.

2 Discard any discolored outer leaves from the cabbage, cut it into 8 wedges, then trim the stem a bit but leave enough on to keep the wedges together. Brush the cabbage on all sides with 2 tablespoons of the oil.

3 Put the cabbage on the grill directly over the fire, cut side down. Close the lid and cook until the bottom browns, about 5 minutes; turn and cook the other side. Transfer to a platter.

4 While the cabbage is grilling, put the pancetta in a small skillet over medium heat. Cook, stirring occasionally, until it renders its fat and the meat crisps, about 5 minutes. Remove from the heat, add the vinegar and remaining 3 tablespoons oil, and whisk to combine; taste and add some salt and pepper. (You can make the vinaigrette up to a day ahead; refrigerate and gently reheat it before using.) Pour the hot dressing over the cabbage wedges and serve.

Cabbage Wedges with Warm Bacon-Cumin Vinaigrette	The classic combination: Substitute diced thick-sliced or slab bacon for the pancetta and add 1 teaspoon cumin seeds along with the vinegar.
Cabbage Wedges with Apple Cider–Caraway Vinaigrette	Lose the meat: For the vinaigrette, whisk together ½ cup good-quality olive oil, 3 tablespoons cider vinegar, 1 teaspoon caraway seeds, and salt and pepper to taste. No need to heat it up.
Ketchup and Soy–Glazed Cabbage Wedges	Sweet and salty: Omit the vinaigrette. Instead of olive oil, brush the cabbage with a mixture of 1 tablespoon each good-quality vegetable oil and sesame oil. Combine 2 tablespoons each ketchup and soy sauce and 1 tablespoon each rice vinegar and minced fresh ginger and whisk until combined. Just before taking the cabbage off the grill, brush the glaze on top, close the lid, and cook for a minute; turn and repeat with the other side.

Thai-Style Coleslaw

Makes: **8 servings**	Time: **15 to 20 minutes**	Ⓜ Ⓥ

When a coleslaw is so simple, it's remarkable how much the type of cabbage can change things: Napa or Savoy make a crisp-tender, salad-like slaw, while red or green cabbage will give you more crunch and intensity. You can make the slaw several hours earlier or even the day before. Just pour off any extra liquid before serving. Serve this no-grill, no-mayo slaw with any simply cooked fish, meat, or poultry, or as part of a Southeast Asian spread. For a grilled spin, see the last variation.

1 small head cabbage (1 pound)

¼ cup fresh lime juice

¼ cup fish sauce

1 tablespoon minced garlic

1 tablespoon sugar

1 small red chile (like Thai), chopped, or
½ teaspoon red chile flakes or more to taste

¼ cup chopped fresh mint

1 Discard any discolored outer leaves from the cabbage, cut it into quarters, and remove the core. Cut across into thin ribbons or shred on the largest holes of a box grater or in a food processor with the shredding disk.

2 Whisk the lime juice, fish sauce, garlic, sugar, and chile together in a large bowl. Add the shredded cabbage and mint and toss with the dressing until completely coated. Serve immediately, or cover and refrigerate until you're ready to serve.

Dijon Coleslaw	Still no mayonnaise: For the dressing, whisk together ¼ cup good-quality olive oil, 2 tablespoons each Dijon mustard and red wine vinegar, and salt and pepper to taste. Substitute 4 chopped scallions for the mint.
Creamy Cabbage and Carrot Slaw	For the dressing, whisk together the juice of 1 lemon, ¼ cup mayonnaise, 2 tablespoons good-quality olive oil, and salt and pepper to taste. Add 2 grated carrots and substitute parsley for the mint.
Grilled or Smoked Slaw	Grilling the cabbage wedges over direct heat before shredding will add a hint of smoke to any of these slaw recipes: After quartering the cabbage, brush the pieces with a good-quality vegetable oil, then put over a medium direct fire, turning once, until browned on the cut sides, about 5 minutes per side. Shred the cabbage as directed and finish the slaw. For a more pronounced smoke flavor, swap out half of the raw shredded cabbage for thinly sliced Smoked Cabbage (page 403).

Ⓓ direct fire   Ⓘ indirect fire   Ⓜ make ahead   Ⓥ vegetarian option

Orange-Glazed Carrots or Parsnips

Makes: 4 servings	Time: 45 to 50 minutes	Ⓘ Ⓜ Ⓥ

Carrots and parsnips cooked this way are terrific hot, warm, or at room temperature. (Use oil instead of butter if you plan to serve them any way other than hot.) They also take to a wide variety of herbs and other simple treatments. Look for the thinnest carrots and parsnips you can find, no wider than 1½ inches at the thick end. If you must use larger ones, cut them lengthwise in half or quarters and trim away any woody core.

To use this recipe for rutabagas and turnips: Peel them, then slice across into 1-inch-thick rounds. Once they're tender, chop into bite-sized pieces and toss with the remaining glaze.

8 tablespoons (1 stick) butter or good-quality olive oil

1½ pounds carrots or parsnips, trimmed and peeled

Salt and pepper

Grated zest of 1 large orange

2 tablespoons fresh orange juice

Chopped fresh parsley, dill, mint, basil, or chervil leaves for garnish (optional)

1 Start the coals or heat a gas grill for medium indirect cooking. Make sure the grates are clean.

2 Melt the butter in a small saucepan over medium heat. Remove from the heat. Sprinkle with salt and pepper and stir in the orange zest and juice. Brush the carrots with the butter; keep the remaining butter mixture warm.

3 Put the carrots on the grill directly over the fire, with the thick ends just over the edge of the coals and the thin ends over indirect heat. Close the lid and cook, turning them every 5 minutes or so, until a knife inserted at the thickest part goes in without resistance, 20 to 40 minutes total. (Cook less if you prefer them more crisp-tender.)

4 Transfer to a cutting board, cut into pieces, and put in a serving dish. Drizzle over the remaining flavored butter and toss to coat. Sprinkle with fresh herbs if you're using them and serve.

• recipe continues →

Maple-Glazed Carrots or Parsnips	Substitute 2 tablespoons maple syrup for the orange zest and juice. Or leave the orange zest in, if you prefer.
Sweet-Hot Glazed Carrots or Parsnips	Omit the orange zest and juice. When the butter has melted, stir in 1 tablespoon each honey and hot sauce (or to taste). No need to garnish.
Lemon-Dill Carrot and Snow Pea Packet	You won't get any grill flavor, but it's such an easy way to prepare a vegetable side. And the packet can be put together hours ahead and refrigerated until you're ready to grill: Slice 12 ounces carrots into ¼-inch coins and 12 ounces snow peas at an angle into ½-inch pieces. Put them in the center of a 12-inch piece of heavy-duty foil and sprinkle with 1 tablespoon chopped fresh dill, 1 teaspoon grated lemon zest, and salt and pepper. Pour over 1 tablespoon water and top with 2 tablespoons butter. Fold over the foil to cover, and crimp the sides shut tightly to keep steam from escaping. Put directly over a medium fire. Close the lid and cook until the vegetables are quite tender, 20 to 30 minutes. To serve, transfer to a bowl and toss; taste and adjust the seasonings and toss again.

4 WAYS TO JAZZ UP GLAZED CARROTS

1. Add ½ cup chopped onion, shallot, scallion, or leeks to the melted butter and cook, stirring, until softened, 2 to 3 minutes.

2. Add ½ cup chopped pitted dates, raisins, dried currants, or dried tomatoes to the melted butter and cook, stirring, until plumped, 2 to 3 minutes.

3. Reduce the butter to 6 tablespoons; whisk together 1 tablespoon each soy sauce and miso and stir into the melted butter.

4. Add up to ½ cup whole or chopped toasted nuts or seeds like walnuts, pecans, pistachios, hazelnuts, sesame seeds, or sunflower seeds right before serving.

D direct fire   I indirect fire   M make ahead   V vegetarian option

Cauliflower with Garlic and Anchovies

Makes: 4 servings	Time: 20 to 25 minutes	D M V

A play on the classic Provençal anchovy and olive oil dip *anchoïade*, this is absolutely delicious with cauliflower—and everything else for that matter. The grilling technique also works for broccoli. You'll definitely need a perforated grill pan for either.

1 head cauliflower (1½–2 pounds)

6 tablespoons good-quality olive oil

6 oil-packed anchovy fillets, chopped, or more to taste

1 tablespoon minced garlic

½ teaspoon red chile flakes, or to taste (optional)

Salt and pepper (optional)

Chopped fresh parsley for garnish

1 Start the coals or heat a gas grill for medium direct cooking.

2 Break or cut the cauliflower into florets about 1½ inches across; put in a bowl.

3 Put the oil, anchovies, garlic, and red pepper if using it in a small skillet over medium-low heat. Cook, stirring occasionally, until the anchovies begin to break up and the garlic just begins to color, about 5 minutes. Taste and add more anchovies or some salt and pepper. Pour half of the oil mixture over the cauliflower; toss to coat evenly with it. Put the florets in a single layer on a perforated grill pan.

4 Put the perforated pan on the grill directly over the fire. Close the lid and cook, shaking the pan occasionally, until the cauliflower is as tender and browned as you like it, 3 minutes for crisp-tender to 10 minutes for fully tender. Transfer to a serving bowl, drizzle over the remaining sauce and the parsley, toss gently, and serve warm or at room temperature.

Lemon-Garlic Cauliflower	Omit the anchovies. Add the grated zest and juice of 1 lemon along with the parsley just before serving.
Cauliflower with Grill-Roasted Red Peppers and Hazelnuts	Toss the florets with 3 tablespoons good-quality olive oil before grilling. After grilling, toss them with ½ cup chopped roasted red peppers (page 34), 2 tablespoons balsamic or sherry vinegar, and 3 tablespoons chopped toasted hazelnuts.
Cauliflower with Toasted Bread Crumbs and Olives	Toss the florets with 3 tablespoons good-quality olive oil and salt and pepper before grilling. Toast ½ cup dry bread crumbs in 2 tablespoons olive oil in a skillet over medium heat until golden. Remove from the heat. While the cauliflower is still warm, toss the florets with ½ red onion, thinly sliced, ½ cup chopped olives, and the toasted bread crumbs. Drizzle with another 2 tablespoons olive oil and a splash of red wine vinegar if you like. Toss, taste and adjust the seasoning, toss again, and serve warm or at room temperature.

Smoked Cauliflower

Makes: 4 servings	Time: 1 to 2 hours	Ⓘ Ⓜ Ⓥ

The smell of this is intoxicating. If you like, you can smoke the head whole, but I prefer to cut it in half or in wedges or steaks (see page 347) to expose more surface area to the seasoning and the smoke. You can cut the smoked cauliflower into pieces and add it to salads, or roughly chop and include it in tacos, wraps, and quesadillas—it's that meaty. I also cut it into big florets to serve with dip before dinner or as a snack. For some dip ideas, see the list below.

1 head cauliflower

About ¼ cup good-quality olive oil

Salt and pepper

1 Start the coals or heat a gas grill for medium indirect cooking. If using charcoal, position the coals so the smoke will be pulled over the cauliflower and out the top vent. Make sure the grates are clean. When the grill is ready, add wood to the fire (see "Smoking," pages 10–12).

2 While the grill comes to temperature, if you like, cut the cauliflower in half through the stem or into steaks (see the headnote). Brush it on all sides with oil. Sprinkle all over with salt and pepper.

3 When the grill fills with smoke, put the cauliflower on the indirect side of the grill. Close the lid and cook until you can insert a skewer or thin knife through the thickest florets with little or no resistance, depending on how tender you want it. This will take up to 2 hours for a whole head, about an hour for cauliflower cut in half, and less for steaks. (Keep the grill full of smoke for up to 30 minutes.) Transfer the cauliflower to a platter and serve, or wait until it's cool enough to handle to cut into pieces and use as you like. Or store in an airtight container in the refrigerator for 4 to 5 days.

---

7 DELICIOUS DIPS FOR SMOKED CAULIFLOWER

Brightly flavored, creamy dips are a nice offset to the smoke flavor of the florets.

1. Green Goddess Dressing (page 334)
2. Basil Mayonnaise (page 461)
3. Lemon Mayo (page 71)
4. Parmesan Herb Dressing (page 335)
5. Za'atar Yogurt Sauce (page 38)
6. Lime Crema Dipping Sauce (page 82)
7. Minted Yogurt (page 323)

Smoked Cabbage	Wonderful substituted for part of the cabbage in any kind of coleslaw; start with about a quarter-head and adjust as you like: Substitute a small to medium head green cabbage for the cauliflower. Cut through the stem end into 1- to 1½-inch slices. Brush with good-quality olive oil; you'll need 2–4 tablespoons. Sprinkle with salt and pepper. You have a lot of leeway with cooking time, as the cabbage will retain crispness for a long time, even after 2 hours on the grill. If the outer leaf covering a slice browns to the point of crispiness, remove it—it will taste bitter.
Smoked Onions	Serve these as rings alongside—or on top of—burgers, or chop them to add smoke to almost anything. They make Easy Onion Jam (page 433) even more incredible. And you can freeze them almost indefinitely so they're always handy: Cut as many large onions as you want (any kind) into 1-inch slices. Brush with about 1 tablespoon oil per onion and sprinkle with salt and pepper. As with cabbage, you have a lot of leeway; after 2 hours, they will be soft but not crazy soft. You'll want to keep them on for at least an hour; after that, it's your call.
Sherry-Smoked Vegetables	Regardless of the quantity of olive oil, substitute half with dry sherry. This new dimension complements all three of these vegetables.

Corn on the Cob

| Makes: **4 servings** | Time: **25 to 30 minutes** | **D** **V** |

Grilled corn is unbeatable. Here's my way of doing it, in which the kernels blacken a bit.

4 ears fresh corn

Salt and pepper

Butter (optional)

1 Start the coals or heat a gas grill for medium direct cooking. Make sure the grates are clean.

2 Shuck the corn, removing the husks and silks.

3 Put the corn on the grill directly over the fire. Close the lid and cook, turning the ears every few minutes, until some of the kernels char a bit, 8 to 12 minutes total. Serve with salt, pepper, and butter if you like.

Spicy Corn on the Cob	After grilling the corn, rub it with butter, then sprinkle with chili powder to taste and serve with lime wedges.
Cheesy Corn	Omit the butter. Crumble or grate about 4 ounces Cotija or Monterey Jack cheese (1 cup) onto a plate. After grilling the corn, sprinkle with chili powder to taste, then brush with Mexican *crema,* mayonnaise, or thinned sour cream, about 1 tablespoon per ear, Roll in the cheese, pressing gently to stick. Season with plenty of pepper.
Cambodian-Style Coconut Corn	Unexpected and haunting flavor: Whisk together ½ cup coconut milk, 2 tablespoons fish sauce, 1 tablespoon turbinado sugar, and 2 chopped scallions in a small bowl. Before grilling, brush the corn with this mixture, pushing down on the brush to get the seasonings into all the nooks and crannies between the kernels. Turn the corn several times for even cooking, basting with the coconut mixture each time.

---

9 FLAVORINGS FOR HOT CORN ON THE COB

1. Freshly grated Parmesan cheese
2. Fresh lemon or lime juice—especially with a few dashes of hot sauce
3. Red chile flakes or cayenne
4. A spice blend like chili powder or chaat masala
5. Sesame seeds or finely chopped pumpkin or sunflower seeds
6. Finely chopped nuts (like hazelnuts, almonds, cashews, or peanuts)
7. Minced fresh herbs (like parsley, mint, chervil, or chives)
8. Mashed Grill-Roasted Garlic (page 464)
9. Softened butter mixed with honey and sriracha or other hot sauce to taste

---

D direct fire   **I** indirect fire   **M** make ahead   **V** vegetarian option

Grilled Corn Pudding

| Makes: 4 to 6 servings | Time: 60 to 70 minutes, largely unattended | Ⓓ Ⓜ Ⓥ |

Like mac and cheese (page 447), corn pudding is always welcome on the picnic table, a perfect partner for most anything barbecued. Grill the corn before mixing up the batter and you've got something extraordinary. You can put this together and bake it when guests arrive, or the day before and reheat it just before serving. Use any of the different variations to grill the corn—the flavor will carry to the pudding.

6 ears corn, shucked and grilled (page 404)

4 tablespoons (½ stick) butter, melted, plus more for greasing the pan

2 cups milk

2 eggs

½ teaspoon salt

1 Heat the oven to 350°F. Butter an 8-inch square baking dish or 9- or 10-inch cast-iron skillet.

2 When the corn is cool enough to handle, cut the kernels from cobs, working downward along the cob over a bowl to collect any juices; you should have about 4 cups corn. Whisk the butter, milk, eggs, and salt together in a large bowl. Stir in the corn. Pour the batter into the baking dish.

3 Bake on the center rack of the oven until a skewer inserted in the center comes out clean and the pudding no longer jiggles but is still soft to the touch, 40 to 50 minutes. Serve with a big spoon, hot or warm.

Cheesy Corn Pudding	Use any cheese you like, so long as it melts well—I like Parmesan, Emmental, Gruyère, and cheddar; goat cheese is also good, as well as mozzarella if you like that stringiness: Stir in ½ cup grated cheese along with the corn. For a double shot of smoke flavor, use a smoked cheese.
Chile-Spiked Corn Pudding	A modern classic heat-meets-sweet combination: When you grill the corn, also grill 2 jalapeños until blackened. Remove the skins, seeds, and stems, chop, and add to the batter along with the corn. If you're not keen on heat, grill a red bell pepper instead, which will add mild flavor and color.
Coconut Corn Pudding	A nice choice to accompany a meal with Southeast Asian flavors: Substitute 1 cup coconut milk for 1 cup of the milk.

Grilled Polenta

| Makes: 4 to 6 servings | Time: 50 to 60 minutes, plus cooling time | Ⓓ Ⓜ Ⓥ |

Grilling is a great way to enjoy leftover polenta—but why wait for the next day? Make a fresh batch earlier in the day, let it cool in a pan, slice, and sear over the fire. These pieces are thicker and creamier inside than the Polenta Squares on page 59. Try both!

2 tablespoons butter, plus more for the pan

½ cup milk (preferably whole)

Salt

1 cup coarse cornmeal

Black pepper

Good-quality olive oil for brushing

¾ cup freshly grated Parmesan cheese

1 Generously grease an 8-inch square baking dish or standard loaf pan with butter. Combine the milk with 2 cups of water and a large pinch salt in a medium saucepan over medium heat. Bring just about to a boil, then add the cornmeal in a steady stream, whisking constantly to prevent lumps from forming. Turn the heat down to low and simmer, whisking frequently, until it has the consistency of thick oatmeal, 10 to 15 minutes. Stir in the butter, taste, and adjust the seasoning with salt and pepper. Pour the polenta into the prepared pan and spread into an even layer. Let stand at room temperature until fully cooled, about 1 hour, or cover and refrigerate overnight.

2 Start the coals or heat a gas grill for medium direct cooking. Make sure the grates are clean.

3 Turn the polenta out onto a cutting board. With a serrated knife, cut it into 1½- to 2-inch squares. Brush the squares with oil on both sides.

4 Put the polenta squares on the grill directly over the fire. Close the lid and cook, turning once, until they brown and are heated through, 4 to 5 minutes per side. Transfer to a platter, immediately sprinkle with the Parmesan, and serve.

---

6 MORE FLAVOR ADDITIONS TO POLENTA

Add any of the first five along with the butter in Step 1.

1. ½ cup chopped pitted olives
2. ¼ cup (or to taste) mashed Grill-Roasted Garlic (page 464)
3. ¼ cup chopped rind of preserved lemons
4. 1 jalapeño chile, seeded and chopped
5. Chopped pine nuts or other nuts
6. Basil Pesto (page 475) or other pesto, brushed on the tops of the slices before grilling

---

Ⓓ direct fire   Ⓘ indirect fire   Ⓜ make ahead   Ⓥ vegetarian option

Dairy-Free Grilled Polenta	Make it vegan: Substitute unsweetened almond milk for the regular milk and olive oil for the butter. Omit the Parmesan and dust with chopped nuts if you like when it comes off the grill.
Grilled Polenta with Basil or Mint	When stirring in the butter, also add ½ cup chopped fresh basil or mint, or a mixture of the two.
Grilled Polenta with Grilled Vegetables	You can amp up the smoky flavor by adding ½ cup chopped grilled vegetables when the polenta is almost done in Step 1. Great choices would be onions (page 433), scallions (page 437), leeks (page 413), roasted red peppers (page 34), and/or escarole or broccoli raab (page 417).

Sort-of-Stuffed Eggplant with Ginger, Sesame, and Soy

Makes: 4 servings	Time: 35 to 45 minutes	Ⓘ Ⓜ Ⓥ

Eggplant can handle direct heat (including getting tossed right into the fire; see page 226), but it's also delicious cut in half and cooked with indirect heat. The longer time off-flame gives the skin and cut surfaces time to crisp up while the flesh develops a rich creaminess that soaks up the seasonings. Scoring the cut side and working in herbs, spices, or aromatics is almost like stuffing it. You can prepare the eggplants for the grill several hours before; cover with plastic wrap and refrigerate. You can also grill them ahead time; they're just as good at room temperature.

2 small eggplants (about 8 ounces each)

¼ cup minced fresh cilantro

2 tablespoons soy sauce

1 tablespoon minced fresh ginger

1 teaspoon sesame oil

Lime wedges for serving

1 Start the coals or heat a gas grill for medium-high indirect cooking. Make sure the grates are clean.

2 Cut the eggplants in half lengthwise for long eggplant, or through the equator for globe eggplant.

Score the cut surface of the eggplants with lots of shallow incisions. Mix the cilantro, soy sauce, ginger, and oil together well in a small bowl. Work the flavor paste over the cut surfaces of the eggplants, pushing it into the slits.

3 Put the eggplant halves on the indirect side of the grill, cut side up. Close the lid and cook until the skin has crisped, the tops are browned, and the flesh is fork-tender, 20 to 30 minutes; rotate and turn about halfway through for even cooking. Transfer to a platter and serve hot, warm, or at room temperature with lime wedges.

Sort-of-Stuffed Eggplant with Ras el Hanout and Mint	"Stuff" the eggplant with a mixture of ¼ cup minced fresh mint, 2 tablespoons good-quality olive oil, 1 tablespoon minced garlic, 2 teaspoons ras el hanout (page 456), and the grated zest of 1 lime.
Sort-of-Stuffed Eggplant with Garlic-Basil Crumbs	"Stuff" the eggplant with a mixture of 3 tablespoons dry bread crumbs and 2 tablespoons each good-quality olive oil, minced garlic, and minced fresh basil.
Sort-of-Stuffed Eggplant with Lemon, Parsley, and Feta	Combine ¼ cup minced fresh parsley, 2 tablespoons good-quality olive oil, 1 tablespoon minced garlic, and the grated zest of 1 lemon in a small bowl to "stuff" the eggplants. When they look almost ready to come off the grill, sprinkle each one with 2 tablespoons crumbled feta cheese and cook for another 5 minutes.

Eggplant with Garlic

Makes: 4 to 6 servings	Time: 25 to 30 minutes	Ⓓ Ⓜ Ⓥ

Among the fastest and easiest ways to prepare eggplant, and super at room temperature, this technique is so reliably good you might just want to make a batch whenever you've got the grill going and save it for another meal. It's perfect tossed with pasta or grains, puréed for spreads or dips, and sliced for sandwiches.

2 medium or 1 large eggplant (1½–2 pounds)

1 tablespoon minced garlic, or more to taste

6 tablespoons good-quality olive oil

Salt and pepper

Chopped fresh parsley for garnish

1 Start the coals or heat a gas grill for medium-high direct cooking. Make sure the grates are clean.

2 Peel the eggplant if you like and cut it across into ½-inch slices. Stir the garlic into the oil along with salt and pepper; brush on the slices on both sides.

3 Put the eggplant slices on the grill directly over the fire. Close the lid and cook, turning and basting with the garlic oil, until the slices are browned and fork-tender, 10 to 15 minutes total. Transfer to a platter, drizzle with any remaining oil, sprinkle with parsley, and serve hot, warm, or at room temperature. Or transfer to an airtight container and refrigerate for up to a few days.

Teriyaki Eggplant	Put 3 tablespoons each soy sauce and mirin (or substitute 1½ tablespoons each honey and water for the mirin) in small saucepan and bring to a gentle bubble. Stir in 2 tablespoons good-quality vegetable oil and 1 tablespoon each sesame oil, minced garlic, and minced fresh ginger. Use this teriyaki sauce to brush on the eggplant slices instead of the garlic oil. Garnish with chopped chives or scallions.
Balsamic-Glazed Eggplant with Garlic and Rosemary	For a lighter flavor and color, try white balsamic vinegar: Combine ¼ cup good-quality olive oil and 1 tablespoon each balsamic vinegar, minced garlic, and minced fresh rosemary; sprinkle with salt and pepper, whisk, and use to brush the eggplant.
Lime and Yogurt–Basted Eggplant	Omit the garlic and oil. Whisk together ½ cup Greek yogurt and the grated zest and juice of 1 lime; sprinkle with salt and pepper. After each side has been over the fire for about 3 minutes, baste the eggplant slices with the yogurt mixture. Garnish with chopped fresh mint.

Ⓓ direct fire   Ⓘ indirect fire   Ⓜ make ahead   Ⓥ vegetarian option

Grill-Steamed Leeks

Makes: 4 servings	Time: 25 to 30 minutes	Ⓓ Ⓜ Ⓥ

Mild and sweet, leeks—at least the root ends—have a silky texture when grilled. Buy leeks with plenty of white on the stalk; you'll be trimming away most of the green. And don't skimp on the rinsing—their multiple layers can hold a lot of unappetizing grit. Don't bother to shake the water off. The steam cooks the leeks and prevents burning. Once they're tender, brush them with oil and grill until both sides develop good color.

4 leeks (1–1½ pounds)

Salt and pepper

Good-quality olive oil

1 Start the coals or heat a gas grill for medium to medium-low direct cooking. Make sure the grates are clean.

2 Trim the root ends of the leeks and cut away the tough green tops. Make a long vertical slit through the center of the leek from the root end through the remaining green part, but not cutting all the way through to the other side. Rinse well to get the sand out from between the layers. Sprinkle both sides with salt.

3 Open up the leeks and put them on the grill directly over the fire, cut side down, pressing down gently with a spatula to make sure the layers fan out over the heat. Close the lid and cook until they have fully softened, 6 to 8 minutes, depending on their thickness. Brush with some oil, turn, and cook until the bottom browns, 1 to 3 minutes. Brush the top with oil, turn, and cook another 1 to 3 minutes. Transfer the leeks to a plate, sprinkle with pepper, and serve hot, warm, or at room temperature.

Grilled Sesame-Soy Leeks	Substitute sesame oil, or a mixture of vegetable and sesame oil for a milder taste, for the olive oil. Before taking the leeks off the grill, brush both sides with soy sauce.
Leeks with Tarragon Vinaigrette	While the leeks grill, whisk together ¼ cup good-quality olive oil, 4 teaspoons fresh lemon juice, 1 tablespoon chopped fresh tarragon, and some salt and pepper in a small bowl until thick. Drizzle over the leeks before serving.
Leeks with Sherry Vinaigrette	While the leeks grill, whisk together ¼ cup good-quality olive oil, 4 teaspoons sherry vinegar, 1 teaspoon each Dijon mustard and minced shallot, and some salt and pepper in a small bowl until thick. Drizzle over the leeks before serving.

Fennel-Orange Slaw with Rosemary and Pickled Red Onion

Makes: 4 to 6 servings	Time: 45 to 55 minutes	Ⓓ Ⓜ Ⓥ

Wonderful and unexpected alongside virtually any grilled entrée—especially chicken—as well as rice dishes and curries. The orange and the anise flavor from the fennel bulb are always simpatico, and the quick-pickled red onion adds a welcome pop of sweet sharpness. Small to medium fennel bulbs are best for this; they can develop a woody core when too large.

½ cup rice vinegar

¼ cup sugar

1 small red onion, halved, thinly sliced, and pulled apart

2 pounds fennel

2 tablespoons good-quality olive oil, plus more for brushing

3 navel oranges

1 teaspoon minced fresh rosemary

Salt and pepper

1 Put the vinegar and sugar in a small nonreactive saucepan and bring to a boil. Remove from the heat, add the onion, and stir to combine. Let sit while you prepare the fire. Or you can do this earlier in the day, cover, and let sit at room temperature.

2 Start the coals or heat a gas grill for medium direct cooking. Make sure the grates are clean.

3 Trim the fennel bulbs, reserving the feathery fronds. Cut the fennel in half from stalk end to base; brush with some oil. Cut the peel from the oranges with a small knife, deep enough to remove the white pith. Slice the oranges across into ¼-inch rounds, then cut the rounds into wedges. Put in a large bowl.

4 Put the fennel on the grill directly over the fire. Close the lid and cook, turning once, until the fennel is crisp-tender and browned or charred in spots, 3 to 5 minutes per side. Transfer to a cutting board and thinly slice across into crescents. Add to the oranges. Use a slotted spoon to transfer the onion to the bowl; reserve the brine. Mince enough fennel fronds to make 2 tablespoons.

5 Add the oil, 1 tablespoon of the brine, the rosemary, the minced fronds, and some salt and pepper. Toss to coat, taste and adjust the seasoning, and serve. Or prepare the slaw up to a day ahead, cover, and refrigerate.

Fennel with Olive Oil and Lemon	A classic Italian combination: Omit the onion, orange, and rosemary. In a large bowl, whisk together 2 tablespoons good-quality olive oil, the grated zest of 1 lemon, 1 tablespoon fresh lemon juice, and a sprinkle of salt and pepper. Grill and slice the fennel as directed and toss in the dressing. Shave some Parmesan cheese into curls over the top and serve.
Celery Root and Orange Salad with Rosemary and Pickled Red Onion	Celery root (also known as celeriac) delivers a flavor somewhere between celery and parsley, plus a wonderful crunch: Substitute 1 celery root (about 2 pounds), peeled, for the fennel bulb. Cut it into ¼-inch slices in either direction. Brush with oil, then grill as directed, 3 to 5 minutes per side. Cut the celery root slices into matchsticks before tossing with the oranges and onion.
Jícama and Mango Salad with Basil and Pickled Red Onion	Substitute about 1 pound jícama, peeled, for the fennel; cut it into ¼-inch slices. Substitute 1 ripe mango for the oranges; peel, cut the flesh from the pit, and thinly slice. For the dressing, substitute ¼ cup chopped fresh basil (preferably Thai) for the rosemary and add the grated zest of 1 lime. Grill the jícama as directed, 6 to 8 minutes per side. Cut the slices into matchsticks and toss with the mango and the dressing.

Grilled Kale with Lemon

Makes: 4 servings	Time: 20 to 25 minutes	D M V

Whether you love kale or hate it, you need to make this. Even though the kale is only on the grill for a matter of minutes, exposure to fire transforms it, infusing the leaves with smoke and a taste you simply can't resist. And did I mention they're super crunchy? Offer them dramatically on a platter as a side dish, or rip or cut the leaves into smaller "chips" and serve them before the main course. Be sure to buy lacinato kale (also called Tuscan or dinosaur kale); the curly variety doesn't grill as well. Stay close while you cook the kale; if you let it go too long, it dehydrates to the point where it will shatter when you try to pick it up.

You can also grill collards this way; cut the grill time down to 1 to 2 minutes per side. And once you get the technique down, you can change up the seasonings; toss the greens with vinaigrettes, seeds or nuts, or chopped olives; or simply drizzle with soy sauce and sesame oil.

1½ pounds lacinato kale

¼ cup good-quality olive oil

Salt and pepper

½ lemon, cut into wedges

1 Start the coals or heat a gas grill for medium direct cooking. Make sure the grates are clean.

2 Cut the stems from the leaves; save them for another use if you like. Rip the leaves into pieces if you like (but not too small). Put the oil in a large bowl. Add the leaves and massage them around until they are completely coated. Sprinkle with salt and pepper, and toss. (You can prepare the kale to this point up to several hours ahead and refrigerate in a plastic zipper bag until you're ready to grill.)

3 Put the leaves on the grill directly over the fire; it's okay if they overlap. Close the lid and cook until the leaves develop some char, 2 to 4 minutes. Turn and cook, spreading them into a single layer as they shrink, until charred on the other side, another 1 to 3 minutes. As they finish, immediately transfer to a platter. Serve with the lemon wedges.

Swiss Chard with Lemon	You can do this with the kale stems if you like, but chard makes a sweeter treat: Use a 2-pound bunch chard. Cut the stems off at the bottom of the leaf, brush them with some of the oil, and sprinkle with salt and pepper; toss the leaves with the remainder of the oil and season. Put the stems on the grill first. Close the lid and cook, turning them at least once, until tender and browned, 2 to 4 minutes per side. Transfer to a cutting board. Put the leaves on the grill and cook as directed in Step 3. Transfer to a bowl. Cut the stems into bite-sized pieces, add to the leaves, and squeeze the lemon over everything. Toss, taste and adjust the seasoning, and serve.
Escarole with Vinegar and Red Pepper	Substitute 2 heads escarole for the kale. After trimming, cut the heads into quarters lengthwise, through the root end. Add 2 tablespoons sherry vinegar or red wine vinegar to the oil along with red chile flakes and salt to taste. Add the escarole to the bowl and work around to coat it thoroughly. Grill as directed until soft and charred in places, 3 to 5 minutes per side. Transfer to a platter and serve; drizzle with more oil if you like.
Broccoli Raab with Lemon and Feta	The leaves of broccoli raab really stand up to the heat of the grill; don't worry when they blacken, it's all flavor—and somehow the bitterness is minimized: Substitute 1½ pounds broccoli raab for the kale. Add 2 tablespoons lemon juice and the grated zest of 1 lemon to the oil. Toss the broccoli raab with this mixture, then grill as directed until the stems are just tender and the leaves soft and charred, 3 to 5 minutes per side. Transfer to a platter, sprinkle with ½ cup crumbled feta cheese, drizzle with a bit more oil, and serve.

Rosemary Mushrooms

| Makes: **4 servings** | Time: **25 to 35 minutes** | Ⓓ Ⓜ Ⓥ |

Of course you can grill plain button mushrooms, but my favorite mushrooms over fire are the more interesting shiitakes, creminis, and portobellos. Portobellos can go right on the grates, as can larger shiitake, button, and cremini mushrooms. For smaller mushrooms, skewer them or use a perforated grill pan.

4 large portobello mushrooms, or 1½ pounds shiitake, button, or cremini mushrooms

⅓ cup good-quality olive oil

1 tablespoon minced shallot, scallion, onion, or garlic

1 tablespoon chopped fresh rosemary

Salt and pepper

1 Start the coals or heat a gas grill for medium direct cooking. Make sure the grates are clean.

2 Rinse and trim the mushrooms to remove any tough stems. Combine the oil, shallot, rosemary, and some salt and pepper in a small bowl. Brush the mushrooms all over with about half of the mixture; reserve the rest. Skewer the mushrooms if they're small or put them in a perforated grill pan.

3 Put the mushrooms on the grill directly over the fire. Close the lid and cook, turning or shaking the pan to cook evenly, until they soften and a knife pierces the center with no resistance, 5 to 20 minutes total depending on the size of the mushrooms. Brush with the remaining oil as they cook. Transfer to a platter. Portobellos can be served whole or cut into wedges or slices. All are good hot, warm, or at room temperature.

Mushroom and Parsley Salad with Red Wine Vinaigrette

This makes a delicious topping for steak. Button or cremini mushrooms work best; leave them whole or cut them into halves or quarters once grilled: Omit the oil, shallot, and rosemary. Whisk together ⅓ cup red wine vinegar and ¼ cup good-quality olive oil in a medium-sized bowl. Add the mushrooms, toss to coat, then grill as directed, without brushing with oil a second time. After grilling, return them to the remaining vinaigrette, add ½ cup chopped fresh parsley, ½ thinly sliced small red onion, and 2 cloves garlic, slivered. Toss to coat.

Ⓓ direct fire   Ⓘ indirect fire   Ⓜ make ahead   Ⓥ vegetarian option

Mushrooms with Soy Vinaigrette	To serve over greens as a big salad, double the dressing: Use a good-quality vegetable oil instead of olive oil, and add garlic; omit the rosemary. Add 2 tablespoons rice vinegar, 1 tablespoon soy sauce, and 1 teaspoon sesame oil to the oil; whisk to combine. If using portobellos, cut them into wedges or slices after grilling. Toss the mushrooms with the remaining vinaigrette after grilling, and serve.
Rosemary Mushroom and Shallot Packet with Port Wine	For when you don't want to fiddle with individual mushrooms on the grill; you can prepare the packet for the grill up to several hours earlier. I like this best using cremini mushrooms: Trim and quarter the mushrooms; peel, trim, and quarter 12 ounces small shallots. Put them all in the center of a 12-inch piece of heavy-duty foil, sprinkle with 1 tablespoon chopped fresh rosemary and some salt and pepper (be generous with the pepper). Drizzle over 2 tablespoons port wine and 2 tablespoons good-quality olive oil. Fold over the foil to cover, and crimp the edges toward the center to seal tightly. Put directly over a medium fire. Close the lid and cook until the mushrooms and shallots are tender enough to be pierced with a skewer, 15 to 25 minutes. There will be lots of juice in the packet; if you want to evaporate most of it down to a glaze, carefully open the packet while it's still on the grill (avoid the releasing steam) and let the juices bubble away.

Okra with Sea Salt

Makes: 4 servings	Time: 25 to 30 minutes	Ⓓ Ⓜ Ⓥ

Okay, let's address the thing about okra: People complain it's slimy. Grilling the whole pods takes that issue entirely out of the equation. You get the grassy, squash-like flavor, along with a little char from the fire, plus a pleasant chewiness. So there's nothing *not* to like about this okra. Look for plump, uniformly colored pods, the smaller the better. Just make sure they're about the same size to ensure even cooking.

1½ pounds okra pods, stem ends trimmed

2 tablespoons good-quality olive oil

2 teaspoons coarse sea salt

1 Start the coals or heat a gas grill for medium direct cooking. Make sure the grates are clean.

2 Put the okra in a bowl. Drizzle with the oil and toss to coat completely. Sprinkle with the salt and toss again.

3 Put the okra on the grill directly over the fire. Close the lid and cook, turning them once or twice, until the pods turn bright green and a knife inserted in the thickest part goes through without resistance, 5 to 10 minutes total. Transfer to a platter and serve hot or at room temperature.

Double Sesame Okra	Perfect for a Chinese- or Korean-inspired menu: Substitute 1 tablespoon each good-quality vegetable oil and sesame oil for the olive oil. Toss the grilled okra with 1 tablespoon toasted sesame seeds before serving and pass soy sauce at the table.
Sweet and Hot Okra	Whisk the oil and salt with a pinch cayenne and 1 teaspoon turbinado sugar; toss the okra in the mixture.
Okra with Indian Flavors	Seed and chop 1 jalapeño chile and put it in a mini food processor or a mortar with 3 tablespoons good-quality vegetable oil and 1 tablespoon each garam masala, chopped garlic, and chopped fresh ginger; process or grind with a pestle to a smooth paste. Transfer to a large bowl. In Step 3, add the grilled okra to the paste and toss until coated; fold in ½ cup yogurt and serve.

Ⓓ direct fire   Ⓘ indirect fire   Ⓜ make ahead   Ⓥ vegetarian option

Spicy Glazed Plantains

Makes: **4 to 6 servings**	Time: **25 to 30 minutes**	Ⓓ Ⓥ

Plantains are a ubiquitous tropical companion to pork, but also go well with chicken, fish, and green vegetables. Make this with ripe plantains—the soft yellow ones with some black spots—as unripe green plantains tend to dry out on the grill.

4 ripe plantains

2 tablespoons good-quality olive oil

1 tablespoon honey

1 tablespoon hot sauce, or more or less to taste

1 Start the coals or heat a gas grill for medium direct cooking. Make sure the grates are clean.

2 Trim away the ends of the plantains, then cut them in half lengthwise, leaving the peel intact. Whisk the oil, honey, and hot sauce together in a small bowl. Brush the cut sides of the plantains with the mixture.

3 Put the plantains on the grill directly over the fire, peel side down. Close the lid and cook until the peel starts to pull away from the plantain, 5 to 8 minutes. Carefully turn the plantains over and cook until the glazed side browns, 1 to 2 minutes. Transfer to a plate, remove the peels, drizzle over the remaining glaze, and serve.

Plantains with Mojo Sauce	This is the classic garlic-fueled citrus sauce usually served with fried green plantains (*tostones*)—and it's just as delicious with grilled sweet plantains: Omit the honey and hot sauce. Whisk ¼ cup each good-quality olive oil and fresh orange juice, 2 tablespoons each fresh lemon and lime juice, 1 tablespoon minced garlic, and ½ teaspoon salt together in a bowl. Brush the plantains lightly with olive oil before grilling, then serve with the mojo sauce drizzled over them.
Plantains with Lime Coconut Cream	You buy a can of coconut cream (*not* cream of coconut) or you can simply skim off the thick layer of cream that floats to the top of canned coconut milk. Just make sure to buy it from a store with good turnover because if it sits too long, it hardens: Omit the oil, honey, and hot sauce. Whisk ¼ cup coconut cream and the grated zest of 1 lime together in a bowl. Brush this on the cut sides before grilling, and drizzle the remainder over the grilled plantains after peeling.
Plantains with Garlic-Ginger Butter Baste	Omit the oil, honey, and hot sauce. Melt 4 tablespoons (½ stick) butter in a small skillet over medium-low heat, add 1 tablespoon each minced garlic and fresh ginger, and cook, stirring, until fragrant and softened, 2 to 3 minutes. Use this to brush the plantains before grilling, and drizzle the remainder over the grilled plantains.

Grill-Baked Potatoes

Makes: 4 servings	Time: 60 to 90 minutes	I M V

Here are the best ways *not* to bake a potato or sweet potato: Put it directly on the fire (you'll incinerate the skin) or wrap it in foil (it'll steam, resulting in soggy skin and a mushy interior). For fluffy insides and a crisp skin, indirect heat is the way to go, then finish with a little time directly over the fire. If you like, add some smoking wood for the first half hour or so, or try rubbing the skin with different seasonings—but just salt and pepper is always fine, too.

4 baking potatoes or sweet potatoes

Good-quality olive oil for brushing

Salt and pepper

1 Start the coals or heat a gas grill for medium indirect cooking.

2 Prick the potatoes in several spots with a knife or fork. Brush them all over with oil and sprinkle with salt and pepper.

3 Put the potatoes on the indirect side of the grill, with the long sides parallel to the fire. Close the lid and cook until you can insert a skewer through the thickest part with no resistance, 60 to 90 minutes, depending on their size. Turn, move, and rotate the potatoes every 30 minutes for even cooking.

4 To crisp the skins, move them directly over the fire until they brown, turning a few times, 2 to 3 minutes per side. Transfer to a plate and serve.

6 IDEAS FOR TWICE-GRILLED POTATOES

1. Before adding the cheese, mash the potato with coconut milk until smooth, then add curry powder or garam masala to taste; use a fresh cheese, like mozzarella or paneer.
2. Mash ½ cup crumbled goat cheese with the potato and stir in 2 chopped cloves garlic and 1 tablespoon minced fresh oregano.
3. Use Parmesan and stir in ½ cup chopped pitted olives.
4. Mash in ½ cup or more Baba Ghanoush (page 23).
5. Mash the potatoes with ½ cup or more chopped Smoked Cauliflower (page 402) or Easy Onion Jam (page 433).
6. Add 1 cup chopped Grill-Roasted Plum Tomatoes (page 444).

Quicker Grill-Baked Potatoes	You can cut the grill time in half by pricking the potatoes with a fork in a few places and cooking them first in the microwave for 5 minutes or so. Then oil, season, and grill them—only for less time.
Twice-Grilled Potatoes	If you grill the potatoes ahead of time, this becomes so fast and easy: When the potatoes are tender, cut them in half lengthwise and scoop the flesh into a bowl, leaving about ¼-inch layer of potato on the skin. Add 1 cup grated cheddar or Gruyère cheese, salt and pepper, and any seasoning you like (see "6 Ideas for Twice-Grilled Potatoes," opposite). Mash with the potato until combined. Refill the skins, put the potatoes back on the indirect side of the grill, close the lid, and cook until the filling is almost hot, then move them directly over the fire for the bottoms to get brown and crisp, 5 to 10 minutes.
Grilled Potato Skins	Always a crowd-pleasing appetizer; again, you can prep the potatoes for these the day before. Cook, drain, and crumble 4 slices bacon, grate 1½ cups cheddar cheese (about 6 ounces), and chop 1–2 scallions to make ¼ cup. Remove the flesh from the potatoes as directed for Twice-Grilled Potatoes; you can save it for another use. Brush the skins inside and out with 6 tablespoons melted butter or good-quality olive oil. Sprinkle the insides with salt and pepper. Put the potatoes directly over the fire, skin side down, close the lid, and cook until brown and crisp, 5 to 10 minutes. Transfer to a platter, top with the bacon and cheese, and return to the grill, on the indirect side this time. Close the lid and cook until the cheese has fully melted. Transfer to a cutting board, sprinkle with the scallions, cut the skins into wedges, and serve with sour cream.

Fingerling or Baby Potatoes with Sea Salt

Makes: **4 servings**	Time: **25 to 30 minutes**	Ⓓ Ⓥ

Toss fingerling potatoes with a little olive oil, then toss again with a generous amount of coarse sea salt and grill until tender, and you've got a crunchy, creamy, salty treat reminiscent of salt potatoes—the waxy potatoes boiled with lots of salt that are a longtime New York State specialty. For even cooking, get potatoes that are roughly the same size; the times here are based on potatoes that are 1 inch wide.

1½ pounds fingerling or baby potatoes

3 tablespoons good-quality olive oil

1 tablespoon coarse sea salt

1 Start the coals or heat a gas grill for medium direct cooking. Make sure the grates are clean.

2 Put the potatoes in a large bowl. Drizzle them with the oil and toss to coat completely. Sprinkle with the salt and toss again.

3 Put the potatoes on the grill directly over the fire. Close the lid and cook, turning them once or twice, until a knife inserted in the center of a potato goes through without any resistance, 10 to 20 minutes total. Transfer to a platter and serve.

Fingerling or Baby Potatoes with Rosemary and Lemon Zest	I love lemon with potatoes: When you season the potatoes, add pepper. Toss the grilled potatoes with 1 tablespoon chopped fresh rosemary and the grated zest of 1 lemon before serving.
Fingerling or Baby Potatoes with Oregano and Garlic	The perfect side for grilled steak or chicken: When you season the potatoes, add pepper. Toss the grilled potatoes with 1 tablespoon chopped fresh oregano and 2 teaspoons minced garlic before serving.
Fingerling or Baby Potatoes with Grill-Roasted Garlic	For a mellow garlic flavor: When you season the potatoes, add pepper. Toss the grilled potatoes with 2 tablespoons mashed Grill-Roasted Garlic (page 464), or more to taste, before serving.

Ⓓ direct fire Ⓘ indirect fire Ⓜ make ahead Ⓥ vegetarian option

Grill Fries

Makes: **4 servings**	Time: **25 to 30 minutes**	Ⓓ Ⓜ Ⓥ

You may never bother with deep-fried potatoes again. The biggest problem is fitting them all on the grill. Use starchy potatoes (called baking, russet, or Idaho); waxy ones and even all-purpose Yukon Golds won't work as well. The skins crisp up nicely so don't bother to peel them. Serve the fries with a flavored mayonnaise (see page 169 for a list) or plain old ketchup.

2 pounds starchy potatoes, peels on and scrubbed well

About 2 tablespoons good-quality olive oil

Salt

Pepper (optional)

1 Start the coals or heat a gas grill for medium direct cooking. Make sure the grates are clean.

2 Fill a large bowl halfway with cold water. Cut the potatoes lengthwise into sticks ¼ to ½ inch thick, ½ inch wide, and 3 inches long. (Or for steak fries, go to 1 inch wide.) As you cut the potatoes, put them in the water to keep them from discoloring; if they're not entirely covered by water, add more as needed. (You can do this several hours ahead; leave the potatoes in the water at room temperature.)

3 When you're ready to grill, drain the potatoes and pat them thoroughly dry with paper towels. Rinse and dry the bowl, then use it to toss the potatoes gently with the oil; add more oil if necessary to make the fries shiny. Sprinkle generously with salt and toss again.

4 Put the fries on the grill in a single layer directly over the fire, perpendicular to the grates. Close the grill and cook, turning as needed, until they develop grill marks and a knife inserted in the center of a fry goes through without resistance, 8 to 10 minutes total. Stay by the grill while these are cooking; you'll need to move and rotate them to cook evenly. Transfer to a dish or platter, sprinkle with more salt and some pepper if you like, and serve hot.

Cottage Fries	Cut the potatoes across into rounds instead of lengthwise into fries; if you've got a mandoline with a waffle-cut blade or an adjustable slicing blade on a food processor, use it, but set it no thinner than ¼ inch.
Smoky Grill Fries	When they're just about ready, sprinkle the fries evenly with 2 teaspoons smoked paprika (pimentón).
Sweet Potato Fries with Garlic and Cumin	Use sweet potatoes, and peel them before cutting. Check on them early and often; sweet potatoes cook faster than regular potatoes. When they're just about ready, sprinkle them evenly with a mixture of 1 teaspoon each ground cumin and garlic powder.

Grill-Braised Potatoes with Marjoram and Garlic

Makes: **4 servings**	Time: **35 to 45 minutes**	Ⓓ Ⓜ Ⓥ

This is a do-ahead dream. Slice the potatoes, combine with the rest of the ingredients, seal in a foil packet, then refrigerate up to several hours until you're ready to grill. In less than 30 minutes, you'll have fork-tender, perfectly seasoned potatoes. And since they're sealed, the flavor is infused with whatever else goes in with them. For large cookouts you can divide the ingredients into individual packets so folks can grab their own. I like to use red or Yukon Gold potatoes but you can also use peeled starchy potatoes like russets.

You can also use this technique with any kind of root vegetable, including sweet potatoes, carrots, parsnips, rutabagas, and turnips, and even sliced winter squash.

1½ pounds potatoes, cut into ¼-inch-thick slices

3 cloves garlic, sliced

2 tablespoons good-quality olive oil

1 tablespoon chopped fresh marjoram

Salt and pepper

1 tablespoon vegetable broth or water

1 Start the coals or heat a gas grill for medium direct cooking.

2 Put the potatoes, garlic, oil, marjoram, and salt and pepper to taste in a large bowl and toss to combine. Transfer to the center of a 12-inch piece of heavy-duty foil and pour over the broth. Fold over the foil to cover, and crimp the sides shut; you don't want any steam escaping from the packet.

3 Put the packet on the grill directly over the fire. Close the lid and cook until the potatoes are fork tender, 20 to 30 minutes.

4 Transfer the packet to a platter; the potatoes will keep hot in it for at least 15 minutes. Be careful of the steam when you undo the foil; transfer to a dish and serve.

● recipe continues →

Ⓓ direct fire   Ⓘ indirect fire   Ⓜ make ahead   Ⓥ vegetarian option

Grill-Braised Potatoes with Herbes de Provence	You can use store-bought but I prefer to combine the herbs myself. If you have a garden, use fresh and triple the quantities of each herb: Omit the fresh marjoram. Instead, toss the potatoes, garlic, and oil with 1 teaspoon each dried marjoram and thyme, and ½ teaspoon each fennel seeds, dried rosemary, and summer savory. Add some salt and pepper. If you like, you can also add 1 teaspoon grated orange zest.
Grill-Braised Potatoes with Capers, Lemon, and Red Onion	Omit the marjoram and garlic. Instead, toss the potatoes and oil with ½ small red onion, thinly sliced, 2 tablespoons each chopped capers and fresh parsley, the grated zest of 1 lemon, and some salt and pepper.
Grill-Braised Sweet Potatoes with Brown Sugar and Ginger	Great for Thanksgiving; also terrific made with peeled sliced sugar pumpkin. The ginger really penetrates the sweet potatoes when prepared this way: Before slicing the potatoes, halve or quarter them if you like. In a large bowl, whisk together 1 tablespoon each vegetable broth, orange juice, and minced fresh ginger. Add 2 tablespoons brown sugar, 1 teaspoon Dijon mustard, and some salt and pepper and whisk again. Add the sweet potato slices and toss to coat evenly. Transfer to the foil, dot the top with about 2 tablespoons butter, seal, and grill as directed.

D direct fire   I indirect fire   M make ahead   V vegetarian option

Creamy Mustard-Garlic Potato Salad

| Makes: **4 to 6 servings** | Time: **35 to 40 minutes** | Ⓜ Ⓥ |

The classic barbecue accompaniment, and one of the few things in the book cooked only on the stove. Use any kind of potato you like; don't bother to peel the thin-skinned varieties like red, fingerling, and Yukon Gold. Adjust the cooking time accordingly and check often. Another option is to use a selection of different-colored potatoes; just cut them all the same size.

1½ pounds potatoes, peeled if you like, cut into bite-sized pieces

Salt

½ cup mayonnaise (to make your own, see page 460)

3 tablespoons white wine vinegar or cider vinegar

1 tablespoon Dijon mustard

1 teaspoon minced garlic, or more to taste

¼ cup chopped scallions

Pepper

1 Put the potatoes in a pot with enough water to cover them and add a large pinch salt. Bring to a boil, then lower the heat so the water bubbles gently. Cook the potatoes until fork-tender but not at all mushy or breaking apart, about 15 minutes. Drain, rinse under cold running water, then drain again.

2 Whisk the mayonnaise, vinegar, mustard, garlic, and scallions together in a medium-sized bowl. Add the potatoes and toss or fold gently (you don't want the cubes to break up) until they're coated. Taste and adjust the seasoning. Serve right away, or refrigerate in an airtight container for up to 3 days.

• recipe continues →

Hawaiian-Style Potato-Mac Salad	This is the potato salad to serve with Huli Huli Chicken (page 192): Hard-boil 2 eggs; chill them in ice water, peel, and chop. While the potatoes are cooking, separately cook 1 cup elbow macaroni until al dente, then drain. Increase the mayonnaise to 1 cup, decrease the vinegar to 2 tablespoons, and omit the mustard, garlic, and scallions. Add the macaroni, eggs, and ½ cup shredded carrots along with the potatoes. If you like, you can also add ½ cup barely cooked green peas. Makes 6 to 8 servings.
Potato Salad with Mustard-Garlic Vinaigrette	Some like potato salad without mayonnaise: Substitute good-quality olive oil for the mayonnaise.
Sweet Potato Salad with Chipotle-Lime Vinaigrette	Substitute peeled sweet potatoes for the regular potatoes, good-quality olive oil for the mayonnaise, and fresh lime juice for the vinegar. Replace the mustard with a canned chipotle chile, mashed with some of its adobo. Keep the scallions and add ½ cup chopped fresh cilantro. Whisk the dressing to combine before adding the potatoes.

16 ADDITIONS TO POTATO SALAD

Add any of these—alone or in combination, as much or as little as you like—to the dressing.

1. Chopped fresh herbs like chives, chervil, dill, parsley, oregano, or rosemary
2. Chopped watercress
3. Chopped pickles (sweet or dill) or cornichons
4. Chopped celery or fennel
5. Chopped red or sweet onion (instead of the scallions)
6. Chopped red bell pepper, fresh or grill-roasted (page 34)
7. Chopped capers or pitted olives
8. Mashed Grill-Roasted Garlic (page 464) instead of the raw garlic
9. Minced fresh chile (jalapeño, Thai, serrano, or habanero), chili powder, pure chile powder, or any hot sauce
10. Mashed anchovies
11. Crumbled cooked bacon or diced ham or prosciutto
12. Grated hard cheese like Parmesan, cheddar, or Manchego, or crumbled feta, queso fresco, or ricotta salata
13. Sliced or grated radishes
14. Curry powder or other spice mixtures (page 456); start with a teaspoon and taste before adding more
15. Cilantro-Mint Chutney (page 474) or its variations, or any store-bought chutney; start with a spoonful and taste
16. Instead of plain mayonnaise, use a flavored mayo (see page 169 for a list of those in the book)

D direct fire   I indirect fire   M make ahead   V vegetarian option

Grilled Onions

Makes: **4 servings**	Time: **40 to 50 minutes, largely unattended**	D M V

Smoky fire-roasted onions—yellow, white, red, or sweet—are one of the true pleasures of the grill. Like stovetop-cooked caramelized onions, they go with absolutely everything: Throw them on burgers, into salads, turn them into savory soups, or enjoy them plain as a side dish or topping. For all types you want a medium or cooler fire; any higher and they'll burn. For a make-ahead, you can throw them on the grill after the entrée comes off and let them cook slowly over the dying fire, then use them later in the week. They'll keep in an airtight container in the refrigerator for 4 to 5 days.

1½ pounds onions, peeled

About 2 tablespoons good-quality olive oil

Salt and pepper

1 Start the coals or heat a gas grill for medium to medium-low direct cooking. Make sure the grates are clean.

2 Cut the onions through the equator (not root end to stem end) into slices at least 1 inch thick. (If the onions are flat-shaped, simply halve them.) Brush the slices with oil and carefully sprinkle with salt and pepper on both sides.

3 Put the onion slices on the grill directly over the fire. Close the lid and cook, turning once, until they brown and are soft all the way through, 10 to 15 minutes per side. Check them a few minutes after you put them on; if they're coloring too quickly, move them to the edge of the fire. Transfer to a platter and serve hot, warm, or at room temperature.

Grilled Shallots or Cipolline	Substitute shallots or cipolline instead of the onions. Keep them whole; pull the shallots apart into separate cloves. Depending on their size, grill time will range from 12 to 25 minutes total; turn them every few minutes. Check on doneness by piercing them with a sharp knife; it should go through with no resistance.
Easy Onion Jam	So delicious with grilled meats or dolloped on a burger: Put the grilled onions in a food processor and add 1 tablespoon each honey and balsamic vinegar, or to taste. Process to a rough paste. Makes about 1 cup.
Grill-Roasted Onion Salad	In a salad bowl, whisk together ¼ cup good-quality olive oil, 1½ teaspoons balsamic or sherry vinegar, 1 teaspoon each minced garlic and fresh thyme, and some salt and pepper. Grill 2 red onions, 2 white onions, and 8 shallots. When they're done, cut the onion slices into quarters. Add them to the dressing and toss. Taste and adjust the seasoning. Serve hot, warm, or at room temperature.

Radicchio with Balsamic Glaze

Makes: 4 servings	Time: 20 to 25 minutes	Ⓓ Ⓜ Ⓥ

With its signature combination of sweet and sour, balsamic vinegar works miraculously to balance the bitterness of radicchio. Grilling brings even more to the party. Substitute endive, chicory, escarole, or romaine lettuce—any and all are a stunning alternative to salad.

4 small or 2 large heads radicchio (about 1 pound total)

2 tablespoons good-quality olive oil

¼ cup balsamic vinegar

1 tablespoon brown sugar or honey

Salt and pepper

1 Start the coals or heat a gas grill for medium-high direct cooking. Make sure the grates are clean.

2 Leaving just enough at the bottom to keep the wedges intact, core the radicchio and cut the heads into halves or quarters, depending on their size. Rub or brush them with the oil. Whisk the vinegar and sugar together in a small bowl until the sugar dissolves.

3 Put the radicchio wedges on the grill directly over the fire, cut side down. Close the lid and cook for a minute or 2, then carefully turn them. Brush or drizzle with the balsamic mixture. Cook until just starting to crisp and char around the edges, another couple of minutes. Transfer to a platter and sprinkle with salt and lots of black pepper. Serve hot, warm, or at room temperature.

Bacon-Wrapped Radicchio	Heat the grill for medium-low or medium direct heat. Omit the oil, vinegar, and brown sugar. Cut the radicchio into quarters. Wrap each piece with 1 slice bacon, securing it with toothpicks if necessary. Grill directly over the heat until the bacon has browned on all sides; to keep from burning, you may need to move the radicchio to the edges of the fire.
Bacon-Wrapped Radicchio with Balsamic Glaze	Follow the preceding variation, but keep the vinegar–brown sugar glaze to brush on the radicchio after the bacon has started to brown. Finish with lots of black pepper.
Radicchio and Fresh Herb Slaw	After grilling the radicchio, allow it to cool. Chop the leaves and toss with about ½ cup each chopped fresh parsley or dill and red onion. Dress with a little good-quality olive oil or mayonnaise and a squeeze of fresh lemon if you like.

Ⓓ direct fire   Ⓘ indirect fire   Ⓜ make ahead   Ⓥ vegetarian option

Hearts of Romaine
with Vinaigrette Marinade

Makes: **4 servings**	Time: **20 to 25 minutes**	Ⓓ Ⓜ Ⓥ

Fire has a wonderful way with already-dressed romaine, softening some parts and charring others. Try to work as much of the vinaigrette into the heads as you can before you put them on the grill so the flavor permeates. The vinaigrette can be made several hours ahead and refrigerated.

3 tablespoons red wine vinegar

1 tablespoon Dijon mustard

Salt and pepper

½ cup good-quality olive oil

4 hearts of romaine lettuce

1 Start the coals or heat a gas grill for medium direct cooking. Make sure the grates are clean.

2 Put the vinegar and mustard in a large bowl with some salt and pepper and whisk to combine. While still whisking, add the oil in a steady stream; keep whisking until thick.

3 Trim the bottoms of the romaine just enough to remove the tough ends but keep the leaves attached. Remove any damaged outer leaves. Transfer the lettuce to the bowl and coat with the vinaigrette, using your hands to work it into the heads as much as you can without bruising the leaves.

4 Put the romaine on the grill directly over the fire. Close the lid and cook, turning once, until softened and darkly colored in places, 2 to 5 minutes per side, depending on how hot the fire is. Transfer to a platter and serve warm or at room temperature with more pepper sprinkled on top.

---

7 MORE VINAIGRETTES TO USE WITH HEARTS OF ROMAINE OR ICEBERG WEDGES

1. Lime-Basil Vinaigrette (page 38)
2. Sherry Vinaigrette (page 395)
3. Mustard-Garlic Vinaigrette (page 431)
4. Tomato-Basil Vinaigrette (page 147)
5. Lime-Miso Vinaigrette (page 392)
6. Warm Pancetta Vinaigrette (page 397)
7. Dijon-Orange Vinaigrette (page 382)

• recipe continues →

Hearts of Romaine with Lemon-Caper Vinaigrette Marinade	For the vinaigrette, whisk ½ cup good-quality olive oil, ¼ cup fresh lemon juice, 1 tablespoon water, 1 teaspoon chopped capers, and the grated zest of 1 lemon together in a large bowl until thick.
Hearts of Romaine Salad with Tomatoes and Red Onion	You can make this with either the main recipe or first variation: In Step 3, just brush the outside of the hearts with the vinaigrette; reserve the rest of it. After grilling the romaine, cut it across into ½- to 1-inch ribbons; discard the bottoms. Transfer the ribbons to the bowl with the dressing and add 1 cup quartered cherry or grape tomatoes, half of a small red onion, thinly sliced, and ½ cup lightly packed torn fresh basil leaves. Toss to combine, taste and adjust the seasoning, and serve.
Iceberg Lettuce with Blue Cheese Dressing	The classic wedge. Iceberg stands up to the grill just fine: For the dressing, combine ½ cup each mayonnaise and crumbled blue cheese, ¼ cup fresh lemon juice or to taste, and some salt and pepper in the large bowl; whisk until smooth. Substitute 1 head iceberg lettuce, quartered or cut into 6 wedges, for the romaine. Brush it with good-quality olive oil. Grill directly over the fire until it just starts to char, about 1 minute on each cut side; keep an eye on it—a minute too long and the leaves will begin to break down. Serve immediately with the dressing drizzled over. Makes 4 to 6 servings.

D direct fire   I indirect fire   M make ahead   V vegetarian option

Scallions with Cilantro and Lime

| Makes: 4 servings | Time: 25 to 30 minutes | D M V |

A Tex-Mex restaurant staple, these are workhorses: as a side dish, used anywhere you'd add raw or cooked onions, added to guacamole or other dips, or chopped for garnish. Cook them fast over a relatively hot fire, or slowly after you've taken other foods off the grill and scatter them on top of the platter. You can prepare any of these versions using spring onions; depending on their thickness, they may take a few minutes longer.

2 bunches scallions

Good-quality olive oil for brushing

Salt and pepper

2 limes, 1 halved, 1 cut into wedges

Tender fresh cilantro sprigs for garnish

1 Start the coals or heat a gas grill for medium-high direct cooking. Make sure the grates are clean.

2 Trim the root ends of the scallions and the ragged ends of the greens; leave as much of the greens on as possible. Brush or rub the scallions with the oil until well coated; sprinkle with salt.

3 Put the scallions on the grill directly over the fire, perpendicular to the grates so they don't fall through. Close the lid and cook, turning once or twice, until deeply colored and tender, 5 to 10 minutes total, depending on their thickness. Transfer to a platter, sprinkle with pepper, and squeeze the juice of the lime halves over all. Serve hot, warm, or at room temperature, garnished with the cilantro and lime wedges.

Scallions with Parsley and Lemon	Substitute lemons for the limes and 2 tablespoons chopped fresh parsley for the cilantro.
Korean-Style Scallion and Lettuce Salad	Substitute sesame oil for the olive oil. While the scallions grill, whisk together 2 tablespoons soy sauce, 1 tablespoon each sesame oil, rice vinegar, and water, 1 teaspoon each sugar and minced garlic, and ½ teaspoon red chile flakes in a large serving bowl. Cut the grilled scallions into 1- to 2-inch lengths and toss into the dressing along with 4 cups torn tender lettuce leaves (any kind). Toss, taste and adjust the seasoning with salt and pepper if you like, toss again, and serve.
Spring Onions with Romesco Sauce	A traditional Catalan offering: Omit the lime and cilantro. Serve the grilled onions with a dollop of Romesco Sauce (page 470).

Buttery Butternut Squash

Makes: **4 servings**	Time: **About 1½ hours, largely unattended**	Ⓓ Ⓥ

Since roasting butternut squash caramelizes and intensifies its flavor, it was a no-brainer to realize grilling with butter brings it to a whole other level. Make this using a small butternut squash or the already-cleaned pieces available in the supermarket. No need to peel the squash before putting it on the grill; it's simple to slice away the skin with a paring knife afterward. Be careful not to let the squash get too soft, or the cubes will mash together when you toss them with the butter and seasoning. And of course this treatment is also delicious with Hubbard squash, kabocha squash, and sugar pumpkins.

2 pounds butternut squash, cut into large pieces and seeded

4 tablespoons (½ stick) butter, melted

Salt and pepper

1 Start the coals or heat a gas grill for medium-high direct cooking. Make sure the grates are clean.

2 Brush the cut sides of the squash with about half of the melted butter, then sprinkle with salt and pepper.

3 Put the squash on the grill directly over the fire, skin side down. Close the lid and cook until a skewer can be inserted through the center of each chunk without resistance, about 1 hour depending on their thickness. Transfer to a cutting board.

4 When cool enough to handle, slice away the blackened skin, then cut the squash into bite-sized cubes. Put in a serving bowl and drizzle with the remaining melted butter. Taste and adjust the seasoning, toss to combine, and serve.

CUTTING WINTER SQUASH

Grilled winter squash is so good you need to know how to cut the hard—and usually large—vegetable confidently and safely.

Here's what I do: First, use a sharp knife suitable to the size of the squash. Carefully cut off either the stem end or a small piece at the side so that the squash has a flat surface down on the cutting board. Make a shallow cut in the center of the top of the squash and adjust the knife so it's securely embedded near the handle, perpendicular to the cutting board.

Keeping one hand on the back of the blade and the other on the handle, rock the knife firmly and slowly back and forth to deepen the cut. Adjust the knife as you work to keep it balanced. When you get to the seeds, you can press down through the remaining flesh more easily; just be sure to always keep your hands above the blade and out of the way. Once the squash splits, remove the seeds and fibers, put the cut side down on the board, and cut the squash into smaller pieces as necessary.

Ⓓ direct fire   Ⓘ indirect fire   Ⓜ make ahead   Ⓥ vegetarian option

Butternut Squash with Pomegranate Seeds and Mint	Use good-quality olive oil instead of butter. Mix together ½ teaspoon each salt and ground sumac and ¼ teaspoon Aleppo pepper or red chile flakes. After brushing the squash, sprinkle with the spice mixture. Grill and cube as directed. Add ½ cup pomegranate seeds and ¼ cup each fresh orange juice and chopped fresh mint to the remaining oil before drizzling.
Butternut Squash with Pecans and Apples	Perfect for Thanksgiving: Whisk ¼ cup good-quality olive oil, 2 tablespoons lemon juice, and 1 tablespoon chopped fresh rosemary together in a large serving bowl with some salt and pepper; set aside. Grill and cube the squash as directed. As it grills, toast ½ cup pecan halves in a dry skillet over medium-low heat, tossing occasionally until fragrant, 5 to 10 minutes. Core and cut 2 apples (peeled or not) into 1-inch cubes; add to the bowl along with the nuts and the squash when ready. Toss with the dressing.
Butternut Squash with Blue Cheese	Omit the butter. Whisk together 6 tablespoons good-quality olive oil and 2 tablespoons sherry vinegar. Brush the squash with some of the vinaigrette, then grill and cube as directed. Sprinkle the cubed squash with ½ cup crumbled blue cheese, drizzle with the remaining vinaigrette, and toss gently.

Acorn Squash with Smoky Maple Butter

Makes: **4 servings**	Time: **40 to 60 minutes**	Ⓓ Ⓜ Ⓥ

A perfect combination of sweet and savory, and it couldn't be easier.

2 acorn squash (1½–2 pounds each)

8 tablespoons (1 stick) butter

1 teaspoon smoked paprika (pimentón)

1 teaspoon ground cumin

Salt and pepper

1 tablespoon maple syrup

1 Start the coals or heat a gas grill for medium direct cooking. Make sure the grates are clean.

2 Cut the squash in half from top to bottom. Use a spoon, serrated grapefruit spoon, or melon baller to remove all the seeds and fibers. If necessary, take a thin slice off the uncut side so the squash half sits on the cutting board without rocking. Melt the butter in small skillet over medium heat. Add the paprika and cumin and stir until fragrant. Sprinkle with salt and pepper to taste. Remove from the heat and stir in the maple syrup. Brush the seasoned butter over the cut sides and interior of the squash. Pour any remaining butter into the wells of the squash. (You can prepare the squash up to this point several hours in advance, cover, and refrigerate until you're ready to grill.)

3 Put the squash on the grill directly over the fire, skin side down. Close the lid and cook until the flesh is fork-tender, 25 to 45 minutes, depending on the size; start checking doneness at 20 minutes. Transfer to a platter and serve.

Acorn Squash Wedges with Smoky Maple Butter	Faster, with more tasty surface area for the flavored butter to coat: Prepare a medium indirect fire. After removing the seeds, cut the squash into 1- to 1½-inch wedges. Increase the butter to 12 tablespoons (1½ sticks). Pour the flavored butter into a large bowl, add the squash wedges, and toss until they are evenly coated. Put the wedges on the grill directly over the fire (use a perforated grill pan if you have one) and cook, turning as needed, until they are well browned, 4 to 8 minutes per side. Move to the indirect portion of the grill, close the lid, and cook until tender, another 10 to 15 minutes. Transfer to a platter, drizzle with any remaining butter, and serve.
Acorn Squash with Soy-Honey-Ginger Butter	Omit the paprika and cumin, substitute honey for the maple syrup, and add 2 tablespoons soy sauce and 1 tablespoon minced fresh ginger to the butter.
Kabocha Squash	This variety, which originated in Southeast Asia, is similar in flavor and texture to pumpkin, but unlike pumpkin its skin is edible. You can use any of these acorn squash treatments with it. When cooking halves, first brush the skin with olive oil.

Ⓓ direct fire Ⓘ indirect fire Ⓜ make ahead Ⓥ vegetarian option

Summer Squash with Sea Salt

| Makes: **4 servings** | Time: **25 to 30 minutes** | **D** **V** |

Summer squash—like zucchini, yellow summer squash, and pattypan—require almost zero preparation for the grill and make for a tasty and colorful side. Select medium to small squash for the best texture. I prefer to grill them cut in half lengthwise, but you can cut them into long slices or rounds.

1½ pounds summer squash or zucchini

Good-quality olive oil for brushing

Salt

1 Start the coals or heat a gas grill for medium direct cooking. Make sure the grates are clean.

2 Trim the ends from the squash and cut in half lengthwise, or through the equator if using pattypan. Brush with oil on all sides, and sprinkle the cut sides with salt.

3 Put the squash on the grill directly over the fire. Close the lid and cook, turning once, until fork-tender, 3 to 5 minutes per side. Transfer to a platter and serve.

Baby Summer Squash with Lemon and Fresh Herbs	Supermarkets sometimes sell these in mixes; otherwise, look to farmers' markets or your garden. And if they've got the blossoms attached, all the better. This side is a stunner, no matter what: Toss the whole baby squash in a large bowl with 2 tablespoons good-quality olive oil and some salt. Grill as directed, turning them to cook evenly; they'll take 5 to 10 minutes total. If using large squash, cut them into bite-sized pieces. Transfer to a serving bowl, toss with the juice of 1 lemon, and sprinkle with ½ cup mixed torn fresh herbs like basil, cilantro, and/or parsley.
Summer Squash with Pesto	Brush the squash with oil, sprinkle with salt and pepper, and grill as directed. Transfer to a platter, brush them with any pesto (page 475), and serve.
Summer Squash, Tomato, and Corn Salad with Lime Vinaigrette	Before you start, boil or steam 4 ears corn until tender, 2 to 3 minutes. (You could grill them if you prefer, but then the smoke flavor of the salad might end up being a bit much.) Remove from the water to let cool. Whisk together ¼ cup fresh lime juice, ⅓ cup good-quality olive oil, 1 teaspoon minced garlic, and some salt and pepper in a large serving bowl. Skewer a basket of grape or cherry tomatoes and brush with oil. Grill the squash as directed. Grill the tomatoes directly over the fire, turning once, just until they start to blister, about 2 minutes per side. Add the tomatoes to the dressing. When the squash come off the grill, cut them into bite-sized pieces, and add to the dressing. Cut the corn kernels from the cobs and add them, too. Toss the salad and serve warm or at room temperature.

Tomatoes with Basil

| Makes: **4 servings** | Time: **20 to 25 minutes** | Ⓓ Ⓜ Ⓥ |

When you grill a tomato, the high heat not only browns and crinkles the skin, it also begins to caramelize the sugars in the flesh as the water evaporates, intensifying the flavor, color, and texture—all in just 5 to 10 minutes. And this can happen hours before you intend to serve them, if you want to go that route.

3 or 4 fresh tomatoes (1½ pounds)

Good-quality olive oil for brushing

Salt and pepper

⅓ cup or more torn or chopped fresh basil leaves

Freshly grated Parmesan cheese (optional)

1 Start the coals or heat a gas grill for medium direct cooking. Make sure the grates are clean.

2 Core the tomatoes and cut each across into 3 or 4 thick slices. Brush them with oil and sprinkle with salt and pepper on both sides.

3 Put the tomato slices on the grill directly over the fire. Close the lid and cook, turning once, until they are soft but not mushy, 3 to 5 minutes per side. (They should be just on the verge of falling apart; you should be able to barely lift them from the grill with a spatula.) Transfer the slices to a platter, sprinkle with basil and some cheese if you like, and serve hot, warm, or at room temperature.

Tomatoes with Basil and Balsamic Syrup	Omit the Parmesan. Drizzle the grilled tomatoes with Balsamic Syrup (page 467) before scattering the basil.
Cherry Tomatoes with Basil and Cream	Substitute 1 pound cherry or grape tomatoes for the tomatoes. Omit the Parmesan. Toss the whole tomatoes with 1 tablespoon good-quality olive oil, season with salt and pepper, and put in a single layer on a perforated grill pan, or skewer them. Grill until heated through and blistered, 2 to 3 minutes per side; if using a grill pan, shake the pan to turn them. Transfer to a serving dish and toss with the basil. A drizzle of warmed cream is divine.
Warm Cherry Tomato Salad with Yogurt and Cilantro	Follow the directions for cooking the cherry tomatoes above. Omit the basil. Whisk together ¼ cup each yogurt and chopped fresh cilantro and 2 tablespoons good-quality olive oil in a serving bowl. Add the grilled tomatoes and gently toss to coat.

Grill-Roasted Plum Tomatoes

Makes: **4 servings**	Time: **1½ to 3½ hours, largely unattended**	Ⓘ Ⓜ Ⓥ

You can dry plum tomatoes on the grill just like you can in an oven—dense, moist, and full of a complex flavor reminiscent of smoked paprika. The longer these are on the grill, the more those characteristics develop. At the very least, you want visible signs of shriveling. Some ideas about timing with other foods: On charcoal grills, make them when you're going to be cooking something else slow-and-low. Or do a batch while you grill something that needs shorter cooking and leave the tomatoes on, stoking the coals a little as the fire dies down, a day or 2 ahead of when you want them. On a gas grill, add wood for at least the first 30 minutes but not more than 60 minutes. If you do refrigerate the tomatoes after grilling, let them come to room temperature before serving. Serve as is, or cut them up to add to salads, pasta, beans, or grains.

4 plum tomatoes (or as many as you have room for)

Good-quality olive oil for brushing

Salt and pepper

1 Start the coals or heat a gas grill for medium to low indirect cooking. Make sure the grates are clean.

2 Cut the tomatoes in half lengthwise. Brush them with oil and sprinkle the cut sides with salt and pepper.

3 Put the tomatoes on the indirect side of the grill, cut side up. If the fire is closer to medium, keep the tomatoes some distance from the heat to avoid charring. Close the grill and cook until shriveled but you can still see signs of moisture, at least 1 hour and up to 3 hours. About halfway through, move and rotate the tomatoes so they cook evenly.

4 Transfer to a platter and serve hot, warm, or at room temperature. These will keep in an airtight container in the refrigerator for up to a week and in the freezer for several months.

Spiced Grill-Roasted Plum Tomatoes	These spices work beautifully with the smoky flavor the grill imparts to the tomatoes: In addition to salt and pepper, sprinkle the cut sides of the tomatoes with ¼ teaspoon each ground cumin and coriander (or cardamom for a floral sweetness). If you like, serve them sprinkled with chopped fresh mint.
Grill-Roasted Plum Tomatoes with Mirin-Soy Baste	Combine ¼ cup each soy sauce and mirin (or substitute 2 tablespoons each honey and water for the mirin) in a small saucepan and simmer over medium heat until reduced to 2 tablespoons. When the tomatoes are about halfway through cooking, brush the cut sides with the baste, then brush them again about halfway through the remaining time. Repeat until no baste remains, up to 10 minutes before they're ready. You can turn them cut side down over direct heat to brown for just a minute or 2, but watch them to protect your investment from burning!
Tabbouleh-Stuffed Grill-Roasted Plum Tomatoes	Plum tomato halves make the perfect single serving–sized container for an appetizer or side: After cutting the tomatoes in half, scoop out the seeds so the cut side is concave. While the tomatoes are cooking, put ¼ cup bulgur in a heatproof bowl and pour in 1 cup boiling water. Cover with a plate and soak until the grains are tender, 15 to 30 minutes. Drain, squeezing out as much water as possible. Toss the bulgur in a bowl with ¼ cup each chopped fresh parsley and mint, 2 tablespoons each good-quality olive oil and fresh lemon juice, and salt and pepper to taste. When the tomatoes are ready, spread them out cut side up and spoon the bulgur mixture on top.

Watermelon Steaks with Rosemary

Makes: 4 to 8 servings	Time: 25 to 30 minutes	Ⓓ Ⓜ Ⓥ

Grilled watermelon treated like a vegetable with savory seasoning is sublime. Most of the water cooks out of it, leaving behind a tasty little "steak" with a pleasantly dense texture. Plus, it looks terrific. You can also do this with any other sliced melon.

1 small watermelon

¼ cup good-quality olive oil

1 tablespoon minced fresh rosemary

Salt and pepper

Lemon wedges for serving

1 Start the coals or heat a gas grill for medium direct cooking. Make sure the grates are clean.

2 Cut the watermelon into 2-inch-thick slices, with the rind intact, and then into halves or quarters, if you like. If there are seeds, use a fork to remove as many as you can without tearing up the flesh too much.

3 Put the oil and rosemary in a small bowl, sprinkle with salt and pepper, and stir. Brush or rub the mixture all over the watermelon slices. (You can prepare the watermelon for the grill up to 2 hours ahead; wrap tightly in plastic wrap to keep it from drying out and refrigerate.)

4 Put the watermelon on the grill directly over the fire. Close the lid and cook, turning once, until the flesh develops grill marks and has dried out a bit, 4 to 5 minutes per side. Transfer to a platter and serve with lemon wedges.

Watermelon Steaks with Sichuan Peppercorns	A wonderful tingling heat along with the sweetness: Use good-quality vegetable oil instead of olive oil. Substitute 2 teaspoons crushed Sichuan peppercorns for the rosemary and salt and pepper. Substitute lime wedges for the lemon.
Watermelon Melts	Great as a side, or served as a vegetarian main fully dressed like burgers on hard rolls: When they're just about ready to come off the grill, top each steak with thinly sliced fresh mozzarella (8 ounces is enough to top all the steaks). Close the lid, cook until the cheese is melted, and serve.
Watermelon and Tomato Salad with Feta and Mint	Use only half of the watermelon and cut it off the rind. Omit the rosemary. After grilling the watermelon, cut it into chunks and put in a serving bowl with 2 fresh tomatoes cut into chunks, 4 ounces crumbled feta cheese, and ½ cup fresh mint leaves. Whisk together ¼ cup good-quality olive oil, the grated rind of 1 lime, and 2 tablespoons lime juice in a small bowl with some salt and pepper. Drizzle over the salad and toss to combine.

Ⓓ direct fire   Ⓘ indirect fire   Ⓜ make ahead   Ⓥ vegetarian option

Smoked Mac and Cheese

Makes: 4 servings	Time: 50 to 60 minutes	Ⓘ Ⓜ Ⓥ

Mac and cheese is a no-brainer for any barbecue. So why bother to grill it? The fat in the cheese and milk absorbs the smokiness from the fire like a sponge. To maximize the exposure to the grill, use a broad pan and don't bother with bread crumbs on the top; you want the cheese sauce naked. And generate lots of smoke right from the get-go. Finally, stir the pasta several times while it cooks—quickly, to keep too much smoke from escaping from the grill—so every noodle gets a dose of it. Other cheeses to try: goat cheese, smoked (or not) Gouda, even mascarpone. All other add-ins apply—bacon, anyone?—but no more than ½ cup.

3 tablespoons butter, plus more for the pan

Salt and pepper

2 cups elbow macaroni or other small cut pasta

3 tablespoons all-purpose flour

2½ cups milk (low-fat is fine)

2 bay leaves

1½ cups grated cheese (like sharp cheddar or Emmental)

½ cup freshly grated Parmesan cheese

1 Generously butter the bottom and sides of a 9- × 12-inch disposable foil pan; put it in another pan for more stability if you like. Bring a large pot of water to a boil and salt it. Add the pasta. Stir occasionally, until the pasta is at the point where it is almost done but you would still think it needed another minute or 2 to become tender. Drain, rinse with cold water, and put it in the prepared pan.

2 Put the 3 tablespoons butter in a medium saucepan over medium-low heat; when it melts, add the flour and stir until completely mixed with the butter to make a roux. Cook for another minute or 2, but don't let it brown. Add a few tablespoons of the milk, stirring until smooth. Continue to add the milk at little at a time, stirring constantly, until the mixture is more liquid than paste. Add the bay leaves, sprinkle with pepper, raise the heat to medium, and cook until small bubbles form around the edge of the pan. Remove from the heat and discard the bay leaves. Add the cheeses and gently stir until the mixture is smooth. Pour the sauce over the pasta and stir to combine; taste and adjust the seasoning if you like. Let sit at room temperature while you prepare the fire, or cover and refrigerate until you're ready to grill. (You can make the recipe up to several hours in advance and refrigerate; the cook time will be 10 to 20 minutes longer.)

3 Start the coals or heat a gas grill for medium indirect cooking. If using charcoal, position the coals so that the smoke will be pulled over the pan and out the top vent. When the grill is ready, add wood to the fire (see "Smoking," pages 10–12).

4 When the grill fills with smoke, put the mac and cheese on the indirect side of the grill. Close the lid and cook until the sauce is bubbling around the edges, 20 to 30 minutes. About halfway through, rotate the pan for even cooking and quickly stir the pasta then and every 5 minutes thereafter. Be sure to keep the grill filled with smoke; you may need to add more wood. Transfer the pan to a rack and let cool for 5 to 10 minutes before serving.

● recipe continues →

Mascarpone Mac and Cheese	Omit the 3 tablespoons butter, flour, and bay leaves. Reduce the milk to ¾ cup. Substitute mascarpone for the cheddar. Cook the pasta as directed and drain. Mix together the milk, mascarpone, and Parmesan in the buttered foil pan. Add the cooked pasta and 1 tablespoon minced fresh sage, sprinkle with salt and pepper, and combine. Proceed with Step 3.
Macaroni and Goat Cheese with Grill-Roasted Red Peppers	Omit the bay leaves, reduce the grated cheddar to 1 cup, and substitute 1 cup soft goat cheese for the Parmesan. After adding the cheeses, stir in 2 roasted red bell peppers (page 34), chopped, and ½ cup each chopped fresh basil and toasted pine nuts.
Chile Mac and Cheese	For a spicy dish, use a hotter chile or add 1 tablespoon chopped canned chipotle chile with some of its adobo sauce: Substitute 2 cups grated asadero or Jack or use cheddar for all of the cheese. After adding the cheese, stir in 2 roasted medium-sized poblano or other mild green chiles (page 34), chopped. Garnish with ¼ cup chopped fresh cilantro.

---

6 GREAT MAC AND CHEESE COMBOS

Any pasta will work with any of the cheeses, so mix these up as you like. Some drier hard cheeses like Parmesan, Asiago, Manchego, and some pecorinos are best when combined with softer cheeses; similarly, very strong cheeses are best paired with mild cheeses. Try

1. Pasta shells with ½ cup cream cheese and 1½ cups pecorino
2. Fusilli or corkscrews with 1½ cups smoked Gouda or mozzarella and ½ cup Parmesan
3. Wagon wheels with 1½ cups goat cheese and ½ cup pecorino or Parmesan
4. Rotini or spirals with 1 cup Gorgonzola and 1 cup Bel Paese or fontina
5. Tube pastas, like penne, rigatoni, and ziti, with 1 cup Manchego and 1 cup Gruyère
6. Orecchiette with 1 cup ricotta and 1 cup Parmesan or pecorino

Panzanella

Makes: **4 to 6 servings**	Time: **45 to 60 minutes**	

With grilled bread, this salad is the perfect vine-ripened tomato delivery system. The fruit's juices will soak into the bread, making for a delicious jumble of tastes, fragrance, and textures. Have all the ingredients prepped, then grill the bread before your main course—and the salad will be ready to go when you are.

About 8 ounces baguette, ciabatta, or other crusty bread (preferably a little dry)

¼ cup good-quality olive oil

2 tablespoons red wine vinegar or fresh lemon juice

2 large fresh tomatoes, cut into bite-sized pieces

1 small red onion, halved lengthwise and thinly sliced into half moons

1 clove garlic, minced or pressed

About ¼ cup roughly chopped fresh basil or parsley

Salt and pepper

1 Start the coals or heat a gas grill for medium-high direct cooking. Make sure the grates are clean.

2 Cut the bread into 1-inch-thick slices. Put the oil, vinegar, tomatoes, onion, garlic, and basil in a large salad bowl. Sprinkle with salt and lots of pepper and toss to coat the vegetables.

3 Put the bread on the grill directly over the fire. Close the lid and cook, turning once, until well toasted, 2 to 3 minutes per side; it's fine if it gets a little charred in places. Transfer the bread to a cutting board. As soon as it cools enough to handle, cut the slices into bite-sized pieces. Add to the bowl and toss until everything is well combined. Let sit until you are ready to eat, at least 10 minutes; you want to give the bread time to absorb the dressing and tomato juices.

Caprese Panzanella	More of a main dish, especially over a bed of salad greens: When you add the bread to the salad, add 8 ounces bocconcini (small mozzarella balls); if you like, halve or quarter them first.
Panzanella with Kale	The stems here add intermittent crunch: Use 2 tablespoons each red wine vinegar and fresh lemon juice (instead of only vinegar). When you toss the salad, add 8 ounces kale (stems and all), finely chopped.
Fattoush	The Lebanese take on bread salad, loaded with fresh herb flavor: Substitute four 6-inch pitas for the bread and grill as directed; cut each into 8 wedges. In a large salad bowl, whisk together 6 tablespoons good-quality olive oil and 2 tablespoons fresh lemon juice with some salt and pepper. Add ½ cup chopped fresh mint or basil, ¼ cup chopped fresh parsley, 1 large fresh tomato, chopped, 1 cucumber, peeled and chopped, and 1 red or yellow bell pepper, chopped. Toss to combine and coat with the dressing, then add the pita wedges and toss again. Taste and adjust the seasoning, then serve.

D direct fire   **I** indirect fire   **M** make ahead   **V** vegetarian option

Sauces and Condiments

The recipes in this book either have seasonings and sauces built in, or send you here—to my arsenal of toppings, sauces, rubs, and other flavor enhancers that will take your grilling from good to great. So whenever you run across something simply sprinkled with salt and pepper, flip through this chapter. And since these are what I consider universal spice blends and condiments, you can use them on nongrilled foods, too.

Virtually all are multipurpose. Like Basil Pesto (page 475): Brush it on chicken cutlets before putting them on the fire, toss hot-off-the-grill shrimp with some before serving, or pass it at the table to drizzle over asparagus or other vegetables. Homemade mayonnaise—and its many flavor variations—is another example. Use it traditionally, to top burgers or dress slaw; surprise everyone with a special dip for Grill Fries (page 427); or brush on fish fillets to keep them moist during cooking.

Fresh salsas are the most versatile of all sauces; I've included many different kinds to enjoy with grilled wedges of pita, chicken and pork cutlets, fish fillets, or even on steak. And be sure to check out the lists throughout this chapter that redirect you to rubs and condiments that appear elsewhere in the book. Then all you need to do is open your mind to the possibilities and grab a spoon.

TIME IN A BOTTLE

I always say: Anything you make at home will be better than what you can buy. But if something's got to give, let it be bottled condiments like ketchup, mayonnaise, mustard, and hot sauce. If you can, get your hands on good-quality, minimally processed, ideally locally produced bottled condiments.

Then consider doctoring them. To balance sweetness in barbecue sauce, for example, try hitting it with a shot of cider vinegar. Whisk honey or balsamic vinegar—or even heavy cream—into Dijon mustard to turn it into something pourable. And ketchup makes a terrific base for dipping sauces (see page 256).

Salsa is a tricky one; I know there are so many good ones out there, with all sorts of different ingredients; and people go through a ton of it. So here are my guiding principles: I don't buy so-called simmering or pasta sauces. Soy, hoisin, and plum sauce: yes. Flavored ketchups and chili sauces, no. Anything with fresh herbs or butter, you've still got to make yourself. And ditto salad dressings; they're just so easy—and the commercial stuff is loaded with junk. To make your own spice blends, see page 456.

One special note about hot sauce—mandatory seasoning in so many grilled dishes. There are thousands, and no two are exactly alike. So in almost all cases, the recipes call for it generically. Use what you like. Just keep in mind that if your sauce is vinegar based, you might not want too much extra vinegar elsewhere in the dish.

D direct fire   I indirect fire   M make ahead   V vegetarian option

Chris's Best Ever Rub

Makes: ½ cup	Time: 5 minutes	Ⓜ Ⓥ

From Chris Schlesinger, cookbook author, restaurateur, and good friend. This is, hands down, the best rub in my repertoire. It's versatile and flavorful, spicy without being hot, and just a touch of sugar promotes a deeply colored crust. Delicious on ribs, salmon, chicken, vegetables—just about anything.

2 tablespoons sugar

2 tablespoons paprika

1 tablespoon salt

1 tablespoon ground cumin

1 tablespoon black pepper

1 tablespoon chili powder (to make your own, see page 456)

Stir the sugar and spices together in a small bowl. Store in an airtight container away from heat and light for up to several months.

> **7 MORE RUBS FOR THE GRILL**
> 1. Smoky Cumin Grill Salt (page 204)
> 2. Baharat Rub (page 254)
> 3. Spiced Brown Sugar Rub (page 112)
> 4. Sweet Ancho-Cumin Rub (page 294)
> 5. Star Anise Grill Salt (page 222)
> 6. Chipotle-Cumin Grill Salt (page 209)
> 7. Lime-Ancho Grill Salt (page 279)

Best Ever Rub with Five-Spice	Incredibly fragrant: Substitute 2 teaspoons five-spice powder for the chili powder.
Best Ever Rub with Chipotle	Amp up the heat level: Substitute 1 teaspoon chipotle chile powder (or to taste) for the chili powder.
Best Ever Rub with Pimentón	Both this rub and Best Ever Rub with Chipotle are great ways for the gas griller to add smoke flavor without having to add wood to the grill: Substitute smoked paprika (pimentón) for the regular paprika.

9 SPICE BLENDS YOU CAN MAKE YOURSELF

Grinding and blending your own toasted spices yields much more potent blends than even the good stuff you get online. If you don't have a spice grinder, use a clean coffee grinder and designate it for the purpose. Once done, store the finished spice mix away from heat and light; unless noted, they'll keep several months.

You can turn any of these (with the exception of Pickling Spice) into a rub by combining 1 tablespoon or more of the spice mix with 1 tablespoon salt; you can also add some brown sugar if you like, up to 1 tablespoon for each of the recipes here.

CURRY POWDER Put 1 tablespoon each black peppercorns, coriander seeds, ground turmeric, and ground ginger in a dry skillet with 1 teaspoon each cumin seeds, fennel seeds, and ground fenugreek. Toast over medium heat, shaking the pan, until fragrant, 3 to 5 minutes. Let cool, then grind to a fine powder. Makes about ¼ cup.

CHILI POWDER Put 2 tablespoons ancho, New Mexico, or other mild chile powder, in a dry skillet over medium heat. Add 1 tablespoon dried oregano (preferably Mexican), 2 teaspoons each cumin seeds and coriander seeds, and ½ teaspoon each cayenne and black peppercorns. Toast, shaking the pan, until fragrant, 3 to 5 minutes. Let cool, then grind to a fine powder. Makes ¼ cup.

JERK SEASONING Grind 1 tablespoon allspice berries, 2 teaspoons dried thyme, and 1 teaspoon black peppercorns to a fine powder. Combine with 2 tablespoons salt, 1 tablespoon each paprika and sugar, 1 teaspoon cayenne, and ¼ teaspoon freshly grated nutmeg. Makes about ¼ cup.

FIVE-SPICE POWDER Grind 2 tablespoons fennel seeds, 1 tablespoon Sichuan or black peppercorns, 1½ teaspoons whole cloves, 6 star anise pods, and one 3-inch cinnamon stick to a fine powder. Makes about ¼ cup.

GARAM MASALA Put the seeds from 10 cardamom pods and one 3-inch cinnamon stick in a dry skillet over medium heat with 1 tablespoon each cumin seeds and fennel seeds, 1 teaspoon whole cloves, and ½ teaspoon freshly grated nutmeg. Cook, shaking the pan, until fragrant, 1 to 2 minutes. Let cool, then grind to a fine powder. Makes about ¼ cup.

ZA'ATAR Toast 2 tablespoons sesame seeds in a small dry skillet over medium heat until fragrant and golden, 5 to 8 minutes. Crush 1 tablespoon dried thyme between your fingers into a small bowl. Add the sesame seeds, 1 tablespoon ground sumac, and salt and pepper to taste; stir to combine. Because of the sesame seeds, refrigerate for up to several weeks. Makes ¼ cup.

BAHARAT Grind 2 teaspoons black peppercorns, ½ teaspoon each whole cloves, cardamom seeds, cumin seeds, coriander seeds, and allspice berries to a fine powder. Put in a small bowl with 2 teaspoons paprika and ½ teaspoon each ground ginger, cinnamon, and nutmeg; stir to combine. Makes about 3 tablespoons.

RAS EL HANOUT Stir together 1 teaspoon each black pepper, paprika, ground ginger, coriander, cinnamon, cardamom, turmeric, and freshly grated nutmeg. Add ½ teaspoon each cayenne, ground fennel seeds, allspice, and cumin, and ¼ teaspoon ground cloves and stir to combine. Makes about 3½ tablespoons.

PICKLING SPICE Combine two 3-inch cinnamon sticks, 5 bay leaves, 2 tablespoons mustard seeds, 1 tablespoon each allspice berries, black peppercorns, coriander seeds, and dill seeds, 1 teaspoon each whole cloves and cardamom seeds, and 1½ teaspoons red chile flakes. Makes about ½ cup.

How to Grill Everything

456

Ⓓ direct fire Ⓘ indirect fire Ⓜ make ahead Ⓥ vegetarian option

Kansas City–Style Barbecue Sauce

Makes: 1½ cups	Time: 20 to 30 minutes	Ⓜ Ⓥ

You can use this to make Kansas City–Style Ribs (page 295) but it's terrific on pork, chicken, turkey, or even tofu "steaks" and kebabs (page 329). Use any of the regional variations as an alternative to the Carolina sauces for pulled pork (page 290), both for saucing the pork and passing at the table.

1 tablespoon butter

¼ cup minced onion

1 cup ketchup

¼ cup brown sugar

2½ tablespoons distilled white vinegar

1 tablespoon honey

1½ teaspoons yellow mustard (the ballpark stuff)

1½ teaspoons Worcestershire sauce

1½ teaspoons chili powder (to make your own, see opposite)

½ teaspoon cayenne

Salt and pepper

1 Melt the butter in a medium saucepan over medium heat. Add the onion and cook, stirring occasionally, until softened, 3 to 5 minutes. Add the remaining ingredients and salt and pepper to taste and whisk to combine.

2 Bring to a boil, then reduce the heat so the mixture bubbles gently. Cook, stirring occasionally, until the flavors develop, 10 to 15 minutes. Use or let cool and store in an airtight container in the refrigerator for up to a week.

> ### 15 MORE BBQ SAUCES AND GLAZES
>
> 1. White BBQ Sauce (page 189) and its variations
> 2. Classic BBQ Sauce (page 198) and its variations
> 3. Lexington-Style BBQ Sauce (page 288)
> 4. Honey-Lime Glaze (page 179)
> 5. Sweet Rosemary-Orange Glaze (page 179)
> 6. Spicy Miso Glaze (page 126) and its variations
> 7. Gingery Honey Glaze (page 207)
> 8. Sweet Miso Glaze (page 209)
> 9. Mustard-Curry Glaze (page 274)
> 10. Honey Dijon Glaze (page 277)
> 11. Sherry-Honey Glaze (page 291)
> 12. Sauce from Char Siu Baby Back Ribs (page 291)
> 13. Spicy Pineapple Glaze (page 300) and its variations
> 14. Maple-Mustard Glaze (page 300) and its variations
> 15. Balsamic-Honey Glaze (page 279)

• recipe continues →

Memphis-Style Barbecue Sauce	Memphis style has a healthy vinegar and black pepper kick: Use 6 tablespoons cider vinegar instead of the white vinegar, omit the honey and chili powder, and use 2 teaspoons black pepper.
Cola Barbecue Sauce	Decrease the ketchup to ½ cup and the brown sugar to 2 tablespoons; omit the honey, mustard, chili powder, and cayenne; and add ½ cup cola soda and 1½ teaspoons smoked paprika (pimentón).
Texas-Style Barbecue Sauce	Texans prefer a more savory sauce: Decrease the ketchup to ½ cup; use cider vinegar; substitute hot sauce for the chili powder; omit the brown sugar, honey, mustard, and Worcestershire; and add 1 cup beef stock.

D direct fire **I** indirect fire **M** make ahead **V** vegetarian option

TOP TO BOTTOM: **Balsamic Syrup (page 467), Romesco Sauce (page 470), Cilantro-Mint Chutney (page 474), Ketchup (page 462), Instant Peach Jam (page 477), and Kansas City-Style Barbecue Sauce (page 457)**

Mayonnaise

Makes: 1 cup	Time: 10 minutes	Ⓜ Ⓥ

Over the years I've made mayonnaise with a blender, food processor, and whisk, and though the machines make things marginally easier, all techniques are foolproof if you follow the suggestions in "Demystifying Mayonnaise," opposite. Additions behave differently depending on your method: Stirred in by hand, bits and pieces speckle the sauce for a more rustic version. Puréed in by machine, the mayonnaise will be smooth and evenly colored.

Mayonnaise is underestimated with grilled food—it works as a baste, topping, or a dip. I love it with baby artichokes (page 38), with fries (page 427), spread on bruschetta (page 21), or dolloped on a chicken breast.

1 egg yolk

2 teaspoons Dijon mustard

1 cup good-quality vegetable oil or olive oil

Salt

Pepper (optional)

1 tablespoon sherry vinegar, white wine vinegar, or fresh lemon juice

1 TO MAKE BY HAND: Put the yolk and mustard in a medium-sized bowl. Beat together with a wire whisk. Begin to add the oil in dribbles as you beat, adding a little more as each amount is incorporated. You'll notice when an emulsion forms; at that point, you can add the remaining oil a little faster. Depending on how fast you beat, the whole process will take about 5 minutes.

TO MAKE BY MACHINE: Put the yolk and mustard in a blender or food processor and turn the machine on. While it's running, add the oil in a slow, steady stream. When an emulsion forms, you can add it a little faster, until all the oil is incorporated.

---

9 SHORTCUT FLAVORED MAYONNAISES

If you're worried about using raw eggs or want to save time, check out these mayonnaises based on store-bought.

1. Lemon Aïoli (page 38)
2. Classic Tartar Sauce (page 70) and its variations
3. Chipotle Mayo (page 99) and its variation Sweet Chili Mayo (page 100)
4. Scallion Mayo (page 256)
5. Pancetta Aïoli (page 140)
6. Pepper Jelly Mayo (page 271)
7. Orange-Mint Aïoli (page 169)
8. Spicy Lime Mayo (page 335)
9. Lemon Mayo (page 71)

Ⓓ direct fire   Ⓘ indirect fire   Ⓜ make ahead   Ⓥ vegetarian option

2 Sprinkle with salt, and pepper if you don't mind the flecks, then stir in the vinegar. Taste and adjust the seasoning. Use immediately or refrigerate in an airtight container for about a week. (Or just a couple days if you add fresh herbs or aromatics).

Garlic Mayonnaise (Aïoli)	Strong stuff, but so addictive: Peel 3 to 8 cloves garlic, as you like. If mixing by hand, mince; if using a machine, chop into a few pieces. Use at least half olive oil, or all if you like. Add the garlic after the last bit of oil has been incorporated in Step 1.
Roasted Pepper Mayonnaise (Rouille)	The classic accompaniment to bouillabaisse; also try this spooned over mussels or clams: Add 1 roasted red, yellow, or orange bell pepper (page 34) in Step 2. If mixing by hand, mince it first; if using a machine, wait until the last bit of oil is incorporated then add the pepper and pulse until the mayonnaise is smooth.
Basil Mayonnaise	So delicious with chicken or fish: Add 1 cup lightly packed fresh basil leaves. If mixing by hand, chop as finely as you can before adding in Step 2; if using a machine, pulse until the mayonnaise is smooth.

DEMYSTIFYING MAYONNAISE

Mayonnaise is an emulsion, meaning two or more ingredients are integrated thoroughly together—in this case oil and eggs are vigorously stirred to a thick, pale yellow cream. Homemade mayonnaise never emulsifies when you add the oil too quickly or will "break" (separate) if you add too much oil for the egg yolk.

To increase the odds of success, be sure your eggs aren't cold to the touch and your oil is at room temperature. Temperature fluctuations can cause some instability.

To add the oil in a slow, steady stream, you can put it in a squeeze bottle or a liquid measuring cup with a spout. Or use a teaspoon to start with a few drops at a time. If you're using a food processor, note that many have a feed tube with a small hole in it specifically for this purpose: You put the oil in the tube and it drips out. But if you've heard that the direction in which you whisk matters, forget it.

For general use, I like grapeseed oil best because of its neutral flavor, especially if I'm planning on serving the mayonnaise with dishes from Asian cuisines, or adding other ingredients. Other seed oils can deliver slightly more flavor and golden color; avoid generic vegetable oil—which is from soybeans and heavy nut oils. Use olive oil if you want a particularly Mediterranean taste, which is often the case, especially with the aïoli variation. For vinegar, I like sherry or white wine vinegar, but try lemon or even lime juice for a brighter flavor.

Ketchup

| Makes: About 4 cups | Time: About 2 hours | Ⓜ Ⓥ |

It's easier to buy ketchup; if you must, try to find one sweetened with sugar, not high-fructose corn syrup. But this is infinitely better. Use this as the foundation for Kansas City–Style Barbecue Sauce on page 457, on burgers, or for dipping Grill Fries (page 427). See page 256 for a list of ways to flavor store-bought ketchup.

¾ cup cider vinegar

2 tablespoons pickling spice (to make your own, see page 456)

2 tablespoons good-quality vegetable oil

1 red or yellow bell pepper, seeded and chopped

1 large onion, chopped

1 celery stalk, chopped

2 cloves garlic, crushed

2 tablespoons tomato paste

6 cups chopped fresh tomatoes (about 3 pounds—but canned are fine; don't bother to drain)

¼ cup brown sugar

Salt

Cayenne

1 Put the vinegar and pickling spice in a small non-reactive saucepan. Bring to a boil, then remove from the heat and let steep until you're ready to use the vinegar, at least 45 minutes.

2 Meanwhile, put the oil in a large pot over medium-high heat. When it's hot, add the bell pepper, onion, celery, and garlic; cook, stirring occasionally, until the vegetables are softened, 8 to 10 minutes. Stir in the tomato paste until it is evenly distributed and begins to color, another minute or 2. Add the tomatoes and stir. Adjust the heat so the mixture bubbles gently; cook, stirring occasionally and scraping the bottom of the pot to prevent sticking, until slightly thickened, 40 to 45 minutes, being careful not to let the tomatoes stick to the bottom and burn.

3 Strain the spiced vinegar (discard the solids) and stir it into the tomato mixture along with the brown sugar and salt and cayenne to taste. Cook until it's just a little thinner than store-bought ketchup, another 40 to 45 minutes. Taste, adjust the seasonings, and remove from the heat. Use an immersion blender to purée the ketchup in the pot. Or let the ketchup cool slightly, pour half into a blender or food processor, and purée, careful not to overfill the container or it will splash out; repeat with the remaining mixture. Cool and serve. Or refrigerate in an airtight container for up to 2 weeks.

Green Ketchup	If you're a gardener, this is a great way to use up green tomatoes at the end of the season: Use 1 green bell pepper instead of red or yellow. For the tomatoes, use 2 pounds green tomatoes and core, peel, and slice 1 pound tart apples (you should have about 6 cups total). Substitute a seeded jalapeño for the garlic if you like. Omit the tomato paste and increase the brown sugar to ½ cup. Add about 1 cup water when you add the green tomatoes and apples in Step 2.
Jamaican Jerk Ketchup	Give your ketchup a little kick in the pants: Substitute Jerk Seasoning (page 456) for the pickling spice and 1 cup mashed ripe banana for 1 cup of the tomatoes.
Black Bean Ketchup	This gets very close to the flavor of hoisin sauce: Substitute Chinese black vinegar for the cider vinegar and five-spice powder for the pickling spice; if you can't find black vinegar, use balsamic. Add ¼ cup rinsed fermented black beans along with the tomatoes.

Grill-Roasted Garlic

I love the mellow flavor of garlic roasted in the oven. It's just as easy to pop the heads on the grill while you're cooking something else. For a smoky flavor, add wood chips to the charcoal fire, or if you're a gas griller, put them in a smoker box (see page 4).

Whole heads garlic, however many you want

Good-quality olive oil

1 Start the coals or heat a gas grill for medium indirect cooking.

2 Remove the loose papery outer coating from the head(s) of garlic, then use a sharp knife to cut across the top of the head to expose the cloves without cutting away too much of them. Drizzle some oil over the top so that it coats between the cloves as well as the exposed tops.

3 Put the garlic on the indirect side of the grill, cut side up. Close the lid and cook until the garlic feels soft when you squeeze it, 45 to 60 minutes. Transfer to a plate.

4 To use, squeeze the individual cloves from their skins. Roasted garlic will keep in the refrigerator in an airtight container for up to a week, or indefinitely in the freezer; remove the cloves from their skins before freezing.

Grill-Braised Garlic	If you're adding wood chips to the fire and want an even more pronounced smoky flavor, this is the way to go: Peel the garlic cloves, put in a disposable foil pan, and add enough good-quality olive oil to coat them thoroughly; start with ¼ cup and add more if needed. Put the pan on the indirect side of the grill. The garlic will become soft much faster this way, but leave the cloves on the grill until they have the degree of smokiness you prefer, adding more wood chips to the fire for as long as needed. Refrigerate the garlic in the olive oil for up to a few days.
Roasted Garlic Mayonnaise	Absolutely delicious for dipping Cottage Fries (page 427): Mash 6 cloves roasted garlic (or more) to a paste with a fork, then whisk in ½ cup mayonnaise.
Roasted Garlic Compound Butter	Melt this over your next steak: Mash 6 cloves roasted garlic (or more) to a paste with a fork, then stir in 8 tablespoons (1 stick) softened butter. Use soft or shape into a log, wrap well in plastic, refrigerate until solid, then cut into slices.

Compound Butter

Makes: about ¾ cup	Time: 10 minutes	Ⓜ Ⓥ

A fancy way of saying "flavored butter." After folding in the extra ingredients, you can leave it in the bowl to serve by the spoonful, or shape it into a log, wrap in plastic, and refrigerate until solid; then cut off pats to set atop grilled meat, poultry, or fish. The main recipe is for the classic maître d'hôtel butter, a rich and piquant combination of parsley, lemon juice, and butter—perfect with steak.

¼ cup chopped fresh parsley

8 tablespoons (½ stick) butter, softened

1 tablespoon fresh lemon juice

Salt

Black pepper (optional)

Use a fork to stir the parsley into the butter in a small bowl. Add the lemon juice, salt to taste, and pepper if you like. Use the butter soft, or roll it as described in the headnote. (You can wrap it tightly and refrigerate for up to a week or freeze for several months.)

Anchovy-Caper Compound Butter	This one has zing. I love it with fish: Omit the parsley. Add 4 oil-packed anchovy fillets and 1 tablespoon chopped capers, mashing until the anchovies are completely broken up and worked into the butter along with the capers.
Lemon-Garlic Compound Butter	Perfect with grilled chicken breasts and vegetables: Decrease the parsley to 1 tablespoon and add 2 cloves garlic, chopped, and the grated zest of 1 lemon in addition to the lemon juice.
Ginger-Scallion Compound Butter	Use with other Asian flavors: Substitute scallions for the parsley and lime juice for the lemon juice. Add 1 tablespoon minced fresh ginger.

---

8 MORE FLAVORED BUTTERS TO MELT OR DRIZZLE OVER GRILLED FOOD

1. Andouille-Garlic Butter (page 78)
2. Beurre Blanc (page 132) and its variations
3. Citrus Butter (page 141)
4. Chive Drawn Butter (page 145)
5. Parmesan Butter (page 175)
6. Black and Blue Butter (page 224)
7. Smoky Maple Butter and its variation Soy-Honey-Ginger Butter (page 440)
8. Garlic-Ginger Butter Baste (page 423)

Ⓓ direct fire   Ⓘ indirect fire   Ⓜ make ahead   Ⓥ vegetarian option

Balsamic Syrup

Makes: ¼ cup	Time: About 15 minutes	Ⓜ Ⓥ

It takes only a few minutes on the stove to transform inexpensive balsamic vinegar into a rich, sweet–slightly sour syrup that's delicious drizzled over grilled foods from sliced watermelon or whole figs to chicken cutlets and eggplant.

1 cup balsamic vinegar

Put the vinegar in a small nonreactive saucepan over medium-low heat. Bring to a boil, then immediately lower the heat so it bubbles gently. Cook until reduced to ¼ cup, 15 to 20 minutes; it should be thickened and syrupy (it will thicken a little as it cools). Use or let cool and store in an airtight container in the refrigerator for months. Serve warm or cold.

Honeyed Balsamic Syrup	Drizzle this over a grilled fruit salad or sundae; it's also a nice way to serve grilled Pound Cake (page 510) and Pain Perdu (page 509): Stir 2 tablespoons honey into the reduced vinegar.
Pomegranate-Balsamic Syrup	Fantastic with steak, pork, or chicken: Substitute unsweetened pomegranate juice for half the vinegar.
Fresh or Dried Fruit Balsamic Syrup	Make your own customized fruit-flavored balsamic syrup: Add ½ cup fresh or ⅓ cup dried berries or chopped fruit to the pan along with the vinegar. If you like, strain the syrup when it's done. If you don't strain it, it will only keep for a week in the refrigerator.

---

6 MORE WAYS TO FLAVOR BALSAMIC SYRUP

Add any of these to the pan along with the vinegar; strain out the solids at the end.

1. Mashed Grill-Roasted Garlic (page 464), to taste (add to the finished syrup)
2. ¼ cup fruity red wine
3. ½ cup fresh orange juice
4. 1 tablespoon black peppercorns
5. A sprig of a strong-flavored herb like rosemary, tarragon, or thyme, or a few sprigs of milder ones like parsley, mint, or basil
6. 5 star anise pods

Ponzu Sauce

Makes: **About 1½ cups**	Time: **Overnight, completely unattended**	Ⓜ Ⓥ

You can buy ponzu in the supermarket, but the flavor is never fresh enough. It's traditionally made with yuzu, a citrus fruit indigenous to China, but the flavor of yuzu juice can be approximated by mixing equal amounts of lemon and lime juice. Look for bonito flakes in the Asian foods section of your supermarket or a health food store. Use ponzu as a dipping sauce for most anything, or as a marinade for poultry, pork, beef, or lamb.

½ cup soy sauce

¼ cup fresh lemon juice

¼ cup fresh lime juice

¼ cup dried bonito flakes, or one 4-inch piece kombu

2 tablespoons mirin (or 1 tablespoon each honey and water mixed together)

2 tablespoons rice vinegar

1 Whisk all the ingredients together in a small bowl. Cover and refrigerate overnight.

2 Strain into an airtight container and refrigerate until you're ready to use it, for up to several days.

Sans Soy Ponzu	What most people are familiar with is actually *ponzu shoyu*, the citrus-vinegar ponzu mixture in combination with soy sauce. Omit the soy for a completely different spin, with the citrus flavors front and center. If necessary, double the remaining ingredients, or dilute the sauce with a little water.
Orange Ponzu	Fresh orange juice brings a wonderful aroma to the sauce: Substitute orange juice for the lime juice.
Ponzu with Ginger and Chives	Absolutely delicious with shrimp: Add 1 tablespoon minced fresh ginger in Step 1. After straining, stir in 2 tablespoons minced fresh chives.

Ⓓ direct fire   Ⓘ indirect fire   Ⓜ make ahead   Ⓥ vegetarian option

Peanut Sauce

Makes: **2 cups**	Time: **35 minutes**	Ⓓ Ⓥ

To use this sauce for chicken or pork skewers, toss the meat with half the sauce before skewering and grilling, then serve with the remainder as a dipping sauce. Peanut sauce is also a nice change of pace with grilled tofu, shrimp, and squid.

3 small dried red chiles (like Thai or piquin), seeded, or cayenne or red chile flakes to taste

3 cloves garlic, peeled

2 shallots, peeled

1 stalk lemongrass, white part only, peeled, trimmed, and thinly sliced (optional)

2 teaspoons ground turmeric

1 tablespoon peanut oil

1 cup coconut milk

½ cup crunchy peanut butter or chopped peanuts

2 tablespoons soy sauce, or more to taste

2 tablespoons fresh lime juice

1 tablespoon brown sugar

Salt

1 Put the chiles, garlic, shallots, lemongrass, and turmeric in a blender or mini food processor and let the machine run until it's a fairly smooth paste; stop and scrape down the sides of the container as necessary.

2 Put the oil in a saucepan or skillet over medium heat. When it's hot, add the paste and cook until fragrant, about 1 minute. Add the coconut milk, peanut butter, soy sauce, lime juice, and brown sugar; whisk until smooth. Bring to a steady but gentle bubble, and cook, stirring occasionally, until the sauce thickens, 10 to 15 minutes. Taste and adjust the seasoning with salt or a little more soy sauce if you like. Serve right away. Or cool and refrigerate in an airtight container for up to a week; warm gently over very low heat or in the microwave before using.

Ginger-Curry Peanut Sauce	Quite nice with chicken and lamb: Substitute one 2-inch piece fresh ginger, peeled and sliced, for the chiles and lemongrass, and 2 tablespoons curry paste (I like red) or curry powder for the turmeric.
Sweet Peanut Sauce	Give it an Indonesian spin: Add ¼ cup ketchup (even better, kecap manis, if you can find it) in Step 2 when you cook the paste.
Simpler Peanut Sauce with Fish Sauce	Use only the chiles, peanut butter, soy sauce, lime juice, and brown sugar. Add 2 tablespoons fish sauce. Purée in a mini food processor or blender to purée, adding a little water or more soy sauce to get the consistency and taste you want. Gently heat in a small saucepan over low heat. Let cool and stir in ¼ cup each chopped scallions and fresh cilantro.

Romesco Sauce

Makes: 2 cups | Time: 45 minutes, including grilling time for peppers | D M V

A rich meld of grill-roasted red peppers and ground almonds that comes from the Catalan region of Spain. It's traditionally served with grilled fish, but it has an affinity for all kinds of fire-cooked food. It tackles steak with gusto and is my personal favorite alongside grilled cauliflower and winter squash. It also makes a wonderful dip or spread on bruschetta or sandwiches.

3 red bell peppers, grill-roasted (page 34), seeded, and peeled

½ cup almonds

1 or 2 cloves garlic, peeled

1 tablespoon sherry vinegar

1 teaspoon smoked paprika (pimentón)

¼ cup good-quality olive oil

Salt and pepper

Put the peppers, almonds, garlic, vinegar, and paprika in a food processor. With the machine running, slowly pour the oil through the feed tube and process until smooth and thick. Season to taste with salt and pepper. Refrigerate in an airtight container for up to 5 days.

Romesco Sauce with Hazelnuts	It's amazing how changing the nuts impacts the flavor: Substitute toasted peeled hazelnuts for the almonds.
Romesco Sauce with Tomatoes	I'm keen on this with beef or eggplant: Substitute 1½ cups cherry tomatoes for the bell peppers. Grill them over a hot direct fire until softened and black in places, 3 to 5 minutes per side. Add to the food processor with the remaining ingredients, and pulse to a paste. Makes about 1½ cups.
Spicy Romesco Sauce	Add heat to any of these variations: Grill 1 or more jalapeño chiles along with the peppers or tomatoes, then seed and add to the food processor.

D direct fire   I indirect fire   M make ahead   V vegetarian option

Black Bean–Tomato Salsa with Corn and Mint

| Makes: 2½ to 2¾ cups | Times: 10 to 15 minutes, if using canned beans | Ⓜ Ⓥ |

More relish than fresh salsa, this hearty blend works two ways: to bolster mild foods like fish and chicken breasts, and to amplify hearty meats. Either way, the balance of earthiness and brightness is always welcome. Feel free to change up the ratios of ingredients in this recipe or use different cooked beans you like, swap tomatillos for tomatoes, leave out the chiles or add even lots—you get the idea.

1 cup cooked black beans, drained and rinsed if using canned

½ cup chopped fresh tomato

½ cup fresh corn kernels

½ cup chopped red onion

1 teaspoon ground cumin

1 teaspoon minced garlic, or to taste

Minced hot fresh chile (like jalapeño, Thai, or habanero), or red chile flakes or cayenne, to taste

¼ cup chopped fresh mint

2 tablespoons fresh lime juice

Salt and pepper

Put everything in a bowl with a sprinkle of salt and pepper. Toss to combine, then taste and adjust the seasoning. If possible, let the flavors develop for 15 minutes or so before serving, but serve within a couple of hours.

Black Bean–Tomato Salsa with Avocado and Basil	A delicious topper for grilled steak: Instead of the corn, pit, peel, and chop 1 ripe avocado. Substitute scallions for the red onion, and basil for the mint.
White Bean–Tomato Salsa with Dill and Lemon	My choice alongside grilled whole fish or fillets: Substitute small white beans for the black beans, dill for the mint, and lemon juice for the lime juice. Omit the corn and cumin and double the tomatoes.
Chickpea Salsa with Pomegranate Seeds	Beautiful and unexpected: Use chickpeas for the beans. Substitute 1 cup pomegranate seeds for the tomato and corn. Increase the mint to ½ cup.

TOP TO BOTTOM: **Papaya-Cilantro Salsa, Fresh Mango Salsa with Basil, and Green Melon Salsa with Mint**

Fresh Mango Salsa with Basil

Makes: 2½ cups	Time: 10 to 15 minutes	Ⓜ Ⓥ

This is the height of simplicity, and the flavors couldn't be more vibrant. The combination of fruit and herbs makes this a natural companion for fish and chicken, and a surprising one for pork. Be sure to use ripe fruit in good condition and fresh herbs with no signs of wilting. This salsa doesn't benefit from refrigeration. Make it right before you start the fire and let it sit out on the counter until it's time to eat.

2 or 3 ripe mangoes, peeled, pitted, and cut into ½- to ¾-inch dice (about 2 cups)

½ cup chopped fresh basil

Juice of 1 lime

Salt and pepper

Put the mango, basil, and lime juice in a small bowl with some salt and pepper. Toss to combine; taste and adjust the seasoning. Leave at room temperature for up to an hour until you're ready to serve.

Papaya-Cilantro Salsa	Substitute ripe papaya for the mango and cilantro for the basil. If you like, add ¼ cup chopped red onion. Another option is to substitute papaya for half the mango.
Green Melon Salsa with Mint	So incredibly refreshing, and pairs nicely with pork: Substitute peeled and seeded honeydew melon for the mango and mint for the basil.
Five-Spice Peach Salsa with Thai Basil	Save this for when tree-ripened peaches are in season: Substitute peaches for the mango and 2 tablespoons orange juice for the lime juice. Use Thai basil; if you can't find it, use regular basil or cilantro. Add ½ teaspoon five-spice powder.

Cilantro-Mint Chutney

Makes: 1½ cups	Time: 15 minutes	Ⓜ Ⓥ

A fresh herb chutney is a little like pesto, only with a smoother texture and brighter flavor—and some heat from chiles. Serve it with grilled meats, poultry, fish, or the flatbreads on pages 486 through 493. If you prefer to have the mint more prominent than the cilantro, swap the measurements; you can also make this with all cilantro or all mint.

1½ cups packed fresh cilantro leaves

½ cup packed fresh mint leaves

1 or 2 Thai or other hot green chiles, seeded if you like, to taste, or red chile flakes to taste

1 1-inch piece fresh ginger, peeled and sliced

½ red onion, quartered

2 cloves garlic, peeled

¼ cup fresh lime juice

½ teaspoon salt, or more to taste

Put the cilantro, mint, chiles, ginger, onion, and garlic in a food processor; pulse until finely ground. Add the lime juice and salt and process until nearly smooth; you may need to add up to ¼ cup water to help form a sauce. Taste and adjust the seasoning and serve. Or refrigerate for up to a day, but serve at room temperature.

Creamy Cilantro-Basil Chutney	Substitute basil for the mint and stir ¼ cup yogurt into the finished chutney.
Cilantro-Mint Chutney with Pistachios	Veering more toward pesto but still different: Add ½ cup pistachios before puréeing.
Coconut-Cilantro Chutney	Coconut adds a bit of sweet chewiness to chutney. Nice paired with pork or shrimp: Add ½ cup unsweetened shredded coconut along with the herbs.

Ⓓ direct fire   Ⓘ indirect fire   Ⓜ make ahead   Ⓥ vegetarian option

Basil Pesto

Makes: **About 1 cup**	Time: **10 minutes**	Ⓜ Ⓥ

In addition to its classic use on pasta, pesto is an essential addition to the griller's sauce repertoire. Spread it on bruschetta, drizzle it over vegetables, brush it on pork or chicken cutlets or paillards, or fish fillets for that matter before putting them on the fire. Toss shrimp in pesto after coming off the grill, use it as a dunk for grilled artichokes, mash a couple of tablespoons of it with butter for a pungent compound butter . . . the list could go on and on. Pesto will keep in an airtight container in the refrigerator for a day or so. Or freeze it, leaving the Parmesan out until you're ready to use it; it will keep for several months.

2 cups packed fresh basil leaves

½ clove garlic, or more to taste, peeled

2 tablespoons pine nuts or chopped walnuts

½ cup good-quality olive oil, or more as desired

Salt

½ cup freshly grated Parmesan or pecorino Romano (optional)

Put the basil, garlic, nuts, and about ¼ cup oil in a blender or food processor with a pinch of salt. Pulse until finely chopped, stopping to scrape down the side of the container if necessary. Add the rest of the oil gradually while still pulsing. Add more oil if you prefer a thinner mixture. Stir in the cheese by hand just before serving.

Mint or Dill Pesto	Super on grilled fish, chicken, or vegetables: Substitute mint or dill for the basil. The garlic is still optional, or try replacing it with a 1-inch piece of ginger. Use a good-quality vegetable oil instead of olive oil, omit the cheese, and add another 2 tablespoons walnuts. Finish, if you like, with a squeeze of lemon juice. Use within a day.
Dried Tomato Pesto	Delicious on bruschetta and grilled potatoes: Decrease the basil to 1 cup. Omit the nuts. Drain the oil from one 8-ounce jar dried tomatoes packed in olive oil into a measuring cup. Add more olive oil if needed to measure ½ cup. Add the tomatoes and oil to the blender with the basil and garlic and process. The Parmesan is optional.
Salsa Verde	Another Italian fresh herb sauce that is absolutely amazing with grilled meat: Omit the nuts and cheese. Substitute parsley for the basil; increase the olive oil to ¾ cup and the garlic to 4 cloves; and add ¼ cup fresh lemon juice and 2 oil-packed anchovy fillets.

Gremolata

Makes: ½ cup	Time: 10 minutes	Ⓥ

Gremolata—fresh parsley combined with the piquant pop of garlic and lemon zest—is the traditional garnish for osso buco (rich braised veal shank). It's a seasoning that's the essence of simplicity but packs a wallop. Sprinkle it over grilled chicken cutlets or paillards or whole fish, fillets, or steaks. You don't need much, just a tablespoon or so; if you like, accompany it with a lemon wedge.

½ cup chopped fresh parsley

Grated zest of 1 lemon

1 teaspoon minced garlic, or more to taste

Toss the parsley, lemon zest, and garlic together in a small bowl to combine. Use this as soon as you can for the best flavor.

Caper Gremolata	The salty-sour taste of capers makes this a good choice for grilled red meats: Add 1 tablespoon chopped drained capers.
Chive-Dill Gremolata	This herb combination works nicely with the lemon; I love this with fish: Replace the parsley with ¼ cup each chopped dill and chives.
Orange-Mint-Ginger Gremolata	These bright flavors will work with just about everything: Substitute mint for the parsley, the zest of a navel orange for the lemon, and 1 tablespoon minced fresh ginger for the garlic.

11 OTHER FRESH HERB SAUCES AND TOPPINGS

1. Parsley-Cilantro Pesto (page 42)
2. Basil-Orange Oil (page 101) and its variations
3. Lemon-Scallion Relish (page 107)
4. Salmoriglio (page 199) and its variations
5. Caper-Shallot Vinaigrette (page 146) and its variation Tomato-Basil Vinaigrette
6. Green Chimichurri (page 229) and its variations
7. Quick Orange-Sage Drizzle (page 286) and its variations
8. Persillade (page 317)
9. Green Goddess Dressing (page 334) and its variations
10. Tarragon Vinaigrette (page 413)
11. Cilantro-Mint Chutney (page 474)

Ⓓ direct fire　Ⓘ indirect fire　Ⓜ make ahead　Ⓥ vegetarian option

Instant Fig Jam

Makes: 1 cup	Time: 30 to 40 minutes	Ⓓ Ⓜ Ⓥ

Put fire and figs together, and you're just minutes away from a naturally sweet jam you can offer as part of a cheese board or on the breakfast table. Aim for a mellow medium fire for this, around 300°F. You want to heat the figs without evaporating their juice or creating a crust on their skins, since you're going to be mashing them.

1 pound ripe figs, stems removed

1 tablespoon good-quality olive oil

Sugar (optional)

1 Start the coals or heat a gas grill for medium direct fire. Make sure the grates are clean.

2 Toss the figs with the oil in a bowl.

3 Put the figs on the grill directly over the fire. Close the lid and cook, turning once, until soft, 5 to 10 minutes total. Transfer to a bowl. Use a potato masher or an immersion blender to reduce the figs to a purée, smooth or a little chunky. Taste and adjust the sweetness level with sugar if you like. Eat right away. Or let cool, then store in an airtight container in the refrigerator for up to 5 days.

Instant Peach Jam	This is fantastic as a spread but it is saucy enough to spoon on dessert. Flavoring ideas include orange or raspberry liqueur, ground cardamom or star anise, or dried chiles: Substitute 1½ pounds peaches for the figs. Cut in half and remove the pits. Don't bother to peel them; the skins will come right off after grilling. Put the peaches skin side down on the grill. Large peaches will take about 20 minutes to fully soften; small to medium, 10 minutes. Don't bother turning them. They should be fork-tender. When cool enough to handle, pull off the skins, then purée as directed. Makes about 2 cups jam.
Instant Apricot Jam	I love apricots, but only in season and preferably from local sources. This, however, is great way to use less-than-optimum fruit, as the fire intensifies their flavor: Substitute 1 pound apricots for the figs. Cut in half and remove the pits. Put on the grill skin side down; they will take 5 to 10 minutes to soften fully. Don't turn them—juice oozes into the well left by the pit and you don't want to lose that to the fire. You'll have to use an immersion or regular blender or food processor for these; a potato masher will not break up their skins.
Fruit Jam Fool	The perfect summer dessert, best enjoyed the day it is made: For 4 servings, beat 1 cup heavy cream to firm peaks with an electric mixer. Gently fold in 1 cup jam, creating swirls of fruit purée in the cream. Spoon into goblets or other glassware; if you like, top each with chopped fresh fruit, berries, or a sprig fresh mint. Cover and refrigerate until you're ready to serve.

Apple Butter

| Makes: ½ cup | Time: 2¼ to 2¾ hours, largely unattended | Ⓘ Ⓜ Ⓥ |

Like the applesauce on page 381, this is another no-work recipe. Only you'll have a thick apple butter to spread on the morning toast, with a hint of smokiness and nary a pot to wash in sight. Throw the apples on a dying charcoal fire and put the lid back on the grill, or adjust the heat on a gas grill if necessary. You can also make this with pears or a mix of pears and apples.

1½ pounds any apples

1–2 tablespoons sugar, to taste

½ teaspoon ground cinnamon

⅛ teaspoon ground cloves

⅛ teaspoon freshly grated nutmeg

Salt

1 Start the coals or heat a gas grill for medium indirect cooking. Make sure the grates are clean.

2 Put the apples on the indirect side of the grill. Close the lid and cook until they're super soft and have noticeably shrunk down; the skins may burst open at some point. Depending on the size and variety of the apple, this can take anywhere from 2 to 2½ hours. Transfer the apples to a platter.

3 When the apples are cool enough to handle, scrape the thickened, soft flesh from the skins and from around the core with a spoon. Put the flesh in a small bowl. Add the sugar, cinnamon, cloves, nutmeg, and a pinch salt and vigorously mix together with a fork until puréed. (This will keep in an airtight container in the refrigerator for 4 to 5 days.)

Maple or Honey Apple Butter	Substitute maple syrup or honey for the sugar.
Five-Spice Apple Butter	An unconventional alternative for your morning toast: Substitute ½ teaspoon five-spice powder or more to taste for the cinnamon, cloves, and nutmeg.
Pumpkin Butter	The flavors of pumpkin pie: Substitute seeded pumpkin pieces (or any kind of winter squash other than spaghetti) for the apples; don't bother to peel them. Taste after adding the sugar and spices; you may need to add more sugar.

Breads and Desserts

Baking over a live fire is one of life's true pleasures. When it comes to bread, the joy comes from connecting with a deep human tradition. Nothing can quite compare to watching naan puff up like a balloon and then tearing into the chewy pillows moments later, savoring the crisp crust and char from the flames. Cornbread and biscuits are natural partners for barbecue, so it makes sense to bake them outside—and it's easy enough in a cast-iron skillet. You can even time the recipe so they'll still be warm when you sit down to eat. Flatbreads are a wonderful vehicle for enjoying kebabs and sliced meat, chicken, or fish; or you can cut them into pieces to serve with a dip. The simplest and best breads for grilling are all included in this chapter.

With sweets baked on a grill, the pleasure comes with an element of surprise. Applying fire to sugar, chocolate, and fruit—let alone cake batter—isn't intuitive, yet I guarantee the results are always memorable. And like bread, the logistics are streamlined: Many of the recipes in this chapter can be partially or fully prepped ahead of time, requiring just a short interlude over the fire for heating, melting, and/or caramelizing. None are involved, relying instead on a few quality ingredients, including seasonal fruit, for outstanding flavor and texture. And did I mention? They're beautiful. That's part of the enjoyment, too.

The Basics of Grilling Quick, Flat, and Yeasted Breads

Before you begin baking bread in the grill—especially if you're new to this process—here are a few general notes: For recipes that call for a pan, it's important to choose one that can stand up to the heat of the fire. For cornbread and biscuits, I use a cast-iron skillet; multi-ply stainless-steel pans also work. All handles must be metal. For corn muffins, you need a heavy-duty tin; thin aluminum will result in scorched bottoms.

You need to tune in to the smell of batters and doughs grill-baking. The moment you detect an aroma from the grill (even if you're thinking, wow, that smells great), check on its progress. It takes just a minute or two for something to go from done to burnt. If you think something is browning too fast, on a gas grill you can turn the heat down or off directly under the pan and leave the other burners turned to the high position. If you're cooking with charcoal, move the pan to the outer edge of the fire and rotate it as necessary to slow the cooking.

Yeast breads always intimidate people, so these recipes are written with lots of cues to give even beginning bakers confidence. These doughs are easy to mix, knead, and shape. They're forgiving to move on and off the grill: When I'm transporting flatbreads to the grill, I just drape them over one arm, open the lid, then throw them on the grill. In many ways baking over fire is easier than in an oven, since you're in more direct and frequent contact with the bread throughout the process.

Whether you're making a quick bread, flatbread, or other yeasted bread, stay close and check early and often. Most of the flatbreads are cooked over a hot fire and need to be turned in a minute or 2; naan and chapati only take 20 to 30 seconds. Make sure you have long-handled tongs ready, as well as a rimmed baking sheet, board, or platter to offload them just as soon as they are done.

Buttermilk Angel Biscuits

Makes: 12 to 14 biscuits	Time: 45 to 55 minutes, plus rising time	Ⓓ Ⓜ Ⓥ

A welcome addition to any barbecue. Since the dough needs to rise for 1 to 1½ hours, have the biscuits cut and in the pan well in advance, ready to go onto the grill as the rest of the meal is coming off. (See the photo on page 190.)

2½ cups all-purpose flour, plus more for kneading

2¼ teaspoons (1 package) instant yeast

1 teaspoon baking powder

1 teaspoon baking soda

1 teaspoon salt

8 tablespoons (1 stick) butter, melted, plus softened butter for the pans

1 cup buttermilk

1 Whisk the flour, yeast, baking powder and soda, and salt together in a large bowl. Stir the melted butter into the buttermilk, then add to the flour and stir it in. With your hands, gather the dough into a ball and transfer to a lightly floured work surface. Knead the dough until smooth, 1 to 2 minutes, then pat it down to a ½- to ¾-inch thickness. Cut the biscuits using a 2½-inch cutter. Pat the scraps together, flatten again, and cut more biscuits.

2 Coat the insides of two 12-inch cast-iron skillets with softened butter. Put the biscuits in the pans, not touching. Cover with plastic wrap and let rise until doubled, 1 to 1½ hours.

3 Start the coals or heat a gas grill for medium-high direct cooking. The grill temperature should be between 500° and 600°F; if using gas, all your burners might be on medium or medium-low, depending on your particular grill. (See "High-Temperature Baking on the Grill," page 500.)

4 Put the skillets on the grill directly over the fire. Close the lid and grill-bake, rotating the pans for even cooking, until the bottoms of the biscuits release easily and are golden brown and the tops have browned in spots, 10 to 15 minutes; start checking the bottoms and rotating the pans after 5 minutes. The biscuits should be springy to the touch, and a toothpick inserted in the center should come out clean. Transfer the biscuits to a clean dish towel or napkin, wrap loosely, and serve warm.

Cheddar-Chive Angel Biscuits	Toss ¾ cup shredded cheddar cheese and ¼ cup minced fresh chives with the dry ingredients before adding the buttermilk mixture.
Sweet Orange Angel Biscuits	Perfect to split and serve like shortcakes with fresh fruit for dessert: Add 2 tablespoons sugar and 1 tablespoon grated orange zest to the dry ingredients before adding the buttermilk mixture. After the biscuits rise, brush the tops with melted butter, and sprinkle lightly with sugar.
Pancetta Angel Biscuits	Finely dice 2 ounces pancetta and cook over medium heat in a small skillet until the fat renders and the meat is crisp. Add the pancetta and rendered fat to the buttermilk along with the butter.

Breads and Desserts

Southern-Style Mini Corn Muffins

Makes: 24 mini muffins (8 to 12 servings)	Time: 20 to 25 minutes	Ⓓ Ⓥ

It's hard to imagine a cookout without cornbread. And when you bake it in a mini muffin pan, the little morsels are hot off the grill in only minutes. Just have the batter ready in the pan when you pull the meat off.

2 tablespoons butter, melted, or good-quality olive oil, plus softened butter for the pan

1½ cups cornmeal

½ cup all-purpose flour

1 teaspoon baking soda

1 teaspoon salt

1 egg

1½ cups buttermilk or yogurt, plus more as needed

1 Start the coals or heat a gas grill for medium-high direct cooking. The grill temperature should be between 500° and 600°F; if using gas, all your burners might be on medium or medium-low, depending on your particular grill. (See "High-Temperature Baking on the Grill," page 500.) Coat the insides of a 24-cup heavy-duty mini muffin pan with softened butter.

2 Combine the cornmeal, flour, baking soda, and salt in a large bowl. Whisk the egg into the buttermilk. Stir the buttermilk mixture into the dry ingredients just enough to eliminate streaks; lumps are okay. Add the melted butter and stir until just incorporated; avoid overmixing. Spoon or pour the batter into the muffin cups, almost to the top.

3 Put the pan on the grill directly over the fire. Close the lid and grill-bake until the muffins have domed and a skewer inserted in the center comes out clean, 5 to 10 minutes; don't walk away from the grill. Transfer the pan to a rack to cool for a few minutes, then transfer the muffins to a clean dish towel or napkin, wrap loosely, and serve warm.

Corny Corn Muffins	Stir 1 cup corn kernels, fresh or frozen, into the buttermilk mixture.
Jalapeño-Cheddar Corn Muffins	Stir ½ cup grated cheddar cheese and 1 tablespoon minced seeded jalapeño chile (or more to taste) into the dry ingredients after combining.
Cast-Iron Corn Bread	For thick wedges, use this technique for the main recipe or the variations: Coat the inside of a 9- or 10-inch cast-iron skillet with butter. Pour the batter into the pan and bake as directed. Grill time might not change much; start checking after 5 minutes. Let cool for 5 minutes, run a knife around the edge to loosen it, and either invert onto a plate or serve from the pan, cut into 8 or 12 wedges.

Paratha

| Makes: **8 to 12 flatbreads (4 to 6 servings)** | Time: **At least 1 hour, largely unattended** | Ⓓ Ⓜ Ⓥ |

Enriched with butter (or oil if you want these to be vegan), paratha have a lovely flaky texture. They're best eaten still warm or at least within a few hours. So before getting started, get a plate with a cloth napkin or clean dish towel ready and, as they finish, pile them up and wrap loosely.

1½ cups whole wheat flour, plus more as needed

1½ cups all-purpose flour, plus more for kneading and dusting

1 teaspoon salt

¾ cup warm water, plus more as needed

About 4 tablespoons (½ stick) butter, melted, or good-quality vegetable oil

1 Whisk the flours and salt together in a large bowl. Add the water and stir with a heavy spoon until the mixture can be formed into a ball and is slightly sticky. If it's dry, add more water, 1 tablespoon at a time, until you get the right consistency; in the unlikely event that the mixture is too sticky, add flour 1 tablespoon at a time. (You can also make this in a food processor. First pulse the dry ingredients together, then add the water through the feed tube.) Turn the dough out onto a lightly floured work surface; knead a few times until it becomes smooth. Cover with plastic wrap or a clean, damp dish towel and let rest at room temperature for at least 30 minutes or up to 2 hours. (At this point, the dough can be wrapped tightly in plastic and refrigerated for up to a day or frozen for up to a week; bring to room temperature before proceeding.)

2 Divide the dough into 8 to 12 even-sized pieces. Flouring the work surface and dough as necessary, roll each piece out to a 4-inch disk. Brush on one side with some of the melted butter. Roll up like a cigar, then into a coil (kind of like a cinnamon bun); set aside until you finish all the pieces. Don't let them touch or they will stick to one another. Press each coil flat, then roll out into a thin disk, about the size of a tortilla.

3 Start the coals or heat a gas grill for hot direct cooking. Make sure the grates are clean.

4 Working in batches, put the paratha on the grill directly over the fire. Quickly close the lid and cook until lightly browned on the bottom, 3 to 5 minutes. Brush the tops with butter, turn with tongs, and brown the second side, another few minutes. Brush the tops with butter, turn, cook for another minute, until lightly browned and cooked through. Transfer to the prepared plate. Repeat with the remaining paratha and butter and serve as soon as possible.

Spinach Paratha	Vegetables and bread in one bite. This works best putting the dough together in the food processor: Cook 1 pound fresh spinach in a little water until it completely wilts. Let cool until you can handle it, then drain well and squeeze the spinach to remove as much water as possible. Add the spinach, a squeeze of fresh lemon juice, and 2 teaspoons good-quality vegetable oil along with the water and process as directed, adding more water or flour as needed.
Paneer Paratha	Crumble or grate 1 cup paneer and mix together with 1 minced jalapeño chile, 2 tablespoons chopped fresh cilantro, and 1 teaspoon garam masala. After rolling out the balls of dough, do not brush with butter, but divide the stuffing between them and flatten the stuffing a bit. Bring the outside edge of each round up to enclose the filling and pinch to seal. Roll each stuffed paratha out from the center to the edges until it is about 6 inches in diameter. Pick up with Step 3.
Chapati	More intense wheat flavor, chewy rather than flaky, and simpler technique: Increase the whole wheat flour to 2¼ cups and decrease the all-purpose flour to 1 cup. Increase the water to 1 cup; you may still need to add a little extra. After shaping the dough into disks, omit brushing it with butter and rolling it. When you are ready to cook the chapati, roll them out to thin (⅛-inch-thick) circles. Let rest for 5 minutes so the dough can relax. Then cook as directed until they puff and blister, 20 to 30 seconds per side (no need to brush with butter). Don't walk away from the grill; these bake incredibly fast.

Naan

Makes: 8 to 12 naan (4 to 6 servings) | Time: 2 to 2½ hours, largely unattended | D M V

This Indian flatbread is traditionally cooked in a blazing hot clay tandoor oven. The process translates perfectly to the grill. Using a little whole wheat flour results in a slightly warmer, more savory flavor, but you can also use only all-purpose flour.

¼ cup yogurt

2 tablespoons good-quality vegetable oil, plus more for the bowl

1 tablespoon sugar

2¼ teaspoons (1 package) instant yeast

3½ cups all-purpose flour, plus more as needed

½ cup whole wheat flour

2 teaspoons salt

1½ cups warm water, plus more as needed

6 tablespoons (¾ stick) butter, melted and still warm

1 Whisk the yogurt, oil, sugar, and yeast together. Stir the flours and salt together in a large bowl. Add the yogurt mixture and combine. Add the water ½ cup at a time, stirring until the mixture comes together in a cohesive but sticky dough; you may need to add another tablespoon or 2 water.

2 Turn the dough out onto a floured work surface and knead by hand for a minute or so to form a smooth dough. Shape into a round ball, put in a lightly oiled bowl, and cover with plastic wrap. Let rise until doubled in size, 1 to 2 hours. Or you can let the dough rise in the refrigerator for up to 8 hours.

3 Punch the dough down. Using as much flour as necessary to keep the dough from sticking to the work surface or your hands, roll it into a snake about 2 inches in diameter, then tear into 12 equal-sized balls. Space the balls out on the work surface. Cover with plastic wrap or a clean, damp dish towel and let rest for 10 minutes. Roll each dough ball into an oval roughly 6 to 8 inches long and 3 to 4 inches wide.

4 Start the coals or heat a gas grill for hot direct cooking. Make sure the grates are clean. Have the melted butter handy.

5 Working in batches, put the naan on the grill directly over the fire. Quickly close the lid. Don't walk away: If the grill temperature is 600°F or above, it will only take 20 to 30 seconds for the first side to brown. It should smell toasty, not burning. Open the lid; the visible side should be bubbled. Quickly turn with tongs, then close the lid. The other side will take about the same time or a little less to cook. When you grab it with tongs, the bread should feel firm and springy, and both sides should be browned in spots, with a little charring. Transfer to a platter and immediately brush with the butter. Repeat with the remaining naan and butter and serve as soon as possible.

Garlic Naan	In Step 2, knead 2 tablespoons minced garlic into the dough.
Scallion Naan	In Step 2, knead ¼–½ cup minced scallions into the dough.
Sesame Naan with Chiles	Stir 2 tablespoons sesame seeds and 1 teaspoon ground cumin with the flour and salt. In Step 3, knead 1 minced hot green chile (like jalapeño or Thai) into the dough.

Lebanese Flatbread

Makes: **8 flatbreads**	Time: **About 1½ hours, largely unattended**	(D)(M)(V)

Man'oushe—an oval-shaped pizza-like bread native to Lebanon—is an insanely good vehicle for the Middle Eastern spice blend za'atar. There are lots of regional variations, but za'atar generally includes dried thyme, toasted sesame seeds, ground sumac, and a little bit of salt. The flavor of the za'atar baked into the bread is almost impossible to describe—let's leave it at "heady." No need to turn the bread over when grilling—the dough is so thin and the fire so hot that it will cook all the way through, bubbling on top and developing some charring underneath. To get these off the grill, use a spatula, not tongs. The olive oil doesn't entirely bake into the bread, so if you use tongs, you'll have hot oil streaming off them.

1 tablespoon instant yeast

2 teaspoons salt

1 teaspoon sugar

1 cup warm water, plus more as needed

3 cups all-purpose flour, plus more as needed

3 tablespoons za'atar (to make your own, see page 456)

3 tablespoons good-quality olive oil

1 Whisk the yeast, salt, sugar, and 1 cup water together in a large bowl. Add the flour and stir with a heavy spoon until the mixture can be formed into a ball; it should be slightly sticky. If it's dry, add more water 1 tablespoon at a time until you get the right consistency; in the unlikely event that the mixture is too sticky, add flour 1 tablespoon at a time. Turn the dough out onto a lightly floured work surface; knead a few times until smooth. Put the dough in a bowl and cover with plastic wrap; let rise until it doubles in size, about 1 hour.

2 Start the coals or heat a gas grill for medium-high direct cooking. Make sure the grates are clean.

3 Whisk the za'atar into the oil in a small bowl.

4 When the dough is ready, transfer it to a well-floured work surface and knead for a few minutes, until smooth and pliable. Cut into 8 equal-sized pieces. Roll each piece into an oval roughly 6 to 8 inches long and 3 to 4 inches wide. Stack them between wax paper or parchment and bring the breads to the grill along with the za'atar oil, a brush, and a baking sheet. Working in batches, just before cooking, brush the za'atar oil over the breads to within ½ inch of the edge; make sure to get plenty of the sesame seeds and thyme that are suspended in the oil.

5 One at a time, use your hands to pick up an oval by the long ends and drop it onto the grate directly over the fire, with the long side perpendicular to the grates. Close the lid and cook until the dough bubbles up on top, the outer edges start to brown, and the bottom develops grill marks; depending on how hot the fire is, this will take 1½ to 3 minutes. Start checking at 1½ minutes, then every 30 seconds after that. Use a spatula to transfer the breads to the baking sheet and repeat with the remaining dough and za'atar oil. Serve warm or within several hours.

Even Easier Lebanese Flatbread	If you don't want to bother spreading the top with the za'atar and oil, omit the oil and add 2 tablespoons za'atar along with the flour; mix it right into the dough. In Step 5, turn the breads after 1 minute, then check for doneness after another 30 seconds.
Lebanese Flatbread with Onion	Halve a small onion and slice into super-thin half moons; separate them. In Step 4, press a few slices of onion into each piece of dough, then roll the dough out and spread with the za'atar oil.
Lebanese Flatbread with Lemon	The lemon adds another dimension to the citrus notes of the sumac in the za'atar: Knead 2 teaspoons grated lemon zest into the dough.

Pita

Makes: 6 to 12 pitas | Time: About 2 hours, largely unattended | D M V

You can buy pitas everywhere, though most are more "flat" than "bread," and the so-called pockets can be a joke. Unless you have access to a specialty bakery, it's tough to find the chewy, slightly puffed rounds that are ubiquitous in the eastern Mediterranean. But they bake up fast on the grill. Make them fresh and cut into wedges for a dip, or serve them whole to wrap around—or, if pockets form, stuff with—grilled kebabs.

3 cups all-purpose or bread flour, plus more as needed

2 teaspoons instant yeast

2 teaspoons salt

½ teaspoon sugar

3 tablespoons good-quality olive oil

1 cup warm water, plus more as needed

Melted butter for brushing (optional)

1 Whisk the flour, yeast, salt, and sugar together in a large bowl. Add the oil and water and mix with a heavy spoon. Continue to add water 1 tablespoon at a time, until the dough forms a ball and is slightly sticky; in the unlikely event that the mixture gets too sticky, add flour 1 tablespoon at a time.

2 Turn the dough onto a lightly floured work surface and knead for a minute to form a smooth, round ball. Put the dough in a bowl and cover with plastic wrap; let rise in a warm spot until it doubles in size, 1 to 2 hours. Or you can let the dough rise more slowly, in the refrigerator, for up to 8 hours.

3 Divide the dough into 6 to 12 even-sized pieces; roll each into a ball. Put each ball on a lightly floured surface and cover with plastic wrap or a clean dish towel. Let rest until they puff slightly, about 20 minutes.

4 On a lightly floured surface, roll each ball out to about ⅛ inch thick. Cover and let rest while you prepare the fire.

5 Start the coals or heat a gas grill for medium-high direct cooking. Make sure the grates are clean.

6 Working in batches, put the breads on the grill directly over the fire. Close the lid and cook, turning once, until they're slightly colored and puffed, 4 to 8 minutes per side. Don't walk away from the grill. To use the pitas folded over fillings, cook them only until soft and pliable, then remove from the fire. If you're going to cut the pita in wedges for a dip or spread, you can grill them longer; move and rotate them for even cooking. Transfer to a platter, brush with melted butter if you like, and serve.

Whole Wheat Pita	Substitute whole wheat flour for 1½ cups of the all-purpose or bread flour.
Poppy Pita	Untraditional but fun, with a subtle sweet taste: Whisk 1 tablespoon poppy seeds with the flour mixture. In Step 2, knead 1 cup chopped onion into the dough until well distributed.
Oregano-Garlic Pita	Before putting the pitas on the grill, stir together ¼ cup good-quality olive oil, 2 cloves garlic, minced, and 1 tablespoon minced fresh oregano. When you turn the pitas over, brush the baked sides with the seasoned oil.

9 KEBABS TO ENJOY IN PITA OR OTHER FLATBREADS

1. Coconut-Rum Shrimp and Pineapple Skewers (page 129) and its variations
2. Chicken and Vegetable Kebabs (page 170) and its variations
3. Chicken Skewers with Italian Sausage and Lemon Wedges (page 171) and its variations
4. Madeira-Style Beef Skewers (page 247) and its variations
5. Balkan-Style Beef Sausages with Kajmak (page 265) and its variations
6. Liver Kebabs (page 267)
7. Filipino-Style Pork Skewers (page 284) and its variations
8. Shashlik with Onions and Grapes (page 318) and its variations
9. Adana Kebabs (page 320) and its variations

Rosemary Olive Oil Bread

| Makes: One 6- to 7-inch boule | Time: 4 to 5 hours, largely unattended | Ⓘ Ⓜ Ⓥ |

This dough is incredibly easy to mix, and the directions for shaping will ensure success. The seasonings are simple but pronounced: The salt is pleasantly prominent, so use a flavorful sea salt if you can, and the rosemary perfumes the whole loaf.

3 cups all-purpose or bread flour, plus more as needed

2¼ teaspoons (1 package) instant yeast

2 teaspoons salt

⅓ cup plus 1 teaspoon good-quality olive oil

1 tablespoon fresh rosemary leaves

1 Whisk the flour, yeast, and salt together in a large bowl to combine. Add the ⅓ cup oil and ¾ cup water and mix with a heavy spoon. Add more water, 1 tablespoon at a time, until the mixture forms a ball and is slightly sticky.

2 Turn the dough onto a lightly floured work surface and knead in the rosemary until the dough feels smooth and the rosemary is distributed throughout. Put the remaining 1 teaspoon oil in a medium-sized bowl, then add the dough, turning it over until it is coated with oil. Cover with plastic wrap and let rise until the dough doubles in size, about 2 hours. Or you can let the dough rise more slowly in the refrigerator, for up to 8 hours.

3 Lightly dust your hands with flour and shape the dough into a ball. Holding the dough with both hands, work around the outside of the ball, stretching and tucking the edges toward the center at the bottom. Pinch together the seam created underneath the loaf. (This will stretch the top slightly and improve the way the bread rises and forms a crust.) Line a colander or large bowl with a well-floured kitchen towel, set the dough in it, and cover with the ends of the towel (this keeps the dough from spreading too much). Let the dough rise for at least an hour and preferably up to 2 hours, until doubled.

4 When the dough is almost ready, start the coals or heat a gas grill for medium-high indirect cooking. Put a 9-inch cast-iron skillet directly over the heat, close the lid, and let heat for 15 minutes.

5 When you're ready to bake, use a sharp knife or razor blade to make an X in the top of the loaf. Move the skillet to the indirect side of the grill. Pick up the loaf with your hand and carefully put it in the middle of the skillet. Close the lid and bake until the crust is golden brown, the bottom sounds hollow when tapped, and the internal temperature registers 190°F on an instant-read thermometer, 30 to 40 minutes. Transfer to a rack to cool to barely warm or room temperature before slicing.

• recipe continues →

Rosemary Olive Oil Rolls	Put these on the grill to bake before your entrée and you'll be enjoying warm crusty rolls with dinner: In Step 3, take handfuls of the risen dough and shape them into 2-inch rolls in the same way you would shape a boule, pinching the seams closed underneath with your fingers. Put the rolls in an oiled 10-inch cast-iron skillet (it's fine if they touch), cover with plastic wrap, and let rise at least 1 hour and up to 2 hours. Prepare a medium-high direct fire. When you're ready to bake, cut slashes into the tops of the rolls, then put the skillet directly over the fire. Close the lid and grill-bake as directed. Baking time will be 8 to 15 minutes; start checking after 5 minutes. Let cool for at least 10 minutes before serving. Makes about 10 rolls.
Rosemary Olive Oil Bread with Olives	Decrease the salt to 1 teaspoon. In Step 2, knead ½ cup thinly sliced pitted oil-cured olives into the dough along with the rosemary.
Rosemary Olive Oil Bread with Walnuts	In Step 2, knead ½ cup chopped walnuts into the dough along with the rosemary.

Skillet Focaccia with Grapes

| Makes: 4 to 6 servings | Time: 16 to 24 hours, largely unattended | Ⓘ Ⓜ Ⓥ |

Since I first wrote about baker and cookbook author Jim Lahey's no-knead bread in 2006, I've experimented with all sorts of different variables. From replacing some or all of the flour with whole wheat or rye to adding yeast to speed up the process, the recipe is so versatile that it's become my go-to bread. That's how I discovered that it makes an amazing focaccia for the grill. And the timing is perfect: The dough is made well in advance. Then you grill-bake it as you just start to prepare the rest of the meal—it will be ready and still warm by the time dinner comes off the grill.

I like this bread with a little whole wheat flour, but using only all-purpose flour instead gives you a slightly puffier focaccia.

2 cups all-purpose flour, plus more for dusting

1 cup whole wheat flour

1¼ teaspoons salt, plus more for the topping

¼ teaspoon instant yeast

1½ cups plus 2 tablespoons warm water

Up to ½ cup cornmeal for dusting

4 tablespoons good-quality olive oil

Leaves from 1 large sprig fresh rosemary

Black pepper

1 cup red or green seedless grapes

1 Whisk the flours, salt, and yeast together in a large bowl to combine. Add the water and stir with a heavy spoon until a sticky, shaggy dough forms; it doesn't have to be completely smooth. Cover the bowl with plastic wrap and let it sit in a warm spot for anywhere between 12 and 20 hours.

2 The dough will be wet and bubbly. Transfer it to a lightly floured work surface; sprinkle the top with a little more flour and fold the dough over on itself once or twice. Use a metal bench scraper, plastic pastry scraper, or spatula to keep it from sticking to the surface as you fold. Cover it loosely with plastic and let rest about 15 minutes.

3 Generously coat a cotton dish towel (not terry cloth) with a layer of cornmeal. Using just enough flour to keep the dough from sticking to the work surface and your fingers, gently and quickly gather the dough into a loose ball and transfer it to the prepared towel; dust the top with more cornmeal. Cover with another clean towel and let the dough rise until it more than doubles in size and will hold the indentation for a moment when you poke it with your finger, 1½ to 2 hours.

4 Put 2 tablespoons of the oil in a small bowl with the rosemary leaves and a sprinkle of salt and pepper. Stir with a small spoon, using the back to muddle the leaves.

5 Start the coals or heat a gas grill for medium-high indirect cooking; 450°F with the grill closed is ideal. Put a 10-inch ovenproof skillet in the grill over the indirect side of the grill; close the lid. Bring the dough, still in the towels, out to the grill, along with the grapes and oil mixture.

6 When the grill is ready and the skillet is scorching hot, after 10 to 15 minutes, carefully remove the

● recipe continues →

skillet and close the lid again. Pour in the remaining 2 tablespoons oil and swirl it to coat. Use the towel to transfer the dough to the skillet. Scatter the grapes on top and drizzle with the rosemary–olive oil mixture. Shake the pan a few times to distribute the dough if necessary, return it to the indirect side of the grill, and close the lid. Bake, undisturbed, until the focaccia almost fills and separates from the pan and is golden on the top and edges, 30 to 40 minutes. (The internal temperature should register between 205° and 210°F on an instant-read thermometer.) Transfer the pan to a wire rack and let the focaccia cool in the pan until you can touch the bottom. Cut into slices and serve.

Skillet Focaccia with Olives and Thyme	Use pitted whole black or green olives instead of grapes and substitute the leaves from 2 sprigs thyme for the rosemary.
Skillet Focaccia with Pecorino, Garlic, and Cracked Pepper	Omit the rosemary and grapes. Add a generous amount of cracked black pepper and 2 tablespoons chopped garlic to the olive oil. Top the dough with ½ cup grated pecorino Romano cheese before drizzling with the flavored oil.
Skillet Focaccia with Red Onion	Omit the rosemary and grapes. Halve a small red onion, slice it thinly, and toss it with the oil in Step 4. Use this to top the dough before baking.

The Basics of Grilling Desserts

When it comes to the last course, the questions of fire intensity and timing are different depending on what kind of fuel you're using. If you're grilling with charcoal, the recipes assume you've already cooked dinner and you've got active, probably waning, coals. If that's the case, right after taking the entrée off the grill, add more briquettes or charcoal to the fire and close the lid to conserve heat. Unless you wait an hour or more, that should keep the fire hot enough to grill dessert. If you're going to be longer than that, you might have to make another addition of coals. Be sure not to let the fire dwindle too low before adding fuel—it's a lot harder to get it back up to heat once you've lost the critical mass of the coals. Another option for charcoalers is that you grill the dessert immediately prior to dinner or right before your guests arrive; it will likely still be warm room temperature when you're ready to dig into it.

For gas grillers, after dinner comes off the grates, you can turn the grill off to conserve fuel if you're not immediately putting dessert on to bake. (See "High-Temperature Baking on the Grill," below.) When you're starting to finish up dinner, heat the grill again for 15 minutes with all the burners on high, then turn them down to the level indicated in the recipe.

High-Temperature Baking on the Grill

It's completely counterintuitive, but you can grill-bake desserts at a very high temperature and get amazing results. The recipes here are a good start. Once you get the knack, you can try other baked

---

CLEAN THE GRATES!

Remember to scour the grates before putting on dessert if what you're grilling is going to make direct contact with them. The last thing anyone wants is the savory taste of dinner mixed up with the sweet flavors of dessert. And for anything going directly on the grill, be sure to also oil the just-scrubbed grates well.

---

favorites. As long as you keep a close eye—and nose—on the pan and the food, checking in long before you think it might be done and rotating and moving it as necessary for even baking, anything is possible.

For many of the recipes in this section, I call for medium-high heat, around 550° to 600°F. Baked at hyper speed, bread pudding is ready in less than 20 minutes, upside-down cake in 15 minutes, and baked apples in 10 minutes. In the oven, each of these would take at least 45 minutes.

Since there's more intense heat coming from below than in an oven, a heavy-duty pan is key. My first choice is cast iron but any flameproof, thick-walled pan will work.

On a gas grill, if you start to smell or see any scorching at all, turn the heat off under the pan and turn it up on the other burners. Over coals, move the pan to a cooler part of the grill. It's fine to shift to a lower temperature; the dessert will just take longer to bake. Be sure to continue to monitor the browning on the bottom when possible and sides since the pan will be exposed to the fire longer.

Chocolate Panini

Makes: 4 servings	Time: 15 to 20 minutes	D M V

S'mores go uptown. You can make these crisp and gooey dessert sandwiches with any kind of bread as long as it's fairly sturdy and sliceable. I like to keep it simple with Italian peasant bread, crusty on the outside with a chewy, open crumb on the inside; baguettes cut at a slight angle are nice, too. For the chocolate, choose what you like to eat, which for me is bittersweet. Serve with a scoop of ice cream if you like.

4 large or 8 small slices bread (½ to ¾ inch thick)

8 ounces chocolate, chopped

2 tablespoons butter, softened

1 tablespoon sugar

1 If using a gas grill, heat it for medium direct cooking. If using a charcoal grill, after taking off dinner, add more coals if necessary and close the lid until ready to cook. In either case, clean the grates.

2 Put half of the bread slices on a baking sheet. Divide the chocolate evenly on top, spreading almost to the edges. Top with the remaining bread.

Spread both sides of each sandwich with the butter; sprinkle with the sugar. (You can do this earlier in the day if you like; wrap the panini in plastic to keep the bread from drying out.)

3 Put the panini on the grill directly over the fire. Close the lid and cook, turning once, until the bread develops grill marks and the chocolate has melted, 2 to 4 minutes per side. Transfer to a plate. Let cool for a minute or 2; cut large sandwiches in halves, quarters, or sticks if you like and serve.

Chocolate-Almond or Other Nut Panini	Before adding the chocolate, spread the bread with almond butter or other nut butter. You'll need ¼ to ⅓ cup.
Chocolate-Strawberry Panini	Put a layer of strawberry slices over the chocolate before topping with the bread. Depending on the size of your bread slices and the size of the berries, you'll need 1 to 2 strawberries per sandwich.
Peanut Butter, Banana, and Chocolate Panini	Ooey gooey good: Spread creamy or crunchy peanut butter on the bread before adding the chocolate; you'll need ¼ to ⅓ cup. Then put a layer of thinly sliced banana over the chocolate before topping with the bread. One large banana is usually enough.

recipe continues →

9 OTHER IDEAS FOR DESSERT PANINI

1. Change up the chocolate: use white or milk chocolate, or use a specialty bar, like one infused with orange flavor.
2. Sprinkle the chocolate with raspberries or blueberries.
3. Add chopped caramels—and sprinkle with some sea salt if you like.
4. Sprinkle the chocolate with chopped nuts or coconut; and for even deeper flavor, toast them first.
5. Add a layer of thinly sliced marshmallows (to make your own, see page 512).
6. Spread one side of the bread with your favorite jam first.
7. Even better, with great crunch: Add a layer of toasted sliced almonds.
8. Sprinkle the chocolate with chopped candied ginger.
9. Add grated orange zest to the butter before spreading it on the bread.

D direct fire I indirect fire M make ahead V vegetarian option

Piña Colada Tacos

Makes: 4 servings	Time: 35 to 45 minutes, plus macerating time	Ⓓ Ⓜ Ⓥ

The fire concentrates pineapple's sweetness, while the toasted coconut adds crunch. This is also delicious made with cubes of fresh mango. You'll need 6-inch skewers.

½ ripe pineapple, peeled, cored, and cut into 1-inch cubes

¼ cup dark rum

¼ cup coconut milk

4 tablespoons (½ stick) butter, softened

4 7-inch flour tortillas

1 tablespoon sugar, or as needed

Lime wedges for serving (optional)

½ cup shredded coconut, toasted (see below)

1 Put the pineapple, rum, and coconut milk in a bowl and toss to combine. Let the fruit macerate for at least 20 minutes, or up to several hours in the refrigerator.

2 If using a gas grill, heat it for medium direct cooking. If using a charcoal grill, after taking dinner off, add more coals and close the lid until you're ready to cook. In either case, clean the grates. If you're using bamboo or wooden skewers, soak them in water for 30 minutes.

3 Spread the butter on both sides of the tortillas, then sprinkle with the sugar. Thread the pineapple cubes onto 4 skewers, letting excess marinade drip back in the bowl.

4 Put the skewers on the grill directly over the fire. Close the lid and cook until the pineapple is caramelized, 5 to 10 minutes per side, depending on how hot the fire is. Transfer the skewers to a platter. Put the tortillas on the grill directly over the fire, close the lid, and cook, turning once, until they lightly brown, 1 to 2 minutes per side.

5 To serve, put a skewer on top of each tortilla, squeeze with some lime if you like, and sprinkle with toasted coconut. To eat, pull out the skewer.

TOASTING COCONUT

Put shredded coconut in a dry skillet over medium-low heat and cook, shaking the pan several times, until golden brown, 5 to 10 minutes; keep an eye on it, as it can burn quickly.

Brown Sugar Pepita-Pineapple Tacos	Omit the coconut milk and rum marinade. Instead, toss the pineapple cubes with a mixture of ¼ cup brown sugar, 1 teaspoon ground cinnamon, and ¼ teaspoon ground cloves. Replace the coconut with chopped toasted shelled pumpkin seeds.
Mandarin Orange Tacos	Substitute 4 to 6 fresh mandarin or seedless clementine oranges for the pineapple and fresh orange juice for the coconut milk. In Step 5, sprinkle each taco with 1 tablespoon chopped fresh mint along with the toasted coconut, and for a Creamsicle effect, add a scoop of vanilla ice cream.
Mixed Berry Tacos	Substitute 1 pound hulled ripe strawberries for the pineapple (cut any very large berries in half) and toss with ¼ cup granulated sugar instead of the rum and coconut milk; the strawberries will only need about 2 minutes per side on the grill. In Step 5, substitute toasted sliced almonds for the coconut, sprinkle with 1 cup raspberries, blueberries, or a mix of the two, and serve with a dollop of whipped cream.

Fig and Sweetened Orange Ricotta Pizza

Makes: 4 pizzas (8 or more servings)	Time: 1½ hours or more if making your own dough, largely unattended	Ⓓ Ⓜ Ⓥ

Pizza for dessert? You bet. Especially when you grill it. To minimize the last-minute work, you can make the pizza dough and the sweetened ricotta the day before and refrigerate them. Then all you do is roll out the dough before dinner and have it waiting to go on the grill. It's easier to handle four smaller pizzas. Over-achievers can then put out all the flavor variations for a dessert buffet. If you find it difficult getting the topped pizzas onto the grill, try putting the crust on the grill first, then quickly applying the toppings before shutting the lid.

3 cups all-purpose or bread flour, plus more as needed

2 teaspoons instant yeast

2 teaspoons coarse kosher or sea salt

2 tablespoons good-quality olive oil

1 cup warm water, plus more as needed

1 cup ricotta cheese

2 tablespoons honey

1 tablespoon grated orange zest

½ teaspoon vanilla extract

8 fresh figs, stemmed and sliced

1 Whisk the flour, yeast, and salt together in a large bowl. Add the oil and water and mix with a heavy spoon. Continue to add water, 1 tablespoon at a time, until the dough forms a ball and is slightly sticky to the touch. In the unlikely event that the mixture gets too sticky, add flour 1 tablespoon at a time until you have the right consistency.

2 Turn the dough onto a lightly floured work surface and knead by hand for a minute until smooth, then form into a round ball. Put the dough in a bowl and cover with plastic wrap; let rise in a warm spot until it doubles in size, 1 to 2 hours. You can cut this rising time short if you're in a hurry, or you can let the dough rise more slowly, in the refrigerator, for up to 8 hours. (You can freeze the dough at this point for up to a month: Wrap it tightly in plastic or put in a zipper bag. Thaw in the refrigerator; bring to room temperature before shaping.)

3 To shape, divide the dough into 4 pieces; roll each piece into a ball. Put each ball on a lightly floured surface, sprinkle lightly with flour, and cover with plastic wrap or a clean dish towel. Let rest until slightly puffed, 25 to 30 minutes.

4 Whisk the ricotta, honey, orange zest, and vanilla together in a small bowl. Refrigerate until you're ready to use it.

5 If using a gas grill, heat it for medium direct cooking. If using a charcoal grill, after taking dinner off, add more coals and close the lid until you're ready to bake. In either case, clean the grates.

6 Roll or lightly press each ball into a flat round, lightly flouring the work surface and the dough as necessary; use only as much flour as you need to keep it from sticking. To stretch the dough, push down at the center and outward to the edges, turning the round as you work. Continue pushing down and out and turning the dough until the round is ¼ to ½ inch thick. Divide the ricotta mixture between the pizzas, spreading it to within 1 inch of the edge, then top with the sliced figs.

7 Put the pizzas on the grill directly over the fire. Close the lid and bake until the bottoms firm up and brown and the topping is cooked through, about 5 minutes; start checking after 3 minutes. The top of the dough will bubble up from the heat underneath but likely won't take on much color. Transfer to a board and use a pizza cutter or long, sharp knife to cut into wedges or small pieces and serve.

Sweetened Orange Ricotta Pizza with Dates and Pistachios	If you find fresh dates, here's where to use them: Instead of the figs, remove the pits from a dozen dates if they have them; slice the dates lengthwise. After spreading the pizzas with the ricotta, sprinkle with 1 cup chopped pistachios; scatter the dates on top. When the pizzas come off the grill, drizzle lightly with ¼ cup honey.
Chocolate-Cherry-Amaretto Pizza with Mascarpone	A little bit boozy and a lot indulgent: Soak 1 cup dried sweet cherries overnight (or longer) in ½ cup amaretto liqueur, to replace the figs. Substitute mascarpone for the ricotta and omit the orange zest. After spreading the pizzas with the mascarpone, drain the cherries and sprinkle them over; top with 4 ounces dark chocolate, chopped. Grill until the chocolate melts.
Chocolate-Banana Pizza with Toasted Walnuts and Coconut	Omit the orange zest. Substitute 1 to 2 sliced bananas (depends on their size) for the figs. In Step 6, sprinkle ½ cup toasted walnut halves over the bananas. When the pizzas come off the grill, sprinkle with ½ cup toasted shredded coconut and drizzle with 2 ounces melted dark chocolate.

Pain Perdu with Balsamic Strawberries

Makes: 4 servings	Time: 15 to 20 minutes	Ⓓ Ⓜ Ⓥ

Breakfast for dessert. Be sure to use sturdy slices of rich bread like challah or brioche, or a relatively tight-crumbed crusty country-style bread. Don't let the bread sit long in the egg mixture—get it in, get it out, and get it on the grill. The combination of strawberries, balsamic vinegar, and black pepper is classically Italian and is a nice foil to the rich, sweet bread.

3 cups sliced hulled strawberries (about 1½ pounds)

2–3 tablespoons sugar

1 tablespoon balsamic vinegar

2 eggs

½ cup milk

1 teaspoon vanilla extract

Pinch salt

4 slices bread

Black pepper (optional)

1 Put the strawberries in a bowl, sprinkle with 1 to 2 tablespoons of the sugar (depending on their sweetness), and toss gently to coat. Add the vinegar and toss again. Let macerate at room temperature until you're ready for dessert, up to several hours.

2 Beat the eggs lightly in a large shallow bowl, then beat in the milk, the remaining 1 tablespoon sugar, vanilla, and salt. Refrigerate until you're ready to use it (or up to several hours).

3 If using a gas grill, heat it for medium direct cooking. If using a charcoal grill, after taking dinner off, add more coals if necessary and close the lid until you're ready to cook. In either case, clean the grates.

4 Give each slice of bread a quick dip in the egg wash on both sides, put on a large plate, and immediately take out them to the grill. Put the bread on the grill directly over the fire. Close the lid and cook until the bread develops grill marks, 2 to 3 minutes per side. Transfer to a clean platter. To serve, top each grilled toast with a spoonful of the balsamic strawberries. Let diners add freshly ground black pepper to their strawberries, if they like.

Pain Perdu with Butter Pecan Ice Cream and Maple Syrup	Even quicker. A delicious mash-up of hot and cold: Omit the strawberries and vinegar. Top each grilled slice of bread with a scoop of butter pecan ice cream and a generous drizzle of maple syrup.
Pain Perdu with Apricot Preserves and Toasted Hazelnuts	Any jam-nut combo works: Omit the strawberries and vinegar. Top each grilled slice of bread with 1–2 tablespoons apricot preserves and 2 tablespoons chopped toasted hazelnuts.
Pain Perdu with Peaches and Blueberries	Replace the strawberries with 3 ripe peaches, peeled and sliced, and 1 cup blueberries; replace the vinegar and sugar for macerating with 2 tablespoons Grand Marnier or other liqueur (grappa is amazing if you like it). Garnish each serving with chopped fresh mint.

Pound Cake with Oranges and Toasted Coconut

| Makes: 6 to 9 servings | Time: 1¼ to 1½ hours, plus cooling time | Ⓓ Ⓜ Ⓥ |

You probably have heard of grilling store-bought pound cake, then topping it. But it's way better with homemade cake. As incentive, I'm providing a recipe and encouraging you to bake it a day or 2 in advance and let it get a little dry. (This is also a great use for leftover pound cake you might have made for another occasion.) Then all you have to do is macerate the oranges and toast the coconut earlier in the day. For a fine, more tender crumb, go with cake flour; for a coarser texture, choose all-purpose.

½ pound (2 sticks) butter, softened, plus more for the pan

2 cups cake or all-purpose flour

1½ teaspoons baking powder

¼ teaspoon freshly grated nutmeg (optional)

½ teaspoon salt

1 cup sugar, plus 1 tablespoon to sprinkle over the oranges

5 eggs

2 teaspoons vanilla extract

6 medium oranges, peeled, sectioned, and seeded if necessary

Grated zest and juice of 1 lime

½–¾ cup shredded coconut, toasted (see page 504)

2 tablespoons chopped fresh mint for garnish

1 Heat the oven to 325°F. Coat the inside of a 9- × 5-inch loaf pan with butter.

2 Whisk the flour, baking powder, nutmeg if you're using it, and salt together in a bowl.

3 Put the ½ pound butter in a large bowl; use an electric mixer to beat it until smooth. Add ¾ cup of the sugar and beat until it's well blended, then add another ¼ cup. Beat until the mixture is light in color and fluffy, scraping down the side of the bowl if necessary. Beat in the eggs one at a time. Add the vanilla and beat until blended. Add the dry ingredients and stir by hand just until smooth; do not overmix and do not beat.

4 Pour and scrape the batter into the prepared pan. Bake until a toothpick inserted into the center comes out clean, 1 to 1¼ hours.

5 Let the cake rest in the pan for 5 minutes, then invert it onto a wire rack. Remove the pan, then turn the cake right side up. Let cool completely. Store at room temperature, covered with wax paper, for up to 2 days.

6 Put the orange sections in a bowl and sprinkle with the remaining 1 tablespoon sugar and the lime zest and juice. Toss lightly to mix. Let macerate at room temperature for 30 minutes or up to several hours.

7 If using a gas grill, heat it for medium direct cooking. If using a charcoal grill, after taking dinner off, add more coals if necessary and close the lid until you're ready to cook. In either case, clean the grates.

8 Cut the pound cake into 1- to 1½-inch slices. Put them on the grill directly over the fire. Close the lid and cook, turning once, until the slices develop grill marks, 2 to 3 minutes per side. To serve, spoon the oranges over the cake with some of their liquid, sprinkle with the coconut, and garnish with the mint.

Polenta Pound Cake with Oranges and Toasted Coconut	Adds a welcome hint of corn flavor to the cake: Substitute cornmeal for 1 cup of the flour.
Yogurt Pound Cake with Oranges and Toasted Coconut	Lighter and even moister: Substitute ¾ cup yogurt for half of the butter.
Pound Cake with Peaches and Raspberries	So good when made with tree-ripened local peaches: Substitute 6 peaches, pitted and cut into wedges, for the oranges, and the zest and juice of a small navel orange for the lime. Just before serving, gently toss 4 ounces fresh raspberries with the peaches.

S'Mores with Homemade Marshmallows

Makes: 48 marshmallows, enough for 48 s'mores	Time: 1 hour, plus 4 hours or more for marshmallows to set up	

Anyone can put together s'mores—but making marshmallows from scratch takes them up a notch. You've got to have a candy thermometer and an electric mixer, but marshmallows aren't that hard to make, and the flavor and texture are far superior to the pucks in bags. Plus, it's a fun project that's sure to impress people of all ages.

Good-quality vegetable oil for the pan

3 1-ounce packages unflavored gelatin

2 cups granulated sugar

1 cup light corn syrup

¼ teaspoon salt

2 teaspoons vanilla extract

½ cup confectioners' sugar

½ cup cornstarch

Graham crackers and bar chocolate as needed for the s'mores

1 Lightly oil a 9- × 13-inch baking pan. Line the bottom and sides with parchment paper, then lightly oil the paper.

2 Put the gelatin in a large heatproof bowl and add ½ cup cold water. Stir to combine.

3 Put the granulated sugar, corn syrup, salt, and ½ cup water in a heavy medium-sized saucepan over high heat and clip a candy thermometer to the side of the pot. Bring the mixture to a boil, stirring just until the sugar dissolves. Once the syrup is boiling, do not stir; that can cause the sugar to crystallize. Let the syrup continue to boil until the temperature reaches 240°F. Immediately remove the pan from the heat. Slowly pour the hot syrup into the bowl with the softened gelatin, mixing continuously with an electric mixer, initially on low speed and then on high speed once all the syrup has been added. Be careful not to pour the syrup directly on the beaters and splatter scalding hot syrup everywhere. Beat until the mixture expands greatly in volume, becomes stiff, and cools, 10 to 12 minutes. Beat in the vanilla. Transfer the mixture to the prepared pan and spread it evenly with a rubber spatula. Let set, uncovered, at room temperature, until firm, at least 4 hours or overnight.

4 Mix the confectioners' sugar and cornstarch together and sift a third of it over a large cutting board. Turn the baking pan over onto the board, unmold the marshmallow onto the sugar mixture, and remove the parchment. Sift more of the cornstarch-sugar mixture over the marshmallow to coat. Cut across into 1½-inch-wide strips, and the strips into 1½-inch squares. Sift the remainder of the cornstarch-sugar mixture over the marshmallows and toss to coat them completely. Working in small batches, put them in a fine-mesh strainer and shake off the excess sugar coating. Store the marshmallows in an airtight container. (They'll keep for up to a couple of weeks.)

5 If using a gas grill, heat for hot direct cooking. If using a charcoal grill, after taking dinner off, add more coals if necessary and close the lid until you're ready to cook.

6 Skewer the marshmallows and toast them over the fire, turning until they're as brown as you like. Sandwich the hot marshmallow with a piece of chocolate between 2 graham crackers. Eat and repeat.

S'Mores with Homemade Orange Marshmallows	Orange and chocolate are made for one another: Substitute 1 teaspoon orange extract for the vanilla and add 2 tablespoons grated orange zest with it.
S'Mores with Homemade Brown Sugar–Bourbon Marshmallows	These are for the grown-ups: Decrease the granulated sugar to 1 cup and the corn syrup to ½ cup. Add 1 cup dark brown sugar and ½ cup bourbon along with them.
S'Mores with Homemade Espresso Marshmallows	For a little pick-me-up: Add 2 tablespoons instant espresso in Step 3 along with the sugar, corn syrup, salt, and water. Omit the vanilla.

Molten Chocolate Cake

Makes: 8 to 10 servings	Time: 25 to 30 minutes, plus cooling time	Ⓓ Ⓜ Ⓥ

Molten chocolate cake has become a classic restaurant dessert, and it's an even bigger hit at home and on the grill—super-easy, fast, dramatic, and loved by all. This is a simplified adaptation of my friend Jean-Georges Vongerichten's recipe. Have ice cream handy to melt over the tops of the slices at the table.

½ pound (2 sticks) butter, plus softened butter for the pan

8 ounces dark chocolate, chopped

4 eggs

4 egg yolks

½ cup sugar

4 teaspoons all-purpose flour

½ teaspoon salt

1 Generously coat the inside of a 9- or 10-inch cast-iron skillet with softened butter; make sure not to miss any spots, or the cake will stick.

2 Put the ½ pound butter in a heatproof bowl and melt it in the microwave or over hot water in a double boiler. Add the chocolate to the hot butter and stir until it's melted.

3 Put the whole eggs and egg yolks in another bowl. Add the sugar and beat with an electric mixer on high speed (or enthusiastically with a whisk) until light and thick, about 1 minute. On low speed (or whisking) beat the egg mixture, flour, and salt into the melted chocolate and butter until combined. Pour the batter into the prepared pan. (At this point you can refrigerate the batter for up to 3 hours; take the pan out of the refrigerator 30 minutes before you intend to bake it.)

4 If using a gas grill, heat for medium direct cooking. The grill temperature should be 500° to 600°F; it could mean all the burners are on medium or medium-low, depending on your particular grill. (See "High-Temperature Baking on the Grill," page 500.) If using a charcoal grill, after taking off dinner, add more coals if necessary and close the lid until you're ready to bake.

5 Put the pan on the grill directly over the fire. Close the lid and grill-bake until the cake puffs up around the edge but the center still jiggles slightly when shaken, 5 to 15 minutes. (It's better to underbake than to overbake the cake; start checking it after 3 minutes.) Let sit for at least 10 minutes before slicing, or the insides will ooze all over the pan.

Molten Chocolate-Raspberry Cake	Mash ½ cup raspberry preserves with 1 cup fresh raspberries. Pour two-thirds of the cake batter into the skillet, dollop the raspberry mash over the top, then cover with the remaining chocolate batter. Bake as directed.
Molten Chocolate–Peanut Butter Cake	Like a luxurious molten peanut butter cup: Combine 2 tablespoons melted butter with ½ cup peanut butter. Stir in ½ cup confectioners' sugar to combine. Pour two-thirds of the cake batter into the skillet, dollop the peanut butter filling over the top, then cover with the remaining batter. Bake as directed.
Molten Chocolate-Marshmallow Cake	S'mores without the graham cracker; if you've got leftover marshmallows from the recipe on page 512, all you need to do is chop them into small pieces: Pour two-thirds of the cake batter into the skillet, sprinkle with 1½ cups miniature marshmallows, then cover with the remaining batter. Bake as directed.

Plum Upside-Down Cake

Makes: **At least 8 servings**	Time: **25 to 30 minutes**	Ⓓ Ⓜ Ⓥ

One of my favorite cakes, and a revelation on the grill. In about half the time it would take to bake in the oven, the crumb becomes tender and moist, the top puffs and turns golden brown, and the fruit topping starts bubbling. For timing as part of a barbecue meal, prepare it through Step 2. Then all you need to do is stir the flour into the buttermilk mixture, spread the batter over the fruit in the skillet, and pop it on the grill when it's freed up. I like this best served warm with whipped cream.

8 tablespoons (1 stick) butter

½ cup brown sugar

1½ pounds small ripe red plums, halved and pitted (if the plums are large and/or hard, slice them to make sure they cook through)

1 cup buttermilk

2 eggs

½ cup granulated sugar

2 cups all-purpose flour

1 teaspoon baking soda

¼ teaspoon salt

1 Melt 4 tablespoons (½ stick) of the butter in a 9- or 10-inch cast-iron skillet over low heat; remove from the heat. Sprinkle the brown sugar evenly over the bottom of the pan and arrange the plums in a single layer over the brown sugar, cut side down.

2 Melt the remaining 4 tablespoons (½ stick) butter. Add it to the buttermilk, eggs, and granulated sugar in a medium-sized bowl and whisk until foamy. In a large bowl, whisk the flour, baking soda, and salt. (You can make the cake ahead to this point. If not grilling within 30 minutes, refrigerate the buttermilk mixture.)

3 If using a gas grill, heat it for medium-high direct cooking. The grill temperature should be 500° to 600°F; it could mean all the burners are on medium or medium-low, depending on your particular grill. (See "High-Temperature Baking on the Grill," page 500.) If using a charcoal grill, after taking dinner off, add more coals if necessary and close the lid until you're ready to bake.

4 When you're ready to bake, gradually add the egg mixture to the dry ingredients and stir until well incorporated. Spoon the batter over the plums and spread gently with a spatula until it's evenly thick.

5 Put the skillet on the grill directly over the fire. Close the lid and bake for 10 minutes, then check. If the cake seems to be browning too fast, turn the heat off under the pan and turn it up on the other burners on a gas grill, or move the pan to a cooler part of the charcoal grill. Close the lid and keep checking every few minutes until the top of the cake is golden brown and a toothpick inserted into the center comes out clean, 5 to 15 minutes more, depending on how hot the fire is. Carefully transfer the skillet to a rack and let the cake cool for no more than 5 minutes.

6 Run a knife around the edge to loosen the cake. Put a serving plate on top of the skillet and carefully invert the hot pan over the plate. The cake should fall out. If it sticks, turn it right side up again, run the knife along the edge again, and use a spatula to gently lift around the edge. Invert again and tap. Remove any stuck fruit from the bottom of the pan with a knife and fit it back into any gaps on the top of the cake.

Pineapple Upside-Down Cake	The original: Instead of the plums, trim, peel, and core 1 fresh pineapple; cut the flesh into ½-inch chunks. Use enough to cover the pan in a single layer; you can save the rest for breakfast.
Pear-Almond Upside-Down Cake	Add a nutty crunch to the gooey cake; small Seckel pears look elegant, but full-sized pears work too: Substitute 3 or 4 peeled, halved, and cored ripe pears for the plums. Substitute ½ cup ground almonds for ½ cup of the flour. Sprinkle ¼ cup toasted sliced almonds over the top before serving.
Gingery Peach Upside-Down Cake	Sweet meets spicy: Sprinkle 3 tablespoons chopped candied ginger over the bottom of the skillet along with the brown sugar and substitute 3 or 4 pitted and sliced ripe peaches for the plums. Add 1 teaspoon ground ginger to the dry ingredients.

Lemony Blueberry Cornmeal Cake

Makes: 8 to 10 servings	Time: 30 to 45 minutes	

In 10 minutes, you can be on your way to the perfect ending to a summer meal. Just put this cake on to grill-bake when you sit down to eat—or bake it before you put your entrée on the grill—and it will be cooled by the time you're ready for dessert. Everything about it is vibrant, and the berries stain the yellow cake violet.

12 tablespoons (1½ sticks) butter, melted, plus softened butter for the pan

1¼ cups all-purpose flour (or cake flour for a finer crumb)

¾ cup yellow cornmeal

2 teaspoons baking powder

½ teaspoon baking soda

½ teaspoon salt

1 cup sugar

4 eggs

1 teaspoon vanilla extract

2 tablespoons grated lemon zest

⅓ cup fresh lemon juice

1¼ cups buttermilk

2 cups fresh or frozen (don't bother to thaw) blueberries, picked over for stems

1 If using a gas grill, heat it for medium-high direct cooking. The grill temperature should be 500° to 600°F; it could mean all the burners are on medium or medium-low, depending on your particular grill. (See "High-Temperature Baking on the Grill," page 500.) If using a charcoal grill, after taking dinner off, add more coals if necessary and close the lid until you're ready to bake. Generously coat the inside of a 9- or 10-inch cast-iron skillet with softened butter.

2 Whisk the flour, cornmeal, baking powder, soda, and salt together in a bowl. Whisk the sugar, eggs, vanilla, and lemon zest and juice together in a large bowl until thick. Add the melted butter. Fold the dry mixture into the wet, without fully incorporating; there should still be some lumps of flour. Add the buttermilk and stir until the mixture is combined. Pour the batter into the prepared pan and scatter the blueberries evenly over the top.

3 Put the skillet on the grill directly over the fire. Close the lid and start checking after 10 minutes. If the cake seems to be browning too fast, turn the heat off under the pan and turn it up on the other burners for a gas grill, or move the pan to a cooler part of the charcoal grill. Bake until the cake pulls away from the side of the pan and a toothpick inserted into the center comes out clean or with a few moist crumbs, 5 to 20 minutes more, depending on how hot the fire is.

4 Carefully transfer the pan to a rack and let cool until you can comfortably touch the pan. Run a knife around the edges of the cake. Put a serving plate on top of the pan and carefully invert it onto the plate. Or cut and serve the cake directly from the pan. This will keep, out of the pan and covered with plastic wrap, at room temperature for up to few days, if it lasts that long.

• recipe continues →

D direct fire **I** indirect fire **M** make ahead **V** vegetarian option

Lemony Cornmeal Cake with Fresh Herbs	Simple and satisfying. Thyme, rosemary, and lavender are all wonderful: Add 1 tablespoon chopped fresh herbs of your choice to the wet ingredients with the zest.
Cranberry Cornmeal Cake with Ricotta	The creaminess helps balance the tart cranberries: Substitute orange juice and zest for the lemon, ricotta cheese for the buttermilk, and fresh or frozen cranberries for the blueberries.
Almond-Cherry Cornmeal Cake	Omit the lemon juice and zest. Substitute almond extract for $\frac{1}{2}$ teaspoon of the vanilla and chopped pitted sweet cherries for the blueberries.

D direct fire   I indirect fire   M make ahead   V vegetarian option

Orange-Nut Zucchini Quick Bread

Makes: 8 to 10 servings	Time: 25 to 40 minutes	Ⓓ Ⓜ Ⓥ

A lightly sweetened olive oil zucchini bread makes an unexpected foundation for ice cream. To eat it warm, have the wet and dry ingredients each combined—but still separate—up to hours before dinner. When the entrée comes off the grill, mix the batter, pour it into the prepared pan, and away you go. Keep an eye on it and be prepared to move the pan around on the grates, as it will bake fast.

½ cup good-quality olive oil, plus more for the pan

2 cups all-purpose flour

1 cup sugar

1½ teaspoons baking powder

½ teaspoon baking soda

1 teaspoon salt

1 tablespoon grated orange zest

¾ cup fresh orange juice

2 eggs

1 cup grated zucchini

½ cup chopped pecans or walnuts

1 If using a gas grill, heat it for medium-high direct cooking. The grill temperature should be 500° to 600°F; it could mean all the burners are on medium or medium-low, depending on your particular grill. (See "High-Temperature Baking on the Grill," page 500.) If using a charcoal grill, after taking dinner off, add more coals if necessary and close the lid until you're ready to bake. Rub the inside of a 9- or 10-inch cast-iron skillet with oil.

2 Whisk the flour, sugar, baking powder and soda, and salt together in a large bowl. Put the ½ cup oil,

orange zest and juice, and eggs in a separate bowl; whisk to combine. (You can prepare the recipe to this point up to several hours ahead; refrigerate the egg mixture.)

3 Pour the wet mixture into the dry ingredients; stir just enough to combine. Don't overmix; it's okay if the batter has lumps. Fold in the zucchini and nuts. Pour the batter into the prepared pan.

4 Put the pan on the grill directly over the fire. Close the lid and grill-bake for 7 minutes. If the top is brown and the sides have pulled away but the bread still isn't cooked through in the center, turn the heat off under the pan and turn it up on the other burners for a gas grill, or move the pan to a cooler part of the charcoal grill. Bake, checking frequently, until the top is golden brown, the bread has pulled away from the pan, and a toothpick inserted into a couple of different places comes out almost entirely clean, 3 to 10 minutes more, depending on how hot the fire is.

5 Carefully transfer to a rack to cool for at least 15 minutes. You can cut and serve this right out of the pan. Wrapped, it will keep at room temperature for a couple days.

• recipe continues →

Vegan Zucchini Bread	Substitute 2 tablespoons ground flaxseed mixed with 6 tablespoons water for the eggs; let sit for at least 3 minutes until it has a gel-like consistency before whisking it with the other wet ingredients.
Carrot-Ginger Bread	Substitute grated carrots for the zucchini. Whisk 1 teaspoon ground ginger into the dry ingredients. Fold up to ½ cup chopped candied ginger into the batter if you like along with the carrots.
Chocolate Zucchini Bread	A strange-sounding but winning combination: Stir 4 ounces dark chocolate, chopped, into the batter along with the zucchini.

D direct fire I indirect fire M make ahead V vegetarian option

Double Orange Olive Oil Cake

Makes: 8 to 12 servings	Time: 40 to 60 minutes	Ⓓ Ⓜ Ⓥ

Like several of the cake recipes in this chapter, here you can prepare the pan and combine the dry ingredients and wet ingredients in separate bowls, then wait to mix up the batter until after dinner comes off the grill, or you can grill-bake it before putting the entrée on to cook; it'll still be warm when you're ready for dessert. This is delicious topped with vanilla ice cream—it gives a kind of orange Popsicle effect.

1 cup plus 1 tablespoon good-quality olive oil

2 cups all-purpose flour

1 teaspoon baking powder

½ teaspoon baking soda

¾ teaspoon salt

1 cup sugar

4 eggs

½ cup milk

1 tablespoons grated orange zest

¼ cup fresh orange juice

1 If using a gas grill, heat it for medium-high direct cooking. The grill temperature should be 500° to 600°F; it could mean all the burners are on medium or medium-low, depending on your particular grill. (See "High-Temperature Baking on the Grill," page 500.) If using a charcoal grill, after taking dinner off, add more coals if necessary and close the lid until you're ready to bake. Generously coat the inside of a 9- or 10-inch cast-iron skillet with 1 tablespoon of the oil.

2 Whisk the flour, baking powder and soda, and salt together in a bowl. Whisk the remaining 1 cup oil, the sugar, eggs, milk, and orange zest and juice together in a large bowl until well combined. Fold in the dry ingredients and stir until well combined, with no large lumps of flour. Pour the batter into the prepared pan.

3 Put the skillet on the grill directly over the fire. Close the lid and start checking after 15 minutes. If the cake seems to be browning too fast, turn the heat off under the pan and turn it up on the other burners for a gas grill, or move the pan to a cooler part of the charcoal grill. Bake, checking every 5 minutes or so, until a toothpick inserted into the center comes out clean, 5 to 15 minutes more, depending on how hot the fire is.

4 Carefully transfer the cake to a rack and let cool for at least 15 minutes before slicing and serving from the pan. This will keep at room temperature, out of the pan and covered with plastic wrap, for up to 4 days.

● recipe continues →

Rum-Soaked Double Orange Olive Oil Cake	For the grown-ups. You can further change up the flavor by using white or dark rum: Make the soak at least an hour or up to 2 days before the cake comes off the grill; if you make the soak more than a couple of hours in advance, refrigerate it, then bring to room temp before using. Put ½ cup sugar, 2 tablespoons butter, and 1 tablespoon vanilla extract in a small saucepan and cook over the lowest heat possible, stirring frequently, until the sugar has melted and the liquid has thickened slightly, 8 to 10 minutes. Let cool, then stir in ½ cup rum. When the cake comes off the grill, immediately pour the soak over the cake; let it sit until you are ready to serve.
Almond Olive Oil Cake	Wonderful topped with berries or cherries: Omit the orange zest and juice. Increase the milk to ¾ cup. Add ½ teaspoon almond extract to the wet ingredients and fold ½ cup sliced almonds into the finished batter.
Grapefruit Olive Oil Cake	Substitute grapefruit zest and juice for the orange.

D direct fire   I indirect fire   M make ahead   V vegetarian option

Chocolate Bread Pudding

| Makes: 8 to 10 servings | Time: 25 to 30 minutes, plus soaking time | Ⓓ Ⓜ Ⓥ |

The secret to a good bread pudding—golden brown and puffed on top and tender, almost creamy on the inside—is to give the bread enough time to fully absorb the mix of milk, cream, and eggs you pour over it. Of course, you can make that time work to your advantage, and assemble and refrigerate it hours in advance. Then put it on the grill as soon as your entrée comes off.

2 tablespoons butter, melted, plus more for the pan

1 cup milk

1 cup cream

1 teaspoon vanilla extract

3 eggs, beaten

½ cup brown sugar

Pinch salt

6 cups bite-sized pieces bread (preferably stale; you can use any kind of bread you like—though I would pass on rye or pumpernickel—and remove the crusts if they are thick)

4 ounces bittersweet chocolate, roughly chopped

1 Generously coat the inside of a 9- or 10-inch cast-iron skillet with butter.

2 Whisk the milk and cream together in a large bowl. Whisk in the melted butter, then the vanilla and eggs. Whisk in the brown sugar and salt. Add the bread and push the pieces down into the mixture so the custard covers them. Stir in the chocolate. At this point, you can leave it in the bowl until the bread has been fully soaked with the custard, or pour it into the prepared pan; allow at least 15 to 30 minutes or up to several hours in the refrigerator.

3 If using a gas grill, heat it for medium-high direct cooking. The grill temperature should be 500° to 600°F; it could mean all the burners are on medium or medium-low, depending on your particular grill. (See "High-Temperature Baking on the Grill," page 500.) If using a charcoal grill, after taking dinner off, add more coals if necessary and close the lid until you're ready to bake.

4 Put the pan on the grill directly over the fire. Close the lid and grill-bake for 10 minutes, then check it. If the pudding seems to be browning too fast, turn the heat off under the pan and turn it up on the other burners for a gas grill, or move the pan to a cooler part of the charcoal grill. Bake, checking every few minutes, until the edge of the pudding puffs up and pulls away from the pan, the top turns golden brown, and a knife inserted in the center comes out clean, 5 to 20 minutes more, depending on how hot the fire is. Carefully transfer the pan to a rack and let cool 10 to 15 minutes before cutting into wedges and serving.

recipe continues →

Chocolate-Banana-Walnut Bread Pudding	This might remind people of Chunky Monkey ice cream, and if not, you'll still like it: First mash 2 ripe bananas to a smooth purée, then whisk in the milk and cream and continue. Add ½ cup chopped walnuts along with the chocolate.
Chocolate-Cherry-Almond Bread Pudding	Add ½ cup each dried sweet cherries and toasted sliced almonds along with the chocolate.
Rum-Raisin Bread Pudding	Add ¼ cup dark or spiced rum along with the vanilla. Substitute ½ cup raisins for the chocolate.

D direct fire   **I** indirect fire   **M** make ahead   **V** vegetarian option

Cherry Clafoutis

| Makes: **6 to 8 servings** | Time: **20 to 25 minutes** | Ⓓ Ⓜ Ⓥ |

This custardy dessert (pronounced kla-FOO-tee), similar to a German pancake, is an excellent way to enjoy all sorts of fruit in season. As with the cakes, you'll need a flameproof skillet, like cast iron or stainless steel; you can't use the traditional ceramic baking dish. For advance prep, have the fruit in the pan and the batter in the refrigerator, mixed up and ready to go.

3 eggs

½ cup granulated sugar

1 teaspoon vanilla extract

¼ teaspoon salt

½ cup all-purpose flour

1 cup milk

1 tablespoon butter, softened

3 cups pitted sweet cherries

Confectioners' sugar for serving

1 Whisk the eggs and granulated sugar together in a medium bowl until thick. Add the vanilla and salt. Whisk in the flour; don't worry if you see little bits of it in the batter. Beat in half the milk until combined, then the rest. Refrigerate the batter until you're ready to use it.

2 Coat the inside of a 10-inch cast-iron skillet with the butter. Pour the cherries into the pan in a single layer. Leave at room temperature until you are ready to bake the clafoutis.

3 If using a gas grill, heat it for medium-high direct cooking. The grill temperature should be 500° to 600°F; it could mean all the burners are on medium or medium-low, depending on your particular grill. (See "High-Temperature Baking on the Grill," page 500). If using a charcoal grill, after taking dinner off, add more coals if necessary and close the lid until you're ready to bake.

4 Pour the batter over the cherries and give the pan a little shake to even everything out. Put the pan on the grill directly over the fire. Close the lid and bake for 7 minutes, then check on its progress. If the pudding seems to be browning too fast, turn the heat off under the pan and turn it up on the other burners for a gas grill, or move the pan to a cooler part of the charcoal grill. Continue to bake, checking every few minutes, until the edge puffs up and pulls away from the pan and the center is set, 3 to 12 minutes more, depending on how hot the fire is. Carefully transfer the pan to a rack and let cool for a few minutes. Sift a little confectioners' sugar over the top, then cut into wedges or spoon out of the pan and serve.

● recipe continues →

Pear or Apple Clafoutis	You won't be able to do this too far ahead or the fruit will discolor. Substitute 4 cups thinly sliced peeled pears or apples (about 2 pounds) for the cherries. Toss the slices with 2 tablespoons sugar before arranging them in the pan.
Berry Clafoutis	Substitute fresh blueberries, blackberries, raspberries, quartered strawberries, or a mix of berries for the cherries.
Grape Clafoutis	Unusual but very good: Substitute grapes for the cherries—any kind, including Concord, green, or red. If you want to add a little smoke flavor to the clafoutis, set the grapes, still on their stems, on the grill directly over the fire (make sure the grates are clean) until they develop grill marks in places, 3 to 4 minutes. Turn the whole bunch over and grill another 3 to 4 minutes, then remove the grapes from the stems. Pit the grapes if necessary and proceed with the recipe.

Apple Crisp

Makes: 6 to 8 servings	Time: 25 to 30 minutes	D M V

You can make a crisp with any kind of fruit; apple is the default and perfect for fall. Prepare the crumble topping in advance and keep it in the refrigerator. Have the fruit ready, then assemble the dessert in the pan right before putting it on the grill.

5 tablespoons cold butter, cut into bits, plus softened butter for the pan

⅔ cup brown sugar

½ cup rolled oats (not instant)

½ cup all-purpose flour

Pinch salt

6 cups sliced cored apples (2 to 2¼ pounds; peeling is optional)

Juice of ½ lemon

1 Put the cold butter, all but 1 tablespoon of the brown sugar, the oats, flour, and salt in a food processor and pulse a few times, until everything is combined but not too finely ground. (To mix by hand, mash it together between your fingers.) Transfer the topping to a bowl and refrigerate until you're ready to use it.

2 Generously coat the inside of a 10-inch cast-iron skillet with softened butter. Toss the apples with the lemon juice and remaining tablespoon brown sugar in a large bowl. When you're ready to grill, spread them out in the prepared pan in an even layer. (You can leave them in the bowl, cover, and refrigerate until you're ready to bake.)

3 If using a gas grill, heat it for medium direct cooking. If using a charcoal grill, after taking dinner off, add more coals if necessary and close the lid until you're ready to bake.

4 When you're ready for dessert, crumble the topping evenly over the apples. Put the skillet on the grill directly over the fire. Close the lid and bake for 5 minutes, then check. If the topping seems to be browning too fast, turn the heat off under the pan and turn it up on the other burners for a gas grill, or move the pan to a cooler part of the charcoal grill. Bake, checking every few minutes, until the topping is browned and the apples are tender, 5 to 20 minutes more. Carefully transfer to a rack and let cool until you are ready to serve.

Raspberry or Blueberry and Peach Crisp	Substitute 2 cups raspberries or blueberries and 4 cups sliced peeled peaches for the apples. Toss the fruit with 2 tablespoons cornstarch along with the lemon juice to help thicken the juices.
Ginger-Plum Crisp	Add 1 teaspoon ground ginger to the topping with the flour. Substitute sliced pitted plums for the apples, and add 2 tablespoons chopped candied ginger along with the lemon juice.
Strawberry-Rhubarb Crisp	Substitute 2 cups hulled and halved strawberries and 2 cups chopped rhubarb stalks for the apples, increase the brown sugar to ¼ cup, and add 2 tablespoons cornstarch along with the lemon juice to help thicken the juices.

---

4 DIFFERENT WAYS TO MAKE THE CRUMB TOPPING FOR A CRISP

In addition to varying the fruit you use to make your crisp, you can change up the topping.

1. **Make it gluten free:** Substitute ¼ cup each rice flour and almond flour for the all-purpose flour; decrease the brown sugar to ⅓ cup.
2. **Make it nutty:** Add ½ cup chopped walnuts or pecans.
3. **Give it some spice:** Add ½ teaspoon ground cinnamon or five-spice powder.
4. **Take it tropical:** Add ½ cup shredded coconut.

Banana with Chocolate and Crushed Peanut Brittle

Makes: 1 serving	Time: 10 to 15 minutes	Ⓓ Ⓥ

The banana peel becomes a cooking vessel on the grill. Slit it lengthwise down one side, then all kinds of sweet things can happen inside. The whole package goes over direct heat—you can even put it on a piece of foil set right on top of coals, if you like. Eat it straight from the peel, or spoon it out as a ready-made topping over ice cream. You can have the banana stuffed and ready to go before lighting the fire.

1 tablespoon butter, softened

2 tablespoons crushed or chopped peanut brittle

2 tablespoons chopped dark chocolate

1 ripe banana (you want a yellow or darker banana)

Ice cream of your choice (optional)

1 If using a gas grill, heat it for medium direct cooking. If using a charcoal grill, after taking dinner off, add more coals if necessary and close the lid until you're ready to cook. In either case, clean the grates.

2 Put the butter, peanut brittle, and chocolate in a small bowl and mash together. Slit the banana from top to bottom along one side, through the top peel but not the bottom peel. Pull the banana open enough so you can push the filling into the slit.

3 Put the banana on the grill directly over the fire, slit side up. Close the lid and cook until the peel turns black, about 5 minutes. Transfer to a plate.

4 To serve, eat right from the peel or spoon over ice cream, angel food cake, or vanilla pudding.

Banana with Brown Sugar and Toasted Pecans	The taste of pralines: Substitute chopped toasted pecans for the peanut brittle and brown sugar for the chocolate. For a double dose of pecan, serve over butter pecan ice cream.
Banana with Marshmallow, Chocolate, and Toasted Walnuts	Banana rocky road: Substitute chopped toasted walnuts for the peanut brittle and add 2 tablespoons chopped or mini marshmallows. One regular-sized marshmallow should be enough for each banana. Kitchen shears making "chopping" it easy; oil the blades, then snip it into small pieces.
Plantain with Honey, Toasted Coconut, and Cashews	Substitute 1 very ripe plantain (the skin should be black) for the banana, chopped cashews for the peanut brittle, and toasted shredded coconut for the chocolate; add 1 tablespoon honey. Grill until fork-tender, about 8 minutes.

Pineapple–Star Fruit Skewers with Orange-Clove Syrup

Makes: 4 servings	Time: 30 to 35 minutes, plus infusing time	D M V

Infused simple syrup is an easy way to add spices to desserts. Here it adds spark to fruit skewers, but you can also brush it on slices of pound cake headed for the grill (page 510). Another candidate for make-ahead: The syrup can be made earlier in the day or week, and the skewers assembled several hours ahead and refrigerated. These are nice served with lightly whipped cream for dipping.

½ cup sugar

Zest of 1 large orange, taken off in strips

1 tablespoon whole cloves

1 small pineapple

2 star fruit

1 Put the sugar, orange zest, cloves, and ½ cup water in a small saucepan over medium heat; stir until the sugar dissolves. Bring to a boil, reduce the heat, and gently bubble for 5 to 10 minutes. Remove from the heat and let sit for at least 30 minutes and up to several hours to let the flavor develop. When you are happy with the flavor of the syrup, strain it and use or refrigerate in an airtight container; it will keep for at least a week.

2 If using a gas grill, heat it for medium direct cooking. If using a charcoal grill, after taking dinner off, add more coals if necessary and close the lid until you're ready to cook. In either case, clean the grates. If you're using bamboo or wooden skewers, soak them in water for 30 minutes.

3 Trim, peel, and core the pineapple, then cut it into 2-inch chunks. Cut the star fruit into ½-inch-thick slices. Skewer the fruit; using 2 skewers makes them easier to turn. Skewer the star fruit through the points of the star on two sides. Brush lightly with the orange-clove syrup.

4 Put the skewers on the grill directly over the fire. Close the lid and cook, turning once, until the pineapple chunks brown in spots, 4 to 8 minutes per side, depending on how hot the fire is; brush the fruit several times with the syrup while it grills. When the fruit is done, brush it once more with syrup. Transfer to a platter and serve hot or warm.

Pineapple-Mango Skewers with Coconut Syrup	Substitute ¼ cup shredded coconut for the zest and cloves. Replace the star fruit with 2 mangoes, peeled, the flesh cut from the pits in 2-inch lengths.
Strawberry-Watermelon Skewers with Lime-Ginger Syrup	Replace the orange zest and cloves with 1 inch thinly sliced fresh ginger (don't bother to peel) and the zest of 1 lime. Substitute 1 small watermelon (preferably seedless) for the pineapple and 2 cups hulled strawberries (cut any large ones in half) for the star fruit.
Melon Skewers with Fresh Mint Syrup	I say cantaloupe, but really any melon is lovely like this: Substitute ¼ cup lightly packed fresh mint leaves for the zest and cloves, adding them after you remove the syrup from the heat. Substitute 2 peeled and seeded cantaloupes for the pineapple and star fruit.

9 OTHER SIMPLE SYRUPS TO MAKE

When making the simple syrup, add these ingredients to the sugar and water; after bringing to a boil, let stand at least 30 minutes and up to several hours to let the flavors develop, then strain. Use the syrup to brush fruit or slices of cake before grilling.

1. **Star Anise Syrup.** Add 5 star anise pods
2. **Clove–Black Pepper Syrup.** Add 2 tablespoons each whole cloves and black peppercorns
3. **Cardamom Syrup.** Add 5 green cardamom pods, crushed with the flat side of a knife
4. **Lemon-Mint Syrup.** Before the syrup cools, stir in ¼ cup fresh mint leaves and the zest of 1 lemon, taken off in strips with a vegetable peeler
5. **Coffee Syrup.** Substitute brewed strong coffee or espresso for all or some of the water
6. **Vanilla Syrup.** Before cooling the syrup, add the seeds from a vanilla bean, along with the scraped pod
7. **Cinnamon Syrup.** Add 3 cinnamon sticks before heating the sugar and water
8. **Tea Syrup.** Before cooling the syrup, add 2 tablespoons loose tea leaves or the contents of 1 tea bag
9. **Orange-Rosemary Syrup.** Add 2 sprigs fresh rosemary before heating the sugar and water Before the syrup cools, add the zest of 1 orange, taken off in strips with a vegetable peeler

Figs with Walnuts and Honey

Makes: 4 servings	Time: 25 to 35 minutes	D M V

Yet another dessert to prep ahead: Have the figs stuffed and ready to go before guests arrive.

8 ripe figs, stemmed

2 tablespoons walnut oil or good-quality olive oil

8 walnut halves, toasted

¼ cup honey

1 Brush the figs with the walnut oil, then cut an X in the stem ends. Push 1 walnut half into each fig.

2 If using a gas grill, heat it for medium direct cooking. If using a charcoal grill, after taking dinner off, add more coals if necessary and close the lid until you're ready to cook. In either case, clean the grates.

3 Put the figs on the grill directly over the fire, stem side up. Close the lid and cook until the fruit softens, 5 to 10 minutes. Transfer to a platter, drizzle with the honey, and serve.

TOASTING NUTS

Spread the nuts in an even layer in a dry skillet over medium heat and toast, shaking the pan occasionally, until golden brown, 8 to 12 minutes, depending on the type of nut. Immediately remove from the skillet to keep them from continuing to color.

Figs with Cinnamon Sugar and Walnuts	Based very loosely on a Turkish dessert made with poached dried figs: Substitute ½ cup ground walnuts for the walnut halves; add ¼ cup sugar and 1 teaspoon ground cinnamon to them, stirring to mix completely. Omit the honey. Brush the figs with the oil but don't cut into them; instead, dredge them in the walnut-sugar mixture until completely coated. Grill as directed, taking care not to let the coating burn.
Figs with Almonds and Honey	Substitute almond oil for the walnut oil and ½ cup toasted sliced almonds for the walnut halves. Don't cut into the figs. After you drizzle the grilled figs with the honey, sprinkle with the almonds.
Maple Figs with Orange Zest	Serve with a dollop of ricotta or mascarpone cheese: Use olive oil, and don't cut into the figs. Use a mixture of 3 tablespoons maple syrup and 1 tablespoon fresh orange juice instead of the honey. After drizzling, garnish with 1 tablespoon grated orange zest.

Breads and Desserts

Sugared Peaches with Candied Ginger Ice Cream

Makes: 4 servings	Time: 30 to 40 minutes	Ⓓ Ⓜ Ⓥ

A quick brush with butter and a dredge in sugar turns into a light burnt-caramel crust on the grill. Top each peach half with vanilla ice cream studded with candied ginger bits and you've got something simple but special. The size of the peaches will determine how many you need. For peaches weighing in at 8 ounces each or less, figure 1 peach per person; for peaches 12 ounces or more, one peach half makes for a generous dessert serving.

1 pint vanilla ice cream, softened just a bit

¼ cup chopped candied ginger

2 or 4 ripe peaches, depending on their size

4 tablespoons (½ stick) butter, melted

¼ cup Demerara sugar, or more as needed

Fresh mint sprigs for garnish

1 Put the ice cream and ginger in a bowl and mash together with a wooden spoon until the ginger is mixed throughout the ice cream. This can be done several days ahead; put it back in the ice cream container and freeze at least a couple hours.

2 If using a gas grill, heat it for medium direct cooking. If using a charcoal grill, after taking dinner off, add more coals if necessary and close the lid until you're ready to cook. In either case, clean the grates.

3 When you're ready for dessert, cut the peaches in half through the stem end and remove the pits. Brush with the melted butter. Put the sugar on a plate and dredge the cut side of each peach in it.

4 Put the peaches on the grill directly over the fire, cut side up. Close the lid and cook until they soften, 10 to 15 minutes depending on their size and ripeness. Turn them cut side down and cook until the sugar caramelizes to a golden brown, 2 to 5 minutes. Transfer to a platter. To serve, put the warm peaches on plates or in dessert bowls, cut side up. Divide the ice cream between them, or pass the ice cream at the table. Garnish with the mint.

● recipe continues →

Ⓓ direct fire   Ⓘ indirect fire   Ⓜ make ahead   Ⓥ vegetarian option

Honeyed Nectarines with Toasted Almond Whipped Cream	Omit the gingered ice cream, butter, and Demerara sugar. Instead, put 1 cup heavy cream in a bowl and whip to soft peaks with an electric mixer. Add 1 tablespoon granulated sugar and 1 teaspoon almond extract and continue to whip until incorporated. Refrigerate until you're ready to serve. Substitute nectarines for the peaches and brush with 2 tablespoons honey before grilling. Serve the nectarines topped with a dollop of whipped cream and a sprinkle of toasted chopped almonds.
Brandied Plums with Candied Ginger Ice Cream	Substitute 4 plums for the peaches. Instead of the butter and sugar, whisk ¼ cup red currant jelly and 2 tablespoons brandy together in a small saucepan over medium-low heat until smooth and melted. Brush the plums with the mixture and grill. Serve with the ice cream, drizzling any remaining glaze over the top.
Sugared Papayas with Brown Sugar Crème Fraîche and Cashews	Replace the gingered ice cream with ½ cup crème fraîche and 2 tablespoons brown sugar, whisked together. Substitute one 1½- to 2-pound ripe papaya for the peaches. Peel with a paring knife or vegetable peeler, cut lengthwise into quarters, and scoop out the seeds. Brush all sides of the papaya with the butter, but sprinkle only the interior with sugar. To serve, dollop each piece of grilled papaya with some crème fraîche and sprinkle with chopped cashews.

D direct fire   I indirect fire   M make ahead   V vegetarian option

Caramelized Five-Spice Oranges

Makes: 4 servings	Time: 20 to 25 minutes	Ⓓ Ⓜ Ⓥ

After the richest barbecue, sometimes you need a light and simple way to end the meal. Get these ready to roll well in advance and plan to serve with virtually any sorbet.

¼ cup sugar

½ teaspoon five-spice powder (to make your own, see page 456)

2 large oranges

¼ cup chopped fresh mint

1 Stir the sugar and five-spice powder together on a small plate. Cut a sliver off the top and bottom of each orange so that it will sit flat on the grates without rolling, then turn them on their sides and cut in half through the equator. Remove any seeds. Press the cut side of each half into the sugar. Let sit until the sugar is absorbed and/or you are ready to grill.

2 If using a gas grill, heat it for medium direct cooking. If using a charcoal grill, after taking dinner off, add more coals if necessary and close the lid until you're ready to cook. In either case, clean the grates.

3 Put the orange halves on the grill directly over the fire, sugared side up. Close the lid and cook until they are warm all the way through, 5 to 10 minutes, depending on how hot the fire is. (Be careful not to let them stay on too long, or their juice will evaporate.) Turn them over and cook just until the cut sides brown, 2 to 3 minutes. Transfer to individual serving plates, sprinkle with the mint, and serve with a knife and fork or with grapefruit spoons, if you have them.

Boozy Caramelized Oranges with Toasted Coconut	Substitute 1 tablespoon toasted shredded coconut for the five-spice powder; pulse with the sugar in a blender or food processor until the coconut is finely chopped. After dipping the oranges in the sugar, cut slits into the cut side of each half and drizzle each with ½ teaspoon of your choice of rum (light, dark, spiced, coconut). Let sit for at least a few minutes before grilling.
Caramelized Ginger Oranges	Sweet and hot: Replace the sugar and five-spice powder with ½ cup candied ginger, pulsed to a coarse powder in a food processor.
Caramelized Grapefruit	A crunchy crust: Replace the granulated sugar and five-spice powder with 6 tablespoons turbinado sugar and substitute grapefruits for the oranges.

Butter-Rum Pineapple Rings

Makes: 6 to 8 servings	Time: 25 to 30 minutes	Ⓓ Ⓜ Ⓥ

Because of pineapple's high sugar content, you can get delicious browning and a little crust simply by giving the rings a turn on the grill in their natural state. Brush them with a spiked butter or dredge them in flavored sugar before putting them on the fire to take them to dessert status. Serve these rings as is, with ice cream or plain cake, or cut into chunks and add to a dessert fruit salad or a sundae. Or grill them earlier in the meal and serve alongside the entrée as whole rings or chopped into a salsa topping. Pineapple is a traditional partner for pork, but I also love it with chicken and turkey.

1 pineapple

8 tablespoons (1 stick) butter

2 tablespoons spiced or dark rum

2 tablespoons coconut milk

1 Cut the top and bottom off the pineapple, then remove the peel by standing the pineapple upright and running the knife down from top to bottom, working all around, without taking much of the flesh. Lay the pineapple on its side and cut it across into 1- to 1½-inch rings. Cut the core out of each ring. (An easy way to do this is to use a small cookie cutter or swivel peeler, or with a paring knife.) If not using immediately, put the rings in an airtight container; they will keep in the refrigerator for up to 2 days.

2 Melt the butter in a small saucepan over medium heat. When it foams, add the rum and coconut milk and bring to a gentle bubble. Cook without boiling, stirring occasionally, until the mixture reduces a bit and gets syrupy, 4 to 5 minutes. Remove from the heat. Brush the pineapple rings on both sides with the glaze; reserve the remaining glaze.

3 If using a gas grill, heat it for medium direct cooking. If using a charcoal grill, after taking dinner off, add more coals if necessary and close the lid until you're ready to cook. In either case, clean the grates.

4 Put the pineapple rings on the grill directly over the fire. Close the lid and cook, turning once, until they develop grill marks and are heated all the way through, 4 to 8 minutes per side, depending on how hot the fire is. Transfer to a plate and serve drizzled with the remaining glaze (reheat it if necessary).

---

6 GLAZES TO USE FOR SWEET OR SAVORY GRILLED PINEAPPLE RINGS

1. Maple-Mustard Glaze (page 300)
2. Sherry-Honey Glaze (page 215)
3. Maple-Orange Glaze (page 128)
4. Sweet Rosemary-Orange Glaze (page 179)
5. Spicy Miso Glaze (page 126)
6. Balsamic-Honey Glaze (page 279)

Ⓓ direct fire Ⓘ indirect fire Ⓜ make ahead Ⓥ vegetarian option

Maple-Bourbon Pineapple Rings	Substitute bourbon for the rum and maple syrup for the coconut milk.
Cardamom Pineapple Rings	Replace the butter, rum, and coconut milk with ¾ cup sugar mixed with 1 teaspoon ground cardamom in a shallow bowl. Dredge both sides of the rings in this before grilling.
Cinnamon-Orange Pineapple Rings	Replace the butter, rum, and coconut milk with ½ cup sugar, 1 teaspoon ground cinnamon, and the grated zest of 1 large navel orange, mixed together in a shallow bowl. Dredge both sides of the rings in this before grilling.

Watermelon with Honey and Lime

Makes: 2 to 4 servings	Time: 10 to 20 minutes	Ⓓ Ⓥ

You've seen savory grilled watermelon (page 446). Now here's an unexpected and refreshing sweet way to end the meal.

2 1- to 1½-inch-thick watermelon slices, halved

Salt

¼ cup honey

Lime wedges for serving

1 If using a gas grill, heat it for medium direct cooking. If using a charcoal grill, after taking dinner off, add more coals if necessary and close the lid until you're ready to cook. In either case, clean the grates.

2 Lightly salt the watermelon on both sides, then brush both sides with the honey. Put the slices on the grill directly over the fire. Close the lid and cook, turning once, until the watermelon browns in spots, 4 to 8 minutes per side, depending on how hot the fire is. Transfer to a cutting board. Cut the slices into quarters or smaller wedges. Serve with the lime wedges.

Cantaloupe with Chile and Lime	Hot, sweet, and cool all at the same time: Substitute 4 wedges peeled cantaloupe for the watermelon. Mix 1 teaspoon salt with 1 to 1½ teaspoons pure chile powder (not chili powder). The amount depends on how hot the chile is that you are using and/or how much heat you like. For mild heat, try ancho powder or smoked paprika (pimentón); if you like the burn, add cayenne or chipotle. You can also use red chile flakes or Aleppo pepper. Sprinkle the chile salt over both sides of the melon slices and grill as directed.
Watermelon with Sweet Sour Cream and Blueberries	The perfect red, white, and blue dessert for Fourth of July: Combine 6 tablespoons sour cream, 2 tablespoons confectioners' sugar, and 1 tablespoon fresh lemon juice (or more to taste). Dollop this on the grilled watermelon slices, sprinkle generously with blueberries, and serve.
Watermelon and Orange Skewers with Simple Raspberry Sauce	In a blender, process 2 cups raspberries (thawed frozen are fine) to a purée. If you like, push the purée through a fine-mesh strainer to remove the seeds—but I rarely bother. Taste and add sugar if necessary. Cut the watermelon into 1- to 1½-inch cubes and thread onto skewers, alternating with peeled orange sections. After grilling, drizzle with the raspberry sauce and garnish with a little chopped fresh mint.

Ⓓ direct fire   Ⓘ indirect fire   Ⓜ make ahead   Ⓥ vegetarian option

**Watermelon with
Sweet Sour Cream
and Blueberries**

Grill-Baked Apple

Makes: **1 serving**	Time: **25 to 30 minutes**	Ⓓ Ⓜ Ⓥ

A party planner's dream. You can have as many apples as you need, stuffed and ready to go before the first guests arrive. Since they cook fast, there's no excuse not to eat them warm. Or just enjoy one yourself as a treat at the end of a long day.

1 apple

1 tablespoon butter, softened

1 tablespoon brown sugar

⅛ teaspoon ground cinnamon, or more to taste

1 Remove the core of the apple carefully, without puncturing the bottom or side. (A swivel vegetable peeler does an excellent job, or use a paring knife.) Mash the butter, brown sugar, and cinnamon with the back of a fork until thoroughly mixed. Stuff the mixture into the cavity of the apple.

2 If using a gas grill, heat it for medium direct cooking. If using a charcoal grill, after taking dinner off, add more coals if necessary and close the lid until you're ready to cook. In either case, clean the grates.

3 Put the apple on the grill directly over the fire. Close the lid and cook until it feels soft when gently squeezed and the filling is melted, 8 to 10 minutes, depending on its size. Transfer to plate and let cool a few minutes before serving.

Grill-Baked Apple à la Mode	Everything but the crust: After coring the apple, widen the opening at the top so that you will be able to fit a small scoop of vanilla ice cream inside after the apple comes off the grill without it spilling over the side. It will melt and mingle with the spices and juices inside the apple.
Grill-Baked Apple with Honey and Nuts	Add some crunch: Omit the cinnamon, butter, and brown sugar. Stuff the cavity of the apple with 2 tablespoons chopped nuts of your choice, then pour in 1 to 2 tablespoons honey to fill the nooks and crannies.
Grill-Baked Apple with Coconut and Dried Cranberries	Sweet and tart: Omit the cinnamon and add 1 to 2 tablespoons each shredded coconut and dried cranberries.

Strawberries Romanoff

Makes: 4 servings	Time: 15 to 20 minutes	Ⓓ Ⓥ

Grilled fruit and ice cream is a fantastic and simple way to top off a barbecue. Just a few minutes over the fire will concentrate the sugars in the strawberries. A perforated grill pan is a real plus here but the berries are big enough that you can put them directly on the grill without worrying about them falling through.

1 pound strawberries, hulled

¼ cup sugar

2 tablespoons Grand Marnier

1 pint vanilla ice cream

1 If using a gas grill, heat it for medium direct cooking. If using a charcoal grill, after taking dinner off, add more coals if necessary and close the lid until you're ready to cook. In either case, clean the grates.

2 Gently toss the strawberries with the sugar to coat. Put them on the grill directly over the fire. Close the lid and cook, rolling them around once, until heated through, about 5 minutes total.

3 Transfer the strawberries to a bowl. Cut them in halves or quarters, depending on their size, and toss with the Grand Marnier. Let them macerate while you spoon out the ice cream, then divide between the bowls and serve, pouring any liquid from the bowl over the top.

Mixed Berries Romanoff	Delicious and colorful: Add ½ cup each raspberries and blueberries to the grilled strawberries before tossing with the Grand Marnier.
Mango and Blackberry Sundae with Mint	Substitute 2 ripe mangoes for the strawberries. Cut the flesh off the pit, then remove the skin. Sprinkle with the sugar on both sides and cook, turning once, until the pieces develop grill marks, 2 to 3 minutes per side. Cube the mango and toss with 2 tablespoons dark rum along with 1 cup blackberries. Serve over vanilla or coconut ice cream, garnished with chopped fresh mint.
Fruit Sundae with Lemonade Syrup	A delicious alcohol-free version you can make with any kind of fruit you choose: Put ⅓ cup each sugar, fresh lemon juice, and water in a small saucepan over medium heat. Bring to a gentle bubble and cook, stirring occasionally, until slightly reduced and syrupy, 2 to 3 minutes. Let cool a bit, then use to brush the fruit of your choice before grilling. After grilling, cut the fruit into pieces if necessary, toss with the remaining syrup, then spoon over the ice cream and serve.

20 Hidden Gems

The hundreds of variations in this book are unique dishes hiding in plain sight. Each treats the main recipe as a template, then spins it into different ingredient and flavor directions. Here are 20 you should try for sure—a list that I hope inspires you to give them all the attention they deserve.

1. Okra Skewers with Green Olive Dipping Sauce (page 42)
2. Halloumi Cheese with Balsamic Glaze and Pomegranate Seeds (page 48)
3. Hot-Smoked Fish Spread (page 62)
4. Spinach-Stuffed Trout with Bacon and Pine Nuts (page 110)
5. Seafood "Boil" (page 143)
6. Balsamic Chicken and Kale Kebabs (page 170)
7. Grill-Roasted Duck Legs (page 212)
8. Carne Asada Fries (page 244)
9. Veal Chops with Grill-Fried Sage Leaves (page 273)
10. Korean-Style Pork Belly or Jowl Sliders (page 297)
11. Smoked Pork and Beans (page 299)
12. Mixed Mushroom Calzones with Rosemary (page 372)
13. Bulgur Salad with Escarole and Orange (page 375)
14. Cambodian-Style Coconut Corn (page 404)
15. Grilled Potato Skins (page 425)
16. Easy Onion Jam (page 433)
17. Tabbouleh-Stuffed Grill-Roasted Plum Tomatoes (page 445)
18. Fruit Jam Fool (page 477)
19. Chocolate Zucchini Bread (page 522)
20. Grape Clafoutis (page 528)

Index

Note: Page references in *italics* indicate photographs.

Index

Converting Measurements

Essential Conversions

Volume to Volume

3 teaspoons	1 tablespoon
4 tablespoons	¼ cup
5 tablespoons plus 1 teaspoon	⅓ cup
4 ounces	½ cup
8 ounces	1 cup
1 cup	½ pint
2 cups	1 pint
2 pints	1 quart
4 quarts	1 gallon

Approximate Weight to Volume

2 ounces	¼ cup liquid or fat
4 ounces	½ cup liquid or fat
8 ounces	1 cup liquid or fat
1 pound	2 cups liquid or fat
7 ounces	1 cup sugar
5 ounces	1 cup flour

Metric Approximations

Measurements

¼ teaspoon	1.25 milliliters
½ teaspoon	2.5 milliliters
1 teaspoon	5 milliliters
1 tablespoon	15 milliliters
1 fluid ounce	30 milliliters
¼ cup	60 milliliters
⅓ cup	80 milliliters
½ cup	120 milliliters
1 cup	240 milliliters
1 pint (2 cups)	480 milliliters
1 quart (4 cups)	960 milliliters (0.96 liter)
1 gallon (4 quarts)	3.84 liters
1 ounce (weight)	28 grams
¼ pound (4 ounces)	114 grams
1 pound (16 ounces)	454 grams
2.2 pounds	1 kilogram (1,000 grams)
1 inch	2.5 centimeters